Road Pricing, Traffic Congestion and the Environment

Road Pricing, Traffic Congestion and the Environment

Issues of Efficiency and Social Feasibility

Edited by
Kenneth J. Button

*Professor of Public Policy, The Institute of Public Policy,
George Mason University, USA*

Erik T. Verhoef

*Researcher, Department of Spatial Economics, Free University
of Amsterdam, Netherlands*

Edward Elgar
Cheltenham, UK • Northampton, MA, USA

H

© KJ Button and Erik Verhoef, 1998

Published by
Edward Elgar Publishing Limited
Glensanda House
Montpellier Parade
Cheltenham
Glos GL50 1UA
UK

Edward Elgar Publishing, Inc.
6 Market Street
Northampton
Massachusetts 01060
USA

A catalogue record for this book
is available from the British Library

Library of Congress Cataloguing in Publication Data
Road pricing, traffic congestion, and the environment : issues of
   efficiency and social feasibility / edited by Kenneth J. Button,
   Erik T. Verhoef.
      Includes bibliographical references.
      1. Roads—Finance.   2. Urban transportation policy.   3. Traffic
   congestion.   4. Transportation, Automotive—Environmental aspects.
   I. Button, Kenneth John.   II. Verhoef, E. T.
   HE335.R583   1998
   388.1'1—dc21   97–52044
                                                                      CIP

ISBN 1 85898 365 7

Typeset by Manton Typesetters, 5–7 Eastfield Road, Louth, Lincolnshire, LN11 7AJ, UK.
Printed and bound in Great Britain by Bookcraft (Bath) Ltd.

Contents

PART III POLITICAL AND SOCIAL FEASIBILITY

Figures

Tables

Contributors

Richard Arnott   Department of Economics, Boston College, Boston, USA

Chang-Hee Christine Bae   Department of Urban Design and Planning, University of Washington, Seattle, USA

Kenneth J. Button   The Institute of Public Policy, George Mason University, Fairfax, USA

André de Palma   Département des Sciences Economiques, Université de Cergy Pontoise, Cergy Pontoise, France

Richard H.M. Emmerink   McKinsey & Company, Amsterdam, The Netherlands

José A. Gomez-Ibañez   John F. Kennedy School of Government and Graduate School of Design, Harvard University, Cambridge, USA

Timothy D. Hau   School of Economics and Finance, The University of Hong Kong, Hong Kong

Olof Johansson-Stenman   Department of Economics, Gothenburg University, Gothenburg, Sweden

Peter Jones   Transport Studies Group, University of Westminster, London, England

David M. Levinson   Institute of Transportation Studies, University of California at Berkeley, Berkeley, USA

Robin Lindsey   Department of Economics, University of Alberta, Edmonton, Canada

Peter Nijkamp   Department of Spatial Economics, Free University, Amsterdam, The Netherlands

Stef Proost   Center for Economic Studies, Katholieke Universiteit Leuven, Leuven, Belgium

Harry W. Richardson   School of Urban Planning and Development, University of Southern California, Los Angeles, USA

Piet Rietveld   Department of Spatial Economics, Free University, Amsterdam, The Netherlands

Daniel Shefer   Center for Urban and Regional Studies, Technion-Israel Institute of Technology, Haifa, Israel

Kenneth A. Small   Department of Economics, University of California at Irvine, Irvine, USA

Thomas Sterner   Department of Economics, Gothenburg University, Gothenburg, Sweden

Kurt Van Dender   Center for Economic Studies, Katholieke Universiteit, Leuven, Belgium

Erik T. Verhoef   Department of Spatial Economics, Free University, Amsterdam, The Netherlands

Preface

Road pricing has been a topic of both academic interest and a discussion of policy debate almost from the moment that Arthur Pigou suggested the idea in 1920. We have both had an interest in the topic for some time and in 1994 felt it appropriate to try to gather some original papers that would both look at the development of the concept over 75 years or so, and highlight some of the current areas of work that are concerned with road pricing issues. A 75-year anniversary volume would have been ideal but the world never works quite like that, so just as it has taken rather longer for road pricing to become a reality so there has been a lag in producing this volume.

The publication of this volume is timely, however, in our opinion. It is appearing just when transport policy is moving away from a tradition of road construction to meet all traffic growth to one of traffic management. The growing concern with environmental issues has influenced this switch but equally there has been a gradual realization that without appropriate management, and in particular pricing, roads are not often being used efficiently and resources are effectively being wasted. Road pricing, while not directly dealing with the environmental concern, does lead to a more rational allocation of road space.

The current debates surrounding road pricing are really at two levels and we have tried to show this in the contributions that we have gathered. The theory of how the price should be calculated has moved on a lot since Pigou's time and we hope this is reflected in the contributions in this volume. Equally, while Pigou's analysis was primarily theoretical, there has been an expanding debate on how in practice road pricing could be operationalized. We have asked a number of experts to look at this issue and their views are set out in several of the contributions in this book.

Finally, and this is no afterthought, an edited volume is only as good as the contributions that appear in it. We would like to thank the authors who have made this volume possible. It takes time to write academic papers and we appreciate the considerable effort that the very busy individuals who helped us in this venture put into their contributions.

Kenneth J. Button
Erik T. Verhoef

PART I

Theory and Practice Before and After Pigou

1. Introduction

Kenneth J. Button and Erik T. Verhoef

1.1 THE CONCEPT OF ROAD PRICING

John Maynard Keynes once suggested that all decision makers are influenced by some defunct economic scribbler. Not everyone would agree. Nevertheless, economic ideas and their resultant policy applications do have an important bearing on our lives. Equally, economists are well known – possibly unjustly in the case of microeconomists – for having trouble in reaching a consensus on how the world works. There are some areas, however, where there exists a considerable degree of agreement. Often, however, as Keynes implies, it takes time for these ideas to permeate the *conscious politique*. Our concern in this volume is with one such idea; the idea of road pricing, advanced roughly 75 years ago by the Cambridge economist, Arthur Pigou.

A consideration of road pricing at this time seems apposite. 'Transport policy is at the cross-roads', says the European Commission's Green Paper on *Fair and Efficient Pricing in Transport* (Commission of the European Communities, 1996). While the pun is ungainly English, it does reflect the current and genuine reassessment of transport policy; a reassessment that transcends the borders of Europe.

The range of challenges facing transport policy makers has increased. In addition to traditional efficiency matters such as congestion and optimization of infrastructure capacity, a variety of environmental and social problems such as noise annoyance, atmospheric pollution and safety now attract the attention of policy makers. The dominance of road transport and its highly intrusive nature poses serious particular difficulties for decision makers and their advisors. The political pendulum has swung back to favouring smaller government and with this has come tighter public sector spending limits and concern about some of the more traditional command and control forms of regulation. The result is a trend towards more private sector involvement in transport and the seeking of innovative means of finance and regulation.

One particular instrument of transport regulation that seems to gain more political and perhaps also gradual public support, is road pricing, much to the satisfaction of many transport economists. This instrument, in all its facets, is the central topic in the present book.

There have been both intellectual and practical developments since Pigou first put forward the idea of road pricing. The basic concept is deceptively easy; apply the price mechanism in the same way as it applies elsewhere. When there is high demand prices should be high to deter excessive use. Intellectually, the key question is one of defining the appropriate price in what is often a complex set of economic and technical circumstances. The key issue from a practical point of view is one of operationalizing the concept, not only in terms of developing technically efficient charging mechanisms but also in gaining political acceptance as a valid policy instrument.

Traditionally, neo-classical economists have been reserved in their advocacy of government intervention in economic processes. This reservation largely comes from their acceptance of a number of basic welfare economic theorems. In particular, under certain conditions a competitive equilibrium, if it exists, is seen as being Pareto efficient. A move from it can only make some people worse off. Consequently, as it is not possible to make a value-free comparison between different Pareto efficient market outcomes, it is logical for the economists only to advocate regulation if these conditions are not fulfilled; a situation that is usually referred to as market failure.

The early neo-classical writers studying market failures frequently illustrated their viewpoints using transport examples. In 1844, Dupuit took a bridge as a useful example for illustrating efficient pricing of public goods; and more than a century later, Coase (1960) considered sparkles from a railway when studying the absence of property rights in relation to the existence of externalities. In the 1920s, the spiritual fathers of road pricing, Pigou (1920) and Knight (1924), used the example of a congested road to make their points on externalities and optimal congestion charges. They argued that road users should be charged their marginal external congestion costs. This has remained the leading principle in the transport economic literature on road traffic congestion, and has also found its way into environmental economics in the guise of the related 'Polluter Pays Principle' (Baumol and Oates, 1988). Given the growth in road traffic and its adverse side-effects, road pricing has become an important contemporary policy issue.

A basic representation of Pigou's economic analysis of road pricing is presented in Figure 1.1. A simple road is assumed with no junctions and uniform lane width. Vehicles are assumed to be identical in terms of their technical characteristics. We are also not concerned with matters such as pollution and safety in this simple framework. In this setting, road users are identical apart from their marginal willingness to pay for a trip, represented by the demand curve D=MPB=MSB (marginal private and social benefits, respectively). Due to congestion, marginal social cost (MSC) exceeds mar-

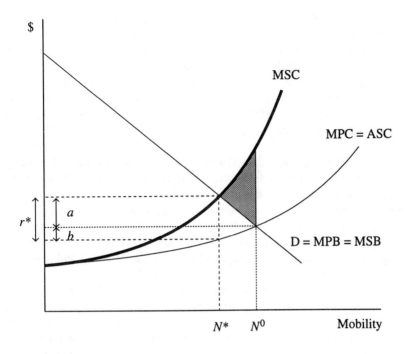

Figure 1.1   The simple economics of road pricing

ginal private cost (MPC); the latter being equal to average social cost (ASC). The free market equilibrium outcome is N^0, and the socially optimal road use at N^*. The road price that accomplishes this optimum is the Pigouvian charge r^*. This is equal to the marginal external congestion costs (MSC–MPC) at the optimum. The welfare gain enjoyed though introducing this charge is given by the shaded area.

1.2   DEVELOPMENTS SINCE PIGOU

Pigou's idea of using road pricing measures to regulate road traffic conges- tion has subsequently given rise to a substantial body of literature. It is not our intention to fully review the post-Pigouvian literature (Chapter 2 by Hau, and Chapter 4 by Arnott, de Palma and Lindsey in this volume do much of this), but seminal works that ought to be mentioned include Wardrop (1952), Walters (1961), and the late Nobel Prize winner Vickrey (1969).

Moreover, Pigou's insights were extended to regulation of road transport externalities other than congestion. Indeed, after 75 years, economists' answers to market failures in road transport typically still rely heavily on the concept of Pigouvian interventions. Under rather stringent assumptions that first-best conditions pertain elsewhere in the economic system and perfectly flexible regulatory policies exist for coping with road transport externalities, there would be little scope for improving on the Pigouvian solution to the problem of external costs of road transport. These assumptions are, however, not usually satisfied. Second-best problems have, accordingly, received ample attention in the recent literature on road pricing. Wilson (1983), and d'Ouville and McDonald (1990) studied optimal road capacity with subopti-mal congestion pricing; Braid (1989) and Arnott, de Palma and Lindsey (1990) consider uniform or step-wise pricing of a bottleneck. Arnott (1979) and Sullivan (1983) look at congestion policies through urban land use strate-gies. Two classic examples on second-best regulation in road transport are Lévy-Lambert (1968) and Marchand (1968), studying optimal congestion pricing with an untolled alternative, an issue that was recently discussed also by Braid (1996) and Verhoef *et al.* (1996) as well as Nijkamp and Shefer in Chapter 8, this volume.

Although Pigouvian principles apply to policies regarding other external traffic costs, the term road pricing is primarily associated with road traffic congestion. Since Pigou's innovative work, a large variety of possible ap-proaches to studying the economics of road traffic congestion and road pric-ing have been developed. An important distinction is between dynamic and static models. Dynamic models of road traffic congestion typically describe equilibrium patterns of variables such as speeds, densities, and arrival rates during the peak. Two types of dynamic approach can be distinguished. First, the 'bottleneck approach' was originally developed by Vickrey (1969), and later refined and extended by Arnott *et al.* (1993), Braid (1989), and others (see the contribution by Arnott, de Palma and Lindsey in this volume). Second is the approach proposed by Henderson (1974, 1981) that uses flow congestion. In contrast to the bottleneck model, travel delays are not com-pletely eliminated in the social optimum (Chu, 1995). In both approaches, the distribution of travel delays and scheduling costs over the peak, and the duration of the peak in the unregulated equilibrium and the social optimum are determined endogenously, and both models have in common that the optimal toll is time-dependent, reaching its maximum for the drivers arriving at the desired arrival time.

Although road traffic congestion is generally accepted as a dynamic phe-nomenon, many analysts rely on static analysis often because of the complex-ity of dynamic models; see for instance the hydro-dynamic model proposed by Newell (1988). However, even within this class of static models academia has not reached a consensus on the fundamentals that should underlie the analyses. An important source of disagreement in static modelling concerns the choice of the output variable in the demand and cost functions. Two main stances can be distinguished: flow-based measures, where output has an explicit per-unit-of-time dimension (De Meza and Gould, 1987; Andrew Evans, 1992, 1993; Else, 1981, 1982 and Nash, 1982), and stock-based measures, such as numbers of trips or densities (Alan Evans, 1992; Hills, 1993).

Analyses using flow-based measures have the advantage of a solid basis in what engineers call the 'fundamental diagram of road traffic congestion'. This depicts the inverse relation between density and speed and, therefore, implies that each road segment has a unique maximum flow. The implication is that the average cost curve is backward-bending. This has initiated debate concerning, for instance, the stability of equilibria on the backward-bending section of the average cost curve. The advantage of stock-based measures is that the representation of demand is nearer reality. It has been observed that road users demand trips, not passages per unit of time, and that flow is an endogenous variable that has only a limited relation to individuals' decisions. In particular, the validity of a demand curve for peak travelling defined over flow has been questioned (Alan Evans, 1992; Hills, 1993).

Many analysts argue that regarding economic efficiency, a refined system of electronic road pricing (ERP) is generally the preferable technical charging mechanism. With ERP, the regulatory charge can be differentiated according to the various dimensions of the marginal external costs of each trip, such as the length of the trip, the time of driving, the route followed and the vehicle used. The main problems with ERP are that it can be expensive to operate and that, since road users only know the price of their trips ex post, the informational signals are not ideal.

Although the Hong Kong experiment, and more recently the Californian FASTRAK, have demonstrated that it is technically possible to operate an ERP scheme successfully (Dawson and Catling, 1986; Hau, 1992; Richardson, this volume), practical applications remain scarce. Lave (1995, p. 464) summarizes the problem as: 'It has been a commonplace event for transportation economists to put the conventional diagram on the board, note the self-evident optimality of pricing solutions, and then sit down waiting for the world to adopt this obviously correct solution. Well, we have been waiting for seventy years now, and it's worth asking what are the facets of the problem that we have been missing. Why is the world reluctant to do the obvious?'

One way of looking at this problem can be seen using Figure 1.1. Although the optimal tax r^* yields the social welfare benefit given by the shaded area, without redistribution of the optimal tax revenues $N^* \cdot r^*$, everybody is worse off due to road pricing, except the regulator. Those remaining on the road incur a net welfare loss of a, consisting of a time gain b, and the necessarily higher road price r^* they have to pay. Those who are taxed off the road incur welfare losses varying from zero, for the initial marginal user, to *a*, for the marginal non-user after road pricing.

Such redistributional effects of road pricing may dominate the efficiency gains (Segal and Steinmeier, 1980). Andrew Evans (1992) questions the desirability of road pricing for this, among other reasons such as the possibility of monopolistic pricing. Borins (1988) goes a step further, and draws the pessimistic conclusion that road pricing will 'inevitably fail because it is an intrinsically unpopular policy in any democratic urban policy'.

Some road users may, however, benefit from road pricing when the heterogeneity of road users is allowed for. The typical case concerns income differences. Following Richardson (1974), most authors conclude that road pricing is likely to be regressive (Layard, 1977; Glazer, 1981; Arnott *et al.*, 1994). Foster (1975), in contrast, stresses that road pricing can be progressive, in particular when society is divided into rich car owners and a poor rest group. Another way of looking at it is that higher income drivers suffer disproportionately from unregulated congestion. It is questionable, though, whether the progressive incidence of welfare losses due to unregulated congestion provides a sound basis for leaving this inefficiency in existence.

Giuliano (1992) notes that such equity considerations may merely 'present an apparently legitimate basis for opposition that is actually motivated by other reasons', and Small (1983, 1992) stresses that road pricing may be progressive given certain redistributions of revenues. Income transfers of road pricing revenues often play an important role in the discussion of its feasibility (Andrew Evans, 1992). Various proposed schemes have been advocated for spending the funds raised so that as many actors as possible benefit (Goodwin, 1989; Jones, 1991; Small, 1992). A questioning of road users in the Randstad, Netherlands (Verhoef *et al.*, 1997) also pointed to the importance road users attach to the allocation of tax revenues. Sheldon *et al.* (1993) from an interview study of London residents, conclude that road pricing is more likely to be accepted if the system is simple, enforcement is guaranteed, and the revenues used in a transparent and equitable manner. May (1992) asserts, however, that 'it has to be expected that any form of road pricing will introduce some inequities. The key is to keep these to a minimum.' Daganzo (1995) approaches the issue from the other side, by proposing a combination of rationing and pricing that reduces the size of money transfers. Else (1986) mentions the possibility of leaving road users a choice between paying a toll or queuing.

Despite problems of social and political feasibility, road pricing in various forms has been, or soon will be introduced in a number of cities (see also Small and Gomez-Ibañez, Chapter 10 this volume). Various types of road pricing exist, and furthermore, road charging in its strict form is only one possible fiscal instrument to deal with road traffic congestion. The Singapore area licensing system offers one example of a well established system, and the toll rings in Norwegian and Swedish cities offer evidence that the political opposition to charging for the use of urban streets, albeit not in a congestion optimizing fashion, can be overcome. Other fiscal instruments offering a quasi road pricing approach are also in use. Parking fees, for example, can approximate to a road price in terms of deterring traffic using city streets, but are second-best in that they poorly differentiate according to trip length or vehicle used.

1.3   THIS BOOK

This book, issued to mark the 75th anniversary of Pigou's pathbreaking writings on road pricing, brings together a number of contributions that reflect both past and present key factors that have dominated and still dominate the public and academic debate on road pricing.

The book consists of three parts. Part I contains three contributions that will give the reader a comprehensive picture of the theoretical and practical developments that have taken place after – and, indeed, before – Pigou. Chapter 2 by Levinson examines the history of turnpikes, which for Britain goes back as far as the year 1656. A number of intriguing parallels with current policy debates arise from this chapter, and Levinson's hypothesis that the rise and decline of turnpikes can in part be explained by trip lengths growing and exceeding jurisdictions' sizes may certainly have great policy relevance for the formulation of contemporary road pricing schemes. Chapter 3 by Hau gives a comprehensive interpretation of the literature on the theory of optimal pricing and investment for roads, as it has emerged since the 1920s. Starting with the elementary model, Hau gives us a tour around the relevant literature and models that have been and can be formulated when relaxing some of the implicit assumptions underlying the most basic model. The fourth chapter by Arnott, de Palma and Lindsey focuses on a particular type of economic model of congestion and road pricing that was originally proposed by the late Nobel Prize winner William Vickrey, and that has received ample attention since: the dynamic bottleneck model. The three authors, who have extended Vickrey's basic bottleneck into various directions and contributed much to this literature themselves, give an overview of the recent developments in this stream of research.

Part II focuses on efficiency aspects, and on second-best alternatives to the theoretical benchmark concept of first-best Pigouvian taxes in a first-best world. Button's Chapter 5 is concerned with the many alternatives that may be considered when road pricing cannot be implemented. The chapter analyses the strengths and weaknesses of these alternatives, and reviews some of the experiences cities have had as a result of adopting such alternatives. In Chapter 6, Proost and Van Dender analyse the relative welfare effects of various tax policies in road transport that constitute a move from fixed vehicle taxes to Pigouvian taxes, based on mileage driven. They discuss both the microeconomic fundamentals of such tax reforms and provide empirical estimates for Belgium and Brussels. Johansson and Sterner, in Chapter 7, focus on the environmental aspects of road pricing. They explicitly acknowledge that the theoretical first-best solution would require a very expensive monitoring and charging scheme, but observe that the additional investment costs for an environmentally benign road pricing scheme, given the system's flexibility that is required to deal efficiently with congestion, need not be very large. Next, Nijkamp and Shefer, in Chapter 8, make a plea for using a system approach when analysing congestion and congestion pricing for urban transport externalities. Otherwise, neglected externality transfers, for example to other parts of the transport network, may outweigh the foreseen benefits, and will usually result in unexpected efficiency and equity effects. Finally Chapter 9 in this part of the book, by Emmerink and Verhoef, is concerned with the relation between road pricing and real time information provision by means of ATIS ('Advanced Travellers' Information Systems') – which will often require comparable technologies. The chapter focuses on the economic principles underlying the analysis of stochastic congestion and the use of pricing and information provision, either in isolation or in combined systems.

Part III is concerned with the political and social feasibility of road pricing. Chapter 10, by Small and Gomez-Ibañez, reviews a variety of examples of road pricing covering a wide range of sites, objectives and implementation strategies. The authors focus on political, institutional and operational features and their impacts on the political and public acceptability of congestion pricing. Richardson and Bae focus on the equity impacts of road congestion pricing. In Chapter 11, they not only provide a comprehensive literature review, but also evaluate the experiences with the Californian FASTRAK scheme in this context. Chapter 12 by Jones investigates public acceptability of road pricing. Based on a number of public surveys, Jones identifies eight key concerns which the public may have about the introduction of road pricing, and suggests some central issues that will have to be addressed before a publicly acceptable scheme can be implemented locally. Finally, Rietveld and Verhoef discuss the social feasibility of Pigouvian transport regulation from various perspectives in Chapter 13. They address the trade-off between efficiency and social feasibility, offer a political economy perspective, and finally present some empirical research that has recently been carried out in The Netherlands on these topics.

All in all, we sincerely hope and believe that this book contains many interesting and sometimes thought-provoking contributions, that will hopefully inspire both transport analysts and policy makers who are nowadays working with, extending, and trying to implement Pigou's intellectual inheritance.

REFERENCES

Arnott, R.J. (1979), 'Unpriced transport congestion', *Journal of Economic Theory*, **21**, 294–316.

Arnott, R., A. de Palma and R. Lindsey (1990), 'Economics of a bottleneck', *Journal of Urban Economics*, **27**, 11–30.

Arnott, R., A. de Palma and R. Lindsey (1993), 'A structural model of peak-period congestion: a traffic bottleneck with elastic demand', *American Economic Review*, **83** (1), 161–79.

Arnott, R., A. de Palma and R. Lindsey (1994), 'The welfare effects of congestion tolls with heterogeneous commuters', *Journal of Transport Economics and Policy*, **28**, 139–61.

Braid, R.M. (1989), 'Uniform versus peak-load pricing of a bottleneck with elastic demand', *Journal of Urban Economics*, **26**, 320–27.

Braid, R.M. (1996), 'Peak-load pricing of a transportation route with an unpriced substitute', *Journal of Urban Economics*, **40**, 179–97.

Baumol, W.J. and W.E. Oates (1988), *The Theory of Environmental Policy*, second edition, Cambridge: Cambridge University Press.

Borins, S.F. (1988), 'Electronic road pricing: an idea whose time may never come', *Transportation Research*, **22A** (1), 37–44.

Coase, R.H. (1960), 'The problem of social cost', *Journal of Law and Economics*, **3** (Oct.), 1–44.

Chu, X. (1995), 'Endogenous trip scheduling: the Henderson approach reformulated and compared with the Vickrey approach', *Journal of Urban Economics*, **37**, 324–43.

Commission of the European Communities (1996), *Green Paper Towards Fair and Efficient Pricing in Transport: Policy Options for Internalising the External Costs of Transport in the European Union*, Brussels: Directorate-General for Transport.

Daganzo, C.F. (1995), 'A Pareto optimum congestion reduction scheme', *Transportation Research*, **29B** (2), 139–54.

Dawson, J.A.L. and I. Catling (1986), 'Electronic road pricing in Hong Kong', *Transportation Research*, **20A** (2), 129–34.

De Meza, D. and J.R. Gould (1987), 'Free access versus private property in a resource: income distributions compared', *Journal of Political Economy*, **95** (6), 1317–25.

Dupuit, J. (1844), 'On the measurement of the utility of public works', in: D. Murphy (ed.) *Transport* (1968), London: Penguin.

Else, P.K. (1981), 'A reformulation of the theory of optimal congestion taxes', *Journal of Transport Economics and Policy*, **15**, 217–32.

Else, P.K. (1982), 'A reformulation of the theory of optimal congestion taxes: a rejoinder', *Journal of Transport Economics and Policy*, **16**, 299–304.

Else, P.K. (1986), 'No entry for congestion taxes?', *Transportation Research*, **20A** (2), 99–107.

Evans, Alan W. (1992), 'Road congestion: the diagrammatic analysis', *Journal of Political Economy*, **100** (1), 211–17.

Evans, Andrew W. (1992), 'Road congestion pricing: when is it a good policy?' *Journal of Transport Economics and Policy*, **26**, 213–43.

Evans, Andrew W. (1993), 'Road congestion pricing: when is it a good policy?: a rejoinder', *Journal of Transport Economics and Policy*, **27**, 99–105.

Foster, C. (1975), 'A note on the distributional effects of road pricing: a comment', *Journal of Transport Economics and Policy*, **9**, 186–7.

Giuliano, G. (1992), 'An assessment of the political acceptability of congestion pricing', *Transportation*, **19** (4), 335–58.

Glazer, A. (1981), 'Congestion tolls and consumer welfare', *Public Finance*, **36** (1), 77–83.

Goodwin, P.B. (1989), 'The rule of three: a possible solution to the political problem of competing objectives for road pricing', *Traffic Engineering and Control*, **30** (10), 495–7.

Hau, T.D. (1992), 'Congestion charging mechanisms: an evaluation of current practice', Preliminary Draft, Transport Division, Washington: The World Bank.

Henderson J.V. (1974), 'Road congestion: a reconsideration of pricing theory', *Journal of Urban Economics*, **1**, 346–65.

Henderson J.V. (1981), 'The economics of staggered work hours', *Journal of Urban Economics*, **9**, 349–64.

Hills, P. (1993), 'Road congestion pricing: when is it a good policy?: a comment', *Journal of Transport Economics and Policy*, **27**, 91–9.

Jones, P. (1991), 'Gaining public support for road pricing through a package approach', *Traffic Engineering and Control*, **32** (4), 194–6.

Knight, F.H. (1924), 'Some fallacies in the interpretation of social cost', *Quarterly Journal of Economics*, **38**, 582–606.

Lave, C. (1995), 'The demand curve under road pricing and the problem of political feasibility: author's reply', *Transportation Research*, **29A** (6), 464–5.

Layard, R. (1977), 'The distributional effects of congestion taxes', *Economica*, **44**, 297–304.

Lévy-Lambert, H. (1968), 'Tarification des services à qualité variable: application aux péages de circulation' ('Pricing of services of varying quality: an application to traffic flow'), *Econometrica*, **36** (3–4), 564–74.

Marchand, M. (1968), 'A note on optimal tolls in an imperfect environment', *Econometrica*, **36** (3–4), 575–81.

May, A.D. (1992), 'Road pricing: an international perspective', *Transportation*, **19** (4), 313–33.

Nash, C.A. (1982), 'A reformulation of the theory of optimal congestion taxes: a comment', *Journal of Transport Economics and Policy*, **26**, 295–9.

Newell, G.F. (1988), 'Traffic flow for the morning commute', *Transportation Science*, **22**, 47–58.

d'Ouville, E.L. and J.F. McDonald (1990), 'Optimal road capacity with a suboptimal congestion toll', *Journal of Urban Economics*, **28**, 34–49.

Pigou, A.C. (1920), *Wealth and Welfare*, London: Macmillan.

Richardson, H.W. (1974), 'A note on the distributional effects of road pricing', *Journal of Transport Economics and Policy*, **8**, 82–5.

Segal, D. and T.L. Steinmeier (1980), 'The incidence of congestion and congestion tolls', *Journal of Urban Economics*, **7**, 42–62.

Sheldon, R., M. Scott and P. Jones (1993), 'London congestion charging: exploratory social research among London residents', Proceedings of Seminar F of the PTRC 21st Summer Annual Meeting, 129–45.

Small, K.A. (1983), 'The incidence of congestion tolls on urban highways', *Journal of Urban Economics*, **13**, 90–111.

Small, K.A. (1992), 'Using the revenues from congestion pricing', *Transportation*, **19** (4), 359–81.

Sullivan, A.M. (1983), 'Second-best policies for congestion externalities', *Journal of Urban Economics*, **14**, 105–23.

Verhoef, E.T., P. Nijkamp and P. Rietveld (1996), 'Second-best congestion pricing: the case of an untolled alternative', *Journal of Urban Economics*, **40** (3), 279–302.

Verhoef, E.T., P. Nijkamp and P. Rietveld (1997), 'The social feasibility of road pricing: a case study for the Randstad area', *Journal of Transport Economics and Policy*, **31** (3), 255–76.

Vickrey, W.S. (1969), 'Congestion theory and transport investment', American *Economic Review*, **59** (Papers and Proceedings), 251–60.

Walters, A.A. (1961), 'The theory and measurement of private and social cost of highway congestion', *Econometrica*, **29** (4), 676–97.

Wardrop, J. (1952), 'Some theoretical aspects of road traffic research', *Proceedings of the Institute of Civil Engineers*, **1** (2), 325–78.

Wilson, J.D. (1983), 'Optimal road capacity in the presence of unpriced congestion', *Journal of Urban Economics*, **13**, 337–57.

2. Road pricing in practice

David M. Levinson

2.1 INTRODUCTION

Proposals to price road use for infrastructure financing, congestion mitigation, or air quality improvement have been surfacing at a regular pace over recent years (Small *et al.* 1989, TRB 1994, Roth 1996). However, the current interest in road pricing needs to fully recognize the long history of turnpikes. In particular, fundamental factors in the historic rise and decline of turnpikes, such as transactions costs, jurisdiction size and trip length, and the nature of the free rider problem (in both the original and modern sense of the term) need to be understood before new efforts are likely to succeed. Hybrid solutions which have been tried in the past, and remain in limited current use, such as lower rates for local traffic and mixed financing between toll revenue and local tax rates may enable new efforts, while theoretically efficient solutions such as pure usage charges remain politically infeasible or economically impractical.

Explanations for the decline of turnpikes in the nineteenth century cite the new modes of transportation, the canal and then the railroad, which diverted a great deal of long distance traffic, while urbanization and its concomitant use of public transport further changed travel patterns (Goodrich 1960, Hilton and Due 1960, Warner 1962, Gray 1967, Bobrick 1986, Smerk 1991, Dilts 1992, Martin 1992, Hood 1993). Yet the railroads brought with them an expansion of the economy and a growth in total traffic, if not an increase in long distance road traffic. But when the automobile–truck–highway system emerged in the twentieth century, toll financing did not resume its previous significance. A positive explanation for both the rise and fall, and the conditions for a significant re-emergence of turnpikes is called for.

This chapter examines the history of turnpikes while developing evidence for an explanatory hypothesis of the choice by jurisdictions to finance roads using tolls. It is posited that jurisdications generally attempt to maximize net benefits to their own residents (voters and road users). Jurisdictions consider the amount of additional revenue raised by tolls from non-residents against the inconvenience of tolls on their own residents and the costs of toll collection when choosing to tax or toll. Whether toll roads are managed by government, quasi-governmental organizations, regulated franchises, or unregulated private firms is a secondary question. The underlying hypothesis predicts that when jurisdictions responsible for managing sections of the road network are relatively small compared to the length of trips, an attempt will be made to shift the financial burden from local residents (local trip-makers) to those who make through trips. The hypothesis can in part explain the rise and decline of turnpikes. When trips by road were long distance (made by out of towners) they were expedient to toll by the simple placement of cordons across which one could not pass without paying a toll. But when long distance trips were diverted to canals and rails, imposing sufficient tolls on local residents to raise the required revenue was politically difficult and inefficient, and the toll financing system collapsed. The hypothesis also suggests that in the present era one is more likely to see tolls on highways constructed by a small jurisdiction (such as Delaware or other states in the northeastern United States), than on those constructed by large states (such as California or other states in the western United States). Furthermore, when roads are financed by a large integrated jurisdiction (like the United States federal government), where all trips are 'local' in that they remain within the large jurisdiction, the motivation to reduce the transaction costs which have traditionally been associated with toll roads is higher than when financing is by a smaller jurisdiction (any state which is a subset of the larger United States).

The burden of the transaction costs of tolls in the smaller jurisdiction falls in part on those who do not vote in the smaller jurisdiction. In the larger jurisdiction, where road use is pervasive (voters and road users are essentially identical groups), there may be no apparent gain to residents by using tolls rather than taxes (aside from the efficiency arguments of congestion pricing), while in the smaller jurisdiction, the benefits of tolls falling on non-residents is clear. This hypothesis does not claim to be a total explanation under all circumstances, a socio-political system like infrastructure financing has many influences. For instance, perfect excludability on roads coupled with the presence of 'free' alternatives, reductions in toll collection costs, ideological trends, regional rivalry and private ownership, may all increase the willingness of a jurisdiction to tolerate tolls even on local residents.

This chapter begins with a review of the status of roads before turnpikes. The weakness of the pre-toll financing system of statute road labor is the progenitor of turnpikes. The next section discusses the factors which led to the expansion and ultimate contraction of turnpikes. Following is a discussion of what has happened since the beginning of the twentieth century, the era of modern roads, which assumed importance first with the bicycle, and more importantly the automobile A wave of turnpike construction beginning with the introduction of limited access highways and lasting to the beginning of the interstate highway system is examined. Finally, current efforts at building toll roads in the post-interstate era and various road pricing schemes are discussed. General conclusions are drawn from an examination of the history.

2.2   ROADS BEFORE TURNPIKES

The roadway network of Britain has been heavily studied, and as English common law has become the underlying standard throughout much of the world, it is a reasonable starting point for understanding the status of roads before the imposition of tolls. This section relies heavily on the history of English roads by the Webbs (1913). It is believed that roads (in Britain and elsewhere) began as trails, running from high ground to fordable points on rivers or seaports. Through a process of cumulative causation – a cleared path attracts more traffic, which helps keep the path clear – these tracks became ensconced as the backbone of the original transportation network. The Roman occupation of Britain resulted in the construction of four main roads, principally for military communication, and numerous minor ones. After the Romans left, road use may have diminished, though certainly did not vanish.

The conception of the road in this period is described as more of a right than an object, a road is a right of passage on another's land, rather than the paved surface owned by some central authority that we imagine today. The highway constituted 'good passage' rather than the beaten track, so if the track were in poor condition, travelers could skirt it. The English word 'road' is of the same root as the word 'ride' – the Middle English 'rood' and Old English 'rad' – meaning the act of riding (Webster's II 1984).

The first English law dealing with roads was the 1285 Statute of Westminster, requiring residents of manors to clear two hundred feet on each side of their roadway of 'bushes, woods, or dykes' where a 'man may lurk to do hurt'. The wide right-of-way was to ensure protection from highway robbery rather than enhance movement. However, the roadways began to deteriorate over the late middle ages and renaissance period. An important cause was the decline of the religious orders associated with Henry VIII's break with Rome, which reduced pilgrimages and levels of traffic on the roads. Monasteries which had maintained roads were no longer able to, while the successors to their property had much less incentive. As cumulative causation works in one direction creating the roads, it also can work in reverse leading to their deterioration through neglect.

The next legal milestone, '2 and 3 Philip and Mary, C.8.', was passed by the Parliament of 1555. This law set the obligation of maintaining public highways upon several parties: the parish and every resident thereof, the newly created Surveyor of Highways for each parish, and the Justices of the Peace within the Parish's Division. Any or all of the parties could be brought before a judicial tribunal if they failed to fulfill their obligation. Parishioners with property were required to send plows, carts and horses to help maintain the roads, while others were required to labor for six consecutive days each year (about two percent of the working year) under the authority of the Surveyor of Highways.

As might be expected with growth in the economy and changes in the price level, over time the penalty for not performing the obligatory labor became less onerous than actually doing the work. By 1649, in some British localities, taxes were beginning to be assessed for road improvements to pay the Surveyor of Highways, formalizing the process. However the system of compulsory labor remained through the 1700s, until finally being eliminated in 1835. With the decline of the feudal manor system, this mechanism of 'financing' road improvements was viewed as more and more inequitable. Furthermore, it became increasingly inefficient as steadily higher and higher quality roads were demanded. The efficient division of labor called for something other than everyone serving the same six day period on roads; it makes little sense to have people responsible for spreading gravel on the roads working (or not working) over the same six days as those who had to dig the gravel.

Similar laws existed in North America, for instance in New York in 1800 all free males over the age of 21 were assessed highway labor 'in proportion to the estate and ability of each', with a minimum of one day and a maximum of 30 days as determined by town highway commissioners. Failure to contribute led to fines which steadily increased over time; commutation of labor cost 62.5 cents per day in 1801 (Klein and Majewski 1991). These laws lasted into the twentieth century in some rural areas, including parts of Texas (Goddard 1994).

The American system collapsed for similar reasons to the British, the mandatory labor was viewed as a burden and the laborers did not contribute their utmost effort. There was no incentive to work hard in general, and particularly so when your co-workers shirked. Unlike money which is fully fungible, labor's value depends on the effort put in as well as the amount of time spent. The stream of money for roads was inconsistent, coming from fines rather than any dedicated revenue, making planning difficult. The districts, which were small, could only draw on local laborers for construction, even if the road which it governed served a broad area.

2.3   THE FIRST TURNPIKE ERA: 1656–1900

2.3.1   Turnpikes in Britain

The initial deployment of turnpikes in seventeenth century Britain, their growth through the eighteenth and early nineteenth century, and decline in the late nineteenth century provides insight into current discussions of private toll roads. The English word 'turnpike' derives from the stretched spiked spear (pike), which is stretched across the road so it could be swung open for toll payers (McShane 1994). Turnpikes were both new and reconstructed roads (Buchanan 1990). In some important cases, the turnpiking of a road was accompanied by its reconstruction, in others, the government subsidized the reconstruction of an existing turnpike.

The first English turnpike is recorded in the Vestry of Radwell, Hertford-shire, which petitioned Parliament for road improvements in 1656. By 1663, Parliament permitted the placement of three toll gates to raise funds for the repair of the Great North Road by the County Justices in Quarter or Highway Sessions (Payne 1956). Some other toll gates followed.

After 1706 in Britain, Parliament chartered 'turnpike trusts' to improve selected roadways. A typical turnpike trust might have well over 80 trustees, though only a dozen or so attended meetings regularly (Payne 1956). The trusts were chaired by the treasurer, while the turnpikes were managed by an appointed surveyor (who generally did not serve as a trustee to avoid the accusation of jobbery). The surveyor supervised maintenance and construc-tion along the road, and was rarely limited to serving on only one turnpike. Ultimately, the collection of tolls was franchised to toll 'farmers', who after paying a fixed sum to the trust, were permitted to collect tolls at specified gates on the turnpike or turnpike system. Initially the toll farmers were local businessmen, but as the system matured the toll farmers became larger and larger organizations, some becoming national in scope by the 1820s.

Pawson (1977) provides the most comprehensive history on the deploy-ment of turnpikes. Figure 2.1 shows the number of turnpike trusts in Britain, approximating the classic 'S-curve' (the cumulative version of a normal distribution) through 1850. The theory underlying the S-curve is straightfor-ward. As knowledge of a technology and realization of its benefits spreads, the rate of adoption increases. Each project acts as a demonstration to poten-tial new users. Furthermore, the advantages to adoption may increase with the number of users if there are network or inter-firm scale, scope, or se-quence economies. As the technology diffuses, those who expect to attain the most benefit adopt it first. After a point, diminishing marginal returns set in. It is expected that, after complete exposure, technology is adopted by those who gain the most, and then by those who gain less and less from it, until it is

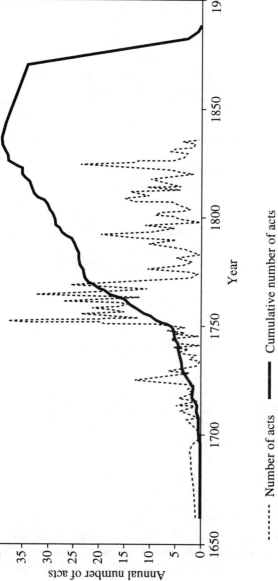

Source: Pawson (1977), Webb (1913)

Figure 2.1 *Turnpikes in Great Britain*

19

fully deployed. The life of technology may be cut short by competing technologies (such as canals and railroads in the case of turnpikes) or because a technological problem is discovered (as in the case of plank roads). Phillips and Turten (1987) describe to basic patterns of British roadways during deployment: radial roads focusing on towns (initially London and later others), and inter-regional roads serving intercity traffic.

In Britain, not everyone was subject to tolls. The government paid an annual fee in lieu of tolls, while residents of the road's locality typically paid a fixed annual fee rather than a per use charge (Payne 1956), thereby enabling some degree of subsidized if not free riding. In economic terms, British turnpikes were viewed as local public goods, with outsiders able to pay for limited use, as with a club good (Cornes and Sandler 1996). It is unlikely the fixed annual fee provided revenue in proportion to the costs of use, though the financial situation in terms of costs and revenues on turnpikes in this era remains to be satisfactorily examined. In other locations, the mails and religious persons were exempt, as were the construction workers improving the roads (Copeland 1963). The tollgates, which generally formed, at minimum, a cordon around the part of the road network operated by a single authority, extracted revenue from trips originating and/or destined for areas outside the toll authority's coverage. The tolls were used to pay off mortgages incurred by the trusts for road improvements, including resurfacing, straightening, and widening the turnpike, constructing footpaths, arching over sewers, and lighting the road in urban areas.

The deployment of turnpikes was not without some opposition. Prior to the turnpiking of a road, it had been open to free passage under English common law. But because 'free' roads were of poor quality, carriages belonging mostly to the rich could not easily pass. The turnpikes, which improved road quality at a price, were thus viewed as a transfer from the poor, who could always pass for free with carts and horses before tolls, to the rich, who gained the most when the roads were improved. This was quite similar to the enclosure movement, which also created similar new property rights. The inequity led to several turnpike riots (Albert 1979). Colliers who resented the placement of tolls between the coal mines and market in Kingswood, Bristol smashed gates and tollhouses during riots in 1727, 1731 and 1749. However, unlike laborers in other sectors who also had resentments, the coal miners were far better organized and had been given fewer dispensations than local traffic elsewhere. To combat these riots, the government in 1727 raised penalties on destroying turnpikes or riverworks to three months in prison and public whipping for the first offense and seven years of transportation (being sent abroad to a penal colony) for the second. Yet the rioters were not deterred. In the 1730s resistance moved to the Gloucester and Hereford regions. The last eighteenth century riot took place in 1758 near Bradford and Leeds, where tolls had been doubled and new gates imposed. In 1843 the Rebecca riots took place in Wales (Duckham 1984), leading to a restructuring of turnpike management.

After the 1843 Rebecca riot, a Welsh commission recommended that turnpikes be consolidated at the county level (Duckham 1984). Further, tolls were to be made uniform throughout the six counties of Wales for each type of good and toll booths were to be placed only every seven miles. Produce was to be exempt and agricultural inputs such as lime only tolled at half the normal rate. In an early recognition of the link between transportation and land use, the road taxes were deducted from the rent paid by tenant farmers. While the counties continued road maintenance, tolls were again farmed. The tolls were auctioned to the highest bidder, who over time became a representative of a national organization who attained one main economy of scale – the spread of risk over multiple operations. Risk was steadily increasing in the mid 1800s due to the railroading of the countryside; as soon as a railroad arrived, toll revenues dropped. When a railroad came in, or for any other good reason, the toll farmers tried to obtain a reduction in their lease payments from the county boards, who only sometimes acquiesced.

It should be noted that revenue dropped when the road board operated tolls themselves (Duckham 1984). Several reasons have been suggested, including higher administrative expenses and less thoroughness in catching toll evaders. A third reason to be noted is that cause and effect are reversed here; because toll revenues dropped, the county road board had to assume toll collection on the turnpike when the toll farmer defaulted. Toll farmers only paid a short period in advance for the right to collect revenue, minimizing capital outlay and providing them the opportunity for renegotiation with some leverage. While the tolls covered maintenance, the county still subsidized major capital expenses through the road rate (general taxes). In 1889 the county took over the road boards and dissolved the turnpikes.

The arrival and deployment of railroads from the late 1820s eroded the market share for inter-city transportation belonging to roads. The railroads, running on steam power, were significantly faster than horse-powered transport, a speed which made up for the increased access costs: the railroad depot may not have been the ultimate origin and destination, and trains ran on fixed schedules. However, since much intercity transport was provided by carriage services, road transport in the mid-1800s more closely resembles a competition between bus and rail than car and rail.

The Webbs (1913) date from the early 1860s the public determination to rid themselves of tolls. Tolls were replaced by local tax revenue in Ireland for funding roads in 1858, and the results were perceived to be adequate. Parliament member George Clive's 1862 retirement was seen as the removal of a key impediment to removing tolls, more precisely, in not renewing the terms of turnpike trusts as had been done in the past. The main complaints against tolls were that they were a costly and wasteful means for collecting revenue, inconvenient to the public, impeded traffic, and that the tax was inequitable. The recommended solution was to vest the roads in a public authority (highway districts or the local highway parish). From 1865, tolls in Scotland were abolished piecemeal. From 1864 onwards, turnpike trusts in Britain were dissolved at a rapid rate as shown on the right side of Figure 2.1. The final turnpike toll was collected November 1, 1895 on the Shrewsbury and Holyhead Road.

The loss of turnpike revenue increased the financial burden on local authorities to finance and maintain roads. Grants from the national government were intended to mitigate these factors. Eventually, authority for the roads moved up to the county level outside urban areas, and was paid for by local taxes sent to the county, town, or special district.

2.3.2   Turnpikes in America

In the United States, turnpike deployment began about a century after Great Britain. In 1785, Virginia authorized tolls on public, tax funded roads, and chartered a short distance turnpike from Alexandria to Berryville (USDOT 1976); Maryland followed suit in 1787 (Klein and Majewski 1994). The first significant US turnpike company was chartered in Pennsylvania in 1792, connecting Philadelphia and Lancaster, and completed two years later (USDOT 1976). To look at the rate of deployment, Table 2.1 shows the number of turnpike companies chartered in several states from 1790 to 1845. Like turnpikes, bridges were private toll facilities. From 1786 to 1798, 59 toll bridges were chartered (Klein 1990). Baer *et al.* (1993) illustrate the basic pattern in New York as a series of roads radiating from that state's main artery, the Hudson River, and later the Erie Canal. In California, most toll roads were deployed in the mining counties of the Sierra Nevada (Klein and Yin 1994).

The Federal Government was not permitted under the Constitution to collect tolls, according to President Monroe, who vetoed attempts to place tolls on the National Road (running from the Potomac River to the Ohio River), which was already beginning to deteriorate less than ten years after its 1813 opening. By the 1830s, Congress turned over the road to the relevant states, who imposed tolls to maintain the road (USDOT 1976).

Much of the American turnpike construction was due to competition between towns to gain trade. The subscribers to turnpikes, as with canals, were a mixed group, including citizens, municipalities, and state governments, as well as foreign nationals in later years. Although the federal government had

Table 2.1   Turnpike incorporation in the United States, 1792–1845

State	1792–1800	1801–10	1811–20	1821–30	1831–40	1841–45	Total
New Hampshire	4	45	5	1	4	0	59
Vermont	9	19	15	7	4	3	57
Massachusetts	9	80	8	16	1	1	115
Rhode Island	3	13	8	13	3	1	41
Connecticut	23	37	16	24	13	0	113
New York	13	126	133	75	83	27	457
Pennsylvania	5	39	101	59	101	37	342
New Jersey	0	22	22	3	3	0	50
Virginia	0	6	7	8	25	0	46
Maryland	3	9	33	12	14	7	78
Ohio	0	2	14	12	114	62	204
Total	69	398	362	230	365	138	1562

Source: Fielding and Klein (1992)

subsidized new turnpikes and roads through land grants in the public lands (western) states prior to 1830, attempts to have the Federal government subscribe to turnpike company stock offerings were thwarted by President Jackson's 1830 veto of the Maysville Road Bill, sponsored by Kentucky to get federal funds for what Jackson deemed a purely local road. It was 20 years before federal subsidies to infrastructure, then railroads, came again (USDOT 1976). Despite the sparse federal involvement, town leaders realized that an early edge in attaining access to other areas, and thus becoming a key cross-roads, would have long term payoffs (Klein and Majewski 1994). Individuals would relocate to the towns with turnpike access, which would attract others individuals, provide revenues to the turnpike, and encourage additional transportation investments. Towns without access would wither.

Klein and Majewski (1994) argue that, after the first few were chartered, turnpike investments were recognized as unprofitable, and were really an example of voluntary private provision of a public good for the good of the public. Towns and their leading citizens were looking for economic spillovers from the roads. Because towns were more autonomous in this era, citizens felt more obligated to contribute. Investors constituting the social elites of towns, invested in turnpikes to promote the town's interest (and only indirectly their own). The voluntary private provision of public goods can be individually rational if the providers' contribution is outweighed by the benefits received from their own contribution (Olson 1965). Furthermore, social pressures were placed on members of the elite to ensure sufficient subscription to new investment. These pressures enforced good behavior (meeting social obligations), due to the repeated interactions of the local business elite, in multiple spheres, which would socially or economically discipline a member who shirked responsibilities. Gray (1967) finds similar practices in the chartering of the Chesapeake and Delaware canal.

Although there is some aspect of voluntary private provision of a public good, with possible private benefit from spillover, in the construction of many turnpikes, other turnpikes were just as surely speculative ventures attempting to be profitable in their own right. Foreign (or even non-local) investment provides evidence of this (USDOT 1976).

In New York, toll booths were spaced at ten mile intervals, thereby allowing local trips to be free riders. The free rider problem was significant. For instance, Massachusetts law exempted people going to and from gristmills or church, people on military duty, on journeys within the town where the tollgate was, or on common and ordinary family business (Rae 1971). Furthermore, shunpikes frequently arose to allow travelers to avoid the road section with the toll booth. These two factors limited the profitability of turnpikes.

Opposition also occurred in the United States, for many of the expected reasons. First was opposition of locals to paying a toll when travel had been free; much of this opposition was mitigated by charters which enabled locals to be free riders. Second there was resentment of those who owned the turnpike, who would get rich (or at least were thought to get rich) at the expense of travelers, and opposition to the corporate form in general, which was new in the early 1800s (Klein and Majewski 1994). Over the long term, this second set of opponents had little effect, as the corporate form has become the dominant means of organizing business. The opposition to urban highways that emerged after the interstate program was initiated was due to destruction of local communities as well as NIMBYism (NIMBY is an abbreviation for Not In My Back Yard), opposition to any noxious facilities nearby. There is no record that opposition in the first turnpike era had any similar causes.

As in Britain, in the United States the driving forces behind disturnpiking were other modes: canals and railroads. At first these modes, particularly canals, killed the competing trunk roads, while in fact promoting the construction of complementary branches (Baer *et al.* 1993). The Erie Canal opened in 1825 and soon found its first victims, the First, Second, and Third Great Western turnpikes, which saw annual revenues decline. Just as the turnpikes declined, the fortunes of towns on the turnpikes declined, while those on the canal rose. Nevertheless, the turnpikes were not immediately put out of business. Turnpikes were not helped by the Supreme Court's 1837 decision in the Charles River Bridge case, which ruled against a nebulous interpretation of the franchises granted by states as exclusive; franchises that roads had hoped to use to delay competing canals and railroads (McShane 1994).

The roads in New York faced a second blow with the advent of major railroad construction beginning in 1848. 'The turnpikes disintegrated in stages, abandoning their road piece by unprofitable piece' (Baer *et al.* 1993, p. 8). By the end of the 1850s New York's major trunk turnpikes were dissolved and became public roads. However, as older turnpikes saw long distance traffic wither and collapse, new feeder roads were being constructed as complements to the railroads. Rose argues that the number of new charters did not diminish greatly until 1875 (Rose 1953). The Lancaster Pike, the first significant turnpike, was not finally dissolved until 1902 (USDOT 1976).

A brief exception to the decline of turnpikes occurred with the emergence (and disappearance) of plank roads between 1846 and 1857 (Klein and Majewski 1994). Plank roads overcame many of the competitive disadvantages suffered by gravel roads, they were smooth and thus enabled faster speeds. They were most prevalent in areas where lumber was cheap. Unfortunately, the planks deteriorated after only a few years, much sooner than expected, and shortly after they were deployed they were abandoned. In New York, the length constructed was over 3500 miles (5800 km) between 1846–53, where the plank roads served principally as branch roads in the Erie Canal and Hudson River regions, as well as radial roads to several upstate cities.

The California turnpike experience differs from that in the eastern states. In addition to beginning about 50 years later in the wake of the gold rush, the rationales for the road differed. California law borrowed heavily from eastern states, including financial requirements that may have hindered the deployment of the new roads (Klein and Yin 1994). In the eastern states toll roads emerged from community enterprise without a significant profit motive, California was far more business-like. It is unclear to what extent the California roads succeeded in being profitable enterprises, some were and some weren't though the exact proportions are not known (Klein and Yin 1994). The principal owners of California's toll roads were resource extraction companies such as mines and lumber companies. In addition, a number of tourist roads were built, including to Yosemite and on Mount Wilson (Klein and Yin 1994).

The argument can be made that some of the toll roads, particularly in California, were required as a component in the production process. For instance roads and mines are complements. A mine without access is useless, but the traffic to the mine does not utilize the full capacity of the road. Because roads exhibit economies of scope – it doesn't matter whether the trip is to the mine (or resort) or not, the road equally serves both – and are lumpy investments (the lanes of a road cannot be made significantly smaller in proportion to the scale of traffic, they represent an indivisibility), the California road owners were trying to reap the rewards associated with the necessary construction of a road. The complementarity between transportation and the points they access has been seen most noticeably in the construction of streetcars and their associated suburbs in the late nineteenth and early twentieth century (Warner 1962) and more recently in developer-financed roads, including some toll roads opening up new areas like the Dulles Greenway in Virginia.

2.4   TWENTIETH CENTURY TURNPIKES

2.4.1 The American Experience

The advent of the bicycle, and then the automobile created a new set of needs for highways. While previously roads had been designed first for pedestrians and animals (pack animals to carry people and goods, cattle and swine being herded to market), wheeled carts and carriages require an improved surface. The technology change of the wide(r)spread adoption of wheeled vehicles led to a change in highway financing in the eighteenth century. Similarly, rubber wheeled vehicles at higher speed required a smoother surface yet again. To support the new vehicle stock, roads needed to be improved with smoother surfaces and more gradual curves that could be taken at higher speeds. In the United States, two highway systems were deployed in the twentieth century to support the automobile. The first 'US Highways' created a national network of paved roads, the second 'Interstates' created a network of grade separated freeways. Both were largely free of tolls. In 1914, before significant federal involvement, but after the beginning of the good roads movements, the United States had 257 293 miles of surfaced roads, of which 75 400 miles were macadam, 1591 were brick, and 2349 were concrete (Flink 1990).

Prior to federal involvement with 'US Highways', some modern twentieth century roads had been toll financed, though this was limited in scope. In 1908, William Vanderbilt started a turnpike company to construct the Long Island Motor Parkway, intended for car enthusiasts in New York (McShane 1994). However the road, only one lane in each direction, never made much money, and had technical problems with its surface. The toll idea was borrowed by Robert Moses, New York's Park Commissioner to fund 'parkways' throughout metropolitan New York from the 1920s (Caro 1974). Ironically, Moses' Northern States Parkway paralleled the Vanderbilt route, and bankrupted it in 1938 (the route became a power line right of way). The DuPont family built a similar private roadway in Delaware (McShane 1994).

Financing in the era of US Highways was principally by gas tax, beginning in Oregon, New Mexico and Colorado in 1919; by 1929 it was national in scope. In 1921 property taxes and general funds paid about 75 percent of the cost of roads, by 1929 21 states no longer used any general funds or property taxes for funding, and most money came from gas taxes (Flink 1990). The federal aid program paid for no more than 7 percent of the road miles in a state; by 1924 this amounted to $15 000 per mile. Beginning in Britain in 1909 came the idea of non-divertability of gas taxes, which said that gas revenue would be spent on roads, not on general budget issues or even for other transport modes. This disappeared in Britain in 1926 (Flink 1990), and later in the United States (1973 for other transport modes and 1993 for general revenue at the federal level).

Before the federal government's involvement in grade separated roads, a number of states, particularly in the northeast, had already chartered turnpike authorities to construct those intercity roads. Proposals by the Roosevelt administration for a transcontinental toll road from 1934 came to naught (Goddard 1994). The Bureau of Public Roads, a long-term opponent of tolls (Goddard 1994) published a report in 1939 'Toll Roads and Free Roads' which argued that tolls would cover less than half the annual cost of a system of interstate roads (Rae 1971). However, their estimates were quite inaccurate given the experience of actual toll roads opened in the next two decades, for instance, a projection of 715 vehicles per day on the Pennsylvania Turnpike, versus actual demand in the tens of thousands (Rae 1971, Gifford 1983). Gifford (1983) argues forcefully that the conclusions of the report to oppose federal toll roads would have been reversed had accurate demand forecasts been used and accepted. Even President Eisenhower thought the interstate system should be toll financed, though Congress, led by Senator Gore, Sr disagreed (Goddard 1994).

Many tunnels and bridges were constructed as toll facilities, both before and during the interstate era. Those before the interstates include the Golden Gate and San Francisco Bay Bridges in the Bay Area and the Holland and Lincoln tunnels and George Washington Bridge in New York.

Just as the first American turnpike was in Pennsylvania, so was the first in the new era of limited access highways. The Pennsylvania Turnpike, constructed in part along the abandoned South Pennsylvania railroad right of way and through already partially bored tunnels, opened in 1940 connecting Pittsburgh with Harrisburg along a higher quality and shorter route than the existing US 30 (The Lincoln Highway) and US 22 (The William Penn Highway). The construction of the South Pennsylvania railroad had begun under the direction of Commodore Vanderbilt and Andrew Carnegie as a competitor to the Pennsylvania railroad, which had a spatial monopoly on long distance freight traffic through the state. Vanderbilt, who owned the New York Central, believed the Pennsylvania railroad was supporting a competitor in New York, and the South Pennsylvania railroad was begun as a competitive response. J.P. Morgan brokered a deal which led to the abandonment of both competitive projects (Cupper 1990). Though the road was built without any federal transportation funds, other New Deal financing sources were used, including a $29.25 million grant from the Public Works Administration and $40.8 million purchase of bonds by the Reconstruction Finance Corporation (Deakin 1989, Cupper 1990). The road was not only the first new era toll road, it was also the first long distance limited access highway built in the United States. The original toll was $1.50 end to end, or just over a penny a mile ($0.006/km), but that was not enough to keep the road uncongested, the first traffic jam occurred (27 000 vehicles on a single day) the sixth day the road was open as Sunday drivers took advantage of views of fall foliage (Cupper 1990). The toll road was extended several times to Ohio and New Jersey, the road was widened and improved in places, and over time the toll has risen to 3.1 pennies/mile ($0.019/km) and traffic flow to 97 million vehicles per year in 1989.

There was considerable controversy over how to treat toll roads in the context of the toll-free interstate highway system, particularly whether states should be compensated for toll roads already constructed. Ultimately 2700 miles (4300 km) of the pre-interstate toll roads were included in the interstate system. Over 4000 miles (6400 km) of toll facilities were built in the period from 1940–60 in over 30 states (Schaevitz 1991). These include the turnpikes shown in Table 2.2, as of 1963, and shown chronologically in Figure 2.2. As can be seen, the toll roads were built largely in the physically smaller eastern and midwestern states, while the large western states relied on 'free' roads. At least two factors help explain this difference. The first is the hypothesis of this research, that the smaller states were raising revenue from the large portion of out-of-state traffic, while in large states it follows that a higher proportion of traffic is local, average trip lengths and their distribution being about equal (which of course is not precisely true, long trip lengths are more often found in the west, though surely flow between states as a share of traffic is less). The second has to do with federal land ownership, which is significantly higher in western states, and led to higher federal matching shares for construction of 'free roads'. In eastern states, the federal match was only 50 percent before the advent of the interstate program, in the public lands states, the match was as high as 85 percent (Gifford 1983).

Since the completion of the interstate system a few additional toll roads have been built, several under private ownership. Some 35 projects over 1900 km in length of new toll roads are under study, design, construction, or

Table 2.2   Miles of toll highways in operation in 1963

State	Mileage in use	Cost ($ thousands)	Period built
Colorado	17.3	6 237	1952
Connecticut	193.9	502 092	1940–59
Delaware	11.2	30 000	1963
Florida	206.6	171 783	1950–64
Georgia	11.1	3 150	1924
Illinois	185.3	445 623	1958–59
Indiana	156.9	280 000	1956
Kansas	240.9	179 500	1956–59
Kentucky	204.7	185 500	1956–64
Maine	112.2	79 406	1955–57
Maryland	42.3	74 000	1963
Massachusetts	124.4	239 000	1957
New Hampshire	77.2	43 524	1950–57
New Jersey	309.2	821 200	1952–57
New York	628.8	1 130 951	1926–60
Ohio	241.0	326 000	1955
Oklahoma	174.3	106 714	1953–57
Pennsylvania	469.3	539 644	1940–57
Texas	30.1	58 500	1957
Virginia	34.6	75 150	1958
West Virginia	86.3	133 000	1954
Totals	3557.6	5 430 994	1940–64

Source: Rae (1971) after Bureau of Public Road data

recently opened, a number are listed in Table 2.3 (Deakin 1989). Some of these roads are intended to accommodate new development, others to serve existing travel demands. The Dulles Greenway, a private road, has been built with major donations of land from adjoining landowners hoping to develop. Along California's SR91, in the median of an existing highway, High Occupancy/Toll lanes were constructed with land control transferred from the state to a private company.

2.4.2   International Experience

While in the United States twentieth-century toll road experience has been almost completely public, the same is not true in other countries. In those countries, private sector toll roads have been constructed with the govern-

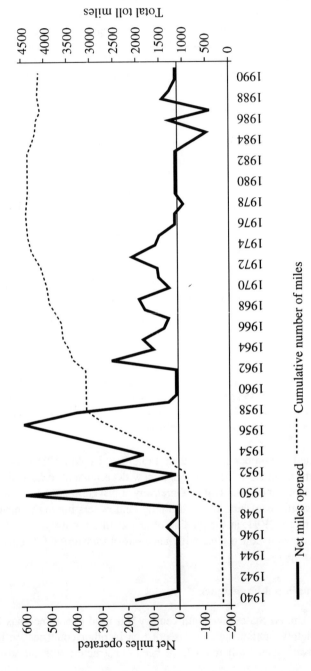

Source: Gomez-Ibañez (1993)

Figure 2.2   Toll roads in the United States 1940–91

— Net miles opened   ······ Cumulative number of miles

30

Table 2.3 Recent public and private toll road projects and proposals

Toll road	Opened	Length	Location	Cost	Ownership
Hardy Toll Road	created 1983	35 km	Houston, TX	$900 million bonds	Harris County Toll Road Authority
Sam Houston Tollway	created 1983	140 km	Houston, TX	$900 million bonds	Harris County Toll Road Authority
North–South Tollway	1990	27 km	DuPage Co. IL		Illinois State Toll Highway Authority
Dulles Greenway	1994	27 km	Loudoun Co. VA	$300 million	Dulles Greenway Consortium
E-470	proposed	77 km	Denver CO		E-470 authority public–private
CA SR91	1994	10 miles	Orange Co. CA	$80 million	California Toll Road Corporation
CA SR-57	proposed	11 miles	Orange Co. CA	$700 million	Perot
CA SR-125	proposed	10 miles	San Diego Co. CA	$400 million	Parsons Brinkerhoff
Midstate Toll Road	proposed	85 miles		$600 million (first 40 miles)	Parsons Corp.
Sawgrass/Deerfield Expwy	1991	23 miles	Ft. Lauderdale Broward Co. FL		Broward Co. Expressway Authority
Bi-County Thruway		28 miles	Tarpon Springs (Tampa) Pasco Co. FL		(maint. by Florida DOT)

Source: Deakin (1989), Schaevitz (1991), Gomez-Ibañez and Meyer (1993)

31

ment's consent. Unlike many toll roads in the US, these roads apply perfect excludability, so no one can free ride the roads. A price for this is longer spacing between exits than traditionally found in the US, where toll roads are more often (though not exclusively) cordons on a state line or across a waterway. A key transportation implication is the increase in back-tracking costs as users must drive beyond a destination to exit and then backtrack, or spend more time in travel on the slower parallel free roads.

France had granted concessions to private and mixed public–private corporations to finance, build, operate and receive revenue from intercity toll roads, while the government retained ownership and the right to repurchase at the end of a fixed time period. By the 1990s France had constructed 6000 km of intercity autoroutes, all but 500 of which are tolled (Gomez-Ibañez and Meyer 1993). However, the 1500 km of urban autoroutes remain untolled. The intercity routes compete with a 30 000 km network of untolled national roads, built to less stringent standards and often not grade separated. The eight major concessionaires originally had significant private sector involvement, but only one, Cofiroute, which operates 732 km, remains so, the rest were taken over by government when they hit financial difficulties. Those difficulties were not solely the product of a free market, rather the government in the 1970s took to regulating prices and allowing them to rise at a rate lower than that of inflation, hurting the companies' balance sheets. The socialist government of Mitterand forced consolidation and conversion of the private companies to mixed public–private companies and implemented cross-subsidies between routes.

Spain began similarly to France, establishing Autopistas, a private concession to operate toll roads. This system was followed by an untolled publicly owned intercity highway system, the Autovias, promoted by the socialized government of Gonzalez. Both systems are about 2000 km in size, the Autopistas system is comprised of 13 companies, nine of which are still private (Gomez-Ibañez and Meyer 1993). In advance of the 1992 Olympics and World's Fair, some new Autopistas routes were established. Gomez-Ibañez and Meyer (1993) conclude that the system as a whole is profitable, though not each route.

Mexico established publicly owned toll roads in the 1950s and constructed about 1000 km by 1970 (Gomez-Ibañez and Meyer 1993). During the 1980s two concessions totaling 215 km were granted to the national development bank, with equity split between the bank, contractors and state governments. In 1989 a program to build 4000 km of toll roads was proposed; the government selected the roads, performed the design and set the initial tolls, which would be permitted to rise with inflation. Twenty-nine new concessions, of an average duration of 11 years, were signed between 1989 and 1991, and roads were opened at the rate of 500 km per year. The toll rates were set high and the roads are thought to be underutilized. The government has subsidized construction on the less profitable routes. There has been a move to privatize the existing publicly owned toll roads.

Malaysia, Indonesia, and Thailand have also experimented with private toll roads (Gomez-Ibañez and Meyer 1993). In Malaysia, a private firm connected with the government received a concession to collect tolls and operate 424 km of road that had already been constructed by the government with the obligation to complete the 785 km road from Thailand to Singapore. The Indonesian government had built 318 km of toll roads and four bridges by 1990. As with Malaysia, firms with government connections were given the authority to build private joint-venture toll roads, where the government provided the right of way and the firm did construction. Thailand has constructed public toll roads in and around Bangkok, and in 1989 signed a concession with a private firm to complete a beltway around the capital and construct spokes. Tolls are to be shared between the public and private roads.

Economists have long suggested widespread road pricing as a solution to the financing and congestion problems. However, comprehensive pricing has only been carried out in a few areas to a limited extent. These experiments have all operated with the government acting as a central planner, dictating road prices to users.

The best example may be in Hong Kong, where in the 1980s a full-fledged test of road pricing technology was implemented (Hau 1992). A sample of 2500 vehicles tested electronic road pricing: each vehicle was fitted with an electronic license plate and tolls were collected at 18 sites buried in the ground. While the system was technically successful, it failed the political test when it was perceived to be just another tax (despite government protestations that it would be revenue neutral) and enabled 'big brother' to monitor travel, a particular concern with the transfer of Hong Kong to the People's Republic of China in 1997.

Since 1975 Singapore has had an area licensing scheme (Hau 1992, McCarthy and Tay 1993), where in order to enter the downtown cordon, cars must possess a license, which can be read as the cars travel at full speed when entering the cordon. The program did significantly reduce vehicle travel into the cordon, though off-peak traffic increased. Hau (1992) concludes that the government is using the area licensing scheme as a traffic management device rather than a revenue generator. McCarthy and Tay (1993) argue that the toll is too high, and that tolled 'peak' period congestion is now lower than the untolled 'off-peak'. They suggest that presence of congestion is insufficient grounds for imposing a toll, and that the congestion externality needs to be estimated explicitly.

Bergen, Norway has established a ring around the central business district and imposed tolls on the traffic crossing that ring. Bergen allows the purchase of a seasonal pass which has zero marginal effect, as there is no immediate out of pocket charge, no delay, and it provides no incentive not to travel after the pass is purchased. Traffic did decline somewhat after the program was put in place. The revenue was used to finance construction of expansion to the toll system. This system has been adopted by Oslo and Trondheim, and considered by many other cities. The tolls use electronic as well as manual collection, and provide volume discounts for frequent users (PRA 1996).

2.5   SUMMARY AND CONCLUSIONS

The pressure to charter turnpikes initially came from the poor results and impracticalities of statute labor for maintaining roads. Toll roads have come in four eras. The first, which lasted from the 1700s and peaked in the early to mid 1800s, saw turnpikes under the control of local companies and trusts chartered by states or Parliament.

The difference between the American and British experience is instructive. In Britain, turnpikes were quasi-governmental organizations which sold bonds to fund construction. In the United States, turnpikes were private companies, granted charters by the state to sell stock, and raise tolls on given roads. Turnpike authorities were permitted to lay out roads and negotiate with property owners whose property they needed to take; legal procedures were implemented when this was a problem. On both continents, the turnpike authority's obligations were similar, to maintain roads at an acceptable standard. In Britain, turnpikes were viewed as local public goods, with some club aspects. In America, turnpikes were privately provided. However, the motivations in the United States include both the case of voluntary provision of public goods – with profits foregone, and the attempt to undertake a profitable enterprise. Free riders were present in both America and England: first, shunpikes enabled the skirting of tolls; second, many classes of trips which crossed the tollgate were exempt; third, trips remaining within the toll cordon raised no revenue. Local residents in Britain and some American towns subsidized the roads through annual taxes, or through municipal subscription to an unprofitable road, but whether these subsidies covered the full private cost of travel by local residents is doubtful. As the competition from canal and rails diverted long distance trips, toll revenue declined, even if local traffic did not, leading to the bankruptcy and abandonment of turnpikes in the United States and disturnpiking and public takeover of the quasi-autonomous trusts in Britain. Because more trips were local to the larger government level (states in the US or counties in England), and revenue could be raised from multiple sources, tolls were removed.

A brief second wave came about with the automobile and the first significant deployment of smooth paved roads. However, in the US most roads were financed by states, and later the federal government by means of a gas tax. With the relatively slow speed of highway travel, most trips remained within states, through trips were not as significant as later in the twentieth century. A number of parkways, however, featuring the property of excludability, were toll financed.

A third and significant wave of toll financing arrived with the deployment of grade separated highways. Because trips become longer distance, more trips were from out of state. Since financing was at the state level, turnpikes were effective for collecting revenue from all users. But when national financing became dominant, the definition of 'local' changed, and new toll roads stopped being built in the US, though international experience varies. Furthermore, unlike earlier roads, grade separated roads are easily excludable, that is, the number of entrances is limited and tolls can be cost-effectively assessed at each. The same is not true of roads without grade separations.

Finally, upon completion of the interstate (intercity grade separated highway) system in the US, new road financing has largely become a local problem again, and new toll roads are being constructed, including some private roads. Because of the length of trips, and because of the ease with which tolls can be collected on these excludable roads, as well as a reduction in toll collection transaction costs on both the government and traveler side with electronic toll collection, tolls are again a feasible option. Road pricing proposals depend on electronic toll collection. Further, cordon tolls are being placed around a number of cities internationally, which will tax non-local residents for traveling on urban streets. The cordons establish excludability for use of a network from outside, though not for any particular link once the network is entered. In places where cordons can easily be established, such as river crossings and ring roads, this is a feasible option for localities wishing to switch the road financing burden to suburban residents. Ironically, the attempts of localities subject to obsolete political boundaries to finance infrastructure for the 'wrong' reason – the offloading of costs on non-residents, creates opportunities to achieve a more efficient infrastructure pricing and financing system.

From the evidence in this chapter, two key conditions required to bring about more widespread use of toll financing emerge. First, a decentralization of the authority for road operation to the point where a significant number of the trips are non-local to the relevant decision-making authority would foster a willingness to use tolls, following the traditional saying 'don't tax you, don't tax me, tax the fellow behind the tree'. Second, a decline in transaction costs to the point where they are equal to or lower than the costs of other revenue streams is necessary, where transaction costs include both delay to users and collection costs for operators. These two factors should shift beliefs about the utility of imposing tolls, as they are designed to toll someone else (not the individual making the decision to support them) and they raise at least as much revenue with the same amount of or less inconvenience.

2.6 ACKNOWLEDGEMENTS

A previous version of this paper was presented at the 43rd North American Meeting of the Regional Science Association International, in Arlington, Virginia, November 14–17, 1996, and at seminars at George Mason University and the University of California at Berkeley. The participants are thanked for their comments. In particular the author would like to thank Mark Hansen, David Gillen, Betty Deakin, Carlos Daganzo, Adib Kanafani, David Klein and Marcus Berliant. This research was funded in part by a Dissertation Fellowship from the University of California Transportation Center and from California PATHS project MOU 275.

REFERENCES

Albert, William (1979), 'Popular opposition to turnpike trusts in early eighteenth century England', *Journal of Transport History*, **2** (5) (Feb.), 1–17.

Baer, Christopher T., Daniel B. Klein and John Majewski (1993), 'From trunk to branch: toll roads in New York, 1800–1860, *Essays in Economic and Business History*, **XI**, 191–209, University of California Transportation Center No. 121, August.

Bobrick, Benson (1986), *Labyrinths of Iron. Subways in History, Myth, Art, Technology, and War*, New York: Henry Holt.

Buchanan, B.J. (1990), 'The turnpike roads: A classic trap?', *Journal of Transport History*, **3** (11) (Sept.), 60–72.

Caro, Robert (1974), *The Power Broker*, New York: Alfred Knopf Publishers.

Copeland, John (1963), 'An Essex turnpike gate', *Journal of Transport History*, **1** (6) (Nov.), 87–94.

Cornes, Richard and Todd Sandler (1996), *The Theory of Externalities, Public Goods, and Club Goods*, Cambridge UK: Cambridge University Press.

Cupper, Dan (1990), 'The Road to the Future', *American Heritage*, May/June, 103–11.

Deakin, Elizabeth (1989), 'Toll roads: A new direction for US highways?', *Built Environment*, **15** (3/4), 185–94. (University of California Transportation Center No. 56 reprint.)

Dilts, James D. (1992), *The Great Road: The Building of the Baltimore and Ohio, the Nation's First Railroad, 1828–1853*, Stanford CA: Stanford University Press.

Duckham, Baron F. (1984), 'Road administration in South Wales: The Carmarthenshire Roads Board, 1845–89', *Journal of Transport History*, **3** (5) (March), 45–65.

Fielding, Gordon J. and Daniel B. Klein (1992), 'Toll roads: learning from the nineteenth century', *Transportation Quarterly*, (July), 321–41.

Flink, James J. (1990), *The Automobile Age*, Cambridge, MA: MIT Press.

Gifford, Jonathan (1983), 'An analysis of the federal role in the planning, design, and deployment of rural roads, toll roads, and urban freeways', Dissertation UCB-ITS-DS-83-2, Institute of Transportation Studies, Berkeley, CA: University of California.

Goddard, Stephen B. (1994), *Getting There: The Epic Struggle Between Road and Rail in the American Century*, New York: Basic Books.

Gomez-Ibañez, Jose and John Meyer (1993), *Going Private: The International Experience with Transport Privatization*, Washington, DC: Brookings Institute.

Goodrich, Carter (1960), *Government Promotion of American Canals and Railroads: 1800–1890*, Westport CT: Greenwood Press Publishers.

Gray, Ralph D. (1967), *The National Waterway*, Urbana, IL: University of Illinois Press.

Hau, Timothy D. (1992), *Congestion Charging Mechanisms: An Evaluation of Current Practice*, Washington, DC: The World Bank.

Hilton, George W. and John F. Due (1960), *The Electric Interurban Railways in America*, Stanford, CA: Stanford University Press.

Hood, Clifton (1993), *722 Miles: The Building of the Subways and How They Transformed New York*, New York: Simon and Schuster.

Klein, Daniel B. (1990), 'The voluntary provision of public goods? The turnpike companies of early America, *Economic Inquiry*, March 1990. (University of California Transportation Center No. 18 reprint.)

Klein, Daniel B. and John Majewski (1994), 'Plank road fever in ante-bellum America: New York state origins, *New York History*, January 1994, 39–65. (University of California Transportation Center No. 243 reprint.)

Klein, Daniel B. and Chi Yin (1994), 'Use esteem and profit in voluntary provision: toll roads in California, 1850–1902', *Economic Inquiry*, **34** (October), 678–92. (*The Private Provision of Frontier Infrastructure: Toll Roads in California 1850–1902*, University of California Transportation Center No. 238, preprint.)

Martin, Albro (1992), *Railroads Triumphant: The Growth, Rejection, and Rebirth of a Vital American Force*, Oxford, UK: Oxford University Press.

McCarthy, Patrick and Richard Tay (1993), 'Economic efficiency vs. traffic restraint: a note on Singapore's area license scheme, *Journal of Urban Economics*, **34**, 96–100.

McShane, Clay (1994), *Down the Asphalt Path: The Automobile and the American City*, New York: Columbia University Press.

Olson, Mancur (1965), *The Logic of Collective Action: Public Goods and the Theory of Groups*, Cambridge, MA: Harvard University Press.

Pawson, Eric (1977), *Transport and Economy: The Turnpike Roads of Eighteenth Century Britain*, New York: Academic Press.

Payne, Peter L. (1956), 'The Bermondsey, Rotherhithe and Deptford Turnpike Trust: 1776–1810', Journal of Transport History **1** (2) (May), 132–43.

Phillips, A.D.M. and B.J. Turten (1987), 'Staffordshire turnpike trusts and traffic in the early nineteenth century', *Journal of Transport History*, **3** (8) (Sept.), 126–46.

Public Roads Administration (PRA) (Norway) (1996), *The Automatic Toll Ring in Trondheim*, Oslo: Directorate of Public Roads.

Rae, John (1971), *The Road and Car in American Life*, Cambridge, MA: MIT Press.

Rose, A. (1953), *Historical American Highways – Public Roads of the Past*, Washington, DC: American Association of State Highway Officials.

Schaevitz, Robert C. (1991), *Private Sector Role in US Toll Road Financing – Issues and Outlook*, Transportation Research Record 1197, 1–8.

Small, Ken, Clifford Winston and Carol Evans (1989), *Road Work*, Washington, DC: Brookings Institution.

Smerk, George M. (1991), *The Federal Role in Urban Mass Transportation*, Bloomington, IN: Indiana University Press.

Transportation Research Board (TRB) (1994), *Curbing Gridlock: Peak Period Fees to Relive Traffic Congestion*, Special Report 242, Washington, DC.

United States Department of Transportation (USDOT) (1976), *America's Highways: 1776–1976*, Washington, DC: Federal Highway Administration, Government Printing Office.

Warner, Sam Bass (1962), *Streetcar Suburbs*, Cambridge, MA: Harvard University Press.

Webb, Sidney and Beatrice Webb (1913), *English Local Government: The Story of the King's Highway*, London: Longmans, Green and Co.

Webster's II New Riverside Dictionary (1984), New York: Riverside Publishing Company.

3. Congestion pricing and road investment

Timothy D. Hau*

I will begin with the proposition that in no other major area are pricing practices so irrational, so out of date, and so conducive to waste as in urban transportation. Two aspects are particularly deficient: the absence of adequate peak-off differentials and the gross underpricing of some modes relative to others. In nearly all other operations characterized by peak load problems, at least some attempt is made to differentiate between the rates charged for peak and for off-peak service. Where competition exists, this pattern is enforced by competition: resort hotels have off-season rates; theaters charge more on weekends and less for matinees. Telephone calls are cheaper at night ... But in transportation, such differentiation as exists is usually perverse.

William Vickrey (1963, p. 452)
Nobel Laureate in Economic Sciences, 1996

3.1 INTRODUCTION

The cost of congestion was regarded by the late Professor William Vickrey to be high. Very roughly, the real economic cost of the transport infrastructure in the US was about three times the total gasoline and vehicular taxes generated by automobile use of city streets (Vickrey, 1963). Yet motorists were always under the misimpression that they pay their way: highway taxes and license revenues were sufficient to cover the highway expenditures made by the US federal and state governments. Even if it were true that gasoline taxes or license fees were increased to meet higher road expenditures, so that motorists were to pay all their way, Professor Vickrey argued back in 1959 – with premonition in hindsight – that the results of not charging motorists for their rush-hour usage can be 'disastrously expensive' (Vickrey, 1960, p. 468; excerpt reprinted in Arnott, et al., 1994, p. 44). Why is it so important to charge users for their use of an item at the margin rather than on average? Professor Vickrey gives us a pedagogical illustration: Each member in a group of conferees meeting for dinner inevitably ends up paying for an expensive steak dinner – instead of most members economizing on the goulash – if, in order to reduce the bookkeeping, the bill is divided evenly amongst the participants. The reason for the excessive consumption is that each person could not lower the group bill significantly by exercising self-restraint unless (s)he is charged according to the true resource costs. Thus everyone in society in fact ends up paying for a costly road system since motorists are not charged at the margin for road use.[1]

Over three decades have passed by since Professor Vickrey enunciated his assessment and recommendations on the urban transportation problem to both the American and British governments. Nevertheless, congestion is ubiquitous as ever in major urban areas and incessant during peak periods and often between the hours. The traditional methods of curtailing congestion remain few, and their usefulness limited. On the supply side, the expansion and improvement of roads is restricted by increasingly tight fiscal, physical and environmental constraints. On the demand side, however, the problem can be addressed by pricing or regulation.[2] This paper argues that the role of peak/off-peak pricing is indispensable in tackling congestion because of its inherent flexibility and power of discrimination. My focus here is on internalizing only the external congestion effects caused by motorists. Congestion is recognized as a significant type of externality from vehicle usage in both developed and developing countries in that it represents a significant share of total estimated road use costs (Newbery, 1988, 1989, 1990; Newbery *et al.*, 1988; Small, Winston and Evans, 1989, Chapter 6).[3]

This paper interprets the literature on the theory of optimal pricing and investment for roads based principally on the work of Herbert Mohring, Robert Strotz, William Vickrey, Alan Walters, Theodore Keeler and Kenneth Small. It aims to integrate their ideas and principles into a single analytical framework (see Newbery, 1989; Winston, 1991; and Hau, 1992a, for details of combining both congestion and road damage). The rigorous and unified non-mathematical framework derived from first principles casts important light on congestion pricing systems and on issues surrounding short-run and long-run marginal cost pricing, scale economies and diseconomies, indivisibilities and cost recovery in the provision of road services. The static models relied upon here differ from the bottleneck model pioneered by William Vickrey (1973), which in turn has been extended by Arnott, de Palma and Lindsey's (1988) dynamic models.

Recent technological breakthroughs in automatic road use charging in a multi-lane setting have brought electronic road pricing much closer to reality. While there are a number of electronic toll collection systems in use in parts of Norway, Italy, Spain, France, America, Britain, Hong Kong, Korea and Japan, to name but a few places, only a few congestion pricing systems are currently operating (Hau, 1992b; 1995). The first is the well-known Singaporean Area Licensing Scheme, which has recently been converted into the smart-card based Electronic Road Pricing Scheme in April 1998. The electronic charging of vehicles entering Trondheim, Norway, during daylight hours on weekdays since 1991 (and perhaps the manual charging of vehicles entering the central business district of Bergen during extended daylight hours on weekdays since 1986) could be viewed as a crude form of congestion pricing. For traffic returning to Paris every Sunday afternoon since 1992, the tolled A-1 expressway imposes a surcharge (of 25 per cent) during peak hours and a discount of equivalent magnitude during the periods before and after the peak. The French scheme has been successful in spreading congestion during the peak hours onto the shoulder periods. With tremendous strides made in technological advances, the electronic charging of congestion tolls is both technically feasible and economically viable (Hau, 1990; Ramjerdi, 1995). This paper therefore attempts to come up with an integrated policy package derived from economic principles to hasten the arrival of road pricing as the urban transport solution.

3.2 CONCEPTUAL GUIDELINES

Rising real incomes result in increased aspirations for the ownership of private automobiles (Hau, 1996). Barring major restraint measures, an increasing number of motor vehicles means that travel demand swells. As municipalities find it increasingly difficult to finance new road construction and improvements, the rate of growth of travel demand outstrips the growth of road capacity. The resulting traffic explosion is an illustration of Downs' (1962, 1992) law of peak-hour expressway congestion, in which commuter traffic ascends rapidly to the level of new capacity in urban areas. Traffic engineers have long been familiar with this 'fundamental law of highway congestion' in which latent demand expands to fill the gap created whenever highway capacity is improved. The only viable solution to this problem is road pricing.

In this section, I set up the conceptual guidelines which allow authorities to improve transport efficiency by curtailing traffic congestion in an efficacious manner while satisfying the World Bank's general guidelines for public sector projects and urban transport policy (World Bank's Operational Manual Statement No. 2.25, 1977; World Bank's Urban Transport Policy Paper, 1986).

In a nutshell, the principles include:

1. implementing short-run marginal cost pricing to generate maximum net benefits for society: *efficiency pricing*;
2. undertaking investment in infrastructure whenever the additional benefits exceed the true resource costs (long-run efficiency) of doing so: *economic viability*;

3. investing in transport services when revenues exceed costs: *financial viability*;
4. maintaining 'fairness' among beneficiaries, for example, via benefit taxa-tion – *equity* – where possible; and
5. using pricing and cost recovery policies to improve the efficiency of managing the public sector – *cost-effectiveness* and *managerial efficiency* – if possible.

3.3   FOUNDATIONS OF ROAD CONGESTION: THE CLASSICAL CASE IN THE SHORT RUN

In the first edition of *The Economics of Welfare* (1920, p. 194), Professor Arthur C. Pigou introduced the idea of a congestion toll by coming up with the famous two-road example. He postulates that one road is wide but rough and slow and effectively of unlimited capacity whereas the other is narrow but smooth and fast, and therefore of limited capacity. He argues that (com-mercial) traffic will distribute itself amongst the two alternative routes until the travel time is the same connecting two points. By imposing a differential tax on the traffic using the narrow road, excessive traffic from the narrow road would be diverted onto the wide road. Total travel time would be lowered and society's welfare enhanced by the imposition of such a Pigouvian toll-tax.[4] Thus far there is no dispute on Pigou's contribution. However, Frank Knight (1924) challenged the idea of imposing a Pigouvian tax (on the difference of the marginal and average costs of a trip) to internalize a nega-tive externality by pointing out that the externality arose because Pigou had implicitly assumed a public road. If (private) property rights on roads are delineated and competitive pressure is present, then self-interested road own-ers would charge users the same differential toll, obviating the need for government intervention in the form of taxation. Even though the two condi-tions are far from being fulfilled in reality, Pigou nevertheless withdrew the two-road illustration from subsequent editions of *The Economics of Welfare*. Be that as it may, Pigou's two-road example remains a classic one, not least because almost all roads are publicly owned and subject to scale economies. Public ownership of roads results in 'market failure' (or perhaps 'government failure', as some would prefer to call it). Where there are private roads, a road without alternatives close by will likely exploit its locational monopoly char-acteristic, threatening a diminution of society's welfare. Are we doomed to suffer from the 'command economy' characteristics of congestion and chronic shortage of funds in roads?

We begin our analysis by following the conventional treatment of the congestion problem in the transport economics literature. Consider a representative driver cruising under low traffic conditions along a given stretch of urban road with fixed beginning and end points (Walters, 1961, 1987; Button, 1986). *Ceteris paribus*, as other vehicles enter the road thereafter, density increases, speed drops and travel time (or delay) lengthens. The causality is as follows: low traffic density yields high speed and not vice versa. Parallelling the theory of fluid dynamics, traffic flow is the product of density, in vehicles per kilometer, and speed, in kilometers per hour. Note that the rectangular area in Figure 3.1(a) is equivalent to traffic flow, expressed in vehicles per hour (see May, 1990, for example). Hence, traffic flow is endogenously determined by traffic density and speed, with traffic flow attaining a maximum at F^{max} with speed at S^m in Figure 3.1(b) (see Haight's 1963 fundamental diagram of road traffic – a flow-density curve – and similar figures in Morrison, 1986). (Touted figures of the 'capacity' of a typical expressway are about 1800 vehicles per lane-hour at 55 kilometers per hour, (Gerlough and Huber, 1975, Chapter 4).

Given a fixed distance of a kilometer of road, say, the traffic engineer's speed-flow curve can be straightforwardly converted to a travel time-flow curve as travel time is the reciprocal of speed, with vehicles–kilometer per lane–kilometer–hour on the horizontal axis (see figure 3.1c). Using a

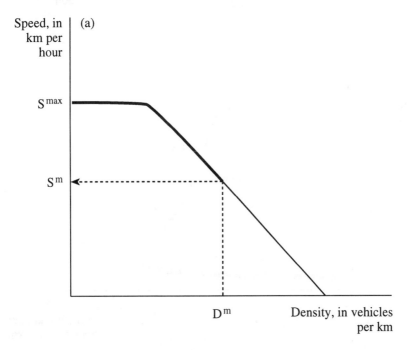

Figure 3.1   Derivation of a travel time-flow curve of an urban highway

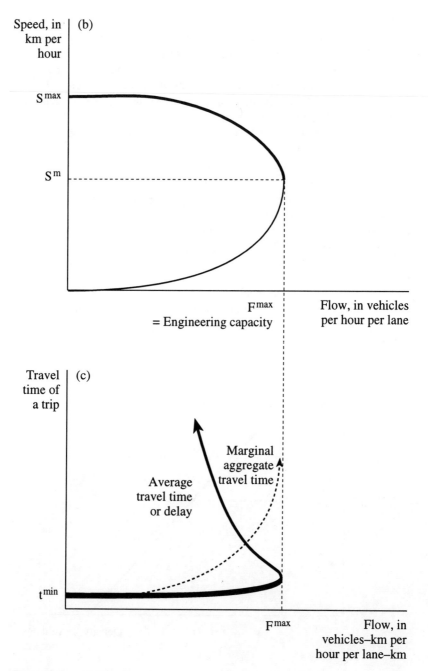

Figure 3.1   continued

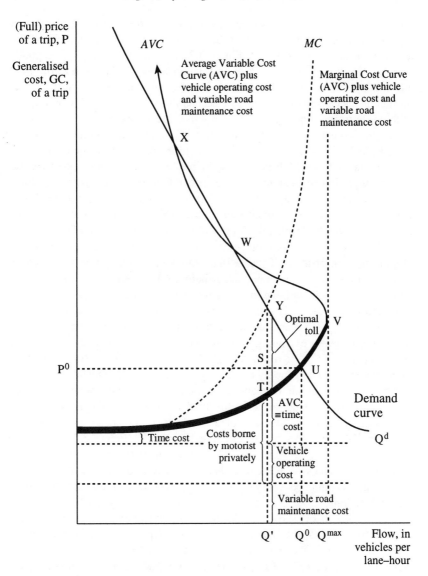

Figure 3.2   Derivation of the marginal cost curve and congestion toll

constant value of time as a shadow price for the representative driver, travel time is then converted to a money basis which yields time cost, called the average variable cost, AVC (see Figure 3.2). Low traffic volume corresponds with relatively high speed, so fuel cost would be high. With high traffic flow and low speed, however, fuel cost would also be kept high because of fuel inefficiencies caused by the alternate acceleration and deceleration associated with dense traffic. These two factors roughly cancel one another out, leading to the plausible assumption that the costs of operating an automobile (which include fuel, oil, maintenance and depreciation costs) are independent of the level of traffic flow (Mohring, 1976, chapter 3). A fixed money cost for the vehicle operating cost can therefore be added to the time cost portion to form the generalized cost – an accepted construct of transport economists. Similarly, the road's variable maintenance cost, which is assumed to be proportional to the traffic level, following Walters (1968, p. 24), can be added up also.[5] So it is the time cost element that is mainly responsible for the upward-sloping portion of the AVC curve. The AVC curve climbs upwards because significant negative interactions occur before traffic reaches maximum basic capacity, Q^{max}; it is variable in the sense that as traffic flow, Q, is increased, congestion delay actually sets in rapidly at a traffic level substantially below the level Q^{max} – contrary to the engineering notion of a constant average variable cost curve extending up to the point Q^{max}. After the engineering or basic capacity, Q^{max}, is reached, AVC becomes an 'inverse supply' curve.[6] Note that the standard supply curve is non-existent in the context of roads.

The 'supply' side can be made to be congruent with the demand side when a conventional demand curve is specified to depend on the travel cost, or price rather, facing a traveller for a single trip.[7] When an initial demand function, Q^d, intersects the AVC curve at point U (Figure 3.2), a (stable) equilibrium is said to exist at Q^0.[8] This is an equilibrium point because travelers' willingness-to-pay curve, that is, the inverse demand function, equals the average variable cost curve – the function upon which travelers base their travel decisions.

Basic price theory says that whenever the average variable cost rises, it means the marginal cost curve lies above it.[9] The vertical difference of the two cost curves is the marginal (external) congestion cost – the additional delay that one driver imposes on the rest. It is not taken into account by the last driver unless he is unusually altruistic. In fact, since each driver chooses whether or not to travel according to the AVC curve – being the decision curve – he or she totally ignores the resulting external congestion cost imposed on fellow motorists. We thus have the optimal point Y at which the marginal cost curve intersects the (peak) demand curve in Figure 3.2. In other words, Q' is the associated optimal output in the sense that the generalized cost, which includes time cost, external congestion cost and other variable costs (that is, constant unit operating cost of a vehicle and variable road maintenance cost), is equated to the price. The (external) congestion cost is the additional time cost that a motorist imposes on others, calculated by taking the increment in average time cost caused by the added trip and multiplied by the number of vehicles in the traffic stream (see note 9). The Pigouvian tax is that optimal toll which closes the wedge between the marginal cost and average variable cost curves by emitting the correct signal and creating appropriate disincentives. (This Pigouvian toll-tax is also known as the net-benefit maximizing, economically efficient, (Pareto) optimal and marginal cost toll.) Hence the marginal cost pricing of trips in the short run (given that a road is fixed) yields a first-best Pareto optimal allocation of resources. The optimal road user charge is then comprised of a congestion toll, shown by distance YT in Figure 3.2, and another component which covers the variable road maintenance cost (see Figure 3.2's legend).

Observe that at the equilibrium point U in Figure 3.2, the resultant throughput is significantly less than the road's maximal flow capacity of point V. The backward-bending 'supply curve' exists when very dense traffic is reached there; a one percent increase in density results in more than a one percent decrease in speed. (That point X (or point W) is a stable (or unstable) equilibrium point can be seen intuitively by perturbing the price level.) We note that many cities are faced with extremely congested situations such as point X, certainly during the peak, if not for most of the day.[10]

3.4   THE WELFARE IMPACT OF CONGESTION PRICING

Here I highlight what I consider to be an important obstacle to introducing congestion pricing. Economists have long known that road pricing results in an improvement in welfare to socicty, yct politicians and the public have always regarded it with skepticism. Why? To economists, the increase in welfare comes about because of the imposition of an externality-corrective tax. Yet, for those motorists remaining on the road, the effect of the toll is similar to a tax increase and the payment made (distance YT) exceeds the monetary value of the time saving (distance ST), so that the 'tolled' are worse off as a group (by the distance YS) under the assumptions of a uniform value of time across the population and a normal downward sloping demand function (see Figure 3.2). When the toll is multiplied by the total number of vehicle-trips undertaken (Q'), the aggregate toll payment clearly exceeds the valuation of the time savings. When the value of travel time varies across the population, the downward sloping nature of demand ensures that the weighted average of the valuation of travel time savings is still less than the toll payment (see Hau,1992a, Appendix). Those who are tolled off the road to an inferior mode or time of travel are definitely worse off, while those who remain on other times of travel or modes – the 'tolled on' – are either worse off, if congestion arises there, or just as well off, if there is no resulting increase in congestion.[11] It turns out that the government, in collecting toll revenues, becomes the main party that is better off (by the area Q' times the distance YT). (The other parties that are clearly made better off are the ones with high values of time.) So unless the congestion toll revenues are recycled and the tolled and the tolled off compensated, it is unlikely that road pricing would become a reality on a widespread basis.[12]

We then ask whether there is a theoretical argument for dedicated funds or earmarking so that society as a whole would benefit from having road pricing implemented. Restated another way, is there a way in which road users can act as beneficiaries and are indirectly 'compensated' for their toll payment by satisfying some commonly accepted notion of fairness, while not violating the first-best pricing rule? I think that the answer is 'yes', although not entirely without qualifications.

3.5   SHORT-RUN EQUILIBRIUM IN TRANSPORT

In a textbook industry such as widgets, the producer uses the revenue which he obtains from selling the good at the market price to pay for all the variable inputs of labor and raw materials, plus the fixed input in the form of quasi-rent on the capital equipment, normally regarded as the accounting profit. However, transport is unusual in that the traveller is both a producer and a consumer simultaneously. The graphs for the textbook commodity are similar to (but not always the same as) the case of roads considered in Figure 3.2.[13] The trip-maker himself supplies some variable inputs, which include vehicle operating cost and time cost, but not the fixed capital infrastructure. Since the competitive level of trips exceeds the efficient quantity in the presence of congestion, and because the quasi-rent of a highway facility would be dissipated due to free competition with public roads, the imposition of an optimal toll would recapture this quasi-rent. Note that because price equals the entire marginal cost of a trip, the optimal toll is equal to the *difference* of SRMC and SRAVC. This is a subtle but crucial distinction between transport and widgets. Despite this difference, short-run equilibrium in transport occurs when the government, in the form of a highway agency, behaves in an optimizing manner just as a private competitive firm would were it possible to organize the industry in a competitive fashion.

To see how this might be done, we introduce the fixed cost, that is, the cost of construction, together with the invariate maintenance, depreciation and operating costs of a road that faces a road agency in Figure 3.3. We then

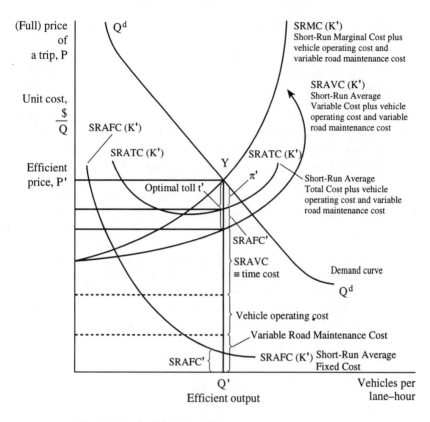

Figure 3.3 Introducing the (short-run average) fixed cost, SRAFC, of a road, short-run optimal toll with economic profit

convert the entire fixed cost into the cost per time period of a unit of capital for utilizing the flow of highway services. This is done in order to make it commensurate with the average variable cost of a trip discussed thus far. The summation of the short-run average fixed cost, SRAFC′, and the average variable cost curve yields the average total cost curve. With marginal cost pricing, the short-run equilibrium output and price is given by the efficient output, Q′, and price, P′, respectively.

3.6   LONG-RUN EQUILIBRIUM UNDER CONSTANT RETURNS

The motorist is oblivious to the capital cost of a road, and his behavior is independent of it. However, from the highway agency's planning point of view, even though the size and capital cost of a road is very much taken into account, once a highway is built it is regarded as sunk. The sunk cost of a road is irrelevant to a planner: only current and future costs, not historical cost, serve as a correct guide to planning future investment. Since the variable road maintenance cost is assumed to be constant, the marginal cost of a trip thus remains unaffected.

In the long run, a highway agency can vary the fixed capital input by road expansion, if the investment is deemed justifiable. Expanding a road until the additional benefit equals the additional cost of building it would yield maximal net benefit to the community. We note that charging the optimal toll of the distance t' in Figure 3.3 seems to be more than sufficient to cover the short-run average fixed cost of the facility. In this case, the optimal toll, t', exceeds the short-run average fixed cost of the facility, SRAFC', by the unit profit difference of π'. In general, there is no *a priori* reason why toll revenue collections cannot cover the non-use-related costs of a given highway facility.

In the case of a textbook commodity, whenever the quasi-rent being earned by a firm's existing capital equipment exceeds its cost, there is an incentive to expand production (following Mohring and Harwitz, 1962, chapter 2). Ultimately, the quasi-rent earned by the existing capital equipment would then be equal to its fixed (opportunity) cost of capital. Upon seeing the existence of economic profits, other firms enter the industry and expand the supply, increasing output and lowering price as a result. The unrestricted mobility of resources and the entry and exit of firms serve as the forces by which profits would be competed away in due course. When capital is freely varying and zero economic profit occurs, long-run equilibrium is reached (see Figure 3.4). This zero profit condition holds under constant returns to scale, where a proportionate increase in all inputs results in the same increase in output. Given fixed factor prices, both average total cost and marginal cost remain constant and flat in the long run. With a slight but crucial modification, this analysis carries over to the case of roads. When the quasi-rent of the existing capital stock exceeds the normal market return on the costs of reproducing the invested capital plus the highway facility's invariate maintenance and depreciation costs, new investment is expected to find its way into that road segment of the highway industry if the appropriate (marginal cost) price signals are given. Equivalently, in the long run, if toll revenues – which recover quasi-rents over time periods – exceed the fixed cost of the existing facility, the highway agency would have the appropriate incentive to expand a stretch of that road until all economic profits are eroded away. As we have seen in the case of roads, the variable cost is composed of user-supplied time and operating costs and are fully self-financing. The non-use related costs are then financed separately by the road agency via the collection of congestion toll revenues. In this way, full costs are covered and the problems of cost recovery and cost allocation disappear. There is no need to raise charges over and above marginal cost – unless one wants to internalize other externalities or to impose a pure tax element.[14]

3.7 OPTIMAL INVESTMENT

Professor Herbert Mohring was the first to show the powerful result that congestion toll revenues would exactly cover the amortized cost of construction, invariate maintenance and depreciation costs of roads in the long run under the technical conditions of constant returns to scale in road construction, maintenance and road use (Mohring and Harwitz, 1962; Mohring, 1965; Arnott and Kraus, 1998). Constant returns to scale in construction and maintenance intuitively means that the cost of building and maintaining an expressway is proportional to the capacity. Constant returns to road use yields an intuitive interpretation: travel time depends solely on the volume–capacity ratio. If the engineering capacity and the traffic flow were doubled, unit travel times would remain the same.[15] By steadily pursuing the policy of marginal cost pricing of a trip via congestion pricing and by expanding or appropriately reducing the capacity of the road until there is zero economic profit, the output (of vehicle–kilometers per lane–km per hour) is considered optimal. At a moment in time for an existing road, output is optimal in the sense that, given the marginal-cost price, the efficient level of trips is achieved. Undertaking either more or less trips would involve lowering the net benefit to the community. In the long run, output would be 'doubly' optimal if it is the efficient level of trips for that link of road which has been optimally built. Diagrammatically, not only does the implementation of a congestion toll internalize the external congestion cost, it can be seen that the toll covers the short-run average fixed cost of the road (Figure 3.4). Clearly, collecting a unit congestion toll would cover the entire average fixed cost of the road and yield zero profit only because the existence of economic profit or loss acts as a quasi-market mechanism in the investment decision of whether to expand or contract highway capacity.

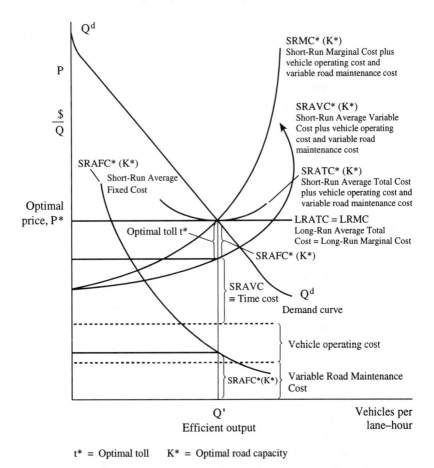

t^* = Optimal toll K^* = Optimal road capacity

Figure 3.4   Long-run equilibrium of an optimally designed road with both optimal pricing and optimal investment

3.8   LONG-RUN VERSUS SHORT-RUN MARGINAL COST PRICING[16]

Intuitively, the long-run marginal cost of producing a trip yields the cost of undertaking a trip to the society when all fixed and variable inputs can be varied continuously in the long run. Proponents of long-run marginal cost pricing argue that the market return to capital investment would presumably be fully covered. Yet the equivalence of short-run and long-run marginal cost pricing holds only in certain cases, including the static demand and single period case considered here. As shown in Figure 3.4, long-run marginal cost pricing would exactly cover all the variable costs, including time cost, vehicle operating cost and variable road maintenance cost, plus the fixed construction, invariate maintenance, depreciation and operating costs of the road. In fact, short-run marginal cost pricing covers the entire capital cost of the facility just as much as long-run marginal cost pricing does, as can be seen in the same diagram. After all, in the long run, the users' marginal willingness-to-pay, the short-run and long-run marginal and average costs are all equal. However, if a road is not optimally constructed but underbuilt, say, then long-run marginal cost pricing would send out too low a price signal, thereby exacerbating congestion. Short-run marginal cost pricing, on the other hand, would give the correct signal of the travellers' true willingness-to-pay and would also yield positive toll revenues and economic profits as a by-product. Short-run marginal cost pricing is the rule to use whether or not long-run equilibrium is reached. Looking at it another way, if short-run marginal cost is below long-run marginal cost at the current output, it means that the road has been overbuilt. But, of course, this does not mean that the size of the expressway should be (or indeed can be) varied instantaneously whenever demand fluctuates daily. Rather, it means that the price ought to be varied according to demand patterns using short-run marginal cost pricing. We shall explore this point further in the section on demand variability.

Indeed, Vickrey has emphatically argued that there can be no solution to the urban transportation problem without peak-load pricing. Time-of-day pricing is an application of the concept of short-run marginal cost pricing. Pursuing economically efficient pricing period by period over the long run would not only guarantee the best use of society's given resources but would also enable road agencies to recover all costs – as an incidental by-product – in the long run. It is therefore recommended that short-run marginal cost pricing – that is, congestion pricing – rather than long-run marginal cost pricing be used whenever cyclical variations in demand are involved.

3.9   TRADING OFF TRAVELLER'S TIME AGAINST THE GOVERNMENT'S RESOURCES

Another way of obtaining the optimal investment level for roads is to answer the following question: what is the minimum cost to the community of road building, taking into account both the highway agency's desire to minimize the fixed cost of capital facilities and the travelling public's desire to save time? By minimizing the sum of these costs, a trade-off is found between individuals' time and the treasury's accounts. Given a non-optimal capital stock (K') associated with a particular highway, as in the previous graph,

Figure 3.3, it can be seen that the least cost for the community involves having a road that is too small, given the demand as depicted. Therefore, there is an incentive for the community to expand the capacity of the road. Long-run equilibrium is reached when the minimum point of the short-run average total cost curve (which equals the short-run marginal cost curve) intersects the demand curve. For the governmental authority, road capacity is a choice variable. By increasing its size, the volume–capacity ratio drops in the short run, and so does time cost. However, the cost from road capacity expansion rises. Intuitively, the highway agency continues to expand the road until the marginal benefit from saving users' time costs is just offset by the marginal cost of an extra unit of capacity.[17] It is at the output Q^* that the valuation of a trip just equals the additional cost to society of taking that trip, plus the vehicle operating cost and the road maintenance cost, given an optimally built road, K^* (see Figure 3.4).[18] By pursuing an efficient pricing policy for each stretch of road, the use of an existing, non-optimal highway network would be optimized. Further, by expanding highway capacity up to the point where the quasi-rent of each capital facility just covers the cost of reproducing it, with zero (economic) profit remaining, the net benefit to the community would be maximized. By symmetry, abandoning or downgrading roads is necessary when economic losses occur. The common practice of not maintaining roads to preset engineering standards is tantamount to an act of disinvesting in roads.

3.10 FIRST-BEST OPTIMAL PRICING AND INVESTMENT[19]

Given an estimate of a speed-flow curve and the corresponding travel-time flow curve, we know how the engineering curves can be converted to a short-run average variable cost curve of a trip, using an estimate of the value of time. Hau (1994) shows how speed-flow and travel time-flow curves are derived empirically for a representative Indonesian road type.[20] Further, a 'supply' elasticity (or cost elasticity, rather) estimate yields a one-to-one correspondence between the short-run average variable cost and the short-run marginal cost (see footnote 9 for formula). A rough estimate of the demand elasticity and the traffic level of a particular road would yield a first order approximation of the proper congestion toll. Now, in order to maximize aggregate net benefit, two operating rules should be followed by the road agency.

First Rule – Optimal Pricing Rule. For each stretch of road, short-run marginal cost pricing is fulfilled by setting a toll equal to the difference of short-run marginal cost and short-run average variable cost. Intuitively, this congestion toll would serve to internalize the (external) congestion cost that a driver imposes on others. In addition, the motorist is charged another component which covers the variable maintenance and operating costs of a road.

Second Rule – Optimal Capacity Rule. Under constant returns and optimal pricing, whenever economic profit is found in the operation of a road link, the capacity of that stretch of road should be expanded. The existence of a loss under short-run (as opposed to long-run) marginal cost pricing suggests that the road has been overbuilt. By altering the capacity of each road over the long run according to the quasi-market signal of profits and losses, the entire highway network's investment level in capacity would be optimized, with the fixed cost of each road covered. Alternatively, the road agency – by trading its direct resource costs against individuals' travel time – can follow the rule of setting the marginal value of user cost savings equal to the marginal cost of investment for an additional unit of capacity. Equivalently, the capacity of a road is expanded until the marginal capital cost equals the marginal (external) congestion cost.

Notice that the optimally designed road has a positive amount of external congestion cost. This results from the road agency's desire to minimize both the sum of the direct cost of the road investment and individual road users' travel time cost. In our simple framework, congestion delay would never be entirely absent, contrary to what motorists and some environmentalists would prefer, because achieving zero congestion is very costly to the community. In other words, an optimal amount of congestion externality is a valid concept, just as an optimal amount of pollution has long been recognized in the environmental economics literature. What if there is no congestion at all on a particular road? Zero congestion means that that stretch of road has been overbuilt (or priced non-optimally) and should perhaps be downgraded or even abandoned. If excess capacity occurs all the time, the road possesses the non-rival consumption characteristic of a public good. Then we are faced squarely with the standard task of provision of public goods. If resources are plentiful, financing the shortfall via general revenue taxation – fully taking into account the social opportunity cost of capital – has been the conventional dictum.[21]

By contrast, a road would sooner or later possess the rival consumption attribute of a private good when demand rises. As a result, a congested road can be regarded as a congested variable-use public facility (or a 'club good', see Buchanan, 1965). With such mixed goods characteristics, the task of providing road services ought to remain with the public sector unless full exclusion is achievable and imperfect competition is of minor concern. Under the condition of constant returns, we have shown that the optimal toll revenue, which also captures the quasi-rent earned from the invested capital and reflects the scarcity value of the facility, would cover the entire fixed cost of the road in the long run. No residual or overhead cost need be allocated. If profit exists, then it is because there is insufficient road capacity (or pricing at a level above marginal cost), and the road is therefore not in long-run equilibrium. The existence of economic profit serves as a surrogate market signal to expand capacity. Updating his earlier work in 1988 on road user charges, Newbery (1990, 1994) estimates that the cost of expanding highway capacity in the United Kingdom is 2.2 pence/km at 1992/93 prices for a private car. This means that transport authorities could simply look at traffic forecasts and decide to expand highway capacity when (external) congestion costs reached 2.2 p/km, and not otherwise.

Similarly, if a road loses money, it suggests that planners may either have invested mistakenly or made overoptimistic forecasts of travel demand, for instance. In that case, marginal cost pricing is still to be adhered to, with the congestion toll set close to nil. A user charge component is also needed to cover the variable road maintenance cost. Thus it may even be worthwhile to abandon a money-losing road and save on any annual invariate maintenance costs that may arise. Efficient pricing, financial viability and cost recovery are therefore entirely consistent with one another under constant returns to scale in long-run equilibrium.

3.11   RELAXATION OF ASSUMPTIONS

Some of the more stringent assumptions employed thus far need to be relaxed. They include: (1) constant value of time, (2) static demand, (3) perfect divisibility, (4) constant returns to scale and (5) variability of road thickness. Here we explore relaxing only the first four assumptions (see Hau, 1992a).

3.11.1   Differences in Time Valuation

The traditional presentation of road pricing assumes a constant value of time (Walters, 1961). The diagrammatic analysis in Figure 3.2 implicitly assumes that every driver is identical and maintains the same time valuation. The question then is what happens when there are heterogeneous motorists, with different time valuations and tastes. A mathematical proof that generalizes the above result of homogeneous drivers to heterogeneous ones with different values of time is shown by Mohring (1976, chapter 4 Appendix) and Strotz (1964), but the intuition behind it is straightforward. Instead of the optimal toll being based on a representative driver's (marginal) value of time, the optimal toll is now a weighted average of the different motorists' marginal valuation of time, weighted by the number of trips taken by those motorists who actually remain on the road. If a traveller's time value and the number of trips are close to the average, he will incur the toll payment that everyone is faced with. If another motorist's time value is higher (lower) than average, he would be willing to pay more (less) than the average toll payment for taking a trip. (Each of them would be willing to, though begrudgingly, pay the difference of the toll and his valuation of time saving.) He thus would end up paying the difference. The constant value of time is reinterpreted as the weighted (marginal) valuations of time, whereas the congestion toll, YT, in Figure 3.2 then can be labelled the weighted congestion toll. For a trip with a very high time value, the money equivalent of the time saved, ST, can be even higher than the weighted congestion toll, YT, thus making the motorist better off. On the other hand, for a trip having a lower than average time value, the user still has to make the average payment and therefore would be made considerably worse off. Nevertheless, they both remain on the tolled road, as opposed to being tolled off, because their individual trips' marginal valuation (or maximum willingness-to-pay) still exceeds (or equals) the generalized cost of their respective journeys. The use of nonconstant values of time would relax the point that congestion pricing would make almost all groups besides the government worse off. By loosening the stringent assumption of a constant value of time across the population, those people with very high values of time would be made better off at the expense of those with low values of time. This intuitive analysis assumes that everyone is faced with the same toll, as in the workings of a competitive economy. Note also that the optimal toll incorporates motorists with both high and low valuations of time but excludes those who are tolled off. With differences in values of time under constant returns, efficient pricing and financial viability are still achievable.

3.11.2 Demand Variability and Peak-load Pricing

Applying short-run marginal cost pricing means that a congestion toll is needed but none when there is excess capacity during the off-peak. With a fixed highway capital stock, the systematic, diurnal nature of travel demand (as opposed to the static, invariant demand character assumed till now) means that the sum of quasi-rents (rather than just the quasi-rent from the single period itself) of the invested capital should be compared with the cost of the highway facility. In other words, when all the quasi-rents over the entire demand cycle are summed up and compared with the capital cost, we can then ask whether expansion of the highway is warranted or not, under constant returns. The conclusions obtained thus far again holds.

An interesting implication is that the entire capital cost of the highway is 'allocated to' and borne by peak travellers, mainly rush-hour commuters. This surprising result may seem 'inequitable', yet it is perfectly consistent with efficiency analysis. After all, it is peak users themselves that create congestion and they that demand the use of heavily congested expressways requiring massive infrastructure developments. Without these peak commuters, the optimal size of the road would be much smaller. The result of allocating all capital costs to users of the peak period is long recognized in the literature on the pricing of public utilities as in Boiteux (1960). The optimal investment rule is then to expand a road until the sum of the quasi-rents over the demand cycle equals the entire capital cost of the facility. By implementing both peak-load pricing and altering the investment level of the highway facility, depending on whether profits are positive or negative, the highway network can again be optimized. Hence, the consideration of demand variability and peak-load pricing would not change the status of our conclusions, in the presence of differences in valuation of time. The fact that the fluctuating demands over the various peak, off-peak and inter-peak periods of a demand cycle are linked by a fixed capital facility and the observation that the consumption of trips must be satisfied by the production of trips during that particular time period combine to yield a simple modification of our result. Pricing, financial viability and cost recovery are again consistent with one another.

Keeler and Small (1977) show rigorously how the Mohring–Harwitz framework developed here is extended to the case of variable demands under peak-load pricing in the presence of independent demands and no indivisibilities.[22] By assuming the demand in each period is in fact dependent on other periods, that is, the case of dependent demands, the derived results still go through (Mohring, 1970).

3.11.3   Indivisibilities

While still retaining the assumption of constant returns, but accounting for differences in values of time and demand variability, we proceed to drop the assumption of a road being finely divisible.

Road construction, in fact, involves significant indivisibilities that cannot be ignored. For example, a road must possess the minimum width for accommodating a standard-sized automobile and should also ideally be bi-directional. In the perfectly divisible case, the long-run average total cost curve enveloping a continuum of closely-packed short-run average total cost curves at their minimum points is made horizontal. A flat LRMC curve also coincides with the corresponding LRATC curve (see Figure 3.4). Due to the presence of indivisibilities, however, the formerly neat and continuous pattern of the LRMC curve is therefore broken (Neutze, 1966). The new long-run average total cost curve is now composed of a finite series of short-run average total cost curves. We note that whenever a short-run marginal cost curve rises above a short-run average total cost curve, profits can be obtained under short-run marginal cost pricing. Thus, if demand happens to intersect the short-run marginal cost curves in the upward-sloping sections of their SRATC curves, then the road makes money in the long run under constant returns. *Per contra*, in the downward-sloping portions of the SRATC curves, the road loses money. When the SRATC is neither rising nor falling (as in Figure 3.4), the road breaks even. With a two-lane road, say, as traffic increases, the road's large fixed cost is spread out by additional traffic, and as congestion sets in, the road begins to make money. When road expansion is justified by cost–benefit analysis, congestion relief results in the road losing money. In other words, as travel demand continues to grow along the trend, adherence to short-run marginal cost pricing suggests that the road would go through an unavoidable cyclical pattern of deficit, surplus, deficit, surplus, and so on. Whether or not one undertakes a road expansion project from two to four lanes depends on a computation of the net benefits, using welfare gain and loss measures, via cost–benefit analysis (see the example in Hau, 1992a, pp. 35–6).

The optimal sequence of decision-making is to first establish the policy of applying marginal cost pricing and then plan future adjustments of the road network according to expected future demand and established pricing policies (Vickrey, 1987). When demand fluctuates, pursuing short-run marginal cost pricing would mean setting different prices, or congestion tolls rather, in response to expected current conditions.

3.11.4   Returns to Scale

The issue of whether constant returns to scale exists or not in road transport is a controversial and important one. Ultimately, it can be answered satisfactorily only via careful econometric analysis of individual cases. The available evidence in road transportation indicates that all three cases exist: decreasing returns to scale, constant returns to scale and increasing returns to scale (see Figure 3.5) – paralleling the case of a competitive private firm and industry – with profit, break even and loss, respectively. (This is but a well-known result of economic theory applied with slight modification to the highway.) It is important to realize at the outset that the case of scale economies, or increasing returns to scale with fixed factor prices under least cost combinations, is merely a case of insufficient demand with respect to the market size in the long run – a point that is sometimes overlooked. This means that if traffic were to grow until congestion delay sets in, congestion toll revenues could be collected. (After all, the short-run marginal cost curve for road use is always non-decreasing, as we have shown in Figures 3.1c and 3.2.) Profits may still occur – due to indivisibilities – despite the fact that the long-run average cost

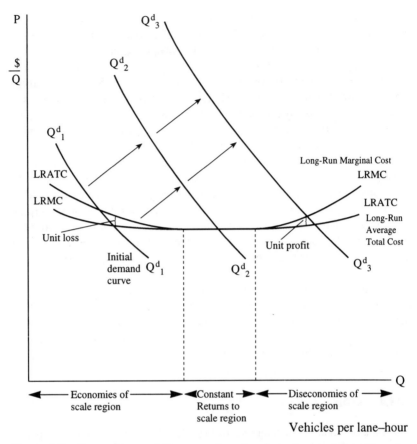

*Figure 3.5   Economies and diseconomies of scale in the provision of road
capacity with the growth of travel demand*

curve is declining. And if traffic were to continue to grow as real incomes and
auto ownership rise, concomitant with expressway expansion, the decreasing
returns region would then be encountered (see Figure 3.5). In the case of
increasing returns with perfect divisibility – commonly known as the natural
monopoly case – efficient pricing will result in losses, beckoning government
subsidization. On the other hand, if travel demand is sufficiently high relative
to engineering capacities of roads, the money-making enterprises would provide much sought-after funds which could be used to finance efficiently
priced but money-losing roads – only if these roads yield positive net benefits
to society.

A. Economies of scale

There is evidence of significant economies of scale in the construction of rural roads (Walters, 1968, pp. 180–82; Mohring, 1976, pp. 140–42). In particular, a two-lane road requires a minimum of a twelve-feet width for each lane and a few feet for shoulders and drainage ditches. What this means is that a substantial proportion of the provision of a road's right-of-way involves dead space. These indivisibilities help contribute to declining unit cost as the large fixed cost of construction and invariate maintenance and depreciation costs are shared over greater amounts of traffic. Thus doubling the width of a two-lane road more than doubles its capacity, the so-called 'shoulder effect' (Hayutin, 1984, pp. 106 and 154). Further, we know that the engineering or basic capacity of a two-lane road is about 2000 vehicles per hour. Since the standard four-lane road has an engineering capacity of 1800–2000 vehicles per lane per hour, doubling the width of a two-lane road almost quadruples its capacity. Further, in order to level hilly terrain and/or fill valleys for transportation purposes, the earth moving costs rise less than proportionately. Hence, for the above three reasons of the existence of large fixed costs in the presence of indivisibilities, the technology of road capacity, and the earth moving costs, we can claim that there are economies of scale associated with the expansion from a two-lane to a four-lane road. Nevertheless, despite the fact that four-lane roads possess two-thirds dead space and eight-lane roads have only half the space for usable road capacity, it is not clear that economies from scale in urban highway construction exist. This is because it is rather difficult to control statistically for the effects of urbanization and separate it from the effects of size. For example, four-lane roads tend to be built in rural areas, where interchanges and overpasses are widely dispersed, and right-of-way costs are low. On the other hand, six-lane or eight-lane roads are built mainly near metropolitan conurbations, where expressway interchanges and overpasses are closely spaced together, and land acquisition costs are high. In practice, the road agency tends to trade off (and avoid) high right-of-way costs with increased tunnelling and overpass construction costs. Lane expansion from a six-lane to an eight-lane expressway at the margin, for example, would increasingly encounter alignment constraints associated with the terrain. This argument is independent of whether the expressway is located near urban areas. Hence all three cases of returns to scale occur, resulting in the classic U-shaped long-run average cost curve, paralleling that of a competitive firm of an industry as we have seen in Figure 3.5.

B. Diseconomies of scale

The discussion thus far centered on economies or diseconomies of scale to road width for single roads, as opposed to a system of roads. Strotz (1964) conjectures, but Vickrey argues convincingly, that there are considerable diseconomies of scale associated with an urban road network. The argument is based on the geometry of road network (see diagrams in Hau, 1992a). As the urban road network expands from a typical single two-lane road to a double two-lane road, say, substantially costlier construction, tunnelling and land acquisition costs are encountered.[23] Either higher construction costs or longer travel time and wait time costs due to the establishment of additional intersections in a road network would contribute to an increase in costs. Just as the congestion toll filled the wedge caused by the difference of short-run marginal and average variable costs, the divergence between long-run marginal and average total cost curves serves as an indicator of the unit profit. In competitive equilibrium, all economic profits are competed away in the long run, so the question that follows is in what sense is the case of diseconomies of scale a 'long run' concept? The presence of economic profits in the long run here is attributable to the rents earned by an invaluable fixed factor of production – land. Intuitively, just as the driver, in the short run, is charged for imposing external congestion costs on others due to his presence on the road, so also should the urban community, in the long run, charge for the increasing use of scarce urban land in a market economy. Put another way, if all factors of production – including land – were doubled, so that a scarcity value could be imputed to land, all economic profits would be competed away and vanish in the long run. Clearly, the supply of land cannot be doubled, so it is the existence of land rents which gives rise to long-run economic profits. Notice that we could no longer use the existence of profits as a surrogate market signal because of decreasing returns to scale. Since the urban road network is supposed to recover substantial amounts of revenue from high land values, relying solely on the profit mechanism and injudiciously investing in urban roads until all economic profits are competed away would result in over-investment in road capacity. With diseconomies of scale and divisibility, all roads generate profits. Performing proper economic appraisal of road projects cannot therefore be circumvented (Dodgson, 1997).

C.   Indivisibilities and scale (dis)economies

The presence of both indivisibilities and scale economies could alter substantially the calculation of optimal tolls and subsidies (Kraus, 1981b). It turns out, perhaps surprisingly, that the existence of indivisibilities serves to improve the state of affairs *vis-à-vis* the road agency. For instance, in the case of rural roads with both scale economies and indivisibilities, there are regions where short-run marginal cost pricing yields profits rather than losses. This is because, with indivisibilities, the long-run marginal cost curve (composed of joined segments of the short-run marginal cost curves) is no longer declining all the way (as in Figure 3.5) but possesses a sawtoothed pattern, alternately cutting its corresponding long-run average total cost curve and short-run average total cost curves (see figure 12 in Hau, 1992a, which is summarized in Figures 3.7b–3.7c). Thus, whenever short-run marginal cost exceeds short-run average total cost at a given traffic level, profit exists and vice versa. It is, therefore, quite conceivable to have a congested road which generates profits even when subject to increasing returns to scale for a sufficiently large discrete change in capacity. The existence of losses does not mean that the road agency should cut back on the provision of highway services that passes the cost–benefit criterion.

How often do we encounter surpluses in the presence of scale economies and deficits in the presence of economies? The answer depends on the extent of the presence or absence of indivisibilities. There are two views on this issue. The first perspective argues that the aggregate road network could be regarded as divisible (see the works by Keeler and Small, 1977; Starkie, 1982). The other view, presented by Walters (1968, chapter 3) and Kraus (1981b), contends that roads are indivisible because the number of lanes – the main measure of highway capacity – is discrete.

The construction of a road or an additional lane may not be finely divisible, but taking the road network as a whole, a single newly constructed facility can be regarded as an incremental addition to the network, resulting in the applicability of the foregoing marginal analysis. Also, often varying some dimensions of road features other than the number of lanes increases the capacity of the road network. For example, the lane width, the provision of auxiliary lanes, horizontal and vertical alignments and the surfacing of road shoulders can all be varied incrementally (Starkie, 1982). One could characterize this view by treating the lane capacity as a continuous variable rather than a discrete one (Small, Winston and Evans, 1989, p. 103). If the road agency follows the twin optimizing rules of pricing and investment, then the road network would be in long-run equilibrium. So with constant returns and a divisible road network, roads would break even. However, some individual roads would make money and some would lose money. On the whole, if the economies and diseconomies of scale roughly cancel one another, the highway budget would be balanced. With indivisibilities, the profit (or loss) regime occurs about half the time but it is unclear what the relative weights would be when travel demand is reasonably assumed to grow over time.

Under decreasing returns and (almost) perfect divisibility, profits always occur as shown in Figure 3.6a. Perfect (and near-perfect) divisibility and an urban road network would mean that marginal cost pricing would always be profitable. This regime of ubiquitous profits disappears once indivisibilities set in sufficiently to admit downward sloping portions of the LRATC curve to occur as in Figure 3.6b. If the extent of indivisibilities progresses from small but significant (Figure 3.6b) to severe (Figure 3.6c), the regions which yield potential losses become larger initially. The symmetry carries over somewhat to the increasing returns to scale case (see Figures 3.7a–3.7c). With perfect (and almost perfect) divisibility in the presence of scale economies (Figure 3.7a), losses would always occur. With scale economies and an intermediate level of indivisibilities (Figure 3.7b), say, smaller regions of profit would become available but would disappear when approaching the neighborhood of the limit (of divisibility).[24] Nevertheless, if one were to accept Walters' (1968) argument that there are significant indivisibilities and scale economies in rural roads (as depicted in Figure 3.7c), we have demonstrated that profits (and losses, of course) would still arise under congestion tolling.[25] Scale economies and financial viability are not necessarily incompatible.

Insights by Newbery (1988, 1989) and Small, Winston and Evans (1989) about the economic implications of the extensive damage that heavy vehicles cause to roads enrich the basic Mohring model. Charging for both the external and variable costs of road damage, by assigning a fee based on vehicle weight per axle (as opposed to weight alone), can go a long way towards covering any deficit arising from congestion tolling. Even if a road network is broadly characterized by increasing returns to scale in building and strengthening roads, the deficit could be closed by scope diseconomies. Diseconomies of scope means that a road network that accommodates both cars and trucks costs more than the sum of an autos-only and a (smaller) trucks-only road system (Winston,

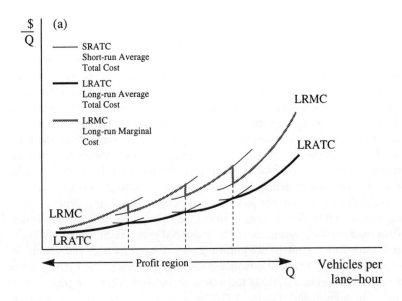

Figure 3.6 Decreasing returns to scale and extent of indivisibilities

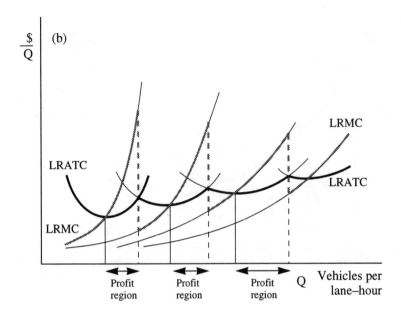

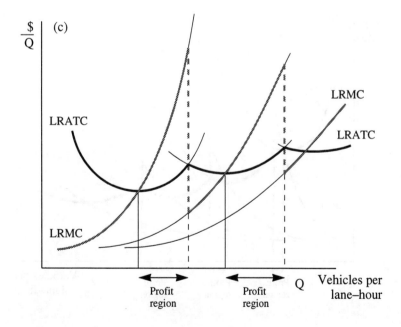

Figure 3.6   continued

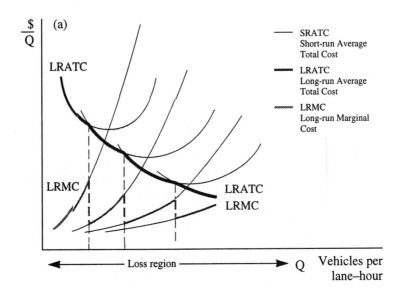

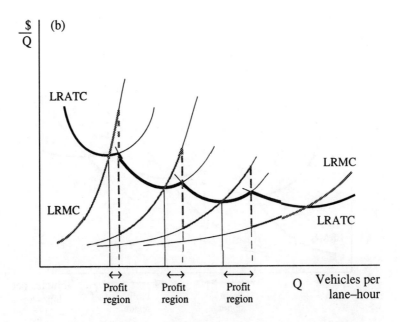

Figure 3.7   Increasing returns to scale and extent of indivisibilities

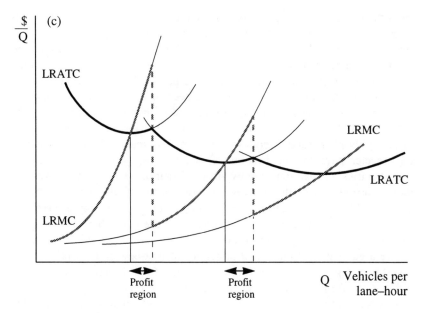

Figure 3.7 continued

1991). So the surplus associated with diseconomies of scope offsets the potential loss from congestion pricing in the presence of scale-specific economies.

Recently, Arnott and Kraus (1998) extends the basic static Mohring-Harwitz result to the intertemporal setting. He shows that the self-financing result of congestible facilities does extend to this new environment in terms of present value. Arnott and Kraus demonstrates that discounted cost recovery in a growing economy depends not only on static returns to scale but also on the technological attributes of road capacity expansion and maintenance.

3.12 CONCLUSIONS

It is hardly surprising that congestion pricing as advanced in the past encountered its share of difficulties. This is because imposing a congestion toll has the effect of a tax increase on trip-makers, despite the fact that it is an externality-corrective tax. In the transport context – unlike in the textbook commodity case – the fact that the traveler is both a consumer and producer has interesting policy implications. With road use, the consumer–producer is a 'perpetrator' and a (willing) 'victim' (of negative externalities), as well as a 'beneficiary' of road use. As a generator and 'perpetrator' of negative externalities such as congestion and pollution, the traveler should be justifiably toll-taxed (as with the polluter pays principle). Yet the traveler also suffers from the congestion and pollution externalities he helps engender. Hence as 'victims' of congestion externalities, perhaps travelers ought to be compensated. However, it has been argued that Pigouvian toll-tax revenues should accrue to the public treasury and should not be used to compensate 'victims' of externalities (Baumol and Oates, 1988, pp. 23–9). The intuition is that motorists would be induced to drive more because the level of compensatory payments would depend on their car usage, so economic efficiency would be violated. In this context, a road fund would be consistent with first-best pricing only if the funds were used in an indirect manner.[26] As a consumer, the traveler pays for the benefits of taking a trip. So travelers are also 'beneficiaries' of road transport by virtue of their use of congested roads and their contributions to the toll revenue component of user charges. In the absence of lump sum transfers, earmarking of toll revenues could serve as a useful device in principle to approximating benefit taxation as a way of satisfying a commonly accepted notion of 'fairness'.[27] Combining these intuitive arguments and our stated principles of first-best optimal pricing and investment suggests that some form of dedicated funds is perhaps necessary – either in the form of a road fund or a transport fund[28] – if congestion pricing is to gain political acceptance. When the proceeds of tolls are channelled back to the users in this way, congestion pricing and road taxes become a (road) user 'fee' (or mobility 'fee') and not regarded as a 'tax' *per se*.

Even without dedicated funds, it is essential to pursue steadfastly efficient pricing in the short run and efficient investment over the long run. Thereafter, the results can be presented for public scrutiny, thereby improving managerial efficiency and public accountability. By exploiting private profit incentives where competitive elements are strong, the competitive tendering and private provision of some transport services could also serve to enhance managerial efficiency in the public sector. However, the welfare gain from managerial efficiency due to private initiatives of road provision via increasingly popular build–operate–transfer (BOT) projects, for instance, should be measured against the welfare loss from monopoly abuse when parallel roads are next to nonexistent. Because many roads possess natural monopoly characteristics and since it is difficult to price various component parts of an integrated road network, the ownership of roads should best reside with the public sector (Newbery, 1994). The market failure resulting from the common property resource problem where no one really owns the roads would still call for the diligent application of optimal pricing and investment rules by an independent public road authority. Thus commercialization is in order rather than privatization.[29] Vickrey (1996) also insists on 'marketization' – that is, the setting of quasi-market prices which enhances efficiency and acts as signals for (dis)investment – in transport and argues strongly against privatization in transportation.

Subject to further research, the idea of setting up a transportation (or road) fund to pursue marginal cost pricing in all its dimensions would enable us to satisfy the quintipartite principles of the World Bank's general guidelines for improving transport efficiency, as stated at the outset of this paper, which is namely to: (1) implement efficiency pricing; (2) meet economic viability; (3) meet (to a considerable extent) financial viability; (4) achieve (some degree of) 'fairness' among beneficiaries; and (5) attain (somewhat) managerial efficiency of the public authority. The conception of such a fund passes many of the tests for a 'good' earmarking arrangement as presented in McCleary (1991).[30] The implementation of marginal cost pricing in the traffic (and loading) dimension could be achieved by employing the recent technological breakthroughs in automatic road use charging. These electronic toll collection devices using smart card technology and automatic classification systems all face remarkable scale economies.[31] Alternatively, less powerful instruments and reversible setups such as area licensing and simple cordon pricing schemes can be used as stepping stones (Glaister, 1991).

NOTES

* Associate Professor of Economics, The University of Hong Kong. This paper draws extensively from research on my 'Economic Fundamentals of Road Pricing: A Diagrammatic Analysis', *World Bank Policy Research Working Paper Series* WPS 1070, The World Bank, Washington DC, December 1992, and research materials published since then. The conclusions in this paper do not reflect the views or policies of the World Bank. I take this opportunity to especially thank my mentor and friend the late Professor William Vickrey – the grandfather of road pricing – without implicating him for my errors. I should like to dedicate this paper to the memory of William S. Vickrey. Further, I thank others with whom I have sparred on road pricing. They include: Esra Bennathan, David Bernstein, Richard Bird, Ken Button, José Carbajo, Shanta Devarajan, Frank Englmann, Phil Goodwin, Clell Harrall, Tatsuo Hatta, Jake Jacoby, Jans Jansson, Frida Johansen, Odd Larsen, Kyu Sik Lee, Lars-Göran Mattsson, Herbert Mohring, Max Neutze, Gabriel Roth, Ken Small, Farideh Ramjerdi, Larry Summers and Sir Alan Walters. While making these acknowledgements, I retain full responsibility for the contents of this paper.
1. Professor Vickrey once told me that he thought that roads in the US were about a quarter to a third overbuilt. Vickrey's views on the severity of the congestion conumdrum remained the same up until his unexpected demise in 1996 (Vickrey, 1996).
2. The regulatory approach suffers from its inability to provide correct market signals to induce the most efficient trips to be undertaken. In contrast to pricing incentives, it generates virtually no revenues for the public sector.
3. Road use costs (both 'private' and 'social') include: (1) congestion (which is borne by road users); (2) pavement wear (which is typically covered by the road agency); (3) air and noise pollution; and (4) costs of accidents (both of which are borne by society at large). This paper deals mainly with congestion pricing (and only tangentially with pavement wear charges) as opposed to marginal social cost pricing, which is defined to include both the private costs and the external costs of congestion, air pollution, noise pollution, accidents, road damages and externalities (see Hau, 1992a).
4. See Beckmann, McGuire and Winsten (1956, figure 4.1); Mogridge (1990, figure 6.3); Jansson (1993, figure 9.4); and Johansson and Mattsson (1995, figure 1.5). In the next

section, we first assume that there are only two alternatives (i.e. periods): a peak and an off-peak.

5. Hence the marginal cost curve, MC, when summed up vertically with the vehicle operating cost and variable road maintenance cost, yields a translated marginal cost curve, *MC*. The same notations apply to the average variable cost curve in Figure 3.2.

6. The relation AVC = AVC(Q) means that time cost depends on traffic level, and not vice versa. The backward-bending portion of the cost curve means that time cost continues to rise when traffic flow is reduced after engineering capacity is reached. The backward-bending portion of the cost curve has been substantiated in the literature (Gerlough and Huber, 1975, chapter 4).

7. Recently, Alan Evans (1992) and Peter Hills (1993) have argued that output should be specified as the number of vehicles over a stretch of roads (that is, density), rather than the number of vehicles per unit of time as used conventionally in Nash (1982), Button and Pearman (1983), De Meza and Gould (1987) and Andrew Evans (1992), for instance. I maintain that the output variable used in the standard analysis is more appropriate because: (i) the (engineering) capacity of a road, in terms of vehicles per hour, is clearly built into the analysis and (ii) any commodity or service consumed clearly takes place in a specific time period (that is, in quantity per unit of time) and is implicit in the demand analysis of the commodity in question. Else (1981) argues that the demand variable is in fact a demand for the number of completed trips, but I argue that it is still necessary to express demand in quantity per unit of time. Hence the number of (vehicle) trips completed per unit time – which is simply the traffic flow – is the correct output specification. Demand and supply as I have interpreted them here are fully consistent with one another.

8. Formally, the functions GC(Q) and $Q^d(P)$ intersect at an equilibrium point, where GC symbolizes the generalized cost. The equilibrium point is expressed as: $Q^d(GC(Q^0)) = Q^0$. Since GC is simply a translation of AVC, the interpretation of one is synonymous with the other.

9. Marginal cost is obtained as follows: MC $\equiv \Delta C(Q)/\Delta Q$ = AVC(Q)+ Q $\cdot \Delta$AVC(Q)/ΔQ = AVC(Q) $\cdot$ (1 + ε) where C(Q) is the cost function, ε is the elasticity of the AVC curve, that is, the rate at which time cost rises with respect to a one percent rise in traffic flow (Walters, 1961). The first term composes of only time cost – where trip time is converted into time cost via the (marginal) valuation of travel time – and the second term is the marginal (external) congestion cost, set equal to the congestion toll. Marginal cost pricing of a trip, P, is achieved by setting P = MC. This is known as the first-best optimal (or efficient) pricing rule: our first optimality rule. (Note that AVC depends parametrically on the capacity level K, and can be expressed as AVC (Q,K). Without loss of generality, the inclusion of the vehicle operating cost and variable road maintenance cost – both being constant with respect to traffic – simply shifts the right-hand side of the equation upwards.) Note further that marginal cost rises asymptotically to the engineering capacity level of Q^{max} and is undefined for the AVC curve at points beyond point V.

10. These major cities include: Bangkok, Bombay, Budapest, Buenos Aires, Jakarta, Mexico City, Pusan, Santiago, Sao Paulo, Seoul, Shanghai and Taipei.

11. The terms 'the tolled' and 'the tolled off' are coined by Zettel and Carll (1964) but their approach differs from our approach and results derived from first principles.

12. Cooperation is greatly enhanced if road users were guaranteed a reduction in motor vehicle-related taxes such as import duties, first registration taxes, annual license fees and/ or fuel taxes (Small, 1992).

13. With standard commodities, both the short-run marginal and average variable cost curves can decline and swing upwards, whereas I have shown that both the short-run marginal and average variable cost curves in transport cannot decline but can only rise upwards.

14. With congestion tolling, note that high purchase taxes and registration/license fees of vehicles (if applicable) ought to be reduced to a level just sufficient to meet the administrative and enforcement costs of collection. If the variable road maintenance cost is constant with respect to the traffic level as we have assumed, an appropriate fuel tax could perhaps be used to approximate usage (as well as to tackle other externalities). As with the

services of public utilities, a pure tax element (such as a value-added tax) could also be imposed on top of the marginal cost of road use to meet general tax revenue requirements.

15. If (1) the capital and invariate maintenance cost of highway capacity, KC, is directly proportional to the engineering capacity, K, that is, KC(K) = aK, where a is a constant, then there exists constant returns to scale in highway construction (and invariate road maintenance). (In mathematical jargon. KC is homogeneous of degree one in capacity.) The engineering capacity is measured by lane-width and is treated as a continuous variable. Further, if (2)(a) traffic can be expressed in terms of a homogeneous unit, Q, in vehicles per lane–hour, and the time cost function AVC(Q,K) depends directly on the traffic flow but is inversely related to the capacity; and (b) if doubling both highway capacity input and the output variable of traffic flow result in the travel time of a trip remaining the same, then there exists constant returns to road use. (Mathematically, the AVC function is homogeneous of degree zero in traffic volume and capacity.) With constant returns to road use, AVC(Q,K) can be formally rewritten as AVC(Q/K), where Q/K is the volume–capacity ratio. Since average vehicle operating and variable road maintenance costs are both independent of the level of output, and capital cost, KC, is proportional to lane expansion, ATC(Q,K) = ATC(Q/K) holds also. These two technical conditions are vital to Mohring and Harwitz's (1962, pp. 85–90) so-called theorem.

16. Prest (1969, p. 8) and Walters (1968, p. 33) argue for short-run marginal cost pricing whereas others like Meyer *et al.* (1959, chapter 4) argue for variants of long-run marginal cost pricing. Since the issue of long-run vs. short-run marginal cost pricing has been with us for some time, a clarification is in order (see the debate between Jordan (1983, 1985) and Vickrey (1985).)

17. Formally, given a particular level of output, the cost-minimizing authority would expand the road up to the point where the marginal valuation in user cost savings due to a unit increase in capacity, $-$ Q $\cdot$ ΔAVC(Q,K)/ΔK, equals the marginal cost of an extra unit of capacity, R(K). R(K), which depends on the level of highway capacity K, is the marginal rental cost per time period of capacity. It includes the invariate maintenance and other operating costs of a road, depreciation and imputed interest on invested capital. The negative sign would offset the inverse relationship of AVC and K, yielding a positive magnitude for the entire term. Alternatively, the road is to be expanded up to the point where the marginal external congestion cost just offsets the marginal cost of investment in capacity. This is the second optimality rule: the optimal investment in capacity rule.

18. The superscript * symbol indicates that that variable is optimized.

19. First-best rules would yield economic efficiency only by assuming that the rest of the economy is marginal cost-priced. When that assumption is not satisfied, the theory of second best, with all its limitations, applies. Verhoef (1996) has recently handled these complex second-best issues in congestion pricing.

20. Estimates for the marginal congestion costs, congestion tolls and revenues for urban road use in Indonesia are reported in Hau (1994).

21. Alternatively, the costs of uncongested rural access roads could be covered by access charges such as annual license fees or local rates (Newbery, 1994). Vickrey (1996) argues strongly for a tax on land values.

22. It is due to the assumption of independent demands that long-run marginal cost pricing (equal to short-run marginal cost pricing) still holds at each time period. The concept of long-run marginal cost pricing is blurred in the case of jointness of demand.

23. Increasing financial costs of construction via tunnelling and/or flyovers, together with high land resumption costs, are consistent with the findings of Hau (1989) for Hong Kong.

24. Perhaps surprisingly, the symmetry of the LRMC curves in Figures 3.6a and 3.7a does not carry over exactly to the other cases in Figures 3.6b, c and 3.7b, c (see Hau, 1992a).

25. Space precludes us from elaborating on the empirical evidence of the scale economy issue (see Hau, 1992a). Walters (1968, pp. 184–5), using Meyer, Kain and Wohl's (1965, p. 205) data, shows that there are diseconomies of scale in the construction of four-lane, six-lane and eight-lane urban road segments. Keeler and Small (1977) find evidence of constant returns to scale for a sample of San Francisco Bay Area roads. Their often cited econometric study is important because of the balance budget implication for congestion pric-

ing. By contrast, using engineering specifications, Kraus (1981a) finds that there are increasing returns to scale in road construction in terms of length of freeway and interchanges but not for overpasses and length of arterials. Meyer and Gomez-Ibañez (1981, pp. 191–2), in assessing the available estimates in the conflicting literature, conclude that economies and diseconomies of scale are 'probably roughly offsetting'. Newbery (1989, 1994, p. 239) observes that '[i]f there are constant returns to expanding road capacity (as seems empirically plausible for those roads carrying the larger fraction of total traffic), then these [efficiency] prices will equal the maintenance costs and the interest on the infrastructural capital involved in an optimally adjusted road network'.

26.   If a road fund were to be set up, compensation would need to be sufficiently indirect to satisfy Pareto efficiency. Thus the funds generated from money-making roads should not be tied to those roads but be made available for road construction and maintenance of the road network in general. The funds from profitable urban roads could be used to finance the fixed capital cost of worthwhile rural roads in a non-distortionary manner, for instance. To what extent can the profits collected from heavily used roads offset the losses arising from the construction of lightly used roads? The answer depends on the extent of the interaction of both scale economies and indivisibilities. A road fund is attractive because of the high marginal cost of raising a tax dollar. Moreover, a road fund run by an autonomous authority would increase the 'linkage' between revenues and expenditures, currently lacking in a politically-based budgeting process, thereby improving managerial efficiency. Without the setting up of such a fund, deficits from lightly used rural roads (with increasing returns to scale) would demand subsidization by the treasury, and would thus compete for tax money valued at a high opportunity cost. By symmetry, surpluses that accrue in heavily utilized urban areas (with decreasing returns to scale) should then be valued at a premium as (toll-)tax revenues. If these welfare losses and premiums offset one another when viewed within the same (transport) sector, then the nominal value of a dollar could be treated at its face value. This allows us to retreat to the standard case of pure efficiency concerns where a dollar is treated as a dollar to whomsoever it accrues. Even if a certain place is found to be faced with mainly increasing returns to scale, the deficit could be closed, in principle, by appealing to the notion of diseconomies of scope (see Hau, 1992a). The surplus associated with diseconomies of scope balances the potential deficit associated with scale-specific economies of road construction or use. The viability of the fund is enhanced by the fact that the maintenance cost of the road pavement is charged twice: once when traffic flow creates congestion, and the second time when traffic loadings cause road damage. Thus, the idea of a trust fund administered by an independent agency according to strict cost–benefit principles is likely to be viable.

27.   Similarly, heavy vehicles ought to incur their 'fair' share of hefty pavement wear fees.

28.   Alternatively, taking the surface transport sector as a whole, a transportation fund ought to be set up. If dedicated funds are set up in this way, indirect 'compensatory' payments can be achieved and would satisfy optimality. I recommend this both because the problem of highway congestion is tied intrinsically to the provision of poor transit alternatives and because public transport plays an important role in most places. The fact is that the production of bus services is subject to increasing returns due to scheduling frequency when passengers' travel time is taken into account (based on the system economy of scale effect or the so-called 'Mohring (1976) effect'). Hence additional funds in the form of a subsidy – preferably a user-side subsidy – is required to meet the financial shortfall arising from (first-best) optimal bus service provision. Road pricing would result in more crowded and inferior public transport services unless bus companies were to run more buses as a supply response. When this results in lower bus fares for passengers, the 'untolled' public transport users and captive riders would then be made better off. (Here the double charging of automobiles via traffic volume and heavy vehicles via loadings would help to close any deficit gap.) Increasingly popular rapid mass transit and light rail systems – both of which are subject to significant scale economies due to its large infrastructure costs – also require capital funds, the construction of which should be based on economic viability. Unless a global view is taken of the congestion problem and more rational time-of-day

pricing practiced on all modes (in contrast to tackling individual, non-optimally priced modes), the urban transportation problem will continue to be pervasive.

29. Newbery (1994) calls for a road authority to be established like a public utility and subject to regulation. Because of roads' natural monopoly attributes, clear safeguards must be put in place via regulation to prevent, for instance, the curtailment of road supply to rake in congestion toll revenues (possibly in concert with environmental lobby groups). Freed from the fiscal shackles that governments face, Newbery argues that the Road Authority, when vested with the capital value of the existing road infrastructure, could finance efficient (but not necessarily profitable) road expansions. One advantage of establishing such an authority is that the politically sensitive issue of the nonhypothecation of tax revenues by the Treasury would be obviated. Further, if the Authority were to be run like an old electricity area board, gas council or water board in the United Kingdom, subcontracting or franchising could take place, all within an open and transparent manner to the (motorist)customer. Newbery (1994, p. 39) puts it aptly by observing that: '[t]he test of commercialisation is whether there is some intermediate allocation of the powers of pricing and investment to a Road Authority and away from the Treasury, subject to regulation on this narrower range of powers, and which nevertheless provides good incentives for efficient management and investment'. The feasibility of Newbery's proposal is buttressed by his estimates showing that the introduction of optimal road user charges in the United Kingdom to replace current road taxes there would adequately cover the cost of the road infrastructure. He also notes that with proper road use charges in place, competing rail services could raise their fares and thus pose less of a drain on government coffers. (Thus introducing road pricing would eliminate the second-best theoretical rationale for continuing to (nonoptimally) subsidize public transport.) Newbery's proposal is fleshed out in Roth (1996), who suggests that the application of commercial principles to roads would reduce congestion and pollution and simultaneously raise funding for roads.

30. The proposal put forth here also satisfies many of the economic, financial and environmental sustainability criteria as set forth in the Development in Practice Series of the World Bank (1996) on priorities for reform in the transport sector.

31. Recent developments in electronic tolling in Norway, Sweden and England point to the fact that travellers do not object to road pricing when the toll revenues are earmarked for both road construction and improvement and/or the provision of better public transport. Indeed, a national survey conducted in England indicates that when people were asked whether they are for or against road pricing, about 57 percent are against it. However, when the question was posed in a different way: would they be supportive of a package approach to road pricing, with the revenues from road pricing used only to finance road construction and/or public transport, 57 per cent of the same surveyed population were in favor of road pricing (Jones, 1991; Goodwin, 1989; Grieco and Jones, 1994). A 1995 House of Commons Transport Committee report in the United Kingdom reveals the results of a survey conducted in Cambridge in 1994: the most effective combination of measures in combatting congestion was public transport improvements coupled with road pricing (Ison, 1996).

REFERENCES

Arnott, Richard, Kenneth Arrow, Anthony B. Atkinson and Jacques H. Drèze (eds) (1994), *Public Economics: Selected Papers by William Vickrey*, Cambridge: Cambridge University Press.

Arnott, Richard, André de Palma and Robin Lindsey (1988), 'Schedule delay and departure time decisions with heterogeneous commuters', *Transportation Research Record*, No. 1197, 56–67.

Arnott, Richard and Martin Kraus (1998), 'Self-financing of congestible facilities in a growing economy', in David Pines, Efrain Sadka and Itzhak Zilcha (eds), *Topics in Public Economics*, Cambridge, UK: Cambridge University Press, Chapter 7, pp. 161–84.

Baumol, William J. and Wallace E. Oates (1975, 1988), *The Theory of Environmental Policy*, first edition, 1975, and second edition, 1988, New York: Cambridge University Press.

Beckmann, Martin, C.B. McGuire and Christopher B. Winsten (1956), *Studies in the Economics of Transportation*, New Haven: Yale University Press.

Boiteux, Marcel (1960), 'Peak-Load Pricing', *Journal of Business*, **33** (2), April, 157–79, translated from the French article 'La tarification des demandes en pointe: application de la theorie de la vente au coût marginal', by H.W. Izzard, as revised by the author, in the *Revue Générale de l'Electricité*, August 1949, **58** (8), 321–40. Reprinted in James R. Nelson (ed.) (1964), *Marginal Cost Pricing in Practice*, pp. 59–89, Englewood Cliffs, NJ: Prentice-Hall, Inc.

Buchanan, James M. (1965), 'An Economic Theory of Clubs', *Economica*, **32**, 1–14.

Button, Kenneth J. (ed.) (1986), *Transportation Research A*, **20A** (2), March, Special issue on 'Road Pricing'.

Button, Kenneth J. and Alan D. Pearman (1983), 'Road pricing – some of the more neglected theoretical and policy implications', *Transportation Planning and Technology*, **8** (1), 15–28.

De Meza, David and J.R. Gould (1987), 'Free access versus private property in a resource: income distributions compared', *Journal of Political Economy*, **95** (6), 1317–25.

Dodgson, John (1997), 'Evaluating transport projects and policies', in Ginés de Rus and Chris Nash (eds), *Recent Developments in Transport Economics*, Chapter 6, pp. 198–231, Aldershot, UK: Ashgate Publishing Limited.

Downs, Anthony (1962), 'The law of peak-hour expressway congestion', *Traffic Quarterly*, **16**, July, 393–409.

Downs, Anthony (1992), *Stuck in Traffic: Coping with Peak-Hour Traffic Congestion*, Washington, DC: The Brookings Institution.

Else, Peter K. (1981), 'A reformulation of the theory of optimum congestion taxes', *Journal of Transport Economics and Policy*, **15** (3), September, 217–32.

Evans. Alan W. (1992), 'Road congestion: the diagrammatic analysis', *Journal of Political Economy*, **100** (1), 211–17.

Evans, Andrew W. (1992), 'Road congestion pricing: When is it a good policy?' *Journal of Transport Economics and Policy*, **26** (3), September, 213–43.

Gerlough, Daniel L. and Matthew J. Huber (1975), *Traffic Flow Theory*, A Monograph, Special Report 165, Transportation Research Board, National Research Council, Washington, DC.

Glaister, Stephen (1991), 'Pricing, investment and capital financing', in Stephen Glaister, Nathaniel Lichfield, David Bayliss, Tony Travers and Tony Ridley (eds), *Transport Options for London*, Chapter 6, pp. 91–116, Greater London Papers No. 18, Greater London Group, London School of Economics and Political Science, London.

Goodwin, Phil B. (1989), 'The rule of three: A possible solution to the political problem of competing objectives for road pricing', *Traffic Engineering and Control*, **29** (10), October, 495–7.

Grieco, Margaret and Peter M. Jones (1994), 'A change in the policy climate? Current perspectives on road pricing', *Urban Studies*, **31** (9), 1517–32.

Haight, Frank A. (1963), *Mathematical Theories of Traffic Flow*, New York: Academic Press.

Hau, Timothy D. (1989), 'Road pricing in Hong Kong: A viable proposal', *Built Environment*, **15** (3/4), 195–214.

Hau, Timothy D. (1990), 'Electronic road pricing: Developments in Hong Kong 1983–89', *Journal of Transport Economics and Policy*, **24** (2), May, 203–14.

Hau, Timothy D. (1992a), 'Economic fundamentals of road pricing: A diagrammatic analysis', World Bank Policy Research Working Paper Series WPS 1070, December, Washington, DC: The World Bank, pp. 1–96.

Hau, Timothy D. (1992b), 'Congestion charging mechanisms for roads: An evaluation of current practice', World Bank Policy Research Working Paper Series WPS 1071, December, Washington, DC: The World Bank, pp. 1–99.

Hau, Timothy D. (1994), 'Estimation of marginal congestion costs, congestion tolls and revenues for urban road use in Indonesia', *Proceedings of the International Conference on Advanced Technologies in Transportation and Traffic Management*, Nanyang Technological University, Singapore, 18–20 May, pp. 77–88.

Hau, Timothy D. (1995), 'Instruments for charging congestion externalities', in Börje Johansson and Lars-Göran Mattsson (eds), *Road Pricing: Theory, Empirical Assessment and Policy*, Chapter 12, pp. 223–34, Boston: Kluwer Academic Publishers.

Hau, Timothy D. (1996), 'Income and car ownership: A cross section and time series exploratory analysis', paper presented at the 71st Annual Conference of the Western Economic Association International, San Francisco, 28 June–2 July, pp. 1–30.

Hayutin, Adele M. (1984), 'Scale economies in highway capacity: Empirical evidence and policy implications', unpublished PhD dissertation, Department of Economics, University of California, Berkeley, California, pp. 1–182. Also available from University Microfilms International, Dissertation Information Service, Ann Arbor, Michigan.

Hills, Peter J. (1993), 'Road congestion pricing: When is it a good policy? A comment', *Journal of Transport Economics and Policy*, **27** (1), January, 91–9.

Ison, Stephen (1996), 'Pricing road space: Back to the future? The Cambridge experience', *Transport Reviews*, **16** (2), 109–26.

Jansson, Jan Owen (1993), 'Government and transport infrastructure – investment', in Jacob Polak and Arnold Heertje (eds), *European Transport Economics*, Chapter 9, pp. 221–43, Oxford, UK: Blackwell Publishers.

Johansson, Börje and Lars-Göran Mattsson (1995), 'Principles of road pricing', in Börje Johansson and Lars-Göran Mattsson (eds), *Road Pricing: Theory, Empirical Assessment and Policy*, Chapter 1, pp. 7–33, Boston: Kluwer Academic Publishers.

Jones, Peter M. (1991), 'Gaining public support for road pricing through a package approach', *Traffic Engineering and Control*, **32** (4), April, 194–6.

Jordan, W. John (1983), 'Heterogeneous users and the peak load pricing model', *The Quarterly Journal of Economics*, **93** (1), February, 127–38.

Jordan, W. John (1985), 'Capacity costs, heterogeneous users, and peak-load pricing', *The Quarterly Journal of Economics*, **95**, November, 1335–7.

Keeler, Theodore E. and Kenneth A. Small (1977), 'Optimal peak-load pricing, investment, and service levels on urban expressways', *Journal of Political Economy*, **85** (1), January, 1–25. Reprinted in Tae Hoon Oum, John S. Dodgson. David A. Hensher, Steven A. Morrison, Christopher A. Nash, Kenneth A. Small and William

G. Waters II (eds) (1995), *Transport Economics: Selected Readings*, Chapter 18, pp. 425–55, Transportation Series 103, published for The Korea Research Foundation for the 21st Century by Seoul Press, Korea.

Knight, Frank H. (1924), 'Some fallacies in the interpretation of social cost', *Quarterly Journal of Economics*, **38**, August, 582–606. Reprinted in Kenneth J. Arrow and Tibor Scitovsky (eds) (1969), *Readings in Welfare Economics*, pp. 213–27, American Economic Association Series, Homewood, Ill: Richard D. Irwin, Inc.

Kraus, Marvin C. (1981a), 'Scale economies analysis for urban highway networks', *Journal of Urban Economics*, **9** (1), January, 1–22.

Kraus, Marvin C. (1981b), 'Indivisibilities, economies of scale, and optimal subsidy policy for freeways', *Land Economics*, **57** (1), February, 115–21.

May, Adolf D. (1990), *Traffic Flow Fundamentals*, Englewood Cliffs, NJ: Prentice-Hall.

McCleary, William A. (1991), 'The earmarking of government revenue: A review of some World Bank experience', *The World Bank Research Observer*, **6** (1), January, 81–104.

Meyer, John R. and José A. Gomez-Ibañez (1981), *Autos, Transit and Cities*, Cambridge, MA: Harvard University Press.

Meyer, John R., John F. Kain and Martin Wohl (1965), *The Urban Transportation Problem*, Cambridge, MA: Harvard University Press.

Meyer, John R., Merton J. Peck, John Stenason and Charles Zwick (1959), *The Economics of Competition in the Transportation Industries*, Cambridge, MA: Harvard University Press.

Mogridge, Martin J.H. (1990), *Travel in Towns: Jam Yesterday, Jam Today and Jam Tomorrow?* London and Basingstoke: The Macmillan Press Ltd.

Mohring, Herbert D. (1965), 'Urban highway investments', in Robert Dorfman (ed.), *Measuring Benefits of Government Investments*, papers presented at a Conference of Experts held 7–9 November, 1963, pp. 231–91, Washington, DC: The Brookings Institution.

Mohring, Herbert D. (1970), 'The peak load problem with increasing returns and pricing constraints', *American Economic Review*, **60** (4), September, 693–705.

Mohring, Herbert D. (1976), *Transportation Economics*, Cambridge, MA: Ballinger Press.

Mohring, Herbert D. and Mitchell Harwitz (1962), *Highway Benefits: An Analytical Framework*, Evanston, IL: Northwestern University Press.

Morrison, Steven A. (1986), 'A survey of road pricing', *Transportation Research A*, **20A** (2), March, 87–98.

Nash, Christopher A. (1982), 'A reformulation of the theory of optimal congestion taxes: A comment', *Journal of Transport Economics and Policy*, **26** (3), September, 295–99.

Neutze, G. Max (1966), 'Investment criteria and road pricing', *Manchester School of Economics and Social Studies*, **34** (1), January, 63–73.

Newbery, David M.G. (1988), 'Road user charges in Britain', *The Economic Journal Supplement (Conference 1987)*, **98** (390), 161–76.

Newbery, David M.G. (1989), 'Cost recovery from optimally designed roads', *Economica*, **56**, May, 165–85. Reprinted in Herbert Mohring (ed.) (1994) *The Economics of Transport*, **I**, Chapter 11, pp. 257–77, The International Library of Critical Writings in Economics 34, An Elgar Reference Collection, Aldershot, Hants.

Newbery, David M.G. (1990), 'Pricing and congestion: Economic principles relevant to pricing roads', *Oxford Review of Economic Policy*, Special Issue on Transport, **6** (2), Summer, 22–38.

Newbery, David M. (1994), 'The case for a public road authority', *Journal of Transport Economics and Policy*, **28** (3), September, 235–53.

Newbery, David M.G., Gordon A. Hughes, William D.O. Paterson and Esra Bennathan (1988), 'Road transport taxation in developing countries: The design of user charges and taxes for Tunisia', World Bank Discussion Paper No. 26, April, Washington, DC: The World Bank, pp. 1–94.

Pigou, Arthur C. (1920), *The Economics of Welfare*, first edition, London: Macmillan and Company.

Prest, Alan R. (1969), *Transport Economics in Developing Countries: Pricing and Financing Aspects*, London: The Trinity Press, Weidenfeld and Nicholson. Excerpt reprinted as 'Public transport pricing and cost recovery', in Gerald M. Meier (ed.) (1983), *Pricing Policy for Development Management*, pp. 216–22, EDI Series in Economic Development, Johns Hopkins University Press, published for The World Bank, Baltimore, MD.

Ramjerdi, Farideh (1995), *Road Pricing and Toll Financing: With Examples from Oslo and Stockholm*, PhD dissertation, Royal Institute of Technology, Department of Infrastructure and Planning, Stockholm, Sweden, Nils J. Schriver AS, Oslo.

Roth, Gabriel (1996), *Roads in a Market Economy*, Aldershot, Hants: Avebury Technical.

Small, Kenneth A. (1992), 'Using the revenues from congestion pricing', *Transportation*, **19** (4), 359–81.

Small, Kenneth A., Clifford M. Winston and Carol A. Evans (1989), *Road Work: A New Highway Pricing and Investment Policy*, Washington, DC: The Brookings Institution.

Starkie, David N.M. (1982), 'Road indivisibilities: Some observations', *Journal of Transport Economics and Policy*, **16** (3), September, 259–66.

Strotz, Robert H. (1964), 'Urban transportation parables', in Julius Margolis (ed.) (1965), *The Public Economy of Urban Communities*, pp. 127–69, papers presented at the Second Conference on Urban Public Expenditures held on 21–22 February, 1964, Resources for the Future, Baltimore, MD: Johns Hopkins University Press.

Verhoef, Erik (1996), *The Economics of Regulating Road Transport*, Cheltenham: Edward Elgar.

Vickrey, William (1960), 'Statement to the Joint Committee on Washington Metropolitan Problems', *Transportation Plan for the National Capital Region*, Hearings, Joint Committee on Washington Metropolitan Problems, 8–14 November, 1959, pp. 454–90. Excerpt reprinted in *Journal of Urban Economics* (1994), **36** (1), 42–65.

Vickrey, William S. (1963), 'Pricing in urban and suburban transport', *American Economic Review: Papers and Proceedings*, **53** (2), May, 452–65. Reprinted in George M. Smerk (ed.) (1968), *Readings in Urban Transportation*, Chapter 4, pp. 120–33, Bloomington: Indiana University Press.

Vickrey, William S. (1973), 'Pricing, metering, and efficiently using urban transportation facilities', *Highway Research Record*, No. 473, 'Price subsidy issues in urban transportation', Highway Research Board, pp. 36–48.

Vickrey, William S. (1985), 'The fallacy of using long-run cost for peak-load pricing', *The Quarterly Journal of Economics*, **95**, November, 1331–4.

Vickrey, William S. (1987), 'Marginal-cost and average-cost pricing', in John Eatwell, Murray Milgate and Peter Newman (eds), *The New Palgrave: A Dictionary of*

Economics, London: The Macmillan Press Limited, **III**, pp. 311–18. Reprinted in Richard Arnott, Kenneth Arrow, Anthony B. Atkinson and Jacques H. Drèze (eds) (1994), *Public Economics: Selected Papers by William Vickrey*, Chapter 10, pp. 197–215, Cambridge: Cambridge University Press.

Vickrey, William S. (1996), 'Privatization and marketization of transportation', in Simon Hakim, Paul Seidenstat and Gary W. Bowman (eds), *Privatizing Transportation Systems*, Chapter 13, pp. 221–48, Westport, CT: Praeger.

Walters, Alan A. (1961), 'The theory and measurement of private and social cost of highway congestion', *Econometrica*, **29** (4), October, 676–99. Reprinted in Matthew Edel and Jerome Rothenberg (eds) (1973), *Readings in Urban Economics*, Chapter 6.2, pp. 417–37, New York: Macmillan.

Walters, Alan A. (1968), *The Economics of Road User Charges*, World Bank Occasional Paper Number 5, International Bank for Reconstruction and Development, Baltimore, MD: Johns Hopkins University Press.

Walters, Alan A. (1987), 'Congestion', in John Eatwell, Murray Milgate and Peter Newman (eds), *The New Palgrave: A Dictionary of Economics*, London: The Macmillan Press Limited, **I**, pp. 570–73.

Winston, Clifford M. (1991), 'Efficient transportation infrastructure policy', *Journal of Economic Perspectives*, **5** (1), Winter, 113–27.

World Bank Operational Manual Statement (1977), 'Cost recovery policies for public sector projects: general aspects', No. 2.25, March, Washington, DC: The World Bank, pp. 1–7.

World Bank (1986), 'Urban transport: A World Bank policy study', Water Supply and Urban Development Department, The International Bank for Reconstruction and Development. Washington, DC: The World Bank, pp. 1–61.

World Bank (1996), *Sustainable Transport: Priorities for Policy Reform*, The Development in Practice Series, Washington DC: The World Bank, pp. 1–131.

Zettel, Richard M. and Richard R. Carll (1964), 'The basic theory of efficiency tolls: The tolled, the tolled-off and the un-tolled', *Highway Research Record*, No. 47, paper presented at the 43rd Annual Meeting of the Highway Research Board, 13–17 January, 1964, Washington, DC: National Research Council, pp. 46–65.

4. Recent developments in the bottleneck model[†]

Richard Arnott, André de Palma and Robin Lindsey

4.1 INTRODUCTION

The basic economic model of urban traffic congestion treats just one margin of individual choice: how many trips to take. In reality the array of decisions facing an individual traveler is far more complex. It is useful to conceptualize the individual as deriving utility from activities (dining in an Italian restaurant, going skiing, meeting Joe over a beer, taking the kids to school, and so on). Given a choice of activities, the individual must decide which activities she will perform and how best to schedule them. The individual's transportation demand is derived from the solution to this choice and scheduling problem. The modern economic theory of urban traffic congestion falls far short of this level of conceptual sophistication, but this is the general direction in which the theory is being developed. Thus far, significant progress has been made in modeling only the individual's participation, departure time and route choice decisions for the morning commute. The seminal paper was by Vickrey (1969). Since Vickrey assumed that traffic congestion takes the form of cars queueing behind a bottleneck, the Vickrey model has come to be termed 'the bottleneck model'; hence the title of this chapter.

The principal innovation of Vickrey's bottleneck model was to endogenize individuals' departure times. In the simple version of the model, each identical morning commuter travels in her own car from home to work along a single road which has a bottleneck of fixed flow capacity. All commuters wish to arrive at work at the same time. But because the bottleneck capacity is finite this is physically impossible; some must arrive early and/or others late. The costs of early and late arrival are termed *schedule delay costs*. Each individual decides when to depart from home so as to minimize trip price, which in the absence of a toll consists of travel time cost and schedule delay cost. Equilibrium requires that the trip price be uniform over the departure period and higher outside this period. Since schedule delay cost cannot be the same for all commuters, travel time cost must adjust over the rush hour in such a way that the equilibrium condition is satisfied. This implies that queueing time must evolve in a particular way over the rush hour, which in turn imposes a particular time pattern of departures from home. Thus, *the evolution of congestion over the rush hour is determined within the model.*

This chapter will explain how this simple modeling innovation has generated a wealth of insights into urban rush-hour auto congestion. The emphasis will be on analytical and economic developments rather than on the model's contributions to practical traffic simulation modeling. Policy insights from the bottleneck model will be mentioned only in passing. The chapter is organized as follows. Section 4.2 works through the analytics of the simple bottleneck model and discusses some of the insights derived from it. Using the same model, Section 4.3 examines the effects of alternative road pricing schemes on congestion. Section 4.4 runs through a list of analytical extensions that have been made to the simple bottleneck model to improve its realism: elastic demand, heterogeneous commuters, simple networks, stochasticity in capacity and demand, and alternative treatments of congestion. Section 4.5 describes preliminary work to make operational the bottleneck model: the construction of a dynamic, network simulation model of metropolitan Geneva by a team headed by André de Palma. Section 4.6 discusses directions for future research. Finally, Section 4.7 concludes.

4.2   THE ANALYTICS OF THE SIMPLE BOTTLENECK MODEL[1]

Every morning a fixed number, N, of identical individuals travel from home (O – origin) to work (D – destination). Drivers are treated as a continuum of measure N. Each individual travels by her own car along the single road joining O and D. Travel is uncongested except at a single bottleneck with a deterministic capacity of *s* cars per unit time. If the arrival rate at the bottleneck exceeds *s*, a queue develops. Travel time from O to D is

$$T(t) = \overline{T} + T^w(t),$$

where $\overline{T}$ is the fixed component of travel, $T^w(t)$ is waiting time (queueing time) at the bottleneck, and *t* is departure time from home. Let $Q(t)$ be queue length (number of cars in the queue) at time *t*. Then

$$T^w(t) = \frac{Q(t)}{s}; \tag{4.1}$$

an individual's queueing time equals queue length at the time she joins the queue divided by the bottleneck capacity (henceforth simply 'capacity'). To simplify algebra and terminology, and without loss of generality, we set $\bar{T} = 0$ so that $T(t) = Q(t)/s$; thus an individual arrives at the bottleneck as soon as she leaves home and arrives at work immediately upon getting through the bottleneck. With $r(t)$ denoting the departure rate, queue length evolves according to

$$\frac{dQ(t)}{dt} = \begin{cases} 0 & \text{for } Q(t) = 0 \text{ and } r(t) \leq s \\ r(t) - s & \text{otherwise} \end{cases} \quad (4.2)$$

In other words, if there is no queue and if the departure rate is less than capacity, then queue length remains zero; otherwise queue length changes at a rate equal to the departure rate minus capacity.

An individual's travel cost excluding any toll depends on her travel time and also on her schedule delay: time early or time late in arriving at work. To simplify, we assume a linear travel cost function:

$$C(t) = \alpha(\text{travel time}) + \beta(\text{time early}) + \gamma(\text{time late}), \quad (4.3)$$

where α is the shadow cost of time spent traveling, β the shadow cost of time early, and γ the shadow cost of time late. We assume as is realistic (Small 1982) that $\gamma > \alpha > \beta$. All individuals have the same official work starting time, t^*. For an individual who arrives early, time early is $t^* - t - T(t)$, and for an individual who arrives late, time late is $t + T(t) - t^*$. Let t_n be the departure time for which an individual arrives on time; that is $t_n + T(t_n) = t^*$. Thus

$$C(t) = \begin{cases} \alpha T(t) + \beta(t^* - t - T(t)) & \text{for } t < t_n \quad \text{(early arrival)} \\ \alpha T(t) + \gamma(t + T(t) - t^*) & \text{for } t > t_n \quad \text{(late arrival)} \end{cases} \quad (4.3')$$

Let $p(t)$ denote the trip price for someone departing at time t. Trip price at time t equals travel cost plus the toll at time t, $\tau(t)$:[2]

$$p(t) = C(t) + \tau(t).$$

4.2.1 No toll equilibrium

In this section, we solve for the no-toll equilibrium and hence assume the toll is zero, so that trip price equals travel cost.[3] The basic idea of the model is that congestion evolves over the period of departures, $\Im$, in such a way that no commuter can strictly reduce her trip price by changing her departure time. With identical individuals this equilibrium condition reduces to the pair of requirements that over $\mathfrak{J}$ trip price be the same for every commuter, whereas outside $\mathfrak{J}$ trip price be at least as high:

$$p(t) \begin{cases} = p \text{ for } t \in \mathfrak{J} \\ \geq p \text{ for } t \notin \mathfrak{J} \end{cases}$$

where p is the equilibrium trip price. The stage is now set to solve for the no-toll equilibrium. Note first that a queue must exist in the interior of the departure interval since otherwise a person departing when there was no queue would face a lower schedule delay cost than either the first or last person to depart, and the same (zero) travel time cost. The bottleneck therefore operates at capacity throughout $\mathfrak{J}$. Letting t_0 and t_e denote respectively the beginning and end of the departure interval, this implies

$$t_e - t_0 = \frac{N}{s}; \tag{4.4}$$

the length of the departure interval equals the number of commuters divided by capacity. The first person departs early (that is, departs at such a time that she arrives early) and faces no queue; hence

$$p(t_0) = C(t_0) = \beta(t^* - t_0). \tag{4.5a}$$

The last person, who departs late, also faces no queue, since joining a queue would increase her travel time without reducing her time late. Hence

$$p(t_e) = C(t_e) = \gamma(t_e - t^*). \tag{4.5b}$$

Combining (4.4), (4.5a), (4.5b), the definition of t_n and the equal-trip-price condition,

$$p(t_0) = p(t_e) = p, \tag{4.5c}$$

one obtains

$$t_0 = t^* - \frac{\gamma}{\beta + \gamma}\left(\frac{N}{s}\right), t_n = t^* - \frac{\beta\gamma}{\alpha(\beta + \gamma)}\left(\frac{N}{s}\right), t_e = t^* + \frac{\beta}{\beta + \gamma}\left(\frac{N}{s}\right), \tag{4.6a,b,c}$$

$$p = C = \frac{\beta\gamma}{\beta + \gamma}\frac{N}{s}. \tag{4.7}$$

Note that t_0, t_e and p are independent of the unit value of time, α. Independence of p implies that queueing delay at any time is inversely proportional to α. Having solved for the equilibrium trip price, it is straightforward to solve for $T(t)$ from (4.3') and (4.5):

$$T(t) = \begin{cases} \dfrac{\beta}{\alpha - \beta}(t - t_0) & \text{for } t \in [t_0, t_n] \\ \dfrac{\gamma}{\alpha + \gamma}(t_e - t) & \text{for } t \in [t_n, t_e] \end{cases}. \qquad (4.8a,b)$$

The intuition for (4.8) is straightforward. Consider an individual who departs early at time $t_0 + \Delta$. Compared to the first person to depart, her travel time cost is $\beta T(t_0 + \Delta)$ higher, while her time early cost is lower by $\beta(\Delta + T(t_0 + \Delta))$. For these to balance out such that the equal trip-price condition is satisfied, $T(t_0 + \Delta) = (\beta/(\alpha - \beta))\Delta$, which yields (4.8a). Equation (4.8b) is explained similarly. Having solved for $T(t)$, $Q(t)$ can be solved using (4.1), and $r(t)$ can thus be solved using (4.2):

$$r(t) = \begin{cases} r_E = \dfrac{\alpha}{\alpha - \beta}s & \text{for } t \in (t_0, t_n) \\ r_L = \dfrac{\alpha}{\alpha + \gamma}s & \text{for } t \in (t_n, t_e) \end{cases}. \qquad (4.9)$$

For early arrival the departure rate is constant and above capacity, so that queue length and travel time increase linearly. For late arrival the departure rate is less than capacity and the queue dissipates linearly.[4] Figure 4.1 depicts the no-toll equilibrium. Cumulative departures from home, ABC, and cumulative arrivals at work, AC, are plotted as functions of time. The slopes of the two curves are the departure rate from home, $r(t)$, and the arrival rate at work, s, respectively. The vertical distance between the two curves at t' equals the number of commuters who have left home by t' minus the number who have arrived at work, and hence equals queue length at t', $Q(t')$. A point on the ordinate indexes a particular individual. Thus the horizontal distance between the cumulative departures and arrivals curves at t' measures an individual's travel time, $T(t')$.

Total travel time (the sum of travel times for all commuters) may be calculated by summing over time increments the number of commuters in the queue in each increment: $\int_{t_0}^{t_e} Q(t)dt$. Graphically, total travel time is therefore given by the area between the cumulative departures and arrivals schedules in Figure 4.1, ABCA. Total travel time costs, TTC, are α times this area. Since commuters arrive at work at rate s throughout the rush hour, total time early is $\int_{t_0}^{t^*} s(t^* - t)dt$: the area under the cumulative arrivals schedule from t_0 to t^*,

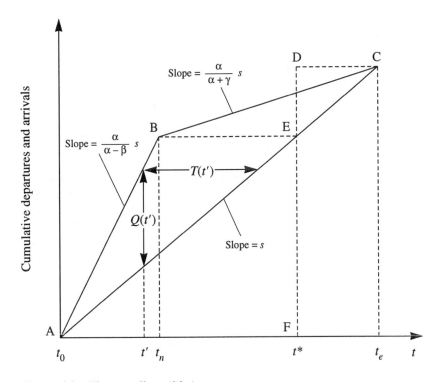

Figure 4.1   The no-toll equilibrium

AEFA. Similarly total time late equals area EDCE. Hence, total schedule delay costs, SDC, equal $\beta(\text{AEFA}) + \gamma(\text{EDCE})$.

Trip price is given by (4.7). Since trip cost equals trip price in the absence of a toll, total travel costs are

$$TC = \delta\left(\frac{N^2}{s}\right),$$
(4.10a)

where $\delta \equiv \beta\gamma/(\beta + \gamma)$, and the corresponding marginal (social) cost of a traveller is

$$MSC = \frac{\partial TC}{\partial N} = 2\delta\left(\frac{N}{s}\right).$$
(4.10b)

Since an individual's trip cost equals travel cost, and since the congestion externality, *CE*, equals marginal cost minus travel cost,

$$CE = MSC - C = \delta\left(\frac{N}{s}\right).\qquad(4.10c)$$

Note that the marginal cost of a driver is independent of when she departs. The reason is that in response to the added driver, other drivers adjust their departure times in such a way that the time pattern of departures, including the added driver, is independent of when the added driver departs. Because of the linearity of the schedule delay cost function, total schedule delay cost and total travel time cost are both half of total travel cost:

$$TTC = SDC = \frac{\delta}{2}\left(\frac{N^2}{s}\right).\qquad(4.11a,b)$$

4.2.2 Social Optimum

The social optimum is most easily established by intuitive reasoning. First the bottleneck should be used to capacity throughout the rush hour, since otherwise schedule delay costs are unnecessarily high. Thus, $t_e - t_0 = N/s$. Second, as noted earlier the departure rate should never exceed capacity, otherwise a queue develops and unnecessary travel time costs are incurred. Third, the schedule delay costs of the first and last persons should be the same; otherwise transferring commuters from one end of the rush hour to the other would reduce total costs. These conditions imply that the rush hour departure interval is the same for the social optimum as for the no-toll equilibrium; so too is the arrival interval and hence total schedule delay costs. Since total travel costs are double total schedule delay costs in the no-toll equilibrium, but equal to total schedule delay costs at the social optimum, total travel costs at the social optimum are only half those in the no-toll equilibrium:

$$TC^o = \frac{\delta}{2}\left(\frac{N^2}{s}\right),\qquad(4.12)$$

where superscript o denotes the social optimum.

Several features of the model and its solution are worthy of note.

- There exist a unique no-toll equilibrium and a unique social optimum.
- The length of the rush hour is equal to the ratio of the number of commuters to capacity, and is therefore endogenous.
- Total schedule delay costs, which the standard analysis of congestion ignores, equal total travel time costs.
- The model is structural in the sense that it provides an explicit treat-

ment of both the congestion technology and users' behavioral decisions (here only departure times). In contrast, the standard model of traffic congestion fails to treat explicitly either individuals' departure time decisions or the 'physics' of congestion.

- Even though the model is dynamic its equilibrium has a time-independent reduced-form representation. The demand curve is vertical at N commuters (since demand is assumed to be inelastic) while the travel cost and marginal social cost curves are given by (4.7) and (4.10b). Thus the standard model of congestion can be viewed as a reduced-form representation of a dynamic model in which the departure rate is endogenous.
- The model treats congestion as history-dependent. The history is captured by the state variable, queue length.
- Optimal capacity can be determined straightforwardly. The marginal benefit of capacity expansion equals $-\partial TC/\partial s$, where TC is given by (4.10a). Equating marginal benefit to marginal cost gives optimal capacity.
- Travel time costs are pure deadweight loss. This points to the potentially very substantial travel cost savings (see equation (4.10a) and equation (4.12)) that can be achieved simply by altering the time pattern of departures, which we show in Section 4.3 can be achieved by tolling.

4.3   TOLLING IN THE BASIC BOTTLENECK MODEL[5]

In this section we show that the social optimum can be decentralized by an optimal time-varying toll. We then briefly consider the relative efficiency of step function tolls.

4.3.1   Decentralization of the Social Optimum via a Toll

The time-varying toll which decentralizes the social optimum can be established by intuitive reasoning. Impose a toll that at each point in time equals the travel time cost of the person who *arrives* at work at that time in the no-toll equilibrium. This induces a new equilibrium in which the equal trip-price condition holds without queueing. The toll simply replaces queueing cost as the rationing mechanism for arrival time slots. Furthermore the toll does not alter the rush-hour interval. It is easy to show that the optimal toll is[6]

$$\tau(t) = \begin{cases} \delta\left(\dfrac{N}{s}\right) - \beta(t^* - t) & \text{for } t \in [t_0, t^*] \\ \delta\left(\dfrac{N}{s}\right) - \gamma(t - t^*) & \text{for } t \in [t^*, t_e] \end{cases},$$

which as one would expect equals the magnitude of the congestion external-ity evaluated at the social optimum. The toll is triangular, rising linearly from zero at t_0 to a maximum at t^*, and then declining linearly to zero at t_e.

4.3.2 Step Tolls

At least in the absence of adequate technology a triangular toll would be very awkward to implement. It is therefore of interest to enquire what proportion of the efficiency gains from tolling can be achieved by imposing an optimal[7] step toll with *n* steps. (A uniform toll is defined simply as a zero-step toll.)

The analytics for step tolls are rather complex for the realistic case $\gamma > \alpha$. For the case $\alpha > \gamma$ Laih (1994) has established that the ratio of the efficiency gain from the optimal step toll to that of the optimal time-varying toll is $n/(n + 1)$. Thus an optimal one-step toll yields half the efficiency gains of the optimal time-varying toll, an optimal two-step toll yields two-thirds of the efficiency gains, and so on. The implication of this result is that, while substantial efficiency gains can be obtained from even an optimal one-step toll, an optimal time-varying toll, which could be imposed via electronic pricing, would do considerably better.

Regardless of the number of toll steps, or the relative magnitude of α and γ, total travel costs have the form:

$$TC^r = \Gamma^r \delta\left(\frac{N^2}{s}\right), \tag{4.13}$$

where *r* denotes the pricing regime and Γ^r is a coefficient that does not depend on *N* or *s*. For the no-toll equilibrium, $\Gamma = 1$ per (4.10a). For the social optimum, $\Gamma = 1/2$ per (4.12). And for the optimal step toll, $\Gamma \in (1/2, 1)$ is a decreasing function of the number of steps.

The bottleneck model demonstrates very effectively the magnitude of the potential efficiency gains that congestion tolls can achieve by changing the time pattern of departures, even without any reduction in the number of trips. As a back-of-the-envelope calculation consider a city of one million people of whom 40 per cent work. Suppose, roughly updating Small's (1982, Table 3, col. 1) estimates, that $\gamma = \$20/hr$, $\alpha = \$10/hr$, and $\beta = \$5/hr$, and that the length of the rush hour is one hour ($N/s = 1$). According to (4.11a) the daily efficiency gains from application of the optimal time-varying toll would be $(5)(20)/(2(25))((4 \times 10^5)^2/(4 \times 10^5) = 0.8 \times 10^6$. With 200 commuting days a year and an annual discount rate of 0.05, this translates into discounted present value efficiency gains of $\$3.2 \times 10^9$, or $8000 per commuter! Comparable gains would presumably be achieved in the afternoon rush hour.[8]

It should be noted that optimal capacity varies according to the tolling regime. Since the marginal benefit from capacity is directly proportional to total travel costs,[9] which are higher the 'coarser' the tolling regime, optimal capacity is higher the coarser the tolling regime, and highest with no toll (or, equivalently, with a uniform toll, since with inelastic demand a uniform toll has no effect on the equilibrium).

One of the best-known results in urban transport economics, due to Mohring and Harwitz (1962), is that if total user costs plus capacity construction costs exhibit constant returns to scale then revenue from the optimal toll exactly covers the cost of constructing optimal capacity. With constant costs to capacity, this result holds in the bottleneck model, which implies that the first-best transport system should be entirely self-financing.[10]

4.4   EXTENSIONS

The simple bottleneck model treated in the previous two sections is a theoretical gem since it generates so many insights with a minimum of analytical clutter. Practical implementation, however, requires considering a wide range of real-world complications, the treatment of which as we shall see yields additional general insights. This section provides a necessarily cursory survey of the substantial theoretical literature which has evolved from the simple bottleneck model. Unless otherwise stated, the extensions are treated one-by-one rather than in combination.

4.4.1   Elastic Demand[11]

Elastic demand is easily handled. Consider the no-toll equilibrium. Equation (4.7) gives travel cost as a function of the number of commuters, $C = C(N,s)$, and since there is no toll, $p = C$. To this pair of equations we add a demand function, $N = N(p)$, yielding three equations in the three unknowns C, p and N.

There is an important qualitative difference between the cases of inelastic and elastic demand in the choice of optimal capacity because with elastic demand *latent demand* must be considered. An expansion of capacity lowers trip price, which induces increased traffic. Whether this affects the marginal benefit from capacity expansion depends on whether trip price equals marginal cost. Let $G(N)$ be gross benefits from N trips and $B(N,s)$ benefits net of total travel costs: $B(N,s) = G(N) - TC(N,s)$. Then

$$\frac{dB}{ds} = \frac{\partial B}{\partial s} + \frac{\partial B}{\partial N}\frac{dN}{ds} = \frac{\partial B}{\partial s} + \frac{\partial B}{\partial N}\frac{dN}{dp}\frac{dp}{ds}$$

(4.14)

$$= -\frac{\partial TC}{\partial s} + \left[\left(\frac{\partial G}{\partial N} - \frac{\partial TC}{\partial N}\right)\frac{dN}{dp}\frac{dp}{ds}\right].$$

The first term on the right-hand side of (4.14) captures the *direct benefit* of the capacity expansion: the benefit that occurs with no change in travel behavior. The second term, in square brackets, captures the *indirect benefit* which comes about because of behavioral changes induced by the capacity expansion: here an increase in the number of trips due to the reduction in trip price caused by the capacity expansion. With no toll the marginal social cost of the induced increase in traffic exceeds the marginal social benefit. Thus the indirect benefit is negative, and in the extreme case of perfectly elastic demand completely offsets the direct benefit. With marginal-cost pricing, however, the indirect benefit is zero because the marginal social benefit of the induced increase in traffic equals the marginal social cost. This is an example of a general principle in economics which surfaces repeatedly in urban transportation. If pricing is efficient (that is with marginal-cost pricing) only the direct effects of a small change need be considered; the indirect effects can be ignored. This is called the *envelope theorem*. But if pricing is inefficient, the envelope theorem does not apply and indirect effects have to be considered. On the assumption that demand is isoelastic, the ranking of optimal capacity by pricing regime turns out to be the same as with fixed demand when $\varepsilon < 1$, and is reversed when $\varepsilon > 1$.

4.4.2 Heterogeneous Individuals[12]

Heterogeneity in individuals introduces a number of interesting complications (Vickrey 1973; Cohen 1987; Newell 1987; ADL 1988, 1992, 1994). In the simple bottleneck model individuals can differ in terms of t^*, α, β and γ. Take first the situation where individuals differ in t^*, and let $W(t^*)$ be the cumulative distribution function of t^*. (In the bottleneck model with identical individuals $W(\cdot)$ is a step function of height N at the common t^*.) Hendrickson and Kocur (1981) consider the case for which in the no-toll equilibrium $W(\cdot)$ crosses the cumulative arrivals schedule once. An example is shown in Figure 4.2. Desired arrival times range from t_0^* to t_e^*, with $s(t_e^* - t_0^*) < N$ so that capacity is insufficient for all N individuals to arrive at their preferred times. As in Figure 4.1, cumulative departures are given by ABC, and cumulative arrivals by AC. The crossing point E occurs at time $t^{**} = W^{-1}[(\gamma/(\beta + \gamma))N]$. As in the model with identical individuals, $(\gamma/(\beta + \gamma))N$ individuals arrive early and $(\beta/(\beta + \gamma))N$ arrive late. The departure rate, queueing pattern and total travel

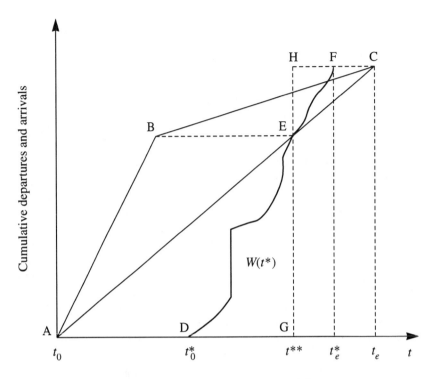

Figure 4.2   No-toll equilibrium with a distribution of t^*

time costs are also the same as in the basic model where all commuters wish to arrive at t^{**}.[13] But total time early is smaller by area DEGD, and total time late by area EHFE. A notable feature of the equilibrium is that, provided $s(t_e^* - t_0^*) < N$, total travel time is not reduced by spreading the distribution of desired arrival times. Staggering work hours is then ineffective for reducing congestion, although it does reduce total schedule delay costs.

Suppose now, still with $s(t_e^* - t_0^*) < N$, that $W(t^*)$ crosses the cumulative arrivals curve three or more times (the number must be odd). The no-toll equilibrium for this case is characterized in ADL (1996b). When cumulative arrivals are running ahead of (respectively behind) cumulative desired arrivals, the departure rate is r_E (respectively r_L) as defined in (4.9). A departure schedule in which individuals depart in strict sequence of increasing t^* constitutes an equilibrium, although it is not necessarily the unique equilibrium. Total travel time costs are still greater than total schedule delay costs, but in contrast to the one-crossing case, lower than with identical individuals.[14]

If $s(t_e^* - t_0^*) > N$, the bottleneck will not operate continuously at capacity, and departures will be concentrated during two or more 'sub-rush hours'.

Total travel time will be considerably less than in the basic model, which has one large rush hour. Indeed, if the slope of $W(t^*)$ is everywhere less than s, everyone can arrive at their preferred time and there will be no queueing at all.

To sum up: If $W(t^*)$ crosses the cumulative arrivals curve once, total travel time is the same as in the basic model. Otherwise, travel time is less and depends on the dispersion of t^* in the population. This points to an important consideration which, with the exception of Henderson (1981), has largely been ignored in the literature on urban traffic congestion. There is typically a tradeoff between the dispersion of work start times and travel time costs. In deciding on his employees' work start times, the individual employer presumably takes into account the private cost of their travel but not the externality cost. Thus when congestion is underpriced, there may be a role for government in encouraging greater dispersion of work start times.

Next suppose individuals differ in terms of α, β and γ, but have the same γ/β and t^*. This means that commuters differ in their absolute shadow costs of travel time and schedule delay, but not in the ratio of their shadow cost of time early to time late. In the no-toll equilibrium commuters order themselves according to their relative cost of travel time to schedule delay, α/β. Those with the lowest α/β (the highest *relative* cost of schedule delay) travel at the peak. In contrast, with the optimal time-varying toll, which eliminates queueing, commuters order themselves according to the *absolute* cost of schedule delay, those with the highest cost traveling at the peak.

Roughly speaking, imposing tolls entails paying with money rather than with travel time. Thus, tolls tend to benefit disproportionately those with a high shadow cost of travel time, who are typically the rich. This may be one of the principal reasons why tolls are so unpopular politically. To counteract this adverse equity effect, several authors have recommended a package approach whereby toll revenue would be allocated to various uses (road construction and maintenance, park and ride facilities, improved transit, general revenues and so on) in such proportions that all major groups end up better off.[15]

Heterogeneity also has implications for optimal capacity. If one defines optimal capacity to be that capacity which minimizes total cost, then cost–benefit practitioners should employ shadow costs of time which are a weighted average of the shadow costs of time in the population, where the weights depend on departure order. One may instead define optimal capacity to be individual-specific: that capacity which maximizes a particular individual's utility. Unless the method of financing is highly progressive, optimal capacity for the poor tends to be lower than for the rich, since expanding capacity is another way of paying with money for reduced travel time and schedule delay, which the rich typically value more.

4.4.3   Networks[16]

The basic bottleneck model assumes that all commuters have the same origin and destination and travel along the same road. In reality the trip pattern in urban areas is highly dispersed, even for commuting trips, and travel occurs on a road network. Network considerations affect the analysis in a variety of ways. Most obviously, with a network each commuter faces not only a departure time choice but also a route choice. The modified equilibrium condition is that each commuter chooses a combination of departure time and route that minimizes her trip price.

For most of this section we assume that commuters are identical. At the end we comment briefly on phenomena that arise with commuter heterogeneity. We consider three tolling regimes: no tolls, optimal tolls on all roads in the network, and tolls on a subset of roads.

a)   No tolls
Analytical research on dynamic network equilibrium has been quite limited. The simple case of one O/D pair connected by two routes in parallel was studied by Mahmassani and Herman (1984) using Greenshields' flow congestion model in which travel speed falls linearly with density. The same network configuration was later studied by ADL (1990b) using the bottleneck model.

Regardless of the 'performance model' (the technology of congestion, for example flow or bottleneck congestion) or the number of routes, equilibrium can be characterized in two steps. The first step involves solving for the equilibrium time pattern of departures on each route taking the number of drivers on the route as given. The second step involves calculating the route split by applying Wardrop's principle that travel cost be equal on all routes that are used, and equal or higher on routes that are not used. This implies that all drivers departing at the same time must experience the same travel time, whatever route they choose. If routes differ in free-flow travel costs, the first drivers to depart take the shortest route. Longer routes start to be used only when travel times on shorter routes have been driven up sufficiently by congestion.

In the case of bottleneck congestion and two routes in parallel that both get used, ADL (1990b) show that equilibrium travel cost is

$$C = \alpha \frac{s_1 \overline{T}_1 + s_2 \overline{T}_2}{s_1 + s_2} + \delta \left(\frac{N}{s_1 + s_2} \right),$$

where $\overline{T}_i$ is the fixed travel cost on route i, $i = 1,2$. Comparing this with (4.7) it is apparent that in terms of costs the network is equivalent to a single route with capacity $s_1 + s_2$ and a fixed travel cost equal to the capacity-weighted average fixed cost on the two routes. This formula generalizes straightforwardly to any number of routes in parallel.

Networks with links in series present a rather different picture than networks with links/routes in parallel. First consider a single O/D pair connected by a series of links each subject to bottleneck congestion. For this configuration, equilibrium is the same as that for a single bottleneck with a capacity equal to that of the smallest bottleneck in the series.[17]

For series networks with more than one origin, equilibrium behaviour is more complex. Kuwahara (1990) studied the network shown in Figure 4.3(a) with two origins, O_1 and O_2, and a single destination, D. Group 1 departs from O_1 and group 2 from O_2. Kuwahara established how the equilibrium departure rates and travel costs of the two groups depend on the capacities of upstream and downstream bottlenecks (s_1 and s_d respectively) as well as the relative size of the groups.

ADL (1993b) built on Kuwahara's analysis by adding a third link to his network, as shown in Figure 4.3(b), and focusing on the welfare effects of capacity expansion. ADL showed that expanding capacity of an upstream bottleneck can, paradoxically, increase total travel costs.[18] In the case of an

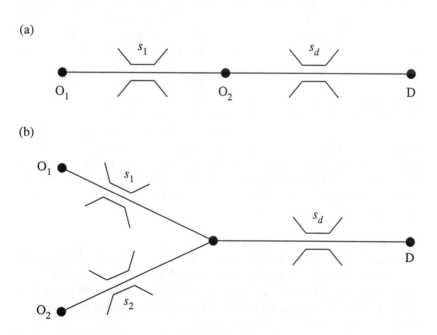

Figure 4.3   Networks with bottlenecks in series

expansion of s_1, this happens when the reduction in queueing time costs for group 1 at s_1 is more than offset by the increase in queueing time downstream, plus the increase in combined schedule delay costs of the two groups, that come about through induced changes in departure rates. In this situation a *reduction* in capacity would be welfare-improving. In lieu of tearing up traffic lanes, this might be accomplished by metering access to the bottleneck in a manner analogous to the practice of metering freeway on-ramps.

This dynamic network equilibrium paradox is reminiscent of the celebrated Braess (1968) paradox for static user equilibrium whereby adding a link to a network results in an increase in total travel costs. In response to the link addition, some drivers alter routes to lower their private costs, but since congestion is unpriced this may entail their switching from routes with lower social costs to routes with higher social costs. The dynamic network equilibrium paradox results not from route choice adjustments, but from *departure time* adjustments. (Note that drivers have no choice of route in Figure 4.3(b).)

Despite its simplicity, the network in Figure 4.3(b) is tedious to treat analytically. Analytical methods become all but unworkable for much larger networks. For this reason, solutions to the dynamic network user equilibrium problem are being sought using algorithmic methods.[19] Because of the large numbers of drivers and road links in large cities, it is inevitable that network models will entail some degree of simplification and aggregation. An important issue that has been largely neglected in the literature is how accurately simulations based on aggregated representations of road networks will describe the effects of network changes. Once such models become operational it will also be interesting to see how closely the simple bottleneck model comes to reproducing the aggregate qualitative and quantitative properties of a metropolitan road network. A few tentative findings are reported in Section 4.5.

A final consideration to keep in mind is that, with inefficient pricing, the cost–benefit analysis of a local change to a network, such as a link expansion, must take into account how the change affects equilibrium flows over the entire network. This is analogous to having to consider the indirect benefits induced by latent demand. Here, however, the indirect benefits come about through changes in route choice.

b)   Optimal tolls on an entire network

While there has been little analytical research on dynamic network equilibrium with no tolls, even less has been devoted to dynamic network equilibrium under various toll regimes. We focus here on the case where optimal time-varying tolls are applied on the whole road network, thereby supporting the system optimum.

Some results for the system optimum with one O/D pair and two routes in parallel were derived by ADL (1990b). As with the basic model, the departure rate on each route is maintained at the capacity of the respective bottle-neck to prevent queueing. This departure rate can be supported as an equilibrium by applying a time-varying toll on each route analogous to the toll for the single bottleneck model. If the two routes differ in fixed travel costs, then a shift in traffic from the shorter to the longer route is also required because in the no-toll equilibrium the shorter route has a longer queue and thus experiences greater congestion. The shift in traffic can be realized by adding to the time-varying toll on the shorter route a positive time-invariant component. Unless the routes differ appreciably in fixed travel costs, the efficiency gains derived from inducing the optimal route split are a small fraction of the gains achieved by eliminating queueing. This suggests that the substantial efficiency gains from time-varying tolls that obtain with the single bottleneck model carry over to networks.

For the networks in Figure 4.3 too it can be shown that the system optima entail no queueing and can be supported by time-varying tolls. One might be tempted to conclude from this that queueing can never be socially optimal on a network characterized by bottleneck congestion. Yet de Palma and Jehiel (1994) have shown that *queuing can be socially optimal*. One of their examples is depicted in Figure 4.4. A single O/D pair is connected by two routes, A and B. Route A has a larger capacity than route B ($s_A > s_B$) and is also shorter $\overline{T}_A < \overline{T}_B$. A link with capacity $s = s_A$ exists upstream of the two routes, but there is no capacity constraint downstream. All travelers are identical. Instead of (4.3), their schedule delay costs are zero if they arrive at D within the time window $[t^* - \Delta, t^* + \Delta]$, and arbitrarily large if they arrive outside the window. (Travel time costs are strictly positive but otherwise immaterial.) To keep the example simple we will assume here that

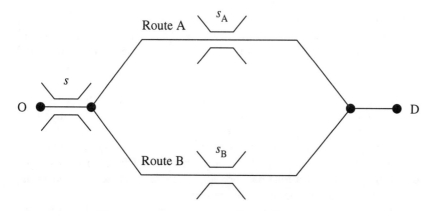

Figure 4.4   Network on which queueing can be optimal

$$(\overline{T}_B - \overline{T}_A)s < 2\Delta s_B. \tag{4.15}$$

It might appear that the most travelers who can be accommodated within the arrival window is $2\Delta s$, which can be achieved by feeding them at rate s onto route A for a period 2Δ. But because route B is longer than route A, a driver can be fed onto route B at time $\overline{T}_B - \overline{T}_A$ earlier than a driver on route A, and both will arrive at the same time. Suppose that $(\overline{T}_B - \overline{T}_A)s_B$ travelers depart on route B before departures on route A begin. The first of the route B drivers arrives at time $t^* - \Delta$ and the last driver at time $t^* - \Delta + \overline{T}_B - \overline{T}_A$. Given condition (4.15), $\overline{T}_B - \overline{T}_A < 2\Delta s_B / s < 2\Delta$; hence the last driver on route B arrives prior to $t^* + \Delta$ and everyone arrives on time.

The maximum number of drivers that can be accommodated without queueing is thus $(\overline{T}_B - \overline{T}_A)s_B + 2\Delta s$. Yet even more can be accommodated by feeding them onto route B at rate s for the period $\overline{T}_B - \overline{T}_A$. While they depart, a queue develops on route B at a rate $s - s_B$. But given (4.15) all drivers taking route B still arrive within the time window. In sum: if the number of drivers falls in the range $((\overline{T}_B - \overline{T}_A)s_B + 2\Delta s, (\overline{T}_B - \overline{T}_A + 2\Delta)s)$, then all drivers can be accommodated within the time window, but only by allowing queueing. Given the assumption that arrival outside the window is much more costly than queueing time, queueing is socially optimal. The assumption of prohibitively costly schedule delay costs outside the arrival time window can obviously be relaxed somewhat and queuing will still occur in the social optimum.

De Palma and Jehiel (1994) provide another example, featuring the cost function (4.3) and two groups of drivers with different values of α, β and t^*, in which queueing is again optimal. These two examples suggest that queueing may be a common feature of the social optimum on networks with bottleneck congestion.

A final word is in order regarding cost–benefit analysis. In contrast to the no-toll equilibrium, the indirect effects of a small policy change on the system optimum can be ignored. Hence the cost–benefit analysis of a small, localized, policy change can ignore how it affects traffic flows on the rest of the network.

c) Tolling on part of the network

Full congestion pricing on an entire road network has never been achieved and is not a realistic prospect in the near future. Impediments to comprehensive pricing include the infrastructure and administration costs, equity concerns and (at least in the US) respect for the constitutional right to freedom of movement that dictates that some routes remain toll-free. Given unpriced congestion on part of a road network, setting optimal tolls on the remaining roads is an exercise in the theory of the second best.

Tolling on part of a road network has been analysed with the bottleneck model by Braid (1995). Braid considers a single O/D pair connected by two parallel routes of equal length.[20] Route 2 can be tolled, but route 1 cannot. Braid shows that the second-best optimal toll on route 2 has two components: a positive time-varying component that prevents queueing on route 2, and a negative uniform component that attracts traffic away from route 1 so as to alleviate congestion on it. The overall toll is negative at the beginning and end of the travel period on route 2, and positive in the middle.

Braid further shows that if routes 1 and 2 have the same capacity, and schedule delay costs are given by (4.3), then twice as much traffic uses route 2 as route 1, and efficiency gains amount to two-thirds those derived from first-best pricing of both routes. By contrast, if the third-best toll is imposed on route 2 (a time-varying toll to eliminate queueing, but with no uniform component), then the two routes carry the same amount of traffic, and only half the efficiency gains from first-best pricing are obtained. This demonstrates clearly the importance of second-best considerations in toll design.

The analysis of second-best road pricing has been extended to allow for elastic trip demand by Verhoef *et al.* (1996). While they use a static model, their results are worth mentioning because they are insightful and carry over without fundamental change to the bottleneck model. With elastic demand, setting a toll on route 2 involves a compromise between reducing total travel, which requires a relatively high toll, and achieving an appropriate division of traffic which (depending on the relative congestibility of the two routes) may dictate a toll that is negative. As expected, the relative efficiency of second-best pricing to first-best pricing declines as the elasticity of demand rises and conflict between the two goals rises. Contrarily, second-best pricing is more efficient the less congestible and shorter is route 2 relative to route 1, because route 2 then carries a larger share of total traffic, leaving less unpriced congestion on route 1. This suggests that priority should be given to tolling short, high-capacity, roads.[21]

Tabuchi (1993) has studied another variant of the second-best pricing problem in which a road subject to bottleneck congestion runs in parallel with a railway. Operating costs of the rail include a fixed cost and a constant marginal cost per rider. The railway is thus congestion-free, but uneconomic to run at low levels of demand. On the assumption of inelastic demand, and average-cost pricing of rail trips, Tabuchi shows that the road share of travel is highest with an optimal fine (that is time-varying) road toll and successively smaller with a step toll, a uniform toll, and no toll. This accords with Braid's analysis of two bottlenecks in parallel. But having an uncongested railway as the alternative mode, rather than a congestible highway, alters the relative efficiency gains of the various road tolls. At sufficiently high levels of demand, a uniform toll yields more than half the efficiency gains from the fine toll. These gains accrue from diverting people from the congested road to the uncongested rail. (By comparison, with inelastic demand and either a single road in isolation or two roads, a uniform toll is worthless.) Additionally, an optimal one-step toll yields more than two-thirds the efficiency gains of the fine toll (compared to precisely two-thirds in Braid's setting).

We conclude this subsection with two observations. First, tolls are likely to be implemented initially, and perhaps exclusively, on major roads. This creates the danger that drivers will try to avoid payment by diverting to minor roads, or 'rat-running'. If tolls are not set according to second-best principles and if minor roads are particularly congestion-prone, tolling can actually *increase* overall travel costs. This is a very real worry that has received inadequate attention in discussions of congestion pricing.

Second, heterogeneity of drivers creates further important network phenomena. Recall that on a single road heterogeneous commuters order their departures in a particular way over the rush hour. This may be referred to as the temporal separation of commuter types. With a network, there is as well the spatial separation of commuter types. The simplest example of this phenomenon occurs where all commuters have the same t^* and the same ratios of α, β and γ, but richer commuters have higher absolute α, β and γ. Consider again Braid's network with a flat toll on route 2. Drivers with high values of time will travel exclusively[22] on route 2; those with lower values on route 1. On large networks, a complicated pattern of temporal and spatial separation of commuter types can emerge.[23]

4.4.4   Stochasticity in Capacity and Demand[24]

The simple bottleneck model assumes that demand and capacity are deterministic. In fact, capacity varies from day to day with the weather, roadwork, accidents, vehicle disablings and so on. Fluctuations also occur in travel demand. It is frequently asserted[25] that more than 50 per cent of time loss due to congestion is 'non-recurrent', stemming from fluctuations in capacity and demand.

Traffic accidents and other disturbances that occur during a given travel period have been incorporated into dynamic network simulations, but have not been treated analytically. This section focuses on analytical work with the bottleneck model that has been done on *day-to-day* fluctuations in capacity and demand. The effects of such stochasticity depend on the extent to which realizations of capacity and demand are anticipated. At one extreme, if they are perfectly anticipated, equilibrium is the same as that which obtains in the deterministic bottleneck model with the particular realization of capacity and demand. At the other extreme, individuals know only the bivariate probability distribution of capacity and demand. More generally, they will obtain from radio and other information sources some, but less than perfect, information about driving conditions. A working assumption is that individuals make travel decisions to minimize expected trip price, with expectations conditioned on the information available to them.

Fluctuations in capacity and demand create fluctuations in travel times and costs. On days when capacity is low or demand is high, travel times will be high, whereas if capacity is high and/or demand is unusually low, there may be no congestion. Except in the extreme case of perfect anticipation, uncertainty about trip price tends to increase over the course of the rush hour, and will have consequences for the equilibrium distribution of trip timing.[26]

Stochasticity also affects optimal design capacity. In the case of perfect information this is easy to analyse. Expected travel cost in pricing regime r is simply the expectation of equation (4.13): $E \cdot [TC^r] = \Gamma^r \delta \cdot E[N^2/s]$, where E is the expectations operator. Let $\hat{s}$ denote design capacity (capacity under ideal conditions) and $\sigma \equiv s/\hat{s} \in (0,1)$ the fraction of capacity available. The marginal benefit of design capacity is $MB(\hat{s}) = -\Gamma^r\delta(\partial/(\partial\hat{s}))E[N^2/\sigma\hat{s}]$. If the probability distribution of σ is independent of $\hat{s}$ (admittedly a strong assumption) then the marginal benefit is proportional to $(1/\hat{s}^2)E[N^2/\sigma]$. Optimal capacity is larger the greater is mean demand, the lower is the mean fraction of capacity available, and (except if N and σ are correlated in an unusual way) the greater is the variability in N and σ. Thus, because capacity availability is both lower on average and more variable in cold weather climates, optimal design capacity for a road in Canada is greater than for a road in California serving the same pattern of demand.

4.4.5 Alternative Treatments of Congestion

The bottleneck congestion technology is attractive because it leads to an analytically tractable model that can be employed to illustrate a wide variety of general insights. The actual technology of urban auto congestion is, however, considerably more complex: there is flow congestion on urban freeways with turbulence at entry points and occasional traffic jams;[27] intersection congestion is predominant in downtown areas, leading in extreme cases to gridlock; and pedestrian and parking congestion are also important.

It remains an open question how urban auto congestion is best treated in simulation models aimed at practical implementation. At least five approaches have been taken: (a) assume that traffic behaves as if there is bottleneck congestion on each link (Ghali and Smith 1997); (b) assume flow congestion on each link (Mahmassani and Herman 1984); (c) assume that capacity on a link depends on queue length (Yang and Huang 1997); (d) assume flow congestion upstream on each link and queueing congestion downstream (Jayakrishnan *et al.* 1994); and (e) assume that travel speed on a link depends on either the entry rate onto that link (Henderson 1974) or the exit rate from it (Chu 1995).

There are at least three major considerations in deciding on the performance model: conceptual soundness, forecasting accuracy, and computational speed. Just as economists often insist that a model has solid microeconomic foundations, so might it be reasonable to require that performance models have a sound foundation in physics. The bottleneck model satisfies this criterion. Unfortunately, however, non-stationary flow congestion models, based on either fluid flow or car following theory, are analytically intractable (Newell 1988) and computationally demanding, even on massively parallel computers. Thus, it may be pragmatic to relax the criterion of sound physical foundations.[28] In Henderson's (1974) formulation, for example, the speed at which a car travels on an entire link depends on the flow rate onto the link at the time the car enters it. This means that a car entering later when the flow rate is relatively low can overtake a car which entered earlier when the flow rate was relatively high. One can impose a 'no overtaking restriction' but this is *ad hoc*. In another formulation, the capacity of a bottleneck depends on the length of the queue behind it (Yang and Huang 1997). This is consistent with the laws of physics; one can imagine the queue as analogous to pressure, and turbulence at the bottleneck as increasing with pressure. But the formulation is physically unrealistic for traffic in that it assumes that a car's behavior depends on what is happening behind the car rather than ahead of it.

The bottleneck model scores well on two of the three criteria: conceptual soundness and computational speed (because of the linearity of the technology). But it has been criticized for giving forecasts that are both quantitatively and qualitatively unrealistic. For example, Chu (1995) argues that, with inelastic demand, application of an optimal toll will lengthen the rush hour, in contrast to the bottleneck model in which the length of the rush hour depends only on the number of travelers and not on the form of pricing.[29] The next section provides a more detailed discussion of a particular dynamic network equilibrium simulation model, METROPOLIS, developed by de Palma *et al.* (1996), that is an intellectual descendant of the Vickrey bottleneck model.

4.5 METROPOLIS

METROPOLIS provides a simulation tool to compute a dynamic equilibrium in a general network. This simulator solves the following problem: Given a directed connected graph, dynamic congestion laws, travel cost functions and an O/D matrix, compute the departure time and route choice equilibrium. The links of the graph correspond to actual streets or to artificial links which connect the centroids (origins and/or destinations) to the actual street network. The bottleneck model is used to describe the congestion technology. The travel cost function is $\tilde{C}(t) = C(t) + \mu\varepsilon$ where ε is a normalized double exponential random variable, μ is a scale parameter which measures the degree of commuter heterogeneity, and $C(t)$ is given by equation (4.3). The O/D matrix specifies the number of commuters making a home-to-work trip between each origin and destination. At equilibrium, no individual can decrease her travel cost by modifying either her departure time or route. This model reduces to Vickrey's model (extended to a network) in the limit as μ tends to zero (see Ben-Akiva *et al.* 1986).

To illustrate an application, the results of the simulator are compared with the no-toll equilibrium of the single bottleneck model, using data for the city of Geneva and its suburbs, which have an area of approximately 200 square miles and 79 300 commuters. The network representation is relatively disaggregated, having 30 000 O/D pairs, 1200 nodes, 300 centroids and 3100 links. Each link is characterized by a fixed travel time and a bottleneck capacity. Values of the schedule delay cost parameters are assumed to be $t^* =$ 8:06 AM, $\alpha = \$6/hr$, $\beta = \$3/hr$ and $\gamma = \$12/hr$; hence $\delta = \$2.4/hr$. (The ratios β/α and γ/α are similar to Small's (1982) estimates.) The dispersion parameter is set at $\mu = 0.5$ and the time step at 1 sec. The origin of time is set at 6:00 AM, and departures are not allowed before this time.

The mean fixed travel time cost per driver is set at $\bar{T} = \$2$.[30] Mean total travel time cost is \$4.094; thus $TTC/N = \$4.094 - \$2 = \$2.094$. Mean schedule delay cost is $SDC/N = \$2.315$, and hence mean total cost is $TC/N = \$2.094 + \$2.315 = \$4.409$. Idiosyncratic utility, $\mu\varepsilon$, has a standard deviation of \$0.64, which is relatively small by comparison.

For the single O/D single bottleneck model, parameters and variables are denoted by hats. To make the bottleneck model comparable with the simulation model, $\hat{N}/\hat{s}$ is chosen to match mean travel equilibrium costs. By equation (4.10a) $\hat{N}/\hat{s} = (T\hat{C}/\hat{N})/\delta$; hence $\hat{N}/\hat{s} = 4.409/2.4 = 1.837$hours $= 110.2$ mins. From (4.6a,b,c), $t_0 = 37.8$ mins, $t_n = 82$ mins, $t_e = 148$ mins and $t_e - t_0 = 110.2$ mins. From (4.11a,b) $T\hat{T}C/\hat{N} = S\hat{D}C/\hat{N} = (\delta/2)(\hat{N}/\hat{s}) = \$2.205$, which is close to the simulated equilibrium values of $TTC/N = \$2.094$ and $SDC/N = \$2.315$. According to the simulated cumulative departures schedule in Figure 4.5, shown by the solid line, the number of commuters who depart between t_0 and t_e, which we take to be $\hat{N}$, is 74 600. Given $\hat{N}/\hat{s} = 110.2$ mins this implies $\hat{s} = 677$ vehicles/min.[31] Finally, from (4.9) $r_E = 1354$ vehicles/min and $r_L = 226$ vehicles/min.

The equilibrium cumulative departures schedule for the single bottleneck model is indicated in Figure 4.5 by the heavy dashed line. The departure rate in the simulated equilibrium reaches a similar maximum value and for a comparable duration of time. But there is no appreciable decrease in the departure rate until near the end of the rush hour, whereas in the bottleneck equilibrium the departure rate drops abruptly below capacity when individuals start to arrive late.

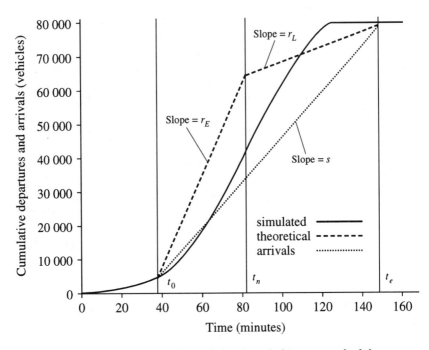

Figure 4.5   The simulated and simple bottleneck departure schedules

To investigate possible reasons for this contrast, METROPOLIS was rerun using successively smaller values of μ. This made no appreciable qualitative difference to the equilibrium departure schedule. We suspect that the geographical dispersion in origins and destinations on the Geneva network is primarily responsible. Individuals making longer trips need to depart earlier to arrive at the (assumed) common preferred arrival time t^*. Differences in trip duration therefore cause the equilibrium departure distribution to be more uniform than for the single O/D single bottleneck model. Further research will be required to determine more precisely how and why dynamic network equilibria differ from the single bottleneck model, and how the latter can be modified or extended to reproduce more closely actual network behaviour.

4.6   DIRECTIONS FOR FUTURE RESEARCH

In this section we discuss quantitatively important aspects of the urban traffic congestion problem that to date have received inadequate attention in bottleneck models.

4.6.1 Parking

Parking is important for a number of reasons: (1) on-street parking affects road capacity; (2) the cost of parking (except with free employer-provided parking) is a large, and often the largest, component of the monetary cost of a car trip; (3) pricing of parking is an important element of urban transport policy and is a critical component of second-best urban transport policy when congestion pricing is not employed; (4) cruising for parking is a major contributor to downtown traffic congestion.

Some theoretical work has been done on parking (Douglas 1975; ADL 1991b; Glazer and Niskanen 1992; Arnott and Rowse 1995) that focuses on the externalities generated by parking decisions. Parking simulation models have also been developed to examine the effects of information provision and other policies on spatial and temporal parking patterns (for example, Young *et al.* 1991; Asakura and Kashiwadani 1995). But research remains to be done to improve understanding of the complex interaction between parking and traffic congestion.

4.6.2 Mass Transit

Compared to the analysis of automobile travel, relatively little work has been done with the bottleneck model on travel by public transit. Departure time and route choice decisions on transit systems have been studied by Sumi *et al.* (1990) and Alfa and Chen (1995) using a schedule delay cost formulation similar to that in the bottleneck model. These studies highlight two features of public transit that distinguish it from auto travel: there is a time table so that departure time choice sets are discrete rather than continuous, and service priority may be random rather than first-come-first-served.

Mode choice has only recently been incorporated into the bottleneck framework. In Tabuchi's (1993) model, mentioned earlier, transit is assumed to be congestion-free. By contrast, Huang and Yang (1995) assume that the arrival rate of passengers at transit stations can exceed capacity, resulting in queues of waiting passengers. Individuals choose between driving and taking transit according to a logit model. Using optimal control methods, Huang and Yang solve for the system-optimal departure rate of travellers on each mode, and for the optimal time-varying toll on each mode that decentralizes the solution.

Much work remains to be done in analysing the joint mode, route and departure time decisions of travellers. Desirable extensions include multiple auto and transit routes, interdependence of automobile and transit congestion, and determination of optimal road and transit capacity, taking into account any economies (or diseconomies) of scale in transit network size, and any economies of transit traffic density.

4.6.3   Intersections

As noted earlier, probably the most important form of congestion in downtown areas is intersection congestion. While intersection congestion has been built into 'microsimulation models' which track individual cars but do not solve for equilibrium (for example, NETSIM), it has yet to be treated in the bottleneck model.

4.6.4   Demand

The treatment of demand in the basic bottleneck model is very simple. The number of trips is a function of trip price, which includes travel time costs, schedule delay costs and toll costs, where the cost of travel time and the cost of time early or late are taken as exogenous. Several authors (for example, Vickrey 1969, 1973; Henderson 1974, 1981) have developed somewhat more sophisticated demand submodels in which individuals choose their allocation of time to maximize utility. But these still fall a long way short of the conceptualization described in the introduction, which is to solve for each individual's trip demand over time and space, derived from the solution to the individual's activity choice and scheduling problem. A satisfactory treatment of demand is actually even more complicated than the above conceptualization suggests, since social activities require schedule coordination.

4.6.5   Work Start Time

It was noted earlier that work start times should be endogenized. The individual employer has to decide on his work start time policy. He will consider how much flexibility to give his employees. In making this decision, he trades off the reduction in wages he can pay his employees as a result of the benefit they derive from more flexible scheduling against the increased problems of schedule coordination within the firm when employees have different work hours. He must also decide on the average work start time. Here the trade off is between the benefits of improved coordination with other firms against the higher wages he has to pay his employees for commuting under congested conditions. Henderson (1981) provides a model along these lines.

4.6.6   Non-commuting Trips

The proportion of urban auto trips whose purpose is not commuting has been increasing steadily over the past few decades, and now over half the trips made even during rush hour are for non-commuting purposes. The simplest way to deal with non-commuting trips is to take them as given (Fargier

1983). But since non-commuters probably have at least as much time-flexibility as commuters, and since the main innovation of the bottleneck model is to endogenize trip timing, this is not very satisfactory. The alternative is to treat explicitly the individual's overall scheduling problem, which would entail solving simultaneously for the timing of commuting and non-commuting trips, but to do this in a way that is both tractable and operational will require a conceptual breakthrough.

4.6.7 Location

The current generation of dynamic network equilibrium models is designed for short-term forecasting and policy simulation. Before these models are applied to longer-term forecasting, as would be needed in the cost–benefit analysis of a transport improvement, it will be necessary to forecast how the locational pattern of trip demand will change. The trends toward subcentering and increased decentralization will probably continue. A further consideration is feedback effects – any major change in transport policy or technology will affect urban spatial structure and the spatial structure of travel demand.

4.7 CONCLUSIONS

The Vickrey bottleneck model is now over 25 years old. At first glance the model appears almost trivially simple. But its innovation, to model the evolution of traffic flow over the rush hour as an equilibrium phenomenon, incorporating commuters' trip-timing decisions, has given rise to a new generation of dynamic urban traffic congestion models that are a quantum level more sophisticated and satisfactory than the previous generation of static rush-hour traffic flow models.

This essay has described the state of the art with respect to the bottleneck model. Economists have contributed primarily to analytical development of the model and to exploration of its economic implications. Transportation engineers/ scientists have focused on its practical implementation via the development of dynamic network equilibrium simulation models and algorithms to solve them. This chapter has focused on the economic contributions.

The new models have already proved their worth in the exploration of vehicle information systems (for example, Jayakrishnan *et al.* 1994). We predict that the next decade will see application of variants of the model to a wide range of policy issues (including congestion pricing) in urban transportation, as well as further model refinement and algorithmic development.

NOTES

†   We would like to thank seminar participants at the Faculty of Commerce, U.B.C., and at the 1995 North American Regional Science Association meetings for insightful comments, and Fabrice Marchal for technical assistance.

1.   This section draws heavily on Arnott, de Palma and Lindsey (ADL hereafter) (1990a), and to a lesser extent on ADL (1993a)

2.   This assumes that the toll is applied when a commuter joins the queue rather than when she traverses the bottleneck. This assumption simplifies the algebra and in no way affects the results.

3.   The derivation of the no-toll equilibrium in this section skirts some technical issues related to existence and uniqueness of equilibrium. Smith (1984) proved existence of equilibrium for a model with bottleneck congestion and a continuum of individuals on the assumption that $\alpha > -p'(x)$, where $p(x)$ is the schedule delay cost function. (For the piecewise linear schedule delay cost function (4.3), the condition $\alpha > -p'(x)$ reduces to $\alpha > \beta$ for early arrivals, and $\alpha > -\gamma$ for late arrivals. The late arrival condition is guaranteed.) Daganzo (1985) proved uniqueness of equilibrium under the additional assumption that $p(x)$ is strictly convex.

     Bernstein (1994) has shown that when the discreteness of individuals is taken into account, a standard Nash equilibrium does not exist. We suspect that this is a 'technical problem' in the sense that, with the introduction of noise that reflects uncertainty about other individuals' departure times, equilibrium would exist.

4.   If, contrary to assumption, $\alpha < \beta$, all early arrivals wish to depart at the same time. A unique equilibrium exists that entails a mass of individuals departing at the same time (ADL 1985).

5.   This section draws primarily on ADL (1990a).

6.   The magnitude of the toll outside $[t_0, t_e]$ must be set so that trip price exceeds the equilibrium trip price; otherwise it is arbitrary.

7.   Unless indicated otherwise we shall assume that, conditional on their form, tolls are set optimally. All optimal tolls so defined entail marginal cost pricing.

8.   There are conceptual difficulties in modelling the afternoon rush hour. Suppose, for example, that one were to assume that everyone left work eight hours after arriving. Then the departure rate from work would be s and there would be no queuing in the afternoon rush hour. The best-known formulation, which ignores the dependence between a driver's departure time from work and her arrival time, is Fargier (1983).

9.   Given (4.13) the marginal benefit of capacity is $-\partial TC'/\partial s = \Gamma^r \delta (N^2/s^2) = TC'/s$.

10.   Small *et al.* (1989) and Kraus (1981) provide very careful analyses of the degree of returns to scale in highway travel, and both find approximately constant costs. To the best of our knowledge no one has investigated this issue for urban streets.

11.   This subsection draws on ADL (1993a).

12.   We draw here on ADL (1988, 1996b).

13.   The crucial property is that $W(t^*)$ cross the cumulative arrivals curve once. As illustrated in Figure 4.2, $W(t^*)$ can be flatter than s over part of the range $[t_0^*, t_e^*]$ and can also have discontinuities.

14.   The social optimum is qualitatively the same as with identical individuals: the departure rate is held at s throughout the departure period, which is the same as for the no-toll equilibrium. The optimum can be decentralized with a time-varying toll that charges each driver the cost of queuing time that she would incur in the no-toll equilibrium if she were to arrive at the same time.

15.   See for example Goodwin (1989), Bayliss (1992), Jones (1992) and Small (1993).

16.   This section draws on ADL (1990b, 1993b).

17.   To see this suppose equilibrium has been established with a single bottleneck of capacity s_1 and add a second bottleneck with capacity $s_2 > s_1$. If bottleneck 2 is located downstream of bottleneck 1, it makes no difference because the upstream bottleneck cannot feed it to capacity. If bottleneck 2 is placed upstream of bottleneck 1, and the equilibrium departure

rate with only bottleneck 1 is always less than s_2, then clearly bottleneck 2 again has no effect. If the equilibrium departure rate exceeds s_2 then a queue will develop at bottleneck 2. But this too is inconsequential because all that matters to drivers is their total travel time, not how long they spend queueing at a particular bottleneck. Bottleneck 2 merely acts as a reservoir for drivers waiting to traverse bottleneck 1. With $s_2 > s_1$, bottleneck 2 can maintain bottleneck 1 at capacity throughout the departure period and so the arrival rate of drivers at the destination is the same as before introduction of the second bottleneck.

18. This paradox (and in fact all the other traffic paradoxes) stems from negative indirect benefits from capacity expansion in the absence of tolling. See Arnott and Small (1994).

19. In the full-blown dynamic network user equilibrium problem, equilibrium departure rates and route splits must be solved for each O/D pair in the network throughout the travel period. Because of the computational burden for networks of even moderate scale, some attention has been focused on the sub-problem of solving for equilibrium route choices while treating the departure rates as given. Currently a number of research teams are developing algorithms to solve the full problem and sub-problems; for a review see Ran and Boyce (1994).

20. Bernstein and El Sanhouri (1994) consider a variant of this in which the two routes can have unequal lengths.

21. Liu and McDonald (1996) adopt a similar modeling framework to Verhoef et al. (1996), except with two travel periods (peak and off-peak). Liu and McDonald find that the welfare gain from second-best pricing as a percentage of the gain from first-best pricing is an increasing and strictly convex function of capacity of the tolled route as a fraction of total capacity.

22. Provided the relative numbers in the two groups fall in a certain range.

23. The interaction between temporal and spatial separation is treated in ADL (1992).

24. This section draws on ADL (1991a, 1995, 1996a).

25. See for example Lindley (1987). This proposition has recently been challenged by Hall (1993).

26. A characterization of the no-toll equilibrium under uncertainty using the bottleneck model is given in ADL (1995). There it is shown that the provision of better, but less than perfect, information about travel conditions can lead through induced changes in departure times to higher expected travel costs. This is another example of how a policy that would be socially beneficial under marginal-cost pricing can be counterproductive in a world of second best.

27. One difficult issue is how to deal with traffic-jam type situations (referred to in the economics literature as hypercongestion) in which flow is positively related to velocity. The flow congestion models treat traffic jams by assuming that velocity, v, is negatively related to density, k, which is consistent with velocity being positively related to flow, f, at high densities ($f = kv$ and $k = k(v)$, implying $f'(v) = k'v + k$). Hypercongestion can be incorporated into the bottleneck model by assuming that bottleneck capacity is negatively related to queue length. The current view, based especially on field studies by Hall and various coauthors (see Hall et al. 1992), is that both these treatments are oversimplified, and that hypercongestion is a transient phenomenon triggered by some stochastic irregularity in flow, which generates a shock wave that travels backwards through the traffic.

28. The relationship between the hydrodynamic approach to traffic flow, as developed in theoretical physics, and engineering traffic flow theory is described in Nagel (1994).

29. Unless, of course, the toll is so high over some portion of the rush hour that the bottleneck is not fully utilized.

30. Fixed travel times and capacities were estimated by B. Dériaz, a consulting company in Geneva (for details see de Palma et al. 1996).

31. Because the cumulative desired arrivals curve has a long flat left-hand tail, some commuters (about 6 per cent of the total) do not experience congestion.

REFERENCES

Alfa, A.S. and M. Chen (1995), 'Temporal distribution of public transport demand during the peak period', *European Journal of Operational Research*, **83**, 137–53.

Arnott, R., A. de Palma and R. Lindsey (1985), 'Economics of a bottleneck', Queen's University, Institute for Economic Research, discussion paper #636.

Arnott, R., A. de Palma and R. Lindsey (1988), 'Schedule delay and departure time decisions with heterogeneous commuters', *Transportation Research Record*, **1197**, 56–67.

Arnott, R., A. de Palma and R. Lindsey (1990a), 'Economics of a bottleneck', *Journal of Urban Economics*, **27**, 111–30.

Arnott, R., A. de Palma and R. Lindsey (1990b), 'Departure time and route choice for routes in parallel', *Transportation Research B*, **24B** (3), 209–28.

Arnott, R., A. de Palma and R. Lindsey (1991a), 'Does providing information to drivers reduce traffic congestion?', *Transportation Research A*, **25A** (5), 309–18.

Arnott, R., A. de Palma and R. Lindsey (1991b), 'A temporal and spatial equilibrium analysis of commuter parking', *Journal of Public Economics*, **45** (3), 301–35.

Arnott, R., A. de Palma and R. Lindsey (1992), 'Route choice with heterogeneous drivers and group-specific congestion costs', *Regional Science and Urban Economics*, **22**, 71–102.

Arnott, R., A. de Palma and R. Lindsey (1993a), 'A structural model of peak-period congestion: A traffic bottleneck with elastic demand', *American Economic Review*, **83** (1), 161–79.

Arnott, R., A. de Palma and R. Lindsey (1993b), 'A dynamic traffic equilibrium paradox', *Transportation Science*, **27** (2), 148–60.

Arnott, R., A. de Palma and R. Lindsey (1994), 'The welfare effects of congestion tolls with heterogeneous commuters', *Journal of Transport Economics and Policy*, **28** (2), 139–61.

Arnott, R., A. de Palma and R. Lindsey (1995), 'Information and time-of-usage decisions in the bottleneck model with stochastic capacity and demand', manuscript.

Arnott, R., A. de Palma and R. Lindsey (1996a), 'Information and usage of free-access congestible facilities', *International Economic Review*, **37** (1), 181–203.

Arnott, R., A. de Palma and R. Lindsey (1996b), *Congestion: A Dynamic Approach*, Cambridge, MA: MIT Press, in progress.

Arnott, R. and J. Rowse (1995), 'Modelling Parking', manuscript.

Arnott, R. and K. Small (1994), 'The economics of traffic congestion', *American Scientist*, **82**, September–October, 446–55.

Asakura, Y. and M. Kashiwadani (1995), 'Parking availability information as a measure of reducing congestion: a simulation approach', paper presented at the Seventh World Conference on Transportation Research, Sydney.

Bayliss, D. (1992), 'British views on road pricing', paper presented at the Sixth World Conference on Transportation Research, France.

Ben-Akiva, M., A. de Palma, and P. Kanaroglou (1986), 'Dynamic model of peak period traffic congestion with elastic arrival rates', *Transportation Science*, **20** (2), 164–81.

Bernstein, D. (1994), 'Non-existence of Nash equilibria for the deterministic departure time choice problem', manuscript.

Bernstein, D. and I. El Sanhouri (1994), 'Congestion pricing with an untolled alternative', Massachusetts Institute of Technology, manuscript.

Braess, D. (1968), 'Uber ein paradoxen der verkehrsplaning', Unternehmensforschung, **12**, 258–68.

Braid, R.M. (1995), 'Peak-load pricing of a transportation route with an unpriced substitute', manuscript.

Chu, X. (1995), 'Endogenous trip scheduling: The Henderson approach reformulated and compared with the Vickrey approach', *Journal of Urban Economics*, **37**, 324–43.

Cohen, Y. (1987), 'Commuter welfare under peak-period congestion tolls: Who gains and who loses?', *The International Journal of Transport Economics*, **14**, 239–66.

Daganzo, C.F. (1985), 'The uniqueness of a time-dependent equilibrium distribution of arrivals at a single bottleneck', *Transportation Science*, **19** (1), 29–37.

de Palma, A. and P. Jehiel (1994), 'Queuing may be efficient in bottleneck models', Department of Economics, Technical report, 1994.9.

de Palma, A., F. Marchal and Y. Nesterov (1996), 'METROPOLIS: A modular system for dynamic traffic simulation', manuscript.

Douglas, R.W. (1975), 'A parking model – the effect of supply on demand', *American Economist*, **19** (1), 85–6.

Fargier, P.H. (1983), 'Effects of the choice of departure time on road traffic congestion: theoretical approach', Proceedings of the 8th International Symposium on Transportation and Traffic Theory, Toronto, Canada, 223–63.

Ghali, M. and M. Smith (1995), 'A model for the dynamic system optimum traffic assignment problem', *Transportation Research B*, **29B** (3), 155–70.

Glazer, A. and E. Niskanen (1992), 'Parking fees and congestion', *Regional Science and Urban Economics*, **22**, 123–32.

Goodwin, P.B. (1989), 'The "rule of three": A possible solution to the political problem of competing objectives for road pricing', *Traffic Engineering and Control*, **30** (10), 495–7.

Hall, F.L., V.F. Hurdle and J.H. Banks (1992), 'A synthesis of recent work on the nature of speed-flow and flow-occupancy (or density) relationships on freeways', paper presented at the 71st annual meeting of the Transportation Research Board.

Hall, W.R. (1993), 'Non-recurrent congestion: How big is the problem? Are traveler information systems the solution?', *Transportation Research C*, **1C** (1), 89–103.

Henderson, J.V. (1974), 'Road congestion: A reconsideration of pricing theory', *Journal of Urban Economics*, **1**, 346–55.

Henderson, J.V. (1981), 'The economics of staggered work hours', *Journal of Urban Economics*, **9**, 349–64.

Hendrickson, C. and G. Kocur (1981), 'Schedule delay and departure time decisions in a deterministic model', *Transportation Science*, **15** (1), 62–77.

Huang, H.-J. and H. Yang (1995), 'A variable trans-modal transport pricing model', manuscript.

Jayakrishnan, R., H. Mahmassani and T.-Y. Hu (1994), 'An evaluation tool for advanced traffic information and management systems in urban networks', *Transportation Research C*, **2C** (3), 129–47.

Jones, P.M. (1992), 'Gaining public support for road pricing through a package approach', paper presented at the Sixth World Conference on Transportation Research, Lyon, France.

Kraus, M. (1981), 'Scale economies analysis for urban highway networks', *Journal of Urban Economics*, **9**, 1–22.

Kuwahara, M. (1990), 'Equilibrium queueing patterns at a two-tandem bottleneck during the morning peak', *Transportation Science*, **24** (3), 217–29.

Laih, C.-H. (1994), 'Queuing at a bottleneck with single- and multi-step tolls', *Transportation Research A*, **28A** (3), 197–208.

Lindley, J.A. (1987), 'Urban freeway congestion: quantification of the problem and effectiveness of potential solutions', *ITE Journal*, **57** (1), 27–32.

Liu, L.N. and J.F. McDonald (1996), 'Economic efficiency of second-best congestion pricing schemes in urban highway systems', University of Illinois at Chicago, manuscript.

Mahmassani, H. and R. Herman (1984), 'Dynamic user equilibrium departure time and route choice on idealized traffic arterials', *Transportation Science*, **18**, 362–84.

Mohring, H. and M. Harwitz (1962), *Highway Benefits*, Evanston, IL: Northwestern University Press.

Nagel, K. (1994), 'High-speed micro-simulation of traffic flow', PhD Thesis, Department of Mathematics, University of Köln, Germany.

Newell, G.F. (1987), 'The morning commute for nonidentical travelers', *Transportation Science*, **21** (2), 74–88.

Newell, G.F. (1988), 'Traffic flow for the morning commute', *Transportation Science*, **22** (1), 47–58.

Ran, B. and D. Boyce (1994), *Dynamic Urban Transportation Network Models, Theory and Implications for Intelligent Vehicle-Highway Systems*, Berlin: Springer Verlag.

Small, K.A. (1982), 'The scheduling of consumer activities: work trips', *American Economic Review*, **72**, 467–79.

Small, K.A. (1993), 'Urban traffic congestion: A new approach to the Gordian knot', *The Brookings Review*, **11** (2), 6–11.

Small, K.A., C. Winston and C.A. Evans (1989), *Road Work*, Washington DC: Brookings.

Smith, M.J. (1984), 'The existence of a time-dependent equilibrium distribution of arrivals at a single bottleneck', *Transportation Science*, **18** (4), 385–94.

Sumi, T., Y. Matsumoto and Y. Miyaki (1990), 'Departure time and route choice of commuters on mass transit systems', *Transportation Research B*, **24B**, 247–62.

Tabuchi, T. (1993), 'Bottleneck congestion and modal split', *Journal of Urban Economics*, **34**, 414–31.

Verhoef, E.T., P. Nijkamp and P. Rietveld (1996), 'Second-best congestion pricing: The case of an untolled alternative', Free University Amsterdam, Tinbergen Institute, Discussion paper TI 94-129; *Journal of Urban Economics*, **40** (3), 279–302.

Vickrey, W.S. (1969), 'Congestion theory and transport investment', *American Economic Review (Papers and Proceedings)*, **59**, 251–60.

Vickrey, W.S. (1973), 'Pricing, metering, and efficiently using urban transportation facilities', *Highway Research Record*, **476**, 36–48.

Yang, H. and H.-J. Huang (1997), 'Analysis of the time-varying pricing of a bottleneck with elastic demand using optimal control theory', *Transportation Research B*, 31B(6), 425–40.

Young, W., M.A.P. Taylor, R.G. Thompson, I. Ker and J. Foster (1991), 'CENCIMM, a software package for the evaluation of parking systems in central city areas', *Traffic Engineering and Control*, **32** (4), 186–93.

PART II

Efficiency Aspects and Second-best Policies

5. Road pricing and the alternatives for controlling road traffic congestion

Kenneth J. Button

5.1 INTRODUCTION

The idea that efficient use of roads requires users to pay for the traffic congestion costs that they impose on urban road networks is long established (Pigou, 1920; Walters, 1961). Such payments, optimally calculated and introduced and enforced at a zero transactions cost, would optimize the use of urban roads and ensure that use would be restricted to those willing to pay for the congestion costs of extra travel time and vehicle operating costs they impose on others.[1]

It is important to note at the outset that here we are only concerned with road pricing in this traditional economic sense as delineated by Pigou – that is, congestion pricing – and not with broader notions which often embrace such things as track cost elements and environmental costs. In practice, these issues are not unrelated (Button, 1991a; Button and Rothengatter, 1997; UK House of Commons Select Committee on Transport, 1994b) but it is helpful for purposes of discussion to define clear lines of demarcation.[2]

While many economists have taken Pigou's (1920) ideas and argued that road pricing offers an efficient and practical means of moving toward optimal traffic conditions in cities there are circumstances when it may not be the ideal approach to adopt.[3] There may be high transaction costs of implementation, enforcement which make it suboptimal in cost–benefit terms or there may be income distribution consequences which, in terms of wider welfare criteria, makes it socially unacceptable. The introduction of road pricing over one part of a network (for example, in only some cities) may distort the allocation of traffic over the entire network, thus reducing overall welfare. At another level, there may be political concern about either the possible exploitation of the system by the administration with it being used to raise sumptuary taxation revenues, or over the ways in which revenues collected from road pricing are spent. Some systems are also seen as posing threats to personal freedoms if they involve collecting information on individuals' travel behavior.

In summary, the difficulty with road pricing is that the world is often rather more complex than even basic partial equilibrium economic models assume, and that in some circumstances road pricing may not be an optimal strategy. The reality of politics also poses problems for those seeking to deploy road pricing although the problems here may lie as much in the way in which the policy is 'sold' as in its political limitations *per se* (Higgins, 1980).

When road pricing is either inappropriate for economic reasons, or simply politically unacceptable, then alternatives must be sought to limit the external costs of traffic congestion. These may take the form of alternative fiscal measures (for example, parking charges, fuel taxation or public transport subsidies) but, equally, direct command and control instruments (for example, traffic management or car bans) are frequently advocated and often used. In either case, they may affect the direct use mode of roads by a particular mode, usually the automobile, but it can also be directed at compliments or substitutes; in fact, any form of measure which attempts to modify the number, mode, time, route or destination of journeys with the aim of reducing traffic congestion.

Pigou was clearly aware of these options when he advocated the use of economic pricing to optimize congestion. Many of the non-road pricing instruments were in use at the time, although the technology and nature of travel behavior meant a somewhat different set of detailed applications. Changes since the 1920s have made some of the non-road pricing alternatives to traffic congestion policy more attractive. Computerization and information systems facilitate more sophisticated traffic management. Equally, however, it is now clear that many of the well-established policies such as infrastructure expansion or public transport subsidies have major caveats associated with them. The nature and range of the portfolio of policy instruments available today, in addition to the greater severity of the congestion problem, differs from that open to Pigou.

In what follows, we initially offer some thoughts as to why, from a microeconomic perspective, there may be problems in implementing a road pricing regime. We then proceed to consider, again in economic terms, the strengths and weaknesses of alternatives. Finally, there is a very brief review of some of the experiences cities have had as a result of adopting such alternatives.

5.2   WHY NOT ROAD PRICING?

As with most economic notions the theory behind road pricing rests upon a number of key assumptions. There have been important theoretical advances in recent years that allow many of these assumptions to be relaxed, but, nevertheless, traffic congestion is a complex phenomenon and modeling is inevitably still crude because of this. The aim here is not to delve into these assumptions too deeply but rather to offer a few comments as to why, in straightforward economic terms, road pricing may not always be the appropriate tool to handle traffic congestion. Of course, there may be other reasons why road pricing has seldom been adopted in practice, ranging from ideological aversion to the price mechanism to pure ignorance of the objectives behind the policy, but we avoid these issues. In reality, of course, the non-economic ones may well be the factors which sway actual policy makers (Lave, 1994; Borins, 1988)! So what seem to be the economic problems? Why should economists look at alternatives to road pricing in some circumstances?

First, some economists (for example, Sharp, 1966) have long argued that the basic idea of road pricing is too simplistic. The information available, despite considerable advances in the technology of mounting traffic flows, is insufficient to calculate the appropriate charge and, in any case, it is dangerous to make assumptions, as many studies do, that the demand curve for road use is smooth and continuous. There may well be kinks or discontinuities in the demand function.[4] Additionally, road pricing, by its nature, is a first-best solution to the congestion problem and, as such, implicitly assumes full marginal cost pricing is the norm throughout the economy. If this is not so then adjustments to the framework are necessary to define second-best criteria.[5] It is also common practice to assume that the road user has accurate knowledge of his own marginal private costs and responds accordingly (Button, 1976).[6] Others economists (for example, Else, 1981; Evans, 1992), accepting that the relevant costs curves are known, have questioned the methodology upon which the calculation of the optimal road price is based.

These types of argument, however, do not destroy the underlying economic case for road pricing but rather indicate that the practical issues are somewhat more complex than some of the simple theory suggests. Indeed, they are probably no more damning of the concept of road pricing *per se* than are similar types of criticism which could be raised against any of the alternatives. What they do reveal is the need to think carefully when translating from abstract economic theory to practical application.

The basic economic theory of road pricing often neglects transaction costs. The actual costs of introducing and enforcing road pricing may be high. In particular, there are trade-offs between the costs of alternative systems of implementing road pricing and the extent to which these systems impose charges which approximate to actual marginal congestion costs. Area licensing systems (of the type used in Singapore) and cordon pricing (of the form used in some Norwegian cities albeit not strictly for road pricing), for example, are both relatively cheap to introduce and enforce but equally both lack spatial and temporal sensitivity.

Recent technical developments involving such things as the use of 'smart cards' as means of payment within an electronic road pricing system suggest the costs of more sophisticated systems are falling and also that the need for centralized data collection, which can impinge on personal privacy, can be avoided. The transaction costs are, nevertheless, still high and are likely to be particularly so in large cities with complex transport networks. They also have the defect that road users, while paying in advance of trip-making, nevertheless only actually know the exact costs of their activities either retrospectively or, at best, when they are actually in the act of making a trip in congested conditions. This may be unavoidable, but it is not an ideal way of influencing travel behavior.[7]

There is the issue of the distribution impacts of road pricing. As a device employed to control the use of scarce road space, road pricing inevitably means that road users as a whole will suffer a loss of welfare – the aggregate beneficiaries, those who are in receipt of the benefits stemming from the revenue generated (Layard, 1977; Foster, 1974; Richardson, 1974). Of course, within the overall picture some groups of road user – for example those with a high valuation for time savings such as those concerned with goods distribution (Button, 1978) – are likely to benefit, but these will be outnumbered by the losers, especially middle income car users. In a general, aggregate sense there may be no concern over the fact that urban car users suffer a diminution of welfare, after all car ownership is highly and positively correlated with income.[8] The difficulties in this argument are twofold. Within the car-owning group there are some who are not high income earners and society may wish to protect them from additional financial burdens. This may relate to specified socioeconomic groups or to those living in certain areas of a city. Second, there are those who, although not car users at present, aspire to car ownership and use, and society may place a high shadow price on not allowing these people to realize their objective.

There is a further form of distribution issue that is relevant. These are problems, highlighted by the Public Choice school of economic thought, of potential capture of the road pricing system by the revenue collecting authorities within the administration (Toh, 1977). Clearly, there may be a case for treating part of any charging system as a pure sumptuary tax – after all most goods and services are taxed so any case for exempting road users has to be made. The danger is that capture of the system by the bureaucracy could lead to abuse of this position and, *ipso facto*, excessive charges being levied. The issue then becomes an empirical one of whether the potential distortions brought about by excessive charges are greater or less than those associated with high levels of congestion.

Linked to the above, there may be concern about the ways in which the revenues from road pricing might be spent. Achieving a Pareto improvement by simply transferring it back to those priced off the road by reducing other forms of road taxation or user fees is hardly satisfactory (especially if it induces a significant 'buy-back effect') but other alternatives raise a wide variety of distribution questions.

A number of possible options have been explored but none are likely to produce an ideal solution. Indeed, most concede to making no effort at economic efficiency but rather pursue a coalition-type approach of setting out alternative ways of allocating the revenues to attain a coalition of voters willing to adopt road pricing.[9] These expenditures often reflect priorities in terms of improving public transit or the road network to appease the claims of particular transport users.

Finally, congestion costs are only one of the externalities associated with urban traffic, there are also the diverse environmental costs of noise, atmospheric pollution, community severance, intimidation, and so on (Button, 1993). In many cases these user-on-nonuser externalities are positively correlated with congestion and the conclusion often drawn is that road pricing would contain some of these adverse third party environmental effects. There is some truth in this but equally road pricing could in some cases, if its application led to excessive temporal and spatial spreading of traffic, result in more environmental intrusion at times (for example early mornings and evenings) and places (for example in residential areas) where only limited nuisance exists currently.[10]

While there may, therefore, be valid economic reasons for looking carefully at the role road pricing has to play one should not be too fearful of seeing the instrument as offering immense potential for pushing urban traffic levels closer to the optimum. Often, as pointed out above, it is simply a question of how to calculate the appropriate charge in specific conditions and then on the best way on imposing it on users. Nevertheless, road pricing is not generally deployed and alternatives are.

5.3 WHAT ARE THE ALTERNATIVES TO ROAD PRICING?[11]

Since there may be both economic and political problems associated with introducing road pricing, even in its crudest form, it is worth considering the implications of pursuing alternative congestion constraining strategies. There are a number of these, and one way to look at them is to 'eye-ball' a simple diagram.[12]

Figure 5.1 is the standard elementary textbook illustration of why urban traffic congestion occurs and why road pricing will optimize this level of congestion. Road users do not take account of the congestion that they

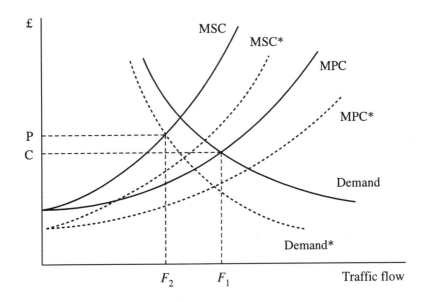

Figure 5.1   The basics of road pricing

impose on others and thus base their trip making decisions on such things as their own marginal private costs of travel time expended and fuel used (MPC) rather than the full (including congestion) marginal costs imposed on all the users of the urban road system (MSC). There may, of course, also be significant environmental costs involved but we ignore these for ease of exposition although in reality additional remedial actions would be required to handle them.

Without road pricing, therefore, the road user will equate MPC with his demand for trip making and a traffic flow of F_1 will ensue. Road pricing is designed to make the road user fully aware of the total congestion costs associated with making a trip. Hence, with a road price of PC, its imposition would lead to a traffic flow of F_2. Of course some congestion remains but the level of congestion is optimized in the sense that the marginal road user is basing his behaviour on knowledge of the full costs of his actions. The marginal benefits a road user enjoys are, thus, equated with these costs.

If there is road pricing then the following alternatives suggest themselves as theoretical possibilities for at least reducing the economic inefficiencies associated with traffic congestion. It should be said at the outset, however, that it is not a straightforward matter to assess the respective attributes of the alternatives. Optimization of congestion requires policy instruments to affect travel behavior in several different ways. Following May (1986), they must bear directly on the traffic creating the problem and be capable of bringing about an acceptable level of response. In the face of uncertainty over outcomes, flexibility is important and, to ensure efficiency, the instrument should bear most heavily on journeys which are the least justified in terms of the benefits they confer. Additionally, there is merit in simplicity and low transactions costs and in instruments which do not simply drive the problem elsewhere to another part of the city, to another area or to a different time period. As we can see, at face value each alternative has its own merits and problems – certainly none is a panacea.

5.3.1   Allow Congestion to Ration Road Space

The result of such a policy would obviously be to leave the traffic flow at F_1 but, in fact, this is not a policy option which should be treated lightly. It is one that most urban authorities tend to rely upon. May (1986), for instance, in an earlier review of traffic restraint measures finds that, in practice, few other methods are used. It has the advantage for the authorities of entailing low transactions costs and may be perceived as equitable in the sense that everyone has the same amount of time available in their lives. Of course, the difficulty is that individuals do not all have the same priorities and, consequently, do not value time in the same way. Also, it does not take a great deal of thought to work out from Figure 5.1 that this approach is wasteful in terms of its overall use of society's resources. The marginal traveler at traffic flow F_1 is imposing considerably more in the way of congestion costs on other road users than he is enjoying benefits from his trip. There are also high costs associated with the wear and tear imposed on the infrastructure. Additionally, since congestion is highly correlated with many environmental effects, the policy would almost inevitably have other serious adverse implications in terms of air pollution, noise levels, and vibration. In the longer term, serious congestion in cities can lead to decentralization and the geographical spread of population and economic activity. This adds a further dimension to the environmental problem.

5.3.2   Parking Charges

Parking policy acts upon a complement to urban road use policies (Verhoef *et al.*, 1995b; Glazer and Niskanen, 1992). Even if there was road pricing there would be a need for an optimal parking pricing policy to both allocate existing spaces efficiently in the short run and to provide guidelines as to the need for investment in capacity in the long run (Button, 1982).[13] Here we are talking about something beyond this; pushing up the price of parking by imposing charges specifically aimed at deterring traffic beyond the level justified simply for allocating parking spaces *per se*. Technically, this will shift the demand curve for road use to the left and reduce the costs of excess road congestion.

The policy could result in an optimal flow but (as with Demand* in Figure 5.1) is more likely to yield improvements rather than an optimal outcome.[14] There are also complexities with terminal policies. They penalize stopping traffic but benefit and, indeed, can encourage through traffic which is in a position to make use of less congested streets at no additional cost (Glazer and Niskanen, 1992). They also have spatial distribution implications in that longer distance terminating traffic has a relatively smaller burden to bear than does shorter distance traffic. How to regulate the costs of using privately supplied parking facilities poses additional problems. The need to zone parking charge areas also means that spatial (as well as temporal) sensitivity is poor. Indeed, such zoning is likely to induce fringe parking effects around the borders of zones (Gillen, 1977). This will affect traffic distribution as well as having environmental and land-use implications.

5.3.3   Public transport subsidies

Subsidies to less congestion-creating transport modes (for example, trams and buses) and to facilities such as 'park and ride' services act to divert car users to a substitute by lowering the latter's price. In terms of the diagram this has exactly the same effect as the parking strategy in that it shifts the demand curve for car use in urban centres to the left. Again, the attainment of a flow of F_2 is theoretically possible but this can only be achieved at a cost.

To obtain significant transfers the cross-elasticity of demand between modes must be high to keep subsidies within manageable levels. Goodwin (1992) and Oum *et al.* (1992) offer surveys of both direct and cross-price elasticities for the use of public transport. The overall impression is one of a highly inelastic demand for such services. The subsidies themselves also pose problems. They are inefficient in the sense that some people switching from cars would have been happy to have done so at lower levels of subsidy than are provided. Their impact can be also be diluted if the transport operator uses the subsidies inefficiently and costs of operations are not minimized. This system may also be captured by other groups, such as organized labor, to extract economic rent. There is evidence that these latter types of problems are not trivial (Pucher *et al.*, 1983).

5.3.4   Fuel Taxation

There is some correlation between fuel use and the amount of congestion on a road. Essentially, the internal combustion engine runs much less efficiently at slow speeds and when there is frequent stopping and starting, than it does at its design cruise speed. Higher fuel taxes, therefore, push up the price of urban driving. Whether this significantly affects urban car use, other than creating a possible very short-term 'knee-jerk reaction' in response to the higher cost is, however, doubtful.[15] It may (see Figure 5.1), push up the MPC to some extent, but in practice the fact that most motorists have a poor knowledge of the MPC for individual trips considerably suppresses the impact. In the longer term the fiscal incentive may lead to more fuel-efficient cars being used with beneficial environmental consequences but with little impact on urban traffic congestion. This is, for example, the basic policy of the UK government in seeking to achieve CO_2 emission targets.

5.3.5 Vehicle License Fees

Most countries impose annual license fees for the right to take a vehicle on the road. Varying these fees influences the total number of vehicles on the road which, while not directly affecting use, has obvious indirect implications for traffic volumes. The advantage of making use of this system is that transaction and administration costs are kept relatively low especially if licensing is already in place serving other (for example policing) functions. The major difficulty from a congestion policy perspective is that the charges do not bear on the amount to which the vehicle is used or upon where and when it is used. Indeed, there is always a danger that a high fixed charge will lead to higher utilization by those with a license.[16]

5.3.6 Road Building

Congestion has often in the past been portrayed (especially by motoring lobbies) as reflecting a shortage of capacity to meet prevailing demand.[17] The traditional response, and one often favored for obvious reasons by engineers, has been to build more capacity to cope with the traffic. In terms of Figure 5.1 this has the effect of pushing the MPC and MSC curves to the right (for example MPC* and MSC*) because any additional vehicle added to a traffic stream will have less impact on congestion if capacity is larger. Given that the divergence between the new MPC and MSC curves is likely to be less at the new traffic flow then congestion costs are reduced although still not optimized. The difficulty with such an approach is that it tends to encounter 'Down's Law'; essentially traffic expands to fill the road space available.

Some economists have taken a somewhat different position on road construction. They have accepted that road pricing is not politically possible and have argued that in this circumstance, capacity should be manipulated so that the shadow price of investment incorporates traffic congestion costs. In other words, investment in infrastructure should be limited in the absence of road pricing since this will in itself contain, although not optimized in a wide sense, excessive traffic levels (Wheaton, 1978). In a way this takes us back to road space allocation by congestion.[18]

5.3.7   Physical Limits on the Quantity of Traffic

Permit systems can be used to limit the number of vehicles entering the urban area to that corresponding to the traffic flow F_2. In the simple framework set out in Figure 5.1 this by definition produces the optimal flow and has the advantage that it circumvents the problem inherent in road pricing of deciding how to dispose of the revenues generated. In a wider, disaggregate sense it is unlikely to yield the benefits of road pricing, however, because of the difficulty of ensuring that the permits actually go to those who gain the greatest benefit from road use. Road pricing achieves this on the basis of the willingness to pay to use the facility. It is more likely that those with the greatest lobbying skills would gain permits under a regime of physical limitation.[19]

5.3.8   Physical Traffic Management

Physical traffic management – such as the use of computerized traffic lights, traffic priority schemes, junction design, bus and car-pool lanes, controls over delivery times and non-parking zones to contain and direct traffic – offers the opportunity to increase the effective capacity of an existing urban road network and in so doing has a similar impact on congestion to the building of new capacity. It also manipulates the generalized cost of using a road network by affecting the travel time and fuel costs of trips. In this way, it impacts on the private marginal costs of trip-making.

From a pure managerial perspective, there are grounds for hoping that traffic management is always conducted efficiently but of itself it does not lead to an optimization of traffic flow. It is akin to good management practice in standard production theory. Good production management ensures that output is produced on the lowest cost curve – it is X-efficient – but it does not ensure that the level of output is at the optimal point on that curve. In our case, it means that the MPC and MSC curves are as low as possible but does not lead to a flow of F_2. There are also often high introduction costs associated with modern management systems and these must be traded-off against the downward shifts in marginal costs attained.

5.3.9   Improved Telematics

A considerable amount of traffic congestion in cities is caused not by the sheer volume of cars, lorries and buses seeking to use roads but by poor information about optimal routing. Some of this is due to ignorance of where and when congestion is occurring and hence the inability to avoid adding to it, but often accidents, breakdowns and other 'incidents' create bottlenecks in the network which are impossible to predict. Improved telematics and information systems can reduce many of these problems. The contentious issue here is not so much to do with the quantity of information as its nature. A 'free market' in information, for example, would lead to all vehicles rushing to routes which, at the time, seem uncongested. The sudden arrival of these cars would soon change the situation.

On-vehicle information and route guidance systems are rapidly being developed and some basic systems are now used in countries like Japan, and taxi cab operators often use them in European cities. Improved information systems can also reduce the amount of certain types of traffic – for example, electronic data interchange (EDI) systems, by increasing load factors and enhancing the productivity of trucks, can reduce the empty running of goods vehicles. Good telecommunications can also improve the productivity of public transport and taxi fleets. In a way this is the information management equivalent of efficient traffic management and, in the same way, it will help improve the internal efficiency of the road network but not optimize its utilization.[20]

5.3.10   Land Use Planning

There has been a long appreciation that transport and land use are interconnected, although our knowledge of this from the casual user is still limited. The planning of urban land use therefore affects the nature and magnitude of travel. Transport demand is largely (although not exclusively) a derived demand associated with the attainment of utility at the final destination.[21] By locating these destinations in particular spatial patterns it is, therefore, possible to influence the aggregate level of travel. A compact city, for example, may generate lower aggregate travel mileage than a dispersed city. Equally, the location of different functions within an urban area can affect the travel behavior of residents.

The difficulty with this type of approach is that it is essentially manipulating the land market to influence the transport market. This poses three types of problem. First, the historical configuration of many urban areas limits the scope for carrying through such policies or makes it prohibitively expensive to do so. This is a particular problem in the older European cities. Second, even when it is possible, the link between land use and transport is a complex one and there is no guarantee that the outcome will be that which is hoped for (Berechman and Gordon, 1996). Third, such manipulation is long term and difficult to reverse which makes the approach rather inflexible. It is difficult, for instance, to see how Los Angeles could suddenly be transformed to substantially reduce the use of the automobile.

Despite these limitations, the urban design may have an important role to play in terms of containing future traffic growth. By making it less desirable to use automobiles in urban areas (for example, through street designs and traffic calming) and offering facilities at a reasonable geographical proximity, there is evidence from countries such as the Netherlands and Germany that car use can be influenced.

5.3.11   Encouraging Alternatives to Transport

Since the demand for transport is generally derived, there are advocates of substituting alternatives for some forms of urban travel. In particular, the encouragement of telecommunications (in the form of telecommuting, teleshopping, and videoconferencing) as a replacement for personal trip-making is pressed as a longer-term strategy.

This type of approach to shifting the demand curve for car use to the left, however, involves entire changes in personal attitudes and activities. This includes not only the transport user but groups such as employers and retailers. How this is be achieved on a significant scale is as yet unclear. Certainly to date, although there is an increase in telecommuting and video conferencing, such changes have largely been resisted by society. There is the problem that without some form of travel restraint measure such as road pricing then time saved by, say, telecommuting, could well be used for other, perhaps, non-business trips (Button, 1991b; Button and Maggi, 1995). There is also the potential that activities such as teleconferencing could stimulate additional travel if it is a complementary activity – the experience of the telephone as a complement to the mail is a historical precedent.

5.4   FISCAL ALTERNATIVES IN PRACTICE

Moving from the theoretical to the more practical, we now turn to provide some brief comments, starting with alternative fiscal measures, on a number of the instruments which are used in practice to regulate urban traffic congestion. There is certainly no claim that the account is exhaustive. It inevitably only scratches the surface of what is actually being done – there are probably as many different approaches to traffic congestion policy as there are urban areas. Here we simply seek to illustrate and to provide guidelines as to the effects of some of the alternative instruments in practice.

Even when road pricing is not adopted, most urban authorities, either implicitly or explicitly, do use a variety of fiscal measures as part of their portfolio of instruments to tackle urban traffic congestion. They also usually combine them with physical controls and other measures hoping for positive synergy effects. This combined use of different instruments, coupled with frequent changes in policy often before the full impact of previous packages have been completely realized, makes it difficult to be precise as to exactly how successful these fiscal alternatives to road pricing have proved to be.

The problem of disentangling the various elements of a portfolio of policy instruments is not the only difficulty. Many of the policies are also aimed at achieving a diversity of objectives (for example, subsidized transport has traditionally been as much to afford mobility to low income groups or areas as to reducing traffic congestion) and it is unclear, therefore, to what extent they are explicit alternatives to road pricing. More recently, issues of congestion policy have merged with matters of environmental protection clouding the picture further.[22] Added to this, urban areas are not homogeneous and differ considerably in form and nature. In consequence, generalizations regarding any form of urban policy is difficult.

What does seem to emerge is that some fiscal alternatives to road pricing have had an effect on traffic congestion. They have produced at least a degree of relief from congestion or have slowed the growth in congestion costs.

Parking charges have for many years been regulated in a large number of cities in part to discourage the use of cars for commuting and shopping purposes. The attention given to the policy has not diminished over time and, indeed, in 1990 Mayor Bradley of Los Angeles proposed parking fees as a substitute for road user fees. The congestion-reducing impact of increasing parking public parking fees has, however, tended in practice to be mixed. One reason for the rather limp response to high parking fees is that many commuters who contribute to rush-hour congestion park free – for example in the USA Willson and Shoup (1990) estimated that 90 per cent of US car commuters park free at work. Further, many parking places are private off-street facilities (for example, up to 60 per cent in UK cities such as Bristol, Oxford, Cambridge, and so on) which makes the direct imposition of high parking fees difficult. This need to deal with private parking if terminal fees are to be an alternative to road pricing has recently come to the fore in New Zealand where the Parliamentary Commission on the Environment has recommended as an anti-congestion measure that employees pay a tax on free parking provided by employers.

Even public parking, and especially on-street parking, policy has seldom been as effective as advocates have hoped. While low enforcement costs and public acceptance have been voiced as specific merits of parking charges there is limited evidence to support such views. The evidence that we do have from countries such as Italy (Ponti and Vittadini, 1990) and the Netherlands (Vleuget *et al.*, 1990) is that such systems are variable in terms of their efficiency in limiting congestion. There is little evidence of public acceptance of high parking fees and they tend to be evaded except in the face of heavy policing and, *ipso facto*, transactions costs. This is, for example, borne out in the London situation where tightening of policing of traffic regulations, including parking policies, on 'Red Routes' was a key element leading to reduced congestion on designated traffic corridors but the policing costs have been high in terms of the commitment of manpower and equipment that has been necessary.

In terms of vehicle taxation, in Europe there has been something of a movement away from high fixed charges such as annual license fees and towards charges more closely linked to transport use. These changes are in part being influenced by developments within the European Community where the Single Market initiative has stimulated the development of more cost-related charging regimes to remove the ability of members to use transport taxation as an instrument in trade discrimination.

Some other countries have, however, explicitly made greater use of fixed charges as an element in their overall urban traffic congestion policy. Hong Kong, for example, trebled annual car tax in 1982 and doubled its purchase tax on cars with a consequential 20 per cent reduction in car ownership. Valletta has higher car taxes than rural Malta – a specific disincentive to urban car ownership. Recently, the nature of some of these schemes has become quite innovative. In Singapore, for example, until May 1990 taxes (for example, registration fees and import duties) made amounted to two thirds of the purchase price of a car. The aim was to contain the growth in the national car park and, equally through such measures as area licensing and parking policies, to limit the use made of the park. Legislative reforms initiated in 1990 brought in a system of 10 year certification of ownership whereby a potential new car owner must enter a public tender to obtain the right to own a car.

The difficulty is that the implementation of this quasi-market approach is that it has tended to lead to speculation in licenses (a problem encountered in many markets for durable products) which in turn questions the efficiency with which licenses actually optimize traffic congestion. Another innovation in Singapore has been the introduction of differential licenses. If a new car is only to be used at weekends, when congestion is low, then there is preferential treatment in terms of lower fees, import duties, and so on. The effects of these policies is less clear cut. The portfolio of transport measures employed in Singapore makes it difficult to isolate the effects of any specific instrument. In Hong Kong, it appears that certainly in the early 1980s the high car taxes had much less impact on traffic in the congested parts of the colony than in the more rural areas suggesting they only partially met their objectives.

The use of high fuel charges has been advocated by some as a tractable and politically acceptable means of controlling congestion even by those who see road pricing as a considerably superior policy instrument (for example, Mohring, 1989). Several countries use them in this way with Singapore, which has a 50 per cent fuel tax, being the most obvious. Detailed analysis of their specific impact on congestion is lacking but overall the evidence tends to show that the long-run fuel price elasticity of demand for car use is low.

The use of carrots, in the form of subsidizing public transport, to attract people away from their cars has tended to be used relatively less in recent years. The policy was, however, widely used in the 1970s and even today some European countries, such as the Netherlands, subsidize the costs of their public transport by 65 per cent or more. Limitations on public expenditure, concern over the effectiveness of the measures when applied to traditional public modes and a feeling that part of any subsidy seems to leak away in higher costs can explain the waning enthusiasm that has been experienced in many countries recently. Where subsidies continue to be used they are now managed more efficiently and objectives are specified more clearly (Button and Costa, 1997). Even so, the impression is that while they may meet certain social needs, with regard to congestion at best they do little more than simply contain the drift to private transport.[23]

In contrast to operating subsidies, the subsidization of investments in less congestion-causing forms of transport, and especially light rapid transit systems, has gained in popularity in recent years (Simpson, 1989). This is obviously a long-term approach[24] but the UK, for instance, has a number of such systems either operational or about to be made so. Other countries such as Portugal have plans to upgrade older systems. The mechanisms for giving public support are generally much tighter than in the past to minimize leakage through excessive X-inefficiency. This is coming about both because of the involvement of private sector suppliers in some cases and via improved public sector management in others. The degree to which even these new public transport systems attract people from their cars, however, is not clear. Recent US evidence (Pickrell, 1989) indicates that very often the forecasts of model transfer to light rapid transit systems have proved to be excessively optimistic. However, and this is perhaps straying away from the central theme of the paper, what is clear is that additional public transport capacity would be required – especially in large cities – in any case, even if road pricing were introduced. It would be needed to accommodate some of those priced from the roads.

5.5   REGULATORY POLICY IN PRACTICE

The range of command and control instruments used by urban authorities to control urban traffic volumes and patterns throughout the world is extensive and, as with fiscal measures, normally come in packages which makes it difficult to assess their impact *vis-à-vis* road pricing alternatives. They are often seen as instruments for tackling several problems rather than being directed specifically at traffic congestion. Continual change in these packages does little to help assess their long-term usefulness.

The most stringent command and control policy is the banning of cars entirely from urban areas. This approach is, in fact, quite widespread in the sense that many cities now have pedestrian areas, but in some cases (as for example is proposed for Amsterdam) more widespread prohibitions are possible in the future. More limited physical controls on the number of vehicles allowed into urban centres have tended to rely either upon permit systems (for example, Milan) or on number plate controls (for example, the odd/even number plates allowed on alternative days in Athens since 1982 and the similar system use in Lagos). One should also include here policies relating to car ownership. Bermuda, for instance, limits households to one car and hire cars are prohibited. In Japan, the policy is that in Tokyo a car license can only be obtained upon proof that off-street parking is available for it.

None of the measures have been entirely successful. In Athens, for instance, the system has been subjected to a high degree of manipulation with scrapped car number plates being fitted to vehicles in use to facilitate all week driving (Matsoukis, 1985). Traffic in areas around the central area also increased which, besides other things, has posed problems for local bus operations. Fraudulent applications for licenses and the use of false number plates were common under the Lagos regime. The sheer disruption to behavior and the relative short-term flexibility of transport systems to cope with such sudden changes can be seen as a partial explanation for this. It is not only manipulation of the system which poses problems; the parking requirement rule in Tokyo has led to distortions in house prices and a response of a rather undesirable kind in residential architecture.

Physical restrictions on the movement of freight transport in cities, for instance in terms of limiting delivery times, restricting the routes that trucks may use, and so on, are also common controls. They are aimed mainly at minimizing the environmental damage caused by such vehicles, but as a secondary objective they are also seen – especially in the cases of controls over deliveries and collections – as removing an impediment to the free flow of traffic (Sharp and Jennings, 1976). The degree to which such instruments are used seem somewhat less than they might be, especially in the UK where few urban authorities make full use of the legal powers with which they are endowed. Lobbying by local business and fears that customers will defect to adjacent areas where collections and deliveries are not so restricted offers one explanation. In any case, the power of delivery and collection controls to reduce traffic congestion is unlikely to be very strong since for purely commercial reasons much of this is already done outside of the normal morning and evening peaks (Button and Pearman, 1981)

The 'science' of physical traffic management has developed considerably over the years. Many European cities now have (albeit often under different names) traffic cell systems (that is, where it is difficult for physical or regulatory reasons to move between cells), mazes (that is, where one-way streets, local closures, and so on make through movements difficult) or traffic calming zones (that is, where speed humps, narrowing of roads, and so on physically slows car traffic and thus pushes up the time costs of auto-trip making). There is evidence from cities such as Gothenburg that such measures can deter through traffic and, as a supplementary benefit, lead to more rapid and reliable public transport services (OECD, 1988). Such systems are, however, often costly to introduce and are inflexible in their nature. Forecasting the impacts of traffic management policies is also particularly difficult across large urban networks (Banister, 1992) which makes lack of flexibility a serious limitation. Enforcement of traffic management regulations is an important element to consider in this context. In London, for example, it is estimated that of 150 000 parking offences in London some 149 000 go undetected (Joseph, 1991). Many of those caught do not pay the fines imposed.

Land-use planning has been seen as a major element in urban transport policy at least since the time of the *Buchanan Report* (United Kingdom Ministry of Transport, 1963). More recent efforts at redesigning land use to minimize car travel is the Dutch strategy of locating new commercial developments around major public transport interchanges (*ABC lokatiebeleid*) – see van Huut (1991). Also, although less directly of immediate relevance to the congestion issue, we find in the former East Germany that, being confronted with transport constraints, industrial development policy is aimed at geographically concentrating economic activities rather than spreading them. At a more micro level, the development of traffic cells as an integral part of the land-use architecture in some western cities (OECD, 1988) and of auto-restraint zones in the USA (Herald, 1977) can be seen as elements of this land-use planning approach.

Since land-use planning is a long-term exercise the ultimate implications for these land use/transportation strategies will not materialize for some time. However, retrospectively, looking back at efforts to engineer travel behavior through land-use planning (for example in the UK context this would embrace such things as new towns and overspill policy) has not been conspicuously successful. There is evidence that traffic cells and pedestrianization have produced some beneficial regeneration effects in central urban areas which, in turn, acts to limit the spread of congestion to suburban sites. At the same time, however, it can lead to additional traffic in the immediate surrounding areas. Bypass facilities are often seen as a key component of land-use/transportation planning which, by causing through traffic to avoid congested core areas, reduce demand for congested road space. In itself, however, the policy may prove of limited effectiveness without accompanying sticks to divert traffic to what is often a physically longer route. In practice, the traffic effects of bypass and circular road construction is difficult to forecast, as witnessed by the case of the M25 motorway around London which attracted considerable, and unexpected, local traffic.

5.6 CONCLUSIONS

Pigou laid down a policy for handling the problems of transport infrastructure access, and transport economists have subsequently refined these to create the modern theory of road pricing. People who have examined the way public policies are determined have found a reluctance on the part of administrators to embrace economic pricing in areas such as road track allocation.[25] Economists are, however, having some success in other related microeconomic policy areas such as industrial regulation, in getting their ideas across. The notion of the polluter pays principle is now widely accepted, and investment appraisal in environmental policy. Debates on the use of road pricing are also part of the wider economic policy dialogues in many cities. In the meantime, other strategies of congestion control are being favored, and these are not always in conflict with economic principles.

There are circumstances where economic logic suggests that road pricing is not the optimum strategy and that alternative policy instruments should be sought to contain excessive traffic congestion. In reality, however, the suspicion is that such policy alternatives do not tend to be adopted for this reason but are preferred for a variety of political reasons or because of a lack of an adequate understanding of what road pricing actually entails and seeks to achieve.

The success of the alternatives in optimizing traffic congestion is variable, and all have their own defects and limitations which must be set against those of road pricing itself. There have been instances where short-term relief from congestion has been possible with the adoption of alternative fiscal or regulatory instruments, but these have proved less enduring in the longer term. In other cases, policies such as freeway constructions without accompanying restrictions on use may well have exacerbated the situation. What also emerges is that applications of alternative policies to road pricing seldom generate outcomes which the textbook model would suggest. Enforcement of the alternatives also often tends to be more difficult than the *ex ante* arguments imply.

NOTES

1. Strict economic theory suggests that internalizing externalities can only completely be achieved through the full allocation of property rights in a competitive market (Coase, 1960). Initially allocating such rights poses potential problems, legally enforcing the system and targeting the purchase rights entails significant transactions costs. Goddard (1997) offers an interesting approach to a quasi-property right method of allocating scarce road space. Pricing externalities is a partial equilibrium approach to optimization that effectively attains a predetermined level of congestion (Bator, 1958; Verhoef, 1996).
2. Strictly, traffic congestion is a 'club good problem' involving the allocation of a fixed asset across a range of users. The environmental issue is one of a strict externality, where activities in one sector impinge on another.
3. Singapore's area pricing scheme is the only major effort to introduce congestion charging. Systems of cordon pricing in Norway and Sweden are effectively revenue-raising policies. There are peak/off-peak tolls on one French motorway to handle different temporal demands on weekends.
4. See Arnott, *et al.* (1990) for a discussion of congestion pricing when there are bottlenecks in the road network.
5. A number of studies have set out second-best criteria for road pricing – for example, Sullivan (1983) and Verhoef, *et al.* (1995a).
6. This also raises questions about drivers having full information regarding traffic conditions (Arnott *et al.*, 1991b).
7. From an administrative perspective, there is also a range of issues concerning the costs and effectiveness of enforcing electronic road pricing, see UK House of Commons Transport Committee (1994a) for details of such practical issues. Much of the recent literature on electronic road pricing ties it in with route guidance systems which introduces a set of wider considerations into the debate.
8. Attached to this is the whole issue of exceptions and direct subsidies for certain groups of road users. While there may be a case for lump sum transfers to selected groups for a variety of reasons, there has been a long history of directly favoring some groups of road users (for example, emergency services) which is unlikely to change.
9. There is growing literature in this field: see Sharp, 1966; Starkie, 1986; Goodwin and Jones, 1989; Jones, 1991; Goodwin, 1992; Small, 1992; and Giuliano 1992.
10. There are also land use and locational implications of introducing road pricing. If other markets are imperfect, road pricing may not lead to environmentally substantial patterns of location and production. It may, for example, affect the location of negative externality generating industries in such a way that overall pollution assesses (Bergh *et al.*, 1997).
11. This section is not claimed to be exhaustive and excludes policies such as education and moral suasion, although these may prove important in fostering such things as spreading work hours (Salomon and Tacken, 1993) and car pooling (see Steininger *et al.*, 1996).
12. May (1986) offers a short outline of many of the possible options.
13. Arnott, *et al.* (1991a) provide a rigorous description of the conditions for an optimal parking change.
14. Verhoef (1996) sets out detailed conditions, whereby the optimal parking charge will result in the same level of congestion as a road price. The distributional consequences, however, would be different.

15. Goodwin's (1992) survey suggests a short-run fuel elasticity price of about –0.16 and a long-run elasticity of about –0.46.
16. The higher the entry fee will reduce the number of potential entrants to the road network, and this is likely to stimulate higher utilization of road space by those who pay the vehicle license fee.
17. The optimal economic road investment strategy is discussed in Vickery (1969).
18. D'Ouville and McDonald (1990) and Wilson (1983) offer alternative models for road investment policy in the context of sub-optimal road user charges.
19. Physical restrictions of other kinds may also affect congestion levels. Experiments on speed limits for UK motorways have been conducted reducing maximum speeds from 70 miles per hour to 50 miles per hour with the results of improved traffic flows.
20. Nijkamp *et al.* (1996) look, in general, at the implications of telematics for travel behavior, and Arnott *et al.* (1991b) provide a detailed examination of the possible implications of improved telemetics on congestion levels. They need not always be positive, especially if they lead to high levels of diversion to poorer quality roads.
21. 'Every day tourism' is an increasingly important area of study and looks at regular urban trips that offer direct utility.
22. For example, see the broad approach advocated in UK Royal Commission on Environmental Pollution (1994).
23. An overall assessment of the longer-term role of public transport in Europe is contained in Stern and Tretvik (1993).
24. For example, it takes 9 to 13 years to approve and implement a scheme in the UK.
25. Frey, *et al.* (1985), for example, surveyed a number of different groups about their attitudes to the use of economic instruments for containing externalities.

REFERENCES

Arnott, R., A. de Palma and R. Lindsey (1990), 'Economics of a bottleneck', *Journal of Urban Economics*, **27**, 11–30.
Arnott, R., A. de Palma and R. Lindsey (1991a), 'A temporal and spatial equilibrium analysis of commuter parking', *Journal of Public Economics*, **45**, 301–35.
Arnott, R., A. de Palma and R. Lindsey (1991b), 'Does providing information to drivers reduce traffic congestion?', *Transportation Research*, **25A**, 309–18.
Arnott, R., A. de Palma and R. Lindsey (1994), 'The welfare effects of congestion tolls with heterogeneous commuters', *Journal of Transport Economics and Policy*, **28**, 139–61.
Banister, D. (1992), 'Transport policy and planning analysis: the first thirty years', paper to the 6th World Conference on Transport Research, Lyon.
Bator, F.M. (1958), 'The anatomy of market failure', *Quarterly Journal of Economics*, **72**, 351–79.
Berechman, J. and P. Gordon (1986), 'Linked models of land use – transport interactions, a review', in B. Hutchison and M. Batty (eds), *Advances in Urban Systems Modelling*, Amsterdam: North-Holland.
Bergh, J.C.J.M van den, K.J. Button and E.T. Verhoef (1997), 'Transport, spatial economy and the global environment', *Environment and Planning* (forthcoming).
Borins, S.F. (1988), 'Electronic road pricing, an idea whose time may never come', *Transportation Research*, **22A**, 37–44.
Button, K.J. (1976), 'A note on the benefits from road pricing', *International Journal of Transport Economics*, **3**, 91–5.
Button, K.J. (1978), 'A note on the road pricing of commercial traffic', *Transportation Planning and Technology*, **4**, 175–8.

Button, K.J. (1982), 'The application of economic principles to the problems of urban car parking', *Economics*, **8**, 83–5.

Button, K.J. (1991a), 'Electronic road pricing, experience and prospects', paper presented at the conference on Economy and the Environment, Neuchatel.

Button, K.J. (1991b), 'Transport and communications', in J.H. Rickard and J. Larkinson (eds), *Long Term Issues in Transport: A Research Agenda*, Aldershot: Avebury.

Button, K.J. (1993), *Transport, the Environment and Economic Policy*, Aldershot: Edward Elgar.

Button, K.J. and A. Costa (1997), 'Economic efficiency gains from public transport regulatory changes in Europe', paper to the 36th Western Regional Science Association Annual Conference, Hawaii.

Button, K.J. and R. Maggi (1995), 'Videoconferencing and its implications for transport, an Anglo–Swiss perspective', *Transport Reviews*, **15**, 59–75.

Button, K.J. and A.D. Pearman (1981), *The Economics of Urban Freight Transport*, London: Macmillan.

Button, K.J. and W. Rothengatter (1997), 'Motor transport, greenhouse gases and economic instruments', *International Journal of Environment and Pollution*, **7**, 327–42.

Coase, R.H. (1960), 'The problem of social cost', *Journal of Law and Economics*, **3**, 1–44.

Else, P.K. (1981), 'A reformation of the theory of optimal congestion taxation', *Journal of Transport Economics and Policy*, **5**, 217–32.

Evans, A.W. (1992), 'Road congestion, the diagrammatic analysis', *Journal of Political Economy*, **100**, 211–17.

Foster, C. (1974), 'A note on the distributional effects of road pricing, a comment', *Journal of Transport Economics and Policy*, **9**, 186–7.

Frey, B.S., F. Schneider and W.W. Pommerehne (1985), 'Economists' opinions on environmental policy instruments: Analysis of a survey', *Journal of Environmental Economics and Management*, **12**, 62–71.

Gillen, D.W. (1977), 'Estimation and specification of the effects of parking costs on urban transport mode choice', *Journal of Urban Economics*, **4**, 186–99.

Giuliano, G. (1992), 'An assessment of the political acceptability of congestion pricing', *Transportation*, **19** (4), 335–58.

Glazer, A. and E. Niskanen (1992), 'Parking fees and congestion', *Regional Science and Urban Economics*, **22**, 123–32.

Goddard, H.C. (1997), 'Optimal restrictions on vehicle use for urban sustainability for Mexico City', *International Journal of Environment and Pollution*, **7**, 357–74.

Goodwin, P.B. (1989), 'The rule of three, a possible solution to the political problem of competing objectives for road pricing', *Traffic Engineering and Control*, **30** (10), 495–7.

Goodwin, P.B. (1992), 'A review of new demand elasticities with special reference to short and long run effects of price changes', *Journal of Transport Economics and Policy*, **26**, 155–70.

Goodwin, P. and P.M. Jones (1989), 'Road pricing, the political and strategic possibilities', in ECMT, *Systems of Road Infrastructure Cost Coverage – Report of the Eightieth Round Table on Transport Economics*, European Conference of Ministers of Transport, Paris.

Herald, W.S. (1977), 'Auto restricted zones, plans for five cities', Report UMTA-VA-06-0042-78-32, Washington, DC: US Department of Transportation.

Higgins, T. (1980), 'Road pricing, a clash of analysis and politics', *Policy Analysis*, **7**, 71–89.

Jones, P. (1991), 'Gaining public support for road pricing through a package approach', *Traffic Engineering and Control*, **32**, 194–6.

Joseph, S. (1991), 'Traffic growth, the problems and the solutions', *Journal of Law and Society*, **18**, 26–134.

Lave, C. (1994), 'The demand curve under road pricing and the problem of political feasibility', *Transportation Research*, **28A**, 83–91.

Layard, R. (1977), 'The distributional effects of congestion taxes', *Economica*, **44**, 297–304.

Matsoukis, E.C. (1985), 'An assessment of vehicle restraint measures', *Transportation Quarterly*, **39**, 125–33.

May, A.D. (1986), 'Traffic restraint, a review of the alternatives', *Transportation Research*, **20A**, 109–21.

Mohring, H. (1989), 'The role of fuel taxes in controlling congestion', in *Transport Policy, Management and Technology Towards 2001*, Ventura: Western Periodicals Company.

Nijkamp, P., G. Pepping and D. Banister (1996), *Telemetics and Transport Behaviour*, Berlin: Springer.

Organisation for Economic Cooperation and Development (OECD) (1988), *Cities and Transport*, Paris, OECD.

Oum, T.H., W.G. Waters and J.-S. Yong (1992), 'Concepts of price elasticities of transport demand and recent empirical estimates', *Journal of Transport Economics and Policy*, **27**, 139–54.

d'Ouville, E.L. and J.F. McDonald (1990), 'Optimal road capacity with a suboptimal congestion toll', *Journal of Urban Economics*, **28**, 34–49.

Pickrell, D.H. (1989), *Urban Transit Projects: Forecast Versus Actual Ridership and Costs*, Cambridge, Massachusetts: US Department of Transportation.

Pigou, A. (1920), *The Economics of Welfare*, London: MacMillan.

Ponti, M. and M.R. Vittadini (1990), 'Italy', in J.-P. Barde and K.J. Button (eds), *Transport Policy and the Environment*, London: Earthscan.

Pucher, J., A. Markstedt and I. Hirschman (1983), 'Impact of subsidies on the costs of urban public transport', *Journal of Transport Economics and Policy*, **17**, 155–76.

Richardson, H.W. (1974), 'A note on the distributional effects of road pricing', *Journal of Transport Economics and Policy*, **8**, 82–5.

Salomon, I. and M. Tacken (1993), 'Taming the peak: Time and timing as travel moderators', in I. Salomon *et al.* (eds), A *Billion Trips A Day: Tradition and Transition in European Travel Patterns*, London: Kluwer Academic Publishers.

Sharp, C.H. (1966), 'Congestion and welfare, an examination of the case for a congestion tax', *Economic Journal*, **76**, 806–17.

Sharp, C.H. and A. Jennings (1976), *Transport and the Environment*, Leicester: Leicester University Press.

Simpson, B.J. (1989), 'Urban rail transit – an appraisal', Transport and Road Research Laboratory Contract Report CR140, Crowthorne.

Small, K. (1992), 'Using the revenues from congestion pricing', *Transportation*, **19** (4), 359–81.

Starkie, D. (1986), 'Efficient and politic congestion tolls', *Transportation Research*, **20A**, 169–73.

Steininger, K., C. Vogal and R. Zettl (1996), 'Car sharing organizations: the size of the market segment and revealed changes in mobility behavior', *Transport Policy*, **3**, 177–86.

Stern, E. and T. Tretvik (1993), 'Public transport in Europe: Requiem or revival?', in I. Salomon *et al.* (eds), *A Billion Trips a Day: Tradition and Transition in European Travel Patterns*, London: Kluwer Academic Publishers.

Sullivan, A.M. (1983), 'Second-best policies for congestion externalities', *Journal of Urban Economics*, **14**, 105–23.

Toh, R. (1977), 'Road congestion pricing: the Singapore experience', *Malayan Economic Review*, **22**, 52–61.

UK House of Commons Select Committee on Transport (1994a), *Charging for the Use of Motorways*, HC-376, London: HMSO.

UK House of Commons Select Committee on Transport (1994b), *Transport-related Air Pollution in London*, HC-506, London: HMSO.

UK Ministry of Transport (1963), *Traffic in Towns*, London: HMSO.

UK Royal Commission on Environmental Pollution (1994), Eighteenth Report: *Transport and the Environment*, London: HMSO.

van Huut, H. (1991), 'The right business in the right place', in *Proceedings of Seminar A*, PTRC Summer Meeting, London.

Vleuget, J., H. van Gent and P. Nijkamp (1990), 'The Netherlands', in J.-P. Barde and K.J. Button (eds), *Transport Policy and the Environment*, London: Earthscan.

Verhoef, E. (1996), *Economic Efficiency and Social Feasibility in The Regulation of Road Transport Externalities*, PhD thesis, Free University of Amsterdam.

Verhoef, E.T., P. Nijkamp and P. Rietveld (1995a), 'Second-best regulation of road transport externalities', *Journal of Transport Economics and Policy*, **29**, 147–67.

Verhoef, E.T., P. Nijkamp and P. Rietveld (1995b), 'The economics of regulatory parking policies', *Transportation Research*, **29A**, 141–56.

Vickery, W.S. (1969), 'Congestion theory and transport investment', *American Economic Review*, **59**, 251–60.

Walters, A.A. (1961), 'The theory and measurement of private and social cost of highway congestion', *Econometrica*, **29**, 676–99.

Wheaton, W.C. (1978), 'Price-induced distortions in urban highway investment', *Bell Journal of Economics*, **9**, 622–32.

Willson, R.W. and D.C. Shoup (1990), 'Parking subsidies and travel choices, assessing the evidence', *Transportation*, **17**, 141–57.

Wilson, J.D. (1983), 'Optimal road capacity in the presence of unpriced congestion', *Journal of Urban Economics*, **13**, 337–57.

6. Variabilization of car taxes and externalities

Stef Proost and Kurt Van Dender

6.1 INTRODUCTION

Car use is heavily taxed in Europe. Usually one distinguishes between two types of tax bases: the possession or purchase of a car, and the use of a car. Registration taxes, purchase taxes, and taxes on annual insurance premiums are linked closely to the ownership of a car. The most important tax on the use of a car is the motorfuel tax. A popular prescription to solve the externality problems linked to car use has been to replace the present ownership-related taxes to use-related taxes and more particularly to motor fuel taxes. It has become known as 'variabilization' of car taxation. In this chapter we will examine the merits of variabilization in more detail.

The Dutch green lobby was the first to defend this idea in the context of greenhouse gas reduction policies: they proposed a strong increase in the tax on motor fuel so as to achieve a reduction of traffic and a decrease in emissions. The tax reform proposed was revenue neutral. As this proposal was difficult to realize in a small country with open borders it could only make sense in a European context. It was taken over by the public transport and green lobby (Kageson, 1993) and received more and more support from the political world. The variabilization proponents make two claims: the reform is feasible and it internalizes better the different externalities. Later on, a double dividend claim has been added to this: one can as well raise the net tax level on cars so that the extra tax revenue can be used to reduce existing distortionary taxes on labour and obtain an increase in employment. The variabilization concept is now known by all policy makers, and most European policy makers support the idea that a motor fuel tax increase is a good thing.

In this chapter we examine the variabilization proposal in two steps. We analyse first what the behavioural effects can be of a variabilization in car taxation. Two effects are distinguished: the effect on car use for given fuel efficiency, and the effect on the fuel efficiency of cars. For the effect on overall car use we will rely mainly on demand theory (De Jong, 1990) and on the use of this theory in Van Dender (1996). For the effect of increased fuel taxes on fuel efficiency we will rely on Khazzoom (1994) and on Walker and Wirl (1993). Next we analyse to what extent an increase in fuel taxes is indeed capable of increasing welfare by internalizing better the different externalities linked to car use. Here we will make use of estimates of external costs by Mayeres, Ochelen and Proost (1996) and of the TRENEN-I model that evaluates second-best pricing options for externalities (De Borger *et al.*, 1997). In the last section we draw some conclusions on the merits of the variabilization proposals.

6.2 THE MICROECONOMIC EFFECTS OF VARIABILIZATION ON CAR OWNERSHIP, CAR USE AND CAR DESIGN

Higher motor fuel taxes have three basic effects on household behaviour. First, for given car characteristics, the household might choose to limit annual mileage or to give up ownership of a car. Next, the household can opt for more fuel-efficient cars and this may give rise to less safe cars. Finally, in a small open country the household could even opt to take fuel abroad. Each of these effects have been studied using different types of models.

6.2.1 Effects of Car Ownership Taxes and Car Use Taxes on Mileage

De Jong (1990) provides one of the few models that explain car ownership and car use (mileage) in a consistent framework. De Jong uses a micro-simulation model that deals with the problem of car ownership in a neo-classical demand model. The consumers' problem is represented in Figure 6.1. This figure represents for a given budget Y, the possible combinations of car kilometres a year and expenses on other goods. The budget set is non-convex. If the household owns a car, this entails a fixed cost C so that, at the maximum, $Y - C$ can be spent on other goods (including public transport). Increasing the number of kilometres makes the individual move along the budget line B_2. When the household does not own a car he can spend Y on other goods and his budget line is just a point on the vertical axis. If we now increase the variable cost of car use, the budget line rotates in the direction of B_1. This has two effects: car use will decrease and, from a certain switching point on, it becomes more economical not to own a car as the number of kilometres driven a year becomes too small compared to the fixed cost of car use. At the budget line B_1 the household prefers not to own a car at all.

When the increase in variable taxes is compensated by a decrease in taxes on ownership, there will be a simultaneous parallel shift upwards of the budget

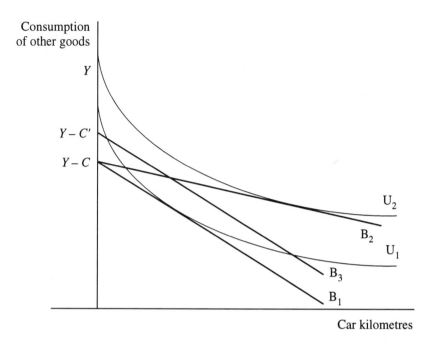

Figure 6.1   Fixed and variable costs of car use

line B_1 to a new budget line B_3. This will increase the ownership of cars again and will have an income effect on the annual mileage. For his sample, De Jong obtains the following two elasticities of private mileage: –0.88 as fixed cost elasticity of which 38 per cent is a direct use effect and 62 per cent is the effect via the change in car ownership; and –1.11 where 59 per cent is through reduced use and 41 per cent occurs via reduced car ownership. The proportions of fixed costs and of variable costs are of the same order of magnitude.

Van Dender (1996) tested the effect of a revenue neutral shift from owner-ship taxes to use taxes under the form of motor fuel taxes. He used a static and a dynamic model that was calibrated with the help of the De Jong elasticities. In the static model (with perfect adaptation of car stocks to desired levels), he found that an increase in both fixed costs and variable costs led to a similar reduction in total car mileage. When fixed costs are used as an instrument, this effect is obtained via a reduction of the car stock and an increase in the annual mileage per car. When variable costs are increased, the mileage per car decreases, but the ownership of cars increases. In the dy-namic model, it is assumed that all the ownership and fixed type of taxes are replaced by variable taxes and that the net tax receipt is identical, at least in the first year. This required an increase in variable costs of car use by 23 per cent.[1] The net effect was only a small decrease in the aggregate mileage (2 per cent) because of the strong expansion of car ownership. The dynamic model also showed some expected results on the second-hand car market. Second-hand cars became less expensive for two reasons. First, because the purchase of a new car has become less expensive, prices of second-hand cars have had to drop. Second, with the technological progress in fuel efficiency, and the increase in the fuel costs, the use of old cars becomes less economical.

In conclusion, the variabilization of car taxes will not lead to a strong decrease in car use, as long as the net tax receipts on automobile use are kept constant. There are two sources of uncertainty in this result. There is the statistical uncertainty in the price elasticity estimates, and there is also the uncertainty in the perception of the different type of car costs by the car users. On this topic there are no clear conclusions in the literature.

6.2.2 Effects of Fuel Taxes on Fuel Efficiency and on Car Use

An increase in fuel taxes will generate a behavioural but also a technological response. The present mix of fuel efficiency and purchase costs embedded in the used car technology will no longer be optimal for the car user. His objective is to minimize the total car user costs and, when the price of fuel changes, it becomes interesting to invest in a more fuel-efficient vehicle. In order to maximize their sales, the car manufacturers will invest in technological progress and make use of existing, more expensive but lighter materials in order to offer a car that has, given the new fuel prices, a lower total user cost. We have all seen how after the first oil shock, the fuel efficiency of medium-sized European[2] cars has improved from some 121/100 km to some 81/100 km and this for a maximum real price increase of some 25 per cent for petrol and 78 per cent for diesel (between 1973 and 1985, De Borger and De Borger, 1988). We are interested in the effect of motor fuel price increases on fuel efficiency and on induced car use.

The effect of higher motor fuel prices on fuel efficiency in Europe has been studied by Walker and Wirl (1993). In their analysis they take into account that the technological development only reacts to expected increases in real motor fuel prices. As the present motor fuel prices are lower than the historical prices, fuel efficiency will only increase if real motor fuel prices are believed to stay more than 30 per cent above the present level. The 30 per cent increase is a threshold that needs to be passed before significant investments in fuel efficiency will be made by car manufacturers. A second factor to be taken into account is the increasing marginal cost of fuel efficiency improvements. Fuel efficiency increases beyond normal technological progress have a cost. This cost increases because for every fuel efficiency improvement, the manufacturer will always first use the cheapest solutions and will need to use more and more exotic technologies to achieve his objective. As an example, consider the cost of improving the fuel efficiency of a medium-sized gasoline car from 6.6 litres in 2005 to 5 litres in 2005. This could necessitate a total increase in car manufacturing costs of 18 per cent of which only half would be paid back to the user by lower fuel costs (Proost, 1997).

The effect of improved fuel efficiency on car use has become known as the rebound effect. The improved car efficiency lowers the net cost of car use. This net cost is the minimized sum of fuel and purchase costs. As the net cost of car use decreases, it becomes interesting for the consumers to make more use of the car. Walker and Wirl (1993) estimate this rebound effect to be equal to 20–50 per cent. This means that when fuel efficiency improves by 10 per cent, car use might increase between 2 and 5 per cent.

6.2.3   Effects of Increased Fuel Taxes on Car Safety

Increased motor fuel taxes lead to higher fuel efficiencies. The higher fuel efficiencies can be achieved by improving the efficiency of the engine, by lowering the horse power of the engine, by lowering the weight and by downsizing the car. Khazzoom (1994) estimated the effect of improved fuel efficiency (generated by the US fuel efficiency standards) on the accident rates. He used data on highway fatalities in the US, and found two types of relationship. First, fuel efficiency, when it is obtained via a reduced engine power, reduces the accident rate. The second relationship concerns the weight and design of the car. A reduction in car weight will not necessarily increase fatalities because some of the lighter (and more expensive) materials also have good safety properties.

The different effects of motor fuel prices on fuel efficiency and car design have been summarized in Table 6.1. The improved fuel efficiency response

Table 6.1   Effects of motor fuel price increase on fuel efficiency and car design

Effects on:	Real price motor fuel increase < 30%	Real price motor fuel increase > 30%
fuel efficiency	no effect	increases but decreasing effect because of increasing marginal cost
induced car use	no induced effect	rebound effect of 20 to 50%
car safety	no effect	small

implies that a budget neutral shift from fixed to variable taxes has to take this into account and increase the motor fuel taxes more than proportionately.

6.3 THE COMPARATIVE WELFARE EFFECTS OF THE FUEL TAX INSTRUMENT

We know from the previous section that there will be almost no net effect of higher fuel taxes on aggregate car use as long as there is no net increase in taxation on car ownership and use. This does not imply that there is no welfare effect from this shift. This will be discussed in Section 6.3.1. Can we expect better results if we allow fuel taxes to increase without any comparative reduction in the level of fixed costs so that net taxation on automobiles increases? Of course car use will decline, but to know whether it is a good policy we need to know not only whether its welfare effects are positive, but also whether there are no better measures to achieve the desired results. This will be the subject of Section 6.3.2.

6.3.1 The Welfare Effect of a Budget Neutral Shift from Ownership to Motor Fuel Taxes

Because the effect on car use is probably very small, the major effect will be via the change in fuel efficiency. We need to distinguish two cases. If the increase in real motor fuel prices is limited (say below 30 per cent), there will be no net effect on fuel efficiency and no net welfare effect. If there is a strong increase in the real motor fuel price, there will be welfare effects. The reduced fuel efficiency will have a welfare cost but also a welfare gain because it will lead to a reduction in the emission of air pollutants. Proost (1997) has estimated the welfare cost (excluding air pollution benefits) for a 100 per cent increase in the real motor fuel price resulting in an increase of fuel efficiency from 6.5 to 5 litres per 100 km. There is a welfare cost because the additional resource costs used to increase the fuel efficiency of cars are balanced only to a small degree by savings in the resource costs of fuel. Efforts to increase the fuel efficiency mainly lead to savings in motor fuel taxes. The motor fuel price accounted in 1995 for 75 per cent of taxes, and with an increase of 100 per cent of the motor fuel price, this will become 92 per cent. The welfare cost could be of the order of 140 ECU/car per year. On the other hand the improvement of the fuel efficiency will lead to a reduction of emissions. If this reduction of emissions is taken as proportional to the fuel emission reduction, we have a reduction of pollutants NO_x, VOC, CO and CO_2 by 25 per cent. The value of this reduction depends on the damage attributed to different air pollutants. If we follow Mayeres, Ochelen and Proost (1996), the avoided air pollution damage would be of the order of 20 ECU per car per year. A fiscally neutral variabilization of car taxation would lead to a net welfare loss of the order of 120 ECU per car per year. In this estimate we have assumed that there are no tax evasion effects by fuelling abroad. If this did happen, the welfare costs could be much higher as the fuel tax has to be increased even more to have budget neutrality. Of course, this result assumes that there is no net effect on the volume of car traffic and on modal choice. If there are effects on the volume of car traffic the welfare evaluation will be different because it has to take into account the change in external costs linked to the volume of car use. This will be discussed in the next section.

6.3.2   The Welfare Effect of an Increase in Motor Fuel Taxes without Reduction in Ownership Taxes

We can expect a net effect on the volume of car use when the motor fuel taxes are increased without any reduction in ownership taxes. The computation of the welfare effect of this policy measure is more complicated because we have to take into account the substitution by other modes of transport as well as the use of the increased tax revenue.

To analyse the welfare effects of higher fuel taxes we use the TRENEN-I model.[3] This model allows us to compute the best equilibrium on the transport market for a given set of policy instruments. The welfare criteria used are the sum of consumer surplus of passenger transport users, the producer surplus of the users of freight transport, the producer surplus of the suppliers of transport means, the tax revenue weighed by the marginal cost of public funds minus the external costs other than congestion. As the model is formulated in terms of generalized costs, congestion is already taken into account in the time cost component of the consumer prices. Similar models are used for the urban and the non-urban transport market. On the non-urban transport market, freight is important.

A brief model description can be found in De Borger *et al.* (1997). The passenger transport market distinguishes between peak and off-peak travel, between motorized and non-motorized travel, between private and public transport (bus and metro); for private transport modes are distinguished by function of vehicle size and the type of fuel (gasoline and diesel). For freight transport, a distinction is made between peak and off-peak traffic, between road, inland waterways and rail, and for trucks a further distinction in function of the size of the trucks is made. It is also important to stress that in TRENEN, unlike in many transportation models, the total number of trips is not fixed. The dominant factor in the welfare evaluation of a policy will be whether the discrepancies between social marginal cost (marginal resource cost + marginal external cost) and consumer prices are increased or not. Given the many externalities in the transport market, perfect pricing is not possible, so that some markets will always be taxed too much and others not enough. A second factor to be taken into account in the welfare evaluation is the use of the net tax revenues collected. When these are used to reduce the labour tax rate, in some cases this can give rise to a double dividend. This means that the change in the net tax revenue collected in the transport sector has a higher value than the consumer surplus in this sector.[4] The externalities taken into account in the TRENEN model exercise are congestion, air pollution, traffic accidents, noise and road usage by trucks.

In order to judge the potential merits of the introduction of higher motor fuel taxes we examine in Table 6.2 the present level of taxes in relation to the total marginal external cost in some of the transportation markets considered in TRENEN. The comparison is made for an unchanged policy case in 2005, where peak and off-peak periods, private and public transport and different fuels are compared. The marginal external congestion cost is the most important external cost and is the dominant problem in the peak periods. The marginal external congestion cost corresponds to the extra time loss of all other road users when one vehicle is added to the traffic volume. This is followed by the marginal accident costs of cars. The marginal accident costs consist of that part of accident costs which is not taken into account by the driver either directly or via his insurance. In the valuation of the marginal accident costs we take into account both the willingness of the victim and of his friends and his family to avoid an accident, and the direct economic costs of an accident. Moreover account is taken of the effect of an extra car on the risk of accidents. The marginal air pollution costs consist of damages linked to particulates, ozone formation, climate change and acid rain. Local as well as regional damages have been taken into account. Comparing the total marginal external costs with the total tax per passenger kilometre, mobility is almost always subsidized by society: the marginal external costs are much higher than the tax per passenger kilometre. This holds for freight and passenger transport and for all modes with one or two exceptions.

The welfare effects of a motor fuel price increase do exist but will be very limited. The major problem is that the motor fuel tax has to be used as instrument to address simultaneously several transportation markets for which the level of external costs differs strongly. The optimal increase in the motor fuel taxes for passenger cars will firstly consist of higher increases for diesel than for gasoline. The reason is that the external air pollution costs of diesel and gasoline cars are not very different so that they should be taxed more or less identically per vehicle kilometre. As diesel cars are more fuel efficient, this requires a proportionally higher tax for diesel. Next a general increase in the tax level on road transport permits better internalization of the marginal

Table 6.2 *Marginal external costs in the urban and non-urban reference equilibrium (2005)*

ECU/passenger km	Congestion	Air pollution	Accidents	Noise	Total external cost	Reference tax
Urban transport						
Peak small gasoline car	1.387	0.024	0.100	0.001	1.512	0.077
Peak small diesel car	1.387	0.022	0.100	0.001	1.510	0.058
Off-peak small gasoline car	0.004	0.021	0.161	0.006	0.192	0.073
Peak bus and tram	0.069	0.014	0.020	0.000	0.103	0.040
Off-peak bus and tram	0.001	0.055	0.082	0.006	0.144	-0.151
Peak subway	0.000	0.017	0.000	0.000	0.017	0.056
Off-peak subway	0.000	0.076	0.001	0.000	0.077	-0.094
Non-urban transport						
Peak small gasoline car	0.781	0.007	0.046	0.000	0.834	0.073
Peak small diesel car	0.781	0.015	0.046	0.000	0.842	0.054
Off-peak small gasoline car	0.008	0.008	0.046	0.000	0.062	0.076
Peak bus	0.042	0.008	0.002	0.000	0.052	-0.012
Off-peak bus	0.001	0.013	0.003	0.000	0.017	0.003
Peak train	0.000	0.005	0.000	0.000	0.005	-0.060
Off-peak train	0.000	0.011	0.000	0.000	0.011	-0.008
ECU/ton km						
Waterways	0.000	0.009	0.000	0.000	0.009	0.0035
Railways	0.000	0.007	0.000	0.000	0.007	0.000
Peak truck	0.138	0.021	0.004	0.001	0.164	0.0077
Off-peak truck	0.001	0.015	0.004	0.001	0.021	0.002

external air pollution and accident costs because they are not too different for the different transport markets considered. When it comes to the internalization of the congestion externalities, the motor fuel tax appears as a very inefficient instrument for two reasons. First is the variation in the congestion costs: they differ strongly between urban and non-urban areas and between peak and off-peak periods. This holds for freight as well as for passenger transport. Any attempt to internalize the external congestion costs in the peak period in the urban areas will always generate large inefficiencies by discouraging too much off-peak traffic. This problem also holds internationally. Too large an international differentiation of motor fuel taxes generates fuelling abroad, which is a pure loss of resources for society (like any tax evasion). Second, is that the size of the externalities is so large that a sharp increase in motor fuel taxes is required, and as a consequence important fuel efficiency efforts are launched. We have seen in the previous section that the fuel efficiency efforts are in this context a waste of resources.

6.3.3   The Welfare Effects of a Motor Fuel Tax Policy Compared with other Pricing Policies

The merits of an increased motor fuel tax have to be compared with those of traditional instruments like car standards and public transportation pricing, and also to new instruments like a kilometre charge and electronic road pricing. We will make this comparison separately for urban and for non-urban transport problems. In this comparison we use two benchmarks. As a starting point we take the base case in 2005 that excludes all policy changes. The second benchmark is called the full optimum in which all perfect pricing instruments and environmental standards for cars can be used to optimize welfare without any implementation costs. The potential welfare gain that can be obtained in this optimum is set equal to 100 per cent. All other policy instruments are compared to this benchmark.

In an urban environment like Brussels[5] one could envisage many combinations of instruments. What we choose to do is, starting from the base case, optimize each time the use of one instrument that is added to the existing tax and regulation structure. Moreover we did not take into account any implementation cost of the new policy measures that are analysed. Table 6.3 summarizes the relative merits of the different individual instruments.

The environmental standards for cars are capable of improving strongly the air pollution externalities. Here they included the imposition of a preheated catalyst for gasoline cars and a particulate filter for diesel cars. The overall contribution of this type of policy instrument is limited because it only addresses the air pollution externalities.

Table 6.3   Relative merits of alternative policy instruments in an urban environment (Brussels 2005)

Policy measure	Relative welfare–efficiency (%)
base case	0
environmental standards for cars	11
public transport pricing	12
motor fuel taxes	< 30
kilometre tax	43
cordon pricing commuters	48
perfect pricing (benchmark)	100

The use of public transport pricing is another favourite policy instrument that is already used intensively in many urban areas. The public transport measure proposed here is to reduce further the prices of public transport in the peak period and to increase the prices in the off-peak period. Indeed, in Table 6.1 we see that in the off-peak period, the subsidies for public transport per passenger kilometre are the highest, but so are the marginal external costs. Combine this with the relatively low discrepancy between taxes and marginal external costs for cars in the off-peak period and this explains why it can make sense to increase public transport prices in the off-peak period. The possibilities to achieve large welfare gains with this instrument are limited because peak public transport was already subsidized in the base case and because the market share of public transport is limited (26 per cent in the base case).

Increased motor fuel taxes are capable of closing the gap between external costs and consumer prices. They can only do this imperfectly (no differentiation over peak and off-peak period) and the measure will generate an unintended effort to improve the fuel efficiency of cars. The figure advanced in Table 6.3 is to be considered as a maximum, as the motor fuel tax can not be differentiated between urban and non-urban areas while it has been assumed in this exercise that it can.

A tax per kilometre has comparable effects to a fuel tax but does not have the two drawbacks of a fuel tax. It does not incite people to switch to more fuel-efficient cars and it can be differentiated between urban and non-urban areas.[6] Its overall efficiency is limited as there is no differentiation in function between the peak and off-peak periods.

A cordon pricing system is the most effective of the individual policy measures considered. It consists of a specific charge for all commuters entering the urban area in the peak period. Its main strength is that it addresses specifically the congestion problem, which was shown to be the major source of external effects. Its main weakness is that only commuter traffic is priced and not the traffic that originates and ends within the city borders. Actually, compared to the base case, the traffic of inhabitants will increase when cordon pricing is used because speed has gone up and generalized prices have been reduced for them. Much higher welfare gains (approximately 80 per cent) can be achieved if more sophisticated forms of road pricing (several cordons in the city centre, and so on) can be implemented. However, no account has been taken of the implementation costs of electronic road pricing. The costs of simple cordon pricing in Brussels could be up to 40 per cent of the gross benefits. This means that simple cordon pricing could still achieve 30 per cent of the maximum welfare gains.

For non-urban transport a similar analysis has been made. The main difference is that now freight transport also has to be taken into account. Table 6.4 illustrates the effects of some individual policy measures that can be added to the base case equilibrium. We see that the effects of environmental standards are limited because environmental externalities are a less important part of the problem in non-urban transport. The scope for improving the pricing of public transport is limited for freight (rail and inland waterways) as well as for passengers. Improved pricing here means raising prices in the off-peak period. Motor fuel tax increases can have some effects. The overall efficiency will be limited due to inefficient fuel efficiency responses and due to tax competition problems with neighbouring countries. Certainly for small countries (like Luxemburg), it might be in their interest not to try to internalize their externalities but to try to extract as much revenue as possible from transit traffic.

Table 6.4   Relative merits of alternative policy instruments for non-urban transport (Belgium 2005)

Policy measure	Relative welfare–efficiency (%)
base case	0
environmental standards for cars	2
public transport pricing	1
motor fuel taxes	< 20
perfect pricing (benchmark)	100

It is clear that only road pricing is able to address specifically the problems of congestion and the problems of charging transit freight traffic for the different externalities it generates. The most sophisticated systems could possibly achieve 80 per cent of the maximal gross benefits, but implementation costs linked to such systems are important, so that the best system might only be able to achieve 50 per cent of the maximal gross benefits.

CONCLUSION

In this chapter we have examined the merits of a switch from ownership type of taxes to motor fuel taxes. We have first examined the potential effects of a budget neutral shift between the two types of taxes. Empirical evidence seems to demonstrate that the net effect on the volume of car use could be negative but small. The main driver of car use will be the average tax level rather than only the variable cost. An effect of higher motor fuel taxes that can not be overlooked is the incentive to switch to more expensive but more fuel-efficient cars. This will happen if the increase of taxes is sufficient to increase the real price of motor fuel beyond the historical maximum.

The welfare effects of a substitution of ownership taxes by motor fuel taxes are likely to be negative. The volume of car use will not change very much. The major welfare cost will be the inefficient effort of car manufacturers and consumers to improve the fuel efficiency of cars. This is a welfare loss because resources are used to save mainly fuel taxes as these constitute already 75 per cent of the pump price in most EU countries.

Some welfare gains can be achieved by increasing the net tax on car use via increased fuel taxes. Welfare gains can be achieved because the present tax levels on automobile use are below the marginal social costs. They will be limited however, because motor fuel taxes can not discriminate between urban and non-urban traffic and can not differentiate between peak and off-peak periods. Moreover they can lead to undesired side effects, like fuel efficiency investments and international tax competition. This conclusion holds certainly for Europe where motor fuel taxes are already very high.

There are more promising instruments to correct the present inefficiencies on the transport markets. Public transport and the environmental regulation of cars have a reduced potential because they have already been used intensively in the past and because they can only address the congestion problems indirectly. The correction of the congestion externalities is the first priority and only the implementation of road pricing can do this efficiently.

ACKNOWLEDGEMENTS

We acknowledge the support of the EU Transport RTD Programme (TEREN-II-STRAN Consortium). Stef Proost has been supported by the Fund for Scientific Research, Flanders.

NOTES

1. These are results for Belgium. The Belgian tax structure can be taken as representative for the tax structure in the other EU countries except Denmark that has much higher ownership and purchase taxes. In the US and Canada, the tax structure on automobile use is characterized by much lower motor fuel taxes so that our empirical results cannot be transplanted.
2. The US case is different because the motor fuel prices and the type of cars are different. Moreover the fuel efficiency of cars has been regulated in the US but not in Europe.
3. The TRENEN-I model has been developed by a consortium consisting of CES-KULeuven, SESO-UFSIA, VIA-Aachen, TCDublin and GRETA-Venice that has been financed by the JOULE-II research program of the EC-DGXII.
4. The condition for obtaining a double dividend is that the net tax wedge on labour decreases. This is only possible if part of the increased transport tax is shifted to non-labour income or to the rest of the world (Bovenberg and Van der Ploeg, 1994).
5. Brussels has 1 million inhabitants and 0.6 million commuters using the transport system. It has congestion problems, but it is certainly not the worst case in Europe.
6. This only holds if an electronic version is used that can be switched on and off when certain cordons are passed.

REFERENCES

Bovenberg, L. and F. Van der Ploeg (1994), 'Environmental policy, public finance and the labour market in a Second-Best world', *Journal of Public Economics*, **55**, 349–90.

De Borger, L. and B. De Borger (1988), 'Energieverbruik in het personenvervoer: recente evolutie en enkele prognoses' (Energy consumption in passenger transport: recent developments and some forecasts), SESO working paper, 109.

De Borger, B., S. Ochelen, S. Proost and D. Swysen (1997), 'Alternative transport pricing and regulation policies: a welfare analysis for Belgium in 2005', *Transportation Research D*, **2** (3), 177–98.

De Jong, G.C. (1990), 'An indirect utility model of car ownership and private car use', *European Economic Review*, **34**, 971–85.

Kageson, P. (1993), *Getting the Prices Right. A European scheme for making transport pay its true costs*, Brussels: European Federation for Transport and the Environment.

Khazzoom, J.D. (1994), 'An econometric model of fuel economy and single-vehicle highway fatalities', in series *Advances in the Economics of Energy and Resources*, Greenwich, CT: JAI Press Inc., 184pp.

Mayeres, I., S. Ochelen and S. Proost (1996), 'The marginal external costs of car use revisited', *Transportation Research D*, **1** (2), 111–30.

Proost, S. (1997), *Economic evaluation of community options to limit CO_2, SO_2 and No_x emissions at the horizon 2005 and 2010 – transport sector*, Study for the European Commission, 27pp.

Van Dender, K. (1996), 'A dynamic partial equilibrium model for passenger car transport', Msc. Paper, Economics department, KULeuven.

Walker, I.O. and F. Wirl (1993), 'Irreversible price induced efficiency improvements: theory and empirical application to road transportation', *The Energy Journal*, **14** (4), 183–205.

7. What is the scope for environmental road pricing?

Olof Johansson-Stenman and Thomas Sterner

7.1 INTRODUCTION

The European political interest in using pricing within the transport sector more efficiently appears to be increasing as witnessed by the European Commission's (1995) Green Paper entitled 'Towards fair and efficient pricing in transport'.

Road pricing is a notion which still, more than 30 years after the seminal papers by Walters (1961) and Vickrey (1963), is used primarily in relation to congestion problems; see Morrison (1986), Hau (1992), Lewis (1993) and Johansson and Mattsson (1995) for surveys. However, the interest in pricing traffic efficiently is now spreading to other areas such as health effects, regional environmental effects, global warming, noise, barrier effects, road damage and accidents; see De Borger *et al.* (1996), Kågeson (1993), Maddison *et al.* (1996), Mayeres (1993), Newbery (1990), Rothengatter (1994) and Verhoef (1994). The main reason for this, aside from a general increase in environmental awareness, is presumably the fact that modern information technology has made various road pricing systems more realistic, at least in the near future.

This paper will focus on the environmental aspects of road pricing. Air pollution from cars consists of many different chemical substances with very different consequences for human beings as well as for the environment in general. The problems arising from pollution may roughly be divided into three sub-categories; global, regional and local problems. Emissions of CO_2 (carbon dioxide) fit in the first category, since it does not matter where and when the emissions occur. Furthermore, since CO_2 emissions are (almost) proportional to fossil fuel use, a fuel tax will deal with this problem in an economically efficient way. Consequently, the global warming problem is hardly an argument for road pricing, even though it is doubtless one of the most serious problems facing the road transport sector today.

Acidification is a typical example of a regional environmental problem. The effects (and thus the costs) differ somewhat with respect to where the emissions occur since both the current pollution pressure and the sensitivity of the ecosystems, soil and underlying rock vary quite dramatically. It is, however, not likely that the effects vary much with respect to the timing of the emission, even though problems related to tropospheric ozone are higher during the summer period.

Local environmental problems, such as health effects, vary with respect to both the time and the location of the emission. The environmental costs depend on the number of persons affected and are therefore, naturally, much larger in a city center (with a high population density) at rush hours on a day with severe inversion problems, than they are far out in the countryside at the same time. As we will show, the relevant exhausts may easily vary by a factor of 100 between different vehicles, and the sensitivity of the environment may vary even more! Multiplying these factors implies that the external local environmental cost of one kilometer driven by a car with poor exhaust characteristics in inner city rush hours may be several orders of magnitude larger than the external cost of a kilometer in the countryside driven by a relatively clean vehicle.

Furthermore, there are a number of other inherent differences between different vehicle-related externalities concerning, for instance, the character-istics of the control technology: for some problems cheap and rapid progress may be expected as a result of research, technical progress or scale, whereas other problems may not be so amenable to easy solution. The different characteristics of these problems suggest that different policy instruments and methods of quantifying the environmental costs might be advisable. Economic instruments which equate the marginal costs of abatement have an advantage over simple regulations with respect to allocative efficiency, and this advantage becomes all the more important the more these marginal costs differ between polluters. This is one fundamental reason why road pricing is particularly relevant for local environmental problems. But these allocative efficiency gains will then have to be compared to the increased investment and operational costs of the system, which will be discussed at a fundamental level at some length in this chapter.

7.2 THE NATURE OF THE DAMAGE FUNCTION AND THE FIRST-BEST SOLUTION

In a first-best world, it is well known from economic theory that an optimal externality correcting charge is equal to the short-run marginal external cost, that is, a Pigovian charge (or tax). The consequences, if strictly applied to the road transport sector, are perhaps not equally well known.

In order to assess the damage function related to air pollution from road transport, the first step is to measure the quantity and composition of vehicle

exhausts. This is by no means a trivial task and the values differ dramatically
with respect to type and age of vehicle, control equipment, traffic conditions,
driving behavior and the current weather situation. There exist a relatively
large number of studies on emission factors for cars, based on 'real' vehicle
fleets under different circumstances, which illustrate this; see for example,
Hassel and Weber (1993), Krawack (1993), Metz (1993), and Michaelis
(1993). So, ideally, the road charge should be differentiated with respect to
all of these variables. For example, it should be more expensive to drive an
old car with poor emission control equipment at peak hours. Similarly certain
aggressive driving styles might be discouraged by higher tariffs and even the
first kilometer of a trip should be more expensive, particularly if it is cold
outside, since the emissions are much larger before the engine and the catalytic converter have had time to warm up, as illustrated in Table 7.1. Thus the
first kilometer driven (especially in cold climate) typically accounts for a
dominating share of total VOC (volatile organic compounds) and CO (carbon
monoxide) emissions even for a fairly long trip![1] Furthermore, the environmental cost, and hence the optimal charge, would also vary with respect to
the population density in the neighborhood and the geographical and various
climatological conditions. Ideally, it should then be much more expensive to
drive outside a hospital in the city center during periods of thermic inversion,
than somewhere in the countryside on an ordinary day.

Table 7.1   *Emission factors in g/km at a highway driving cycle for a car
with a catalytic converter at different outside temperatures for
the first and second km driven, and for a warm engine,
respectively*

Temperature °C	First km driven VOC g/km	CO g/km	Second km driven VOC g/km	CO g/km	Warm engine VOC g/km	CO g/km
22	2.6	21.0	0.07	0.16	0.02	0.12
–7	15.7	123.1	1.38	11.0	0.25	0.80

Source: Laurikko *et al.* (1995).

The local and regional damage function can easily vary by a factor of 10–
100 for different vehicles and a factor of 10 for geographical location. In
addition we should remind the reader of the variations with respect to the
current wind situation (maybe a factor of at least three according to Leksell
and Löfgren, 1995), driving behavior (Rouwendal, 1996), and fuel (quality as

well as chemical composition, including the use of 'reformulated' fuels, alcohols or ethers, and so on) which might have a substantial effect.

These findings clearly show a potential role for strongly differentiated road charges. On the one hand there are a number of ways in which we could achieve considerable reductions in vehicle emissions. On the other hand the environmental effect of these reductions also varies strongly. Thus the cost of uniform environmental improvements such as requiring ultra-clean cars and very clean fuels all over the board may seem to be very large, compared to the rather limited environmental benefit in rural areas, for example. In an environment of rapid technological progress, and great diversity in perform-ance, there appear to be considerable gains from a policy instrument which would guide the environmentally best vehicles to the most sensitive areas, such as the city centers, but still allow cheaper (older and less environmen-tally sophisticated) vehicles to be used in less sensitive areas.

As long as we stay in the frictionless world of first-best, we can assume that there are no costs to the collection and processing of information. For example, we implicitly assume that the charges would without any costs be instantaneously visible to the driver through some kind of display system in the car (for example similar to a fare meter in a taxi).

In order to obtain a first-best solution we need of course also to differenti-ate the charge perfectly with respect to the variables which determine all the other external costs, such as congestion, noise, external accident costs, barrier effects, road wear and tear, and dirtying.

7.3   SECOND-BEST SOLUTION

It should be clear then that, in reality, we cannot obtain this ideal first-best solution and the corresponding social benefits. Or, rather, it would be too expensive to obtain all of these potential benefits since the system investment and operation costs (which we have so far neglected) would go to infinity when the level of sophistication goes to infinity (which would be necessary to make use of all of the potential allocative efficiency gains). Note that the system costs as defined here include the cost to the driver of processing all the information he would be receiving, and calculating the consequences of alternative traffic decisions. Hence, we have to rely on a second-best solution, which will then be a trade-off between allocative efficiency gains and system investment and operation costs.[2] This is illustrated in Figure 7.1 where the allocative efficiency gains of various road pricing systems are plotted against the investment and operation system costs. It is implicitly assumed that, for a given system cost, the system with the largest social net benefit is chosen. The optimal system cost (C*) will then be a measure of the optimal level of

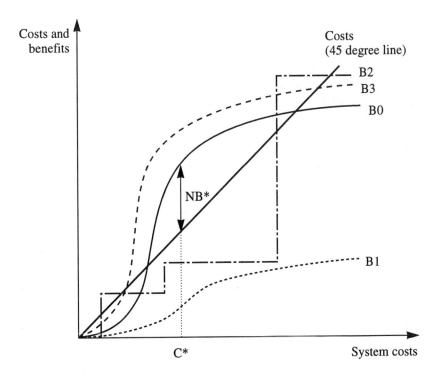

*Figure 7.1   The trade-off between allocative efficiency gains and system
costs for road pricing systems of different levels of sophistication*

system sophistication. C^* is found as the system cost where the net benefit,
that is, the allocative efficiency gains B_0 minus the investment and operation
system costs (drawn as a 45 degree line), is maximized and equal to NB^*.

However, it should be noted that it is not obvious that we will have a
unique interior solution. First, we may have a lower corner solution, that is, it
may be optimal not to have road pricing at all. This is illustrated by the lower
dotted benefit curve B_1, and in this case it is clear that the optimal solution is
found at the origin. In fact, currently this is most likely the case for most
villages and smaller cities. Second, we may have discontinuities and multiple
local optima. Consider an example where we have three major technical
options, according to the benefit curve B_2. The simplest is an area pricing
system with very low system cost, but also relatively small allocative efficiency gains. Then there is an intermediate system consisting of semi-
automatic road tolls in a ring around the town. The most advanced system is a
satellite-based GPS (Global Positional System) where the charges may be
distance-related and varied between different zones in the city.[3] This system

is the most expensive but provides the largest allocative efficiency gains. It might then be the case that both the simplest and the most advanced systems are superior to the intermediate one. Actually, we think that this example provides more than an academic curiosity, and that the most promising options are often between advanced high-tech solutions with a large potential steering impact, and very simple and cheap systems.

In reality, of course, there exist many alternatives within this broad system characterization. For example, the differentiation by environmental characteristics within the advanced system could be done in a more or less sophisticated manner. The simplest system would be a number of environmental classes to which a vehicle could belong. This might be determined once and for all, or revised at yearly inspection and maintenance check ups. The most advanced option would be based on on-board real-time monitoring of actual exhausts.[4]

It should generally be clear that if a road pricing system with non-negligible investment and operational costs is to be socially profitable we must have substantial steering impact from the system on the magnitude and composition of road traffic. If, as is sometimes proposed, a system is designed in order to raise revenues without affecting the traffic at all, we will definitely end up with a socioeconomic deficit from that system equal to the system investment and operation costs.[5]

The above analysis is already complex, but the governmental decision is even more complicated. All of the costs and benefits in the analysis are highly uncertain and are quite likely to change rapidly. Further, the costs of future more advanced systems are also unknown. Still, a decision has to be taken regarding when to introduce a road pricing system, what technical solution to choose and for what geographical scope (for example, only in city centers, more regional or even national systems), how to calculate the appropriate charges, and how to make the system publicly acceptable.

The uncertainty *per se* is an important factor for these choices, that is, the uncertainty should not only affect the outcome of the system, but also what system to choose. The major difference from optimizing a deterministic system, where all variables are assumed to be known with certainty, is that there is a type of 'quasi-option value' which may be a very important component when dealing with uncertainty. In particular, it seems important to choose a flexible system, so that the benefit will be relatively stable over a large range of outcomes, and the costs should not increase rapidly due to possible surprises. One consequence, in practice, is that one may be skeptical to invest in systems with large and expensive ground-based infrastructure in terms of toll-stations and so on, if one thinks that such systems may soon be outcompeted by technically more advanced systems with less fixed infrastructure. This is one reason why we indicated that the main options may be between very simple and rather advanced systems, and that it may be less wise to focus on the intermediate systems (which tend to be the ones most often discussed).

This also illustrates the fact that it is indeed likely that the curves in Figure 7.1 will change over time (for example to the benefit curve B_3) due to technical progress. Since the development of information technology in general, and ITS (Intelligent Traffic Systems) in particular, is very rapid, it seems likely that this trade-off will go in the direction of more sophisticated systems over time. It is now possible to use much more advanced features than it was only ten years ago and it will most likely be possible to use even more advanced equipment in the future. This will be discussed further in Section 7.6.

7.4 VALUING THE ROAD TRANSPORT EMISSIONS

In order to be able to discuss the likely allocative gains from environmental road pricing in relation to their cost, it is necessary to have some idea of the magnitude of the environmental external costs at stake. We have already emphasized how complicated and variable these costs are, but nonetheless it is necessary to have some approximate idea of the orders of magnitude involved. In this section we will calculate approximate environmental costs differentiated by some of the most important variables. This includes different vehicle types and vintages as well as a geographical differentiation. We will not be attempting to quantify the effects of different fuels, weather, driving behavior or a number of other albeit important but secondary variables. Nor will we look at actual performance from individual vehicles, but rather at some representative average figures. Since road pricing systems are designed to work for a relatively long time period, it is clearly important to also consider the expected emissions in the future. For this reason, we will present the environmental cost per km for vehicles of different vintages.

The estimated environmental costs from road transport are based on the officially used values for transport infrastructure investments in Sweden (SIKA, 1995), which are largely based on the calculations by Leksell and Löfgren (1995). These calculations, in turn, made strong use of the survey-based studies by Sælendsminde and Hammer (1994) and Wiedlert (1993). On the basis of the willingness to pay figure from Sælendsminde and Hammer (1994), Leksell and Löfgren calculate the economic valuation of the *inhaled* dose as 4 SEK/mg NO_x, 4 SEK/mg VOC and 40 SEK/mg particles (the contributions by CO and SO_2 were considered small and dropped). The average health cost in Göteborg would then be 48 SEK/kg NO_x equivalent. The reader should bear in mind that Göteborg is a fairly small city of half a million inhabitants; the corresponding costs for larger and more densely populated cities would presumably be much higher. The valuations used in our calculations can be summarized as shown in Table 7.2.[6] The differentiation between the average values for cities and the city center is based on Leksell and Löfgren (1995) and Leksell (1996, personal communication). The health cost from particulate matters in the countryside arises from calculations of carcinogenic effects through food production.

By way of comparison we use Bell (1994) who analyses the environmental valuations used by different public institutions in the USA (Table 7.3). The values are based on total environmental costs including health effects. However, they are calculated based on rather varying conditions, for example, with regard to population density and climatological conditions. There are also some European studies such as Bleijenberg *et al.* (1994) who calculate

Table 7.2   Environmental values used in this study

	Regional environmental effects SEK/kg	Health effects, SEK/kg		
		Countryside	City, average	City center
VOC	17	0	49	245
NO$_x$	40	0	49	245
Particulate matters	0	180	904	4520

Note: Exchange rate: 7.8 SEK/USD, April, 1998.

Source: SIKA (1995) and Leksell (1996).

Table 7.3   Environmental values used by 37 government, utility and research agencies in the USA

	CO$_2$ Cent/kg	VOC USD/kg	NO$_x$ USD/kg
Minimum	0.2	0.34	0.04
Maximum	8.4	21.2	40
Average	2.5	6.0	8.2
Median	2.0	3.3	4.2

Note: Bell uses 1990 USD.

Source: Bell (1994).

external environmental costs in Holland rather close to the average in Table 7.3 except for CO_2 which is higher. Mayeres *et al.* (1996) calculate urban external costs from road transport in Belgium and arrive again at similar values for VOC but somewhat higher for NO_x. They also give values for PM which correspond fairly well to the city average figures used in Sweden. As illustrated, there are some studies with lower and higher environmental costs estimates than the ones used by the authorities in Sweden. Still, the order of magnitude seems to be comparable in many studies.

The environmental cost per km driven, which we are interested in, is then simply found by multiplying the emission factors by the environmental values which are differentiated for different geographical locations. The emission factors used here are based on Ahlvik *et al.* (1996). This study is rather unique for several reasons. First, the average numbers are corrected for cold-starts, climate, driving cycle and deterioration of emission-reduction systems over time. Second, they attempt to quantify future emission factors based on existing decisions on future emission factors within the European Union, on foreseeable technical improvements, and on expected improved fuel quality. In addition, they present comparable figures for alternative fuels which will not be discussed further here. However, it should be stressed that these future numbers are not a forecast of the future. Instead they are 'an assessment of what will be technologically and economically possible with regard to existing propositions of future emission standards' (Ahlvik *et al.*, 1996, p. 1). Even though the meaning of this is not perfectly clear (since 'economically possible' is not precisely defined), this assessment is still very interesting. The technological change will be discussed further in Section 7.6.

In Table 7.4 below, we calculate the environmental costs separately for city centers, average urban areas and the countryside, based on Ahlvik *et al.* (1996) by implicitly assuming that the emission factors per km are equal in the countryside and in the city centers. This, however, is not quite correct, and in reality the emission factors are larger for urban transport; see for example, Hassel and Weber (1993). For this reason, the ratio between the environmental costs in urban areas and in the countryside will be even larger than shown in Table 7.4. The emission figures show what may reasonably be expected of new vehicles in each respective class and vintage. However, there is obviously no mechanism to ensure that this technical progress actually occurs. Whether or not it will occur depends both on the preferences of the buyers, the price of cleaner technology and, most relevantly here, the policy instruments used. Within vintages there is normally quite a difference between different vehicles, and in the actual vehicle stock at any one moment in time there are many different vintages, so that the overall difference in emission characteristics (and thus environmental cost) is therefore much

Table 7.4   Estimated emission factors and environmental costs for different vehicles over time

Vintage	Estimated average emissions			Local and regional environmental costs		
	VOC g/km	NO$_x$ g/km	Pm mg/km	Countryside SEK/1000km	City, average SEK/1000km	City center SEK/1000km
Passenger cars, gasoline						
1988	2.50	1.53	37	115	346	1270
1993	1.19	0.50	18	45	144	540
1996	0.89	0.26	13	29	97	369
2000	0.46	0.17	7	16	54	202
2005	0.20	0.08	3	7	24	90
2010	0.08	0.04	1.2	3	10	38
Passenger cars, diesel						
1988	0.67	1.14	451	142	638	2624
1993	0.13	0.68	89	47	168	648
1996	0.13	0.63	56	39	127	479
2000	0.07	0.35	33	22	73	274
2005	0.04	0.25	22	15	49	186
2010	0.02	0.04	16	5	22	92
Heavy trucks, diesel						
1988	1.25	16.6	580	689	1824	6365
1993	0.33	13.0	340	527	1330	4542
1996	0.37	11.5	300	467	1181	4036
2000	0.28	8.2	200	334	837	2849
2005	0.21	5.8	150	236	597	2039
2010	0.15	4.1	100	167	419	1427
Buses, diesel						
1988	1.30	13.2	500	528	1402	4896
1993	0.76	10.0	210	415	1032	3502
1996	0.72	9.7	200	402	999	3383
2000	0.40	7.3	150	300	742	2508
2005	0.30	4.9	100	202	500	1690
2010	0.15	3.2	70	131	325	1103

Note: Exchange rate: 7.8 SEK/USD, April, 1998.

Sources: Emission factors, Ahlvik *et al.* (1996); environmental costs are calculated, assumptions in text.

greater than shown in Table 7.4, probably of the order of at least 100:1, maybe even 1000:1 for the worst 'offenders'.

Going back to the data in Table 7.4 for cars of different vintages, it is interesting to compare the average environmental costs in the countryside and the corresponding costs in the city center. There is a stable pattern over the entire period showing that the values in the city are about three times higher than in the countryside and in the center they are still higher, again by a factor of 3 or 4. The difference in health-related external costs is of course still very much larger since there are virtually none in the rural areas. As can be seen from Table 7.2, our figures do, however, imply a relatively high regional environmental cost, particularly for NO_x. This may be a reflection of the relative seriousness of acidification (and eutrophication) in Sweden. In regions where this problem is smaller and where cities are larger and more densely populated, the differences between rural and urban (center) values would (for this reason too) be even greater than in Table 7.4.

However, as can also be seen from these calculations, the future emissions may be very much lower than the present ones, which should imply a corresponding decrease in environmental costs. The decrease is particularly dramatic for passenger cars, which according to these figures will reduce their environmental costs to only a few per cent for vintage 2010 compared to the 1988 vintage. So, even though the relation between the urban environmental costs and the ones in the countryside remains rather stable over time, the *absolute* level of these costs seems to decrease rather drastically. This would strongly reduce the comparative advantage of any advanced road pricing system with regard to environmental benefits.

Johansson (1997a) shows that also indirect emission effects, due to the fact that emissions per kilometer driven will typically increase due to congestion, should be included in the optimal traffic charge. Furthermore, it was demonstrated that these indirect effects may, under some circumstances, be very important. However, the importance of these effects will also decrease when the overall emissions decrease.

7.5   FUTURE ENVIRONMENTAL VALUATIONS

It should, however, be emphasized that the above calculations were built on the implicit assumptions that the environmental valuations per emission unit will be constant over time. But this is hardly likely. Although the future is very uncertain it seems more likely that we will value the environment more highly in the future due to various facts, including in particular increasing income, but there may also be contradicting factors. A positive income elasticity is typically found in empirical studies of environmental valuation, but it is not equally clear that this income elasticity is larger than one; that is, that the income *share* of environmental valuations increases with income. This is often seen as an indication of whether or not environmental goods are luxury goods. The conventional view seems to be that environmental goods are luxury goods, for instance since poor people need to focus on more basic consumption. The so-called environmental Kuznetz curve, that is, that environmental quality seems to increase with national income after a certain income level, is sometimes seen as an indication of this fact. McFadden and Leonard (1993) argued for instance that 'environmental goods should be a "luxury good"' (p. 22). On the contrary, Kriström and Riera (1996) argue, based on many empirical studies, that the income elasticity for environmental goods most often seems to be lower than one.

Assuming an average growth rate of 1.5 per cent/year between 1988 and 2010 implies a total growth by 39 per cent. An income elasticity equal to one would then imply a corresponding increase in environmental valuations, whereas an income elasticity of 0.5, 2 and 5, would imply an increase in environmental valuations by 18, 92, and 414 per cent, respectively.[7] Still, these increases would not suffice to outweigh (but only partially diminish the effect of) the emission reduction for passenger cars.

But there are also other things which will change in the future. Our knowledge will increase. This effect may go in either direction for various pollutants, that is, we may find that some emissions turned out not to be as harmful as expected, whereas other emissions turned out to be more harmful than previously believed. Perhaps the second alternative is more likely due to the possibility of finding that 'new' substances, that is, substances not previously studied, are harmful. A further complication in this context is that individual sensitivity to various toxic substances is likely to be very high and may increase (namely the apparent increase in asthma). This naturally creates large individual differences in valuation. A contradictory effect may occur from the fact that the marginal damage costs may be increasing in pollution levels, which would imply that the valuations per emission unit would decrease as the air quality improves.

It may also be that the individual valuations need not be reflected in political valuations, for example because of so-called 'political failures'. Furthermore, it is possible that individuals may have some special 'public preferences' which makes it very difficult to aggregate individual private preferences. These public preferences can for example be based on deontological or right-based ethics, as opposed to a teleological utilitarianism, see for example Howarth (1995).

7.6 TECHNICAL CHANGE IN ITS AND ROAD-PRICING SYSTEMS

So, it may not seem reasonable that environmental effects *per se* justifies an advanced road-pricing system. However, some external costs, notably congestion costs, are very difficult to deal with effectively without using road charges. In a situation where time-differentiated road pricing is to be implemented anyway, it is not obvious that the *additional* system costs need to be very high for differentiating the charges with respect to important emission characteristics and other variables important for the environment.

It may be illustrative to consider the similarity with other technically advanced goods, where the development cost constitutes the dominating cost share and where the production costs are very limited. The additional cost of a CD player in a computer is today almost negligible, but was very expensive only a few years ago. The same applies to the processors, memories and other parts of a computer. Even though there exist a very large number of PC components with varying capacity, it is today almost impossible to find a new PC with a slower processor than a Pentium type. Still, only five years ago such fast processors did not exist. The price versus technical characteristics for knowledge-intensive products (that is, for goods where research and development costs constitute a large fraction of the price of the good) is illustrated in Figure 7.2.

The development of ITS seems similar, although the scale is of course much lower. Even if it is costly today to differentiate the charges with respect to environmental characteristics, weather situation, traffic situation, and so

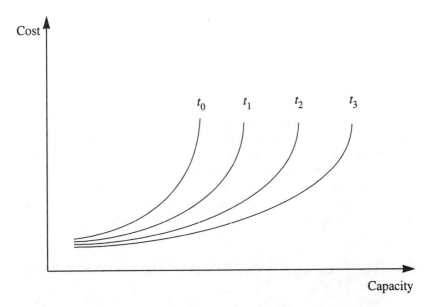

Figure 7.2   Typical development of the cost (or price) of a knowledge-intensive product with different capacity over time ($t_3 > t_2 > t_1 > t_0$)

on, it need not be so in the future. For this reason, it seems likely that we will see more sophisticated systems over time. We will thus have a situation in which both the benefits and costs in Figure 7.1 are falling rapidly and it is far from easy to judge the net consequences for an overall optimization.

7.7 ROAD-PRICING VERSUS CONVENTIONAL POLICY INSTRUMENTS

At present we observe a wide-varying mix of policy instruments applied to the regulation of transport emissions. While we certainly do believe in the potential for both simple and advanced road-pricing schemes in the future, it is also clear that this does not mean that they should necessarily replace all the other policy instruments such as regulations and fuel taxes currently used.

One example where the system costs of upgrading the sophistication of road pricing probably exceed benefits is the problem already mentioned of cold-starts. Obviously the system needs to be quite complicated in order to differentiate between the first kilometer when the car motor and catalytic converter are cold and emissions very high. This could be done by on-board monitoring, but it would probably be very costly. It is likely that technological fixes such as the more widespread use of electric pre-heating of the motor (and/or converter) can deal with this problem separately. There are presumably simple administrative ways of encouraging and mandating such solutions that are cheaper than building them into a road-pricing model.[8]

Another example is the global warming issue where environmental damage does not depend on when and where you drive but does depend on the original source of your fuel. Obviously, onboard systems for road pricing will have to be extremely sophisticated to differentiate between fossil methanol and bio-methanol, so a simple tax on the *fossil* carbon content of the fuel is always going to be a superior instrument for this problem.

The most important policy instrument so far, in order to deal with local and regional traffic air-pollution problems, is the set of emission standards. The emission factors in our calculation example above were treated as given. In reality they are of course not; the future emission figures simply represent a single estimate of what is 'technically and economically possible' and there is a trade-off between more expensive cars and cleaner air. A natural question is, then, if it would be a better alternative not to have emission standards and to charge the distance driven optimally instead? Theoretically, in a first-best world with no control and operation costs, and with exogenous technical change, the answer would be yes. This is because with emission standards we would theoretically have non-optimally clean cars in the countryside, and perhaps not sufficiently clean cars in the city-centers and so on. If, on the other hand, one had no emission standards but (first-best) optimal environmental charges (per distance driven), then it would be very much more expensive to drive in the city-center and an optimal mix of vehicles would result. In reality, however, there are several factors which would appear to make it unwise to abandon emission standards. Due to economics of scale in car production, time-dependent production costs, costly monitoring and uncertainties about the actual effects of road pricing, it would seem prudent to combine it with some form of emission standards.

Furthermore, at present one cannot rule out the possibility that local and regional environmental problems from road transport may be solved almost completely through better technology at a modest cost in the perspective of a few decades. It may be useful to think of a comparison with drinking-water supply. The drinking-water quality is in many western countries rather good almost everywhere. Still, the individual willingness to pay for various drinking-water qualities will probably vary rather dramatically, since the sensitivity with regard to different bacteria varies strongly in the human population. In a way, one could argue that this indicates large economic losses, since some people will, from an economic point of view, have unnecessarily good quality, whereas others may have too poor a quality. However, these conclusions are probably not correct when taking control and information costs into account. It is certainly not difficult to imagine the information problems and associated costs with a dramatically varying drinking-water quality, and it seems likely that these costs are often larger than the potential gains in allocative efficiency (from equalizing marginal benefits and marginal costs). This is perhaps a somewhat extreme example, and the road transport sector is probably far from a situation like this at current. Still, the point is that it seems that we are moving in this direction, and it is not clear how close we will finally end up.

7.8   THE FUTURE ROLE OF EMISSION STANDARDS AND ENVIRONMENTAL CLASSES

But even if we will rely heavily on environmental standards in the future too, it is far from straightforward to *design* these standards, even if we disregard problems related to the economic valuation of different substances. The most obvious decision criterion for an economist would be to weight costs and benefits of a standard improvement, and to choose the alternative where the social net benefit, that is, social benefits minus social costs, is maximized; see for example, Crandall *et al.* (1986) or Hahn (1995). Assuming an interior solution and sufficient differentiability, this would occur where the marginal benefit, calculated during the whole lifetime of the car, would equal the marginal cost of the improvement. However, naturally, this is easier in theory than in practice. First, the costs are generally unknown to the authorities, and car manufacturers have generally no incentives to reveal their true (or expected) costs. Second, there may be an important indirect benefit of improvements due to the (at least partly) irreversible technical progress. For this reason, it will be less costly to reach a future norm if some technical progress is made today.

A system based on environmental classes for vehicles is an interesting intermediate option between environmental road pricing, where the charge per kilometer is differentiated with regard to environmental characteristics (and other variables), and the pure command and control strategy based on emission standards. In Sweden such a system has been used since 1992 where annual and sales taxes depend on the emission factors. Currently, there are two different standards for passenger cars, where the strongest standard (environmental class 1) is exempted from annual tax on car ownership for the first five years.

There are several arguments in favor of a system based on environmental classes for vehicles. First, it would constitute incentives for car manufacturers to make cost-efficient improvements beyond the current emission standards. Although this system will theoretically be less efficient (in an allocative sense) than a perfect road-pricing system, or a system based on driving distance rather than on car ownership, it will still provide important incentives at a rather modest administrative cost. It is also probably cost-efficient that some companies are on the technological front regarding emission technology, and some companies are 'followers', which will introduce similar technology a few years later.

Second, it may be part of a second-best strategy due to incomplete and asymmetric information. Since, as mentioned above, the authorities have very limited information concerning the costs of stronger emission standards, environmental classes may be a way of buying important information! If, for example, environmental class 1 vehicles are subsidized by 5000 SEK, relative to the compulsory class 2 standards, and 50 per cent of the cars produced are of class 1, then we may conclude that the additional cost to the manufacturers for producing class 1 cars instead of class 2 currently are less than 5000 SEK/car for about 50 per cent of the vehicles. Furthermore, perhaps the fraction of class 1 vehicles was only 25 per cent last year. Then the authorities can make a reasonably good prediction about the average additional cost next year and so on, and judge whether or not the compulsory standards should be strengthened. Third, such classification can serve as useful information also for road pricing purposes. In addition, it will probably be necessary to have some kind of inspection or control system for the vehicles in different classes, in order for the system to work as intended. If there were two or three classes for new cars and a couple for buses and other heavier vehicles, then there might also be a number of classes for older vehicles of various types. Such a set of vehicle classes could be used for the calibration of tariffs in various intermediate systems such as the setting of differentiated fees for access to urban centers, or differentiated mileage taxes in intra-urban freight traffic.

Fourth, it would provide incentives to 'environmentally aware' consumers, and companies with a 'green' image, to buy more environmentally-friendly vehicles. As is well known, green labeling is today an important selling argument and it is frequently and successfully used in advertisements in many countries. However, 'mainstream economics' has very little to say about these phenomena which are ultimately based on altruistic concern (broadly defined). Recently, however, the interest in economics and altruism has increased considerably; see Zamagni (1995) for a good overview. Still, the policy conclusions regarding how the optimal charge should be adjusted for these altruistic concerns is far from straightforward. Johansson (1997b) shows that the result depends heavily on the nature of the altruistic concern, for example whether there are 'warm-glow' effects present or if the altruistic concern is environment-focused or 'pure'.

It should be noted that the effectiveness of a system based on environmental classes would be very scale-dependent too. The effects both as technology forcing, and as buyer of cost information, would be very limited if implemented only in a single country (such as in Sweden) or region. In addition, the administrative and operational costs would also be much larger per vehicle. So, to work properly it should preferably be implemented in a larger area, such as the European Union or NAFTA.

Currently, it is possible within the European Union to have a system with different environmental classes as long as the standards for the varying classes are equivalent to emission standards already decided for future implementation in the EU. The second argument above is then totally invalid with the present European law. However, as argued, if a system based on environmental classes were to be implemented in the European Union, the information from this system could be a very important input in the process of *deciding* the future emission standards.

With such a system, the role and character of the *compulsory* emission standards would then presumably change. Their importance for pushing technology ahead would diminish and their role might be more of a safe minimum standard applicable to general conditions. The main driving forces for emission-related technology used in vehicles would then be cost reductions within the system of environmental classes, and within the road-pricing system for vehicles driven intensively in the city centers.

7.9 SUMMARY AND DISCUSSION

In this paper, we have discussed the scope for environmental road pricing in the future. Although no conclusive answer is given, we have focused on a number of important factors and trends which individually point in various directions. First, for environmental road pricing to be important, we must have that the environmental costs vary strongly with respect to variables which we may not consider with conventional policy instruments. It was concluded that this criterion is fulfilled for local and regional environmental costs, but not for the global warming problem. Second, the environmental costs must be sufficiently large for the allocative efficiency gains in turn to be sufficiently large to outweigh the investment and operational system costs. This was found to be less clear, at least in the future due to a possible rather dramatic emission reduction. However, it was argued that road pricing is virtually the only policy instrument to deal with congestion in an effective way, and that the *additional* investment and operational cost for including some environmental aspects into the system need not be very large. It was also argued that the additional cost of more technically advanced systems will probably decrease in the future.

Still, it was argued that environmental standards will probably be important in the future too, for several reasons, and that a system based on different environmental classes may be an interesting intermediate option in a world with imperfect and costly information. The purchase tax, the annual tax, and urban road pricing could then be differentiated with respect to these classes.

Another important issue is whether or not it is in itself an advantage or a disadvantage to adopt a new technology (such as advanced road pricing) early. An advantage might be that suppliers may provide a road pricing system to a discounted price, in order to increase their probability of selling systems to other cities too. On the other hand, it is likely that there are substantial economics of scale in the production of these systems, and that these prices therefore are likely to be reduced over time. Furthermore, the risk of adopting a concept which turns out not to be competitive may be substantial. The consequences might be quite dramatic, such as being left with a technically advanced system which does not work, and where the only firm which is capable of modifying it and providing replacement parts is bankrupt. So, even though advanced road-pricing systems clearly have a large long-term potential as such, it may, from a local government perspective, be a more attractive alternative to wait and see. Then, when the technology is developed and demonstrated in practice at a large scale, it is possible to choose a reliable technical solution where much of the likely initial problems are solved. This may be one of the most important reasons, apart from the political feasibility issue, why there are still no 'real' road-pricing systems implemented anywhere in the world.

NOTES

1. The pattern for particulate emissions is likely to be similar. The fuel consumption, and hence CO_2 emissions will also increase the first km when it is cold, but this effect is less dramatic. NO_x (nitrogen oxides) emissions from the *engine* will typically not increase as a result of cold-starts. But since the catalytic converter will not work properly before it is warmed up, the NO_x emissions too will in general increase somewhat; see for example Holman *et al.* (1993),
2. See Verhoef *et al.* (1995) for a derivation of such second-best regulations during various restrictions.
3. It might also be based on modern telephony systems such as the GSM and it might incorporate other features such as weather or congestion signals emitted over radio frequencies or similar technology.
4. Actually, new cars in California are equipped with a simple version of real-time monitoring. However, this equipment is not used for pricing purposes, but for the authorities to check whether or not the car maintenance is taken care of properly for the emission control system to work as intended.
5. Unfortunately, the system design for the proposed systems in Sweden (Stockholm and Göteborg) seems to have been done primarily to raise revenues, and not to correct for negative externalities.
6. The CO_2 emissions are valued at 0.38 SEK/kg CO_2 (irrespective of where the pollution occurs),
7. $GDP_{2010} = GDP_{1988}\ 1.015^{22} = 1.39\ GDP_{1988}$. A constant income elasticity ε implies that the environmental valuation V can be written $V = V_0\ GDP^{\varepsilon}$. The ratio between the environmental valuation 2010 and 1988 is then found as $V_{2010}/\ V_{1988} = (GDP_{2010}/GDP_{1988})^{\varepsilon} = 1.39^{\varepsilon}$.
8. Examples include making the necessary heaters mandatory in cold climates as well as making the necessary electricity available at parking meters and so on. In a somewhat longer time framework, it is possible that such external electric pre-heating will be unnecessary too; due to technical fixes of the vehicle, some technological solutions already exist.

REFERENCES

Ahlvik, P., A. Laveskog, R. Westerholm and K.-E. Egebäck (1996), *Emissionsfaktorer för fordon drivna med biodrivmedel* (Emission factors for bio-fuel vehicles), Motortestcenter (MTC) vid AB Svensk Bilprovning, Stockholms Universitet, samt Tekniska Högskolan i Luleå.

Bell, K. (1994), *Valuing Emissions from Hermiston Generating Project*, Convergence Research, Seattle.

Bleijenberg, A.N., W.J. van den Berg and G. de Wit (1994), *Maatschappelijke Kosten van het Verkeer: Literatuuroverzicht* (Social costs of transport: Literature review), Centrum voor Energiebesparing en Schone Technologie, Delft.

Commission of the European Communities (1995), *Towards fair and efficient pricing in transport – policy options for internalizing the external costs of transport in the European Union*, Green Paper, ISBN 92-77-99209-3, Catalogue no. CB-CO-95774-EN-C.

Crandall, R.W., H.K. Gruenspecht, T.E. Keeler and L.B. Lave (1986), *Regulating the Automobile*, Washington, DC: Brookings.

De Borger, B., I. Mayeres, S. Proost and S. Wouters (1996), 'Optimal pricing of urban transport – a simulation exercise for Belgium', *Journal of Transport Economics and Policy*, **30**, 31–54.

Hahn, R.W. (1995), 'Choosing among fuels and technologies for cleaning up the air', *Journal of Policy Analysis and Management*, **14** (4), 532–54.

Hassel, D. and F.-J. Weber (1993), 'Mean emissions and fuel consumption of vehicles in use with different emission reduction concepts', *The Science of the Total Environment*, **134**, 189–95.

Hau, T. (1992), 'Congestion charging mechanisms for roads', World Bank, Working Paper WPS 1071.

Holman, C., J. Wade and M. Fergusson (1993), *Future Emissions from Cars 1990 to 2025: The importance of the cold start emission penalty*, Godalming, UK: World Wide Fund for Nature.

Howarth, R.B. (1995), 'Sustainability under uncertainty: a deontological approach', *Land Economics*, **71** (4), 417–27.

Johansson, B. and L.-G. Mattsson (eds) (1995), *Road Pricing: Theory, Empirical Assessment and Policy*, Boston: Kluwer Academic Publishers.

Johansson, O. (1997a), 'Optimal road pricing: simultaneous treatment of time losses, increased fuel consumption, and emissions', *Transportation Research*, **2D** (2), 77–87.

Johansson, O. (1997b), 'Optimal Pigouvian taxes with regard to altruism', *Land Economics*, **73** (3), 297–308.

Krawack, S. (1993), 'Traffic management and emissions', *The Science of the Total Environment*, **134**, 305–14.

Kriström, B. and P. Riera (1996), 'Is the income elasticity of environmental improvements less than one?', *Environmental and Resource Economics*, **7**, 45–55.

Kågeson, P. (1993), *Getting the Prices Right. A European Scheme for Making Transport Pay its True Costs*, Transport and Environment 93/6, ISBN 91 558 7721 4.

Laurikko, Juhani, Lennart Erlandsson and Reino Abrahamsson (1995), 'Exhaust Emission in Cold Ambient Conditions; Considerations for a European Test Procedure', SAE-paper, VTT, MTC, SNV.

Leksell, I. (1996), Personal communication, Department of Applied Environmental Science, Göteburg University.

Leksell, I. and L. Löfgren (1995), *Värdering av lokala luftföroreningseffekter*, KFB-rapport 1995:5. In Swedish but with an English summary of 6 pages: *Valuation of the local effects of air pollution. How to place monetary values on health effects of exhaust emissions in urban areas*, Swedish Transport and Communication Research Board.

Lewis, C. (1993), *Road Pricing: Theory and Practice*, London: Thomas Telford.

Maddison, D., D. Pearce, O. Johansson, E. Calthrop, T. Litman and E. Verhoef (1996), *The True Cost of Road Transport, Blueprint 5*, CSERGE, London: Earthscan.

Mayeres, I. (1993), 'The marginal external cost of car use – with an application to Belgium', *Tijdschrift voor Economie en Management*, **38** (3), 225–58.

Mayeres Inge, Sara Ochelen and Stef Proost (1996), 'The marginal external costs of urban transport', Public Economics Research Paper Nr 51, CES, Department of Economics, Katholieke Universiteit Leuven.

McFadden, D.L. and G.K. Leonard (1993), 'Issues in the contingent valuation of environmental goods: methodologies for data collection and analysis', in J.A. Hausman (ed.), *Contingent Valuation: A Critical Assessment*, New York: North-Holland.

Metz, Robert (1993), 'Emission characteristics of different combustion engines in the city, on rural roads and on highways'. *The Science of the Total Environment*, **134**, 225–35.

170   *Efficiency aspects and second-best policies*

Michaelis, Laurie (1993), 'Global warming impacts of transport', *The Science of the Total Environment*, **134**, 117–24.

Morrison, S.A. (1986), 'A survey of road pricing', *Transportation Research*, **20A**, 87–97.

Newbery, D.M. (1990), 'Economic principles relevant to pricing roads', *Oxford Review of Economic Policy*, **6** (2), 22–39.

Rothengatter, W. (1994), *External Effects of Transport*, Project for the UIC, Paris, Interim report, Infras Zurich, IWW Karlsruhe.

Rouwendal, J. (1996), 'An economic analysis of fuel use per kilometre by private cars', *Journal of Transport Economics and Policy*, **30**, 3–14.

Sælendsminde, K. and F. Hammer (1994), *Verdsetting av miljøgoder ved bruk av samvalgsanalyse* (Valuing environmental goods by using stated preference methods), Rapport 251/1994 Transportøkonomisk Institutt, Oslo.

SIKA (1995), *Översyn av samhällsekonomiska kalkylvärden för den nationella trafikplaneringen 1994–1998* (An overhaul of the socio-economic parameter values used in the national traffic planning 1994–1998), SAMPLAN Nr: 1995:13.

Verhoef, E. (1994), 'External effects and social costs of road transport', *Transportation Research*, **28A**, 273–87.

Verhoef, E., P. Nijkamp and P. Rietveld (1995), 'Second-best regulation of road transport externalities', *Journal of Transport Economics and Policy*, **29**, 147–67.

Vickrey, W.S. (1963), 'Pricing in urban and suburban transport', *American Economic Review*, **59**, 251–61.

Walters, A.A. (1961), 'The theory and measurements of private and social cost of highway congestion', *Econometrica*, **29**, 676–99.

Wiedlert, S. (1993), *Värdering av miljöfaktorer* (Valuation of environmental factors), Transek Consultancy Inc.

Zamagni, S. (ed.) (1995), *The Economics of Altruism*, Aldershot, UK and Brookfield, US: Edward Elgar.

8. Urban transport externalities and Pigouvian taxes: a network approach

Peter Nijkamp and Daniel Shefer

8.1 CITIES IN MOTION

Spatial accessibility and urban development are parallel phenomena. As a result of profound changes in industrial structure, social organization and advanced technology, modern societies tend to move towards intricate networks in which transport and communication play a critical and structuring role (see Banister *et al.*, 1995). This holds not only for global, transborder or interregional networks, but also – by way of fractal representation – for urban transport networks. As the urbanization rate is increasing in most industrialized countries, more people in urban areas are dependent on well functioning infrastructure networks. Physical movement is a necessary and indigenous component of the intricate pattern of interactions that make up urban life. The relationship between urban development and urban transport, however, is an ambiguous one, not only because the causality of influence is mutual, but also because of differences between fast and slow dynamics in urban growth and urban infrastructure. As is known from the theory of non-linear dynamics, such phenomena may lead to unexpected bifurcations in the form of catastrophic behaviour or chaotic evolution (see Nijkamp and Reggiani, 1993). Especially infrastructure capacity limits increasingly cause disturbances in modern city life, to such an extent that gridlocks seem to emerge (see Horn *et al.*, 1995). This uneasy relationship between transport and urban development was already recognized some forty years ago in a classic paper by Clark (1957), who focused on the issue: 'transport: maker and breaker of cities'. The main problem is that in a growing urban economy transportation tends to reach the limits of infrastructure capacity, resulting in various kinds of negative externalities which have in turn a negative impact on the performance of the city (see also Kanemoto, 1980).

The issue was recently revisited by Hall (1992), who gave an interesting historical perspective on the relationship between transport technology and urban form. He distinguished four epochs in the past 150 years all of which ended up with a crisis in the urban transport system.

1. *The pre-public-transport city* (until approx. 1850). Such cities were relatively small and dense, while most personal travel was on foot. These cities had a steep density gradient, but were unable to grow beyond their historical boundaries. A breakthrough towards the development of larger cities was only possible thanks to the invention and introduction of a new transport system, namely horse trams and commuter railways.

2. *The early-public-transport city* (until the turn of the last century). The 'streetcar suburbs' allowed for a rapid expansion of cities, which also emerged as a result of the industrialization wave. The growth of these cities, however, was severely hampered by the low speed and lay-out of public transport, resulting in a social housing crisis for the workers. More rapid transit systems appeared to be necessary.

3. *The late-public-transport city* (until World War II). New (electrified) forms of public transit systems were introduced, both as surface transport (trams) and as subterranean transport (subways). This allowed for a drastic rise in commuting distance and resulted in a rich variety of urban activity patterns. The rise in welfare, however, enabled the large-scale introduction of the car, a mode that was largely incompatible with the traditional urban structure.

4. *The car-oriented city* (after World War II). In various cities, private car use became the dominant transport mode, thus causing a new crisis in urban public transit systems. In some cases, public transport has lost the battle (for example, Houston, Los Angeles); in other cities, there is an ongoing fight with varying degrees of success for public transport, depending to a large extent on the degree of dedicated policy support for urban transit. As a result, several archetypes of cities have evolved: strong centre cities, weak centre cities and edge cities.

Seen from a historical perspective, urban development and transportation are thus closely intertwined phenomena. Agglomeration economies are principal driving forces for urban growth, whereas the resulting diseconomies of scale caused by high density leads to congestion and environmental decay which erode the basis for a continuing growth. Clearly, it would be interesting to speculate on new urban forms, such as compact city design. The feasibility of such concepts will depend on future transportation and communication technology and on the possibilities of internalizing the externalities of high densities. Transport creates no doubt many benefits to urban areas, but generates at the same time many social costs which – especially in densely populated cities – may offset the urbanization benefits. This provokes the question whether there is an optimal level of mobility in urban areas that is both Pareto-efficient and sustainable for the entire urban transport system and that is based on sound economic principles.

It is clear that the relationship between the city and its transport is one of 'close enemies': both are dependent on each other and both cause headaches to each other. Urban policy makers faced with the above conflictuous relationship have – in most cases in vain – tried to develop urban transport policies that would maximize the benefits of the transport sector while minimizing the evils. This alliance was not always very successful, and it sometimes seriously affected the urban quality of life. In any case, it has to be admitted that urban policy makers have been extremely creative in developing a formidable variety of urban transport policies aimed at coping with the above-mentioned dilemma. Many of them have, however, often been based on ad hoc policy wishes rather than on solid economic evaluation principles and mechanisms. We will give a concise overview in the next section.

8.2   URBAN TRANSPORT POLICIES

The concern for urban accessibility has provoked a wide variety of public policy initiatives. There are several reasons for justifying government interventions in the (urban) transport sector (for an overview, see Fokkema and Nijkamp 1994). Transportation creates a variety of external effects (both positive and negative) (compare Faiz, 1993; Faiz *et al.*, 1990) and has far-reaching distributional implications (in terms of access for different groups). In the context of our paper we will address three major classes of negative externalities of transport in the city, namely congestion, environmental decay and road safety (see Shefer, 1994).

It should be recognized that these three types of externality are by no means identical (see also Litman, 1995). Congestion is an externality that mainly causes disturbance and costs to other travellers (road users in the case of automobiles, passengers in case of public transport). It is an externality that is essentially internal for the transport mode concerned, although it may have negative implications for environmental quality and perhaps positive implications for traffic safety (see Shefer, 1994; Shefer and Rietveld, 1997). Environmental pollution caused by transport mobility has wide-ranging impacts, not only on other travellers but also on all urban citizens and on the environment at large (including even global warming). Nevertheless, most of the environmental disturbance (noise, air pollution) is felt inside the city itself, so that these externalities are largely internal to the urban area; they do not influence traffic safety or congestion. Finally, a major and important source of transport externalities is formed by road accidents (see Verhoef, 1994). These are mainly caused to other road users, although not necessarily travellers belonging to the same mode (for example, a collision between a train and a car). Thus, these externalities are largely internal with regard to the transport sector as a whole. The combinations of the various cases are schematically depicted in Figure 8.1. A complication in the case of fatalities in the transport sector is that normally an insurance system does exist that largely covers the economic costs caused by accidents, so that these externalities are financially internalized. The pattern of externalities dealt with in this paper are sketched concisely in Figure 8.2.

affected people

externalities	travellers	non-travellers
mode-internal	congestion fatalities	disturbance
mode-external	fatalities	noise pollution

Figure 8.1   A typology of externalities in the transport sector

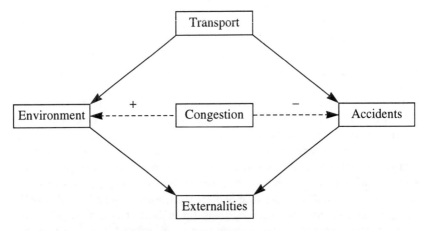

Figure 8.2   Various externality relationships in a transport system

As mentioned above, a variety of policies may be distinguished that serve to alleviate the negative externalities caused by urban transport (see also Horn *et al.* 1995). The following three archetypes can be distinguished:

8.2.1 Command and Control Measures

This policy strategy presupposes a strict and consistent urban policy that is feasible and acceptable, and can be enforced. There is a great diversity of such policies, for example:

- *technological*: catalytic converters, noise standards, tail pipe emission standards, compulsory seat belts, periodic car inspection, clean fuel programmes (including electric cars), telematics, and so on.
- *spatial*: car free zones, pedestrianization, parking restrictions, selective city centre entry by cars (for example, based on license plate numbers), tele-centre strategies, and so on.
- *regulations*: traffic calming measures, speed limits in urban districts, high occupancy vehicles, flex-time strategies, and so on.

Such regulatory measures are in general regarded as fairly effective, but nevertheless non-efficient, as the shadow prices of such interventions are largely unknown or not recognized.

8.2.2 Market-based Measures

This approach takes for granted that either the transaction costs of command and control measures are too high to warrant strict government intervention, or the government has insufficient insights to correct market failures (so-called government failures; see Barde and Button, 1990). The idea behind market-based measures is that the market offers the best available democratic possibilities for alleviating negative externalities of transport by having the users (travellers) pay for the damage caused (see also Gomez-Ibañez and Small, 1994). In this framework, again, several possibilities can be envisaged:

- *Pigouvian tax*: a charge imposed on the traveller or car driver to the amount of the marginal social cost of the transport activity concerned (ensuring a Pareto-efficient allocation of resources). Theoretically, this policy strategy is preferable in a market system, but its implementation encounters great difficulties as a result of high transaction costs caused by the 'large number' case and circumnavigating behaviour of travellers. In the present contribution we will focus our attention mainly on the latter issue.
- *Area licensing schemes*: a system in which entry into the city (centre) has to be paid for on the basis of a fixed toll (examples are Singapore, Oslo, Bergen, Trondheim). An overview is contained in Orski (1992).

At present, the city of Stockholm is planning to introduce such a system, although it is based on a political compromise (the Dennis package) in which new toll road systems (inner-city and tangential) and significant improvements to public transit systems are simultaneously envisaged. The system is a two-edged sword: it will reduce private car use and increase public transport, while funding the public transport improvements (partly) from toll revenues (for more details, see Ramjerdi 1992a, 1992b).

- *Tradeable driving or emission permits*: tradeable permits have in the past few years gained popularity in environmental policy (see Tietenberg, 1985, 1986); they have recently been advocated as a tool in transportation policies for sustainable cities (Goddard, 1995; Nijkamp and Ursem, 1995; and Vleugel, 1995). In this context it is interesting to refer to a recent paper by Goddard (1997) who describes a tradeable permit system for large cities (for example, Mexico City). The basis for the permits which he uses is the number of days someone can use the car. A permit system with a limitation on the number of days for driving the car has the capability to reduce the number of cars in the urban area in both the short run and the long run. The basic idea is to set the total supply of permits to achieve specified targets for ambient air quality and congestion reduction. These permits may be sold or distributed through grandfathering. The grandfathering of existing vehicles avoids serious political resistance to this mechanism. Everyone has a permit to use the car on, for instance, three days a week only. When someone wants to use the car on more days, or when he wants to buy a new car, he has to buy a permit from someone else. The permits can be bought and sold, leased, rented or lent. In this way the total amount of cars used is limited both in the present and in the future, since the number of permits is fixed. The system will require enforcement, but a judicious choice of the magnitude of fines and a reasonable probability of being caught should be enough to encourage substantial compliance (Goddard, 1995). The system will, however, require a fair amount of administration of all transactions. The danger of this system is thus that the transactions do not take place because of insurmountable transaction costs. This is an important issue that needs to be studied further in policies focussing on tradeable permits schemes.

It is widely recognized in the literature (see for example Meyer *et al.*, 1965; Sharp, 1966; and Vickrey, 1963) that such market-oriented transport principles may lead to first-best solutions, but often fail to generate sufficient public support because of distributional implications.

8.2.3   Urban Land Use and Physical Planning Measures

It is clear that the last policy strategy has much more of a structuring influence on mobility patterns in urban areas. Urban form, land use, environment
and energy use are closely related phenomena (see Cervero, 1986, 1989;
Giuliano, 1992; Newman and Kenworthy, 1989). Such policies normally
assume three different forms:

- *housing*: location and type of dwellings to be built;
- *employment*: location and type of buildings to be constructed (for
  example, offices, industrial plants, public facilities);
- *infrastructure*: site and type of infrastructure to be built.

Clearly, these three categories are mutually linked and make up the constitu-
ents of a sustainable city, a concept that is related to both urban morphology
and urban compactness (see Breheny, 1992). It should be recognized that the
social costs of transport externalities and the spatial-economic price gradients
of dwellings and employment locations are closely linked. Thus internalizing
negative externalities at the outset in the location and rent of a built environment seems to be a more appropriate strategic policy for a sustainable city, as
it has a long-term spatially structuring impact.

In reality we find many mixed policies, especially a combination of pricing
policies and standards. Even though such a policy is not Pareto efficient, it
may offer an effective, or even a least-cost, solution, subject to a given
accepted standard level of emission (or critical threshold value). Nevertheless, the remainder of the paper will consider only pure cases of Pigouvian
taxes for negative externalities caused by urban transport. We will address in
particular the issue of the systemic effects of such taxes as a result of circumnavigating behaviour of road users who are confronted with unpleasant tolls
(or charges) on a given urban road. This will be the topic of the next section.

8.3   TRANSPORT EXTERNALITIES AND PIGOUVIAN
         TAX: A STANDARD APPROACH

In the light of the rapid growth in negative externalities caused by urban
transport, policy intervention seems to be inevitable. Pigouvian taxes are
from a welfare-theoretic viewpoint regarded as a solid policy instrument (see
the classical arguments by Pigou, 1920; Knight, 1924; Walters, 1961, 1968;
and Vickrey, 1968). We will now in a series of successive steps describe the
urban network implications of imposing a Pigouvian tax on urban road systems.

Consider a simple network with a number of trip-makers on two possible
and equal alternative links between origin A and destination B (see Figure
8.3a). A certain congestion is assumed, and links I and II have y and $(x - y)$
travellers, respectively. Since both roads have equal characteristics, travellers will be indifferent as to their choice of road. Thus, it is reasonable to
assume that in equilibrium, the number of travellers will be divided equally
between the two alternative roads. Combining the marginal private costs
(MPC) curves of both routes in one scheme, we can easily identify a break-
even point (see point A in Figure 8.4, where $y = (x - y)$ and thus $y = 1/2x$). If
the two links would have different capacities (and thus different congestion
levels), an analogous argumentation would of course apply. Let us now
assume that, because of the continuous growth in the number of trips

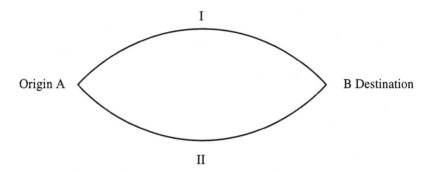

Figure 8.3a   Equal alternative roads

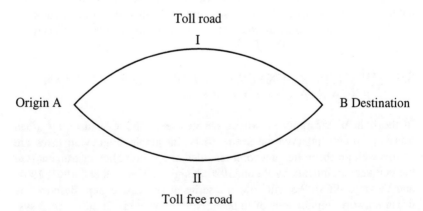

Figure 8.3b   Different alternative roads

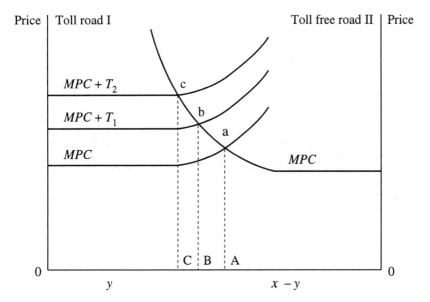

Figure 8.4   Trip distribution between two alternative roads (with fixed demand)

between A and B and the ensuing road congestion gradually setting in, the transport authority contemplates imposing a road pricing scheme (a toll) on link I (see Figure 8.3b).

The level of the toll is designed to control for externalities, that is, to be equal to the marginal social damage generated by an additional traveller. In the conventional approach to congestion externalities, road externalities in a congested situation are limited to the time delay imposed by an additional traveller on all other travellers already on the road. Consequently, it is clear that the marginal social costs created by an extra road user can be expressed as follows (see also Figure 8.5):

$$MSC_1(q) = AC(q) + [AC(q) - AC(q-1)] \cdot (q-1)$$

where:

MSC_1 = marginal social costs caused by an extra traveller 1
AC = average social costs (or marginal private costs)
q = vehicles per hour

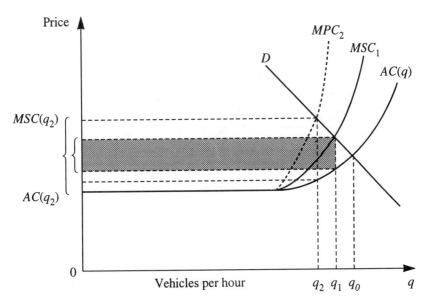

Figure 8.5   Shift in the marginal social cost curve

In such circumstances, a toll equal to the amount of the marginal social costs will reduce the number of travellers on the toll road from q_0 to q_1, although there will be a shift to the other road. The extent to which a user charge will generate substitution does not only depend on the degree of elasticity of demand, but also on the question whether the toll is imposed prior to the construction or opening of a new road or vice versa. We assume that the transport system concerned does not generate other externalities, positive or negative (for example, on housing prices or rent gradients in the urban territory at large). If the demand for travel is inelastic (fixed demand), then it is reasonable to assume that the imposition of a toll on road I will cause an increase in the number of travellers on the alternative road II. This increase in number of travellers on road II will exasperate an already congested situation as depicted in the face-to-face diagram in Figure 8.4. As a result of the toll (T_1) on road I, the number of travellers on this road decreases from 0A to 0B and at the same time, because of the inelastic demand, the number of travellers on road II increases by an equal amount, from 0A to 0B.

The above standard results will now in subsequent sections be extended by investigating the case of multiple source externalities and system efficiency, respectively.

8.4   MULTIPLE SOURCE EXTERNALITIES

Although in the traditional approach to road congestion, externalities are confined to the (direct and indirect) time delay costs, we will in this section expand on this limited approach and incorporate in the discussion also road safety and environmental pollution aspects. As was shown in Figure 8.2, both safety and pollution are closely linked to road congestion.

First, we will look at congestion and safety. We maintain that there exists a direct, functional relationship between road congestion and traffic safety; that is, road safety tends to increase with the rise in the level of congestion. The reason for that conjecture is embedded in the observation that congestion slows down traffic speed. Thus, in an extreme situation – when congestion results in a gridlock – travel speed will approach zero, and so will the number of road accidents. It is therefore possible to show that some of the rapidly increasing costs in time delays may be compensated by increasing road safety (for a further treatment of this hypothesis, see Shefer, 1994). Furthermore, for some supporting empirical evidence the reader is referred to Shefer and Rietveld (1997). The marginal social cost curve will then shift to the right, becoming less steep. In such circumstances, the socially optimal toll level may be smaller than in the case in which no consideration is given for road safety. A smaller toll will inadvertently reduce the number of travellers by a smaller number.

Next, we will examine the relationship between congestion and pollution. In recent years, several studies in the US have revealed a negative functional relationship between traffic congestion and urban air quality. For example, it was found that emissions of carbon monoxide (CO) and hydrocarbons (HC) from automobiles are twice as large at 15 mph as they are at 30 mph (see Faiz, 1993; Faiz *et al.*, 1990).

Similarly, Hanks and Lomax (1992) found that 15 per cent of the total cost of congestion is due to excess fuel consumption.[1] That is, congestion decreases the efficiency of fuel consumption and, thus, proportionally increases the amount of air pollution emissions per vehicle mile of travel. The projected continuous increase in congestion on urban highways will therefore inadvertently result in a reduction in the average speed of vehicles; conversely, their emission of pollutants will grow at an ever increasing rate. An increase in pollution emission from vehicles as a result of an increase in congestion implies higher social costs imposed not only on road travellers, but also on the population residing in the vicinity of the road alignment, and perhaps on the entire urban community (see also Figure 8.1). In order to internalize these negative externalities, it is necessary to impose a higher level of tolls so as to capture the combined social costs imposed by time delays and pollution emissions. Higher tolls will shift the conventional, marginal social cost to the left, from MSC_1 to MSC_2, making it steeper as depicted in Figure 8.5. Since

$$MSC_2 > MSC_1$$
$$\text{and } AC(q_2) - AC(q_1) < 0$$
$$[MSC_2(q_2) - AC(q_2)] > [MSC_1(q_1) - AC(q_1)]$$

Thus, the socially optimal toll will reduce the number of travellers even further, from $0q_1$ to $0q_2$. This will result in an even larger number of travellers choosing the alternative route by switching from Road I with toll to Road II without toll.

Whatever the net result of these countervailing forces, it is abundantly clear that a socially optimal pricing policy must take into account all these externalities which apparently will directly affect the distribution of travellers on the links of the transport network.

8.5   SYSTEM EFFICIENCY

In this section we will investigate the implications of the above ideas for the overall system efficiency concerning the two links under consideration. Utilizing Wardrop's second principle, we define system efficiency as the equilibrium point at which – in case of inelastic demand – average travel time, or total travel time on the network, is at a minimum (see Emmerink *et al.*, 1995). If we return to our simplified example and assume that travellers have an identical value of time, it is necessary to evaluate the net effect of the imposition of a toll on Road I on the average travel time on the two roads combined (or on the total travel time). As the density on Road I (toll road) decreases, travel speed increases up to the legal speed limit, for example 55 mph; therefore, travel time of road users decreases (that is, average travel time decreases) (see Figure 8.6). The decrease in average travel time on Road I affects smaller amounts of travellers, however; concomitantly, the flow on Road II decreases because of increasing congestion as does, too, the speed of travel or the average travel time.

The relationships among traffic flow F, speed S and density D, as depicted in Figure 8.6, are as follows: $F = S \cdot D$, or $D = F/S$, $S = F/D$. Thus, the elasticity of (flow) density with respect to speed, holding capacity constant, can be expressed as follows:

$$\eta = \frac{\partial D}{\partial S} \cdot \frac{S}{D}$$

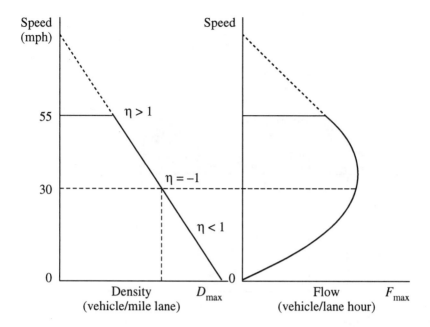

Figure 8.6   Relationships among speed, density and flow

That is, the flow of traffic is *increasing* as long as the elasticity is greater than 1 and the density is also increasing. But the flow of traffic is *decreasing* after the elasticity is less than 1 and density is continuing to increase. The flow eventually will approach zero, $F \to 0$ at which point density is maximized, that is a grid-lock.

Since average travel time rapidly increases with increasing congestion, and affects in addition a larger number of travellers (who now choose to travel on Road II, the road without toll), the weighted average of travel time on the two roads, or the total travel time, is greater than it was when no toll road was imposed (see Verhoef *et al.*, 1996). If, however, there are two types of travellers, one having a greater value of time than the other, a toll road may reduce the average value of time in the following manner.

Suppose the two alternative roads in our simplified transport network are depicted by two cost functions (see Figure 8.7). The lower cost function depicts Road II (without toll), and the higher cost function Road I (with toll). The choice between the two alternative roads will then depend upon the value of time of the individual and the length of travel time.

The left hand side of Figure 8.7 depicts the added travel time required by the travellers in lieu of the congestion, that is, the opportunity costs of time.

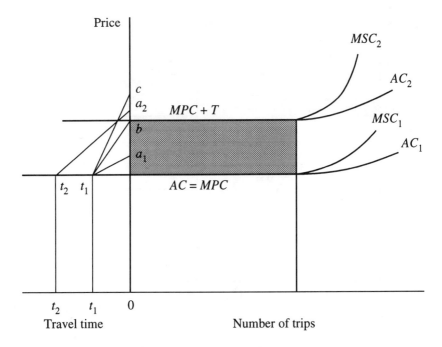

Figure 8.7   Value of time and choice of road

Thus, lines t_1a_1, t_1b and t_1c represent equal time lost but the three different travellers whose value of time is progressively increasing, that is, the opportunity cost of time is progressively increasing. The lines t_1a_1, and t_2a_2 are parellel to each other. They represent the value of time lost by the same individual but line t_2a_2 represents greater time lost. This is the reason why line t_2a_2 lies parallel and above line t_1a_1.

The value of time is inherent in the individual's characteristics (socioeconomic level, trip purpose, and so on; see, for example, Gronau, 1974), whereas the length of travel time between A and B is closely linked to congestion density (see also Figure 8.7).[2] When the additional travel time, because of congestion, increases from $0t_1$ to $0t_2$, the same individual will choose to travel on Road I (the toll road), where the travel cost without congestion is equal only to $MPC + T$. On the other hand, individuals whose value of time is higher, as depicted by the steeper slope of t_1c, will choose Road I even though a toll is imposed on it. The reason is that the traveller's value of travel time and the length of travel time imposed by congestion on Road II (without toll) are greater than the travel cost on Road I (with toll), where no congestion exists. Thus, we can observe that owing to differences in the value of time, some travellers will choose to travel on Road II (without toll), while others whose value of time is higher, will choose Road I (the toll road), at a given level of congestion. In equilibrium, the total cost of travel for each individual on either road must be equal (Pareto optimum).

To test for the socially optimum allocation of travellers on the two roads, it is necessary to evaluate both the *average* and the *total value of time* and to ascertain that they are at a minimum. The optimal solution will depend upon road capacities, the level of demand for travel and the size of each of the two types of travellers.

We can illustrate the traveller's route-choice process in a more formal way, as follows:

if

$$V_i(t_2 - t_1) > T \qquad (8.1)$$

then choose road I (with toll); if, however,

$$V_j(t_2 - t_1) < T \qquad (8.2)$$

then choose road II (without toll), where:

T = toll
V_i = value of unit of time of individual i
V_j = value of unit of time of individual j
t_1 = travel time on road I (with toll)
t_2 = travel time on road II (without toll).

Thus, if the value of time saved while travelling on the toll road is greater than the toll, the individual rational traveller will prefer to travel on the toll road. On the other hand, if the value of time saved on the toll road is less than the toll, then a rational traveller will choose road II, that is, the road without the toll.

Although the travellers who select road I are better off, it is necessary from a social welfare point of view to evaluate the total value of time spent travelling on the entire network where a toll is imposed, compared to a road system where there is no toll. The preferred network will be the one with the minimum total value of time spent on travelling.

8.6 CONCLUSIONS

The analysis in this paper – presented in a simplified form – has convincingly demonstrated that charging road users with a Pigouvian tax may seemingly be very appealing, but may provoke intriguing research and policy questions. The 'large number case' accompanied with multiple pollution sources makes the imposition of a Pigouvian environmental tax in an urban transport system extremely complicated. Due to the circumnavigating behaviour of rational actors the result may be that under certain conditions the performance of the travel system may worsen. This means that urban policy-makers have to be very cautious regarding the application of Pigouvian taxes in a dynamic urban transport network (see also Ran and Boyce, 1994).

Next, another caveat is worth mentioning, namely the interdependence between different transport externalities, through which it may happen that counteracting and co-acting forces may come about at the same time, so that the net effects are unknown and unpredictable. This means that much behavioural research on the trip pattern of urban travellers under various Pigouvian tax regimes will be necessary before an unambiguous policy recipe can be derived. As mentioned, differences in time values between urban trip-makers may cause another major uncertainty for a balanced taxation policy regarding transport on urban roads. And finally, it has to be mentioned that the distributional impacts of externalities to non-travellers may be different on different routes or links. Clearly, there may also be distributional conse-quences of taxation in terms of spending the money collected (which may affect the social acceptability of Pigouvian taxes), but this issue which is closely related to public finance has been left out of consideration in this paper. Thus, the idea of a Pigouvian tax is – despite its theoretical elegance – still fraught with many difficulties.

ACKNOWLEDGMENT

The authors wish to thank Richard Emmerink, Piet Rietveld and Erik Verhoef for constructive comments on a first version of this paper.

NOTES

1. In 1989 the average annual cost of congestion in large urban areas in the US was estimated to be $780 million, of which close to $120 million was due to excess fuel consumption (Hanks and Lomax 1992, p. 56).
2. Individuals with a value of time depicted by the slope of the curve $t_1 a_1$ will choose to travel on the road without a toll, that is, Road I. The concept discussed here is somewhat related

to the economic literature concerning 'rationing/discriminating by waiting time' (see Barzel, 1974, 1989 and Nichols *et al.*, 1972).

REFERENCES

Banister, D., R. Capello and P. Nijkamp (eds) (1995), *European Transport and Communications Networks*, Chichester: John Wiley.

Barde, J.Ph. and K. Button (eds) (1990), *Transport Policy and the Environment: Six Case Studies*, London: Earthscan.

Barzel, Y. (1974), 'A theory of rationing by waiting', *Journal of Law and Economics*, **17** (1), 73–96.

Barzel, Y. (1989), *Economic Analysis of Property Rights*, Cambridge: Cambridge University Press, pp. 13–27.

Breheny, M.J. (ed.) (1992), *Sustainable Development and Urban Form*, London: Pion.

Clark, C. (1957), 'Transport: maker and breaker of cities', *Town Planning Review*, **28**, 237–50.

Cervero, R. (1986), 'Jobs–housing imbalances as a transportation problem', Research Report NCB-ITS RR-86–9, Institute of Transportation Studies, University of California, Berkeley.

Cervero, R. (1989), 'Jobs–housing balancing and regional mobility', *APAJournal*, 136–50.

Emmerink, R.H.M., K.W. Axhausen, P. Nijkamp and P. Rietveld (1995), 'Concentration, overreaction, market penetration and Wardrop's principles in an ATIS environment', *International Journal of Transport Economics*, **22** (2), 123–41.

Faiz, A. (1993), Automobile emissions in developing countries. Relative implication for global warming, acidification and urban air quality', *Transportation Research*, **27A** (3), 167–86.

Faiz, A,, M. Walsh and A. Varma (1990), 'Automobile pollution: issues and options in developing countries', WPS 492, Washington, DC: The World Bank, Infrastructure and Urban Development Department.

Fokkema, J.C. and P. Nijkamp (1994), 'The changing role of governments: the end of planning history?', *International Journal of Transport Economics*, **XXI** (2), 127–45.

Giuliano, G. (1992), 'Is job housing balance a transportation issue?', *Transportation Research Record*, No. 1305, 305–12.

Goddard, H.C. (1997), 'Optimal restrictions on vehicle use for urban sustainability for Mexico City', *International Journal of Environment and Pollution*, **7** (3), 1997, 357–74.

Gomez-Ibañez, J.A. and K.A. Small (1994), *Road Pricing for Congestion Management*, National Cooperative Highway Research Program Synthesis of Highway Practice, No. 210, Washington: National Academy Press.

Gronau, R. (1974), 'Price and value of time', *TRB Special Report*, no. 149, Washington, 180–83.

Hall, P. (1992), 'Transport: maker and breaker of cities', in A.M. Mannion and S.R. Bowlby (eds), *Environmental Issues in the 1990s*, Chichester: John Wiley, 265–76.

Hanks, J.W. Jr and T.J. Lomax (1992), 'Roadway congestion estimates and trends', Research Report 1131–4, College Station Texas, Texas A&M University System.

Horn, B., K. Hashiba and V. Feypell (1995), 'Fighting traffic congestion: an agenda for the future', *IATSS Research*, **19** (2), 6–15.

Kanemoto, Y. (1980), *Externalities in a Spatial Economy*, Amsterdam: North-Holland.

Knight, F.H. (1924), 'Some fallacies in the interpretation of social cost', *Quarterly Journal of Economics*, **38**, 592–606.

Litman, T. (1995), 'Transportation cost analysis for sustainability', *IATSS Research*, **19** (2), 68–78.

Meyer, J.R., J.F. Kain and M. Wohl (1965), *The Urban Transportation Problem*, Cambridge, MA: Harvard University Press.

Newman, P.W.G. and J.R. Kenworthy (1989), *Cities and Automobile Dependence*, Brookfield: Gower.

Nichols, D., E. Smolensky and T.N. Tideman (1972), 'Discrimination by waiting time in merit goods', *American Economic Journal*, **61** (3:1), 312–23.

Nijkamp, P. and A. Reggiani (1993), *Interaction, Evolution and Chaos in Space*, Berlin: Springer-Verlag.

Nijkamp, P. and Th. Ursem (1995), 'Market solutions for sustainable cities', Research Paper, Dept. of Economics, Free University, Amsterdam.

Orski, C.K. (1992), 'Congestion pricing: promise and limitations', *Transportation Quarterly*, **46**, 157–67.

Pigou, A.C. (1920), *Wealth and Welfare*, London: Macmillan.

Ramjerdi, R. (1992a), 'Cost-benefit analysis and distributional consequences of an area licensing scheme for Stockholm', *Transport Policies* (Proceedings 6th World Conference on Transport Research), Lyon, 2043–54.

Ramjerdi, F. (1992b), 'Road pricing in urban areas: a means of financing investment in transport infrastructure or of improving resource allocation: the case of Oslo', *Transport Policies* (Proceedings 6th World Conference on Transport Research), Lyon, 2055–65.

Ran, B. and D. Boyce (1994), *Dynamic Urban Transportation Network Models*, Berlin: Springer-Verlag.

Sharp, C. (1966), 'Congestion and welfare', *Economic Journal*, December, 806–17.

Shefer, D. (1994), 'Congestion, air pollution, and road fatalities in urban areas', *Accidents Analysis and Prevention*, **26** (4), 501–9.

Shefer, D. and P. Rietveld (1997), 'Congestion and safety on highways: towards an analytical model', *Urban Studies*, **34** (4), 679–92.

Tietenberg, T.H. (1985), *Emissions Trading: an Exercise in Reforming Pollution Policy*, Washington, DC: Resources for the Future.

Tietenberg, T.H. (1986), 'Economic instruments for environmental regulation', *Oxford Review of Economic Policy*, **6** (1), 17–33.

Verhoef, E. (1994), 'External effects and social costs of road transport', *Transportation Research*, **28A**, (4), 273–87.

Verhoef, E., P. Nijkamp and P. Rietveld (1996), 'Second-best congestion pricing: the case of an untolled alternative', TRACE Discussion Paper 94–129, Tinbergen Institute, Amsterdam, *Journal of Urban Economics*, **40** (3), 279–302.

Vickrey, W. (1963), 'Pricing in urban and suburban transport', *American Economic Review*, **53**, 452–65.

Vickrey, W. (1968), 'Congestion charges and welfare', *Journal of Transport Economics and Policy*, **2**, 107–18.

Vleugel, J. (1995), *De Milieugebruiksruimte voor Duurzaam Verkeer en Vervoer* (Environmental Utilisation Space for Sustainable Traffic and Transport), Delft: Delftse Universitaire Pers.

Walters, A.A. (1961), 'The theory and measurement of private and social cost of highway congestion', *Econometrica*, **29** (4), 676–97.
Walters, A.A. (1968), *The Economics of Road User Charges*, Baltimore, MD: Johns Hopkins University Press.

9. The economics of information and pricing in transport networks with stochastic congestion

Richard H.M. Emmerink and Erik T. Verhoef

9.1 INTRODUCTION

Due to ever-increasing levels of car ownership and car usage in most countries, and a relatively slow expansion of road infrastructure, congestion has become one of the most urgent problems in metropolitan areas. The social costs due to congestion have been estimated to be in the order of 2.0 per cent of GDP in the EU (EC, 1995). Because of a variety of financial, environmental and social reasons, governments and societies seem increasingly reluctant to apply the traditional instrument of road infrastructure capacity expansion to relieve congestion. Consequently, public policy makers are studying other instruments to resolve (part of) the congestion problem. In this paper, the impact of two such instruments, road pricing and the provision of traffic information to drivers, is analysed. Road pricing has been given attention since the early works of Pigou (1920) and Knight (1924). The provision of traffic information to drivers has only recently gained momentum. The large research programmes in Europe (the DRIVE I, II and III programmes) and the US (the IVHS programme, and currently the ITS programme) provide some idea of the interest and expectations that governments have in such instruments.

Both road pricing and the provision of traffic information may increase the efficiency of existing transport networks. In theory, road pricing is the so-called first-best instrument to tackle the congestion problem, as it is in principle capable of directing traffic flows toward socially optimal levels. However, road pricing has triggered much public and political opposition, as it may leave most road users worse off, whereas primarily the government renders benefits in terms of tax revenues raised. In contrast, the provision of traffic information will only under exceptional conditions direct the traffic flows toward socially optimal levels. However, there has always been much public and political support for this high-tech solution to address the congestion problem. This can mainly be explained by the fact that the introduction of sophisticated information provision systems will by far not induce income transfers comparable to those arising with road pricing. The combination of road pricing and the provision of traffic information might therefore provide an interesting policy alternative; not least because of the likely technical complementarity.

Various researchers have been analysing the impact of road pricing and information provision. The models used were generally based on either the well-known four-step transport model (Ortúzar and Willumsen, 1994), or the bottleneck model, originally proposed by Vickrey (1969) and later extended into various directions by Arnott, De Palma and Lindsey (1990, 1991, 1992, 1993, 1994). In this paper, an alternative approach is chosen. This is done for two main reasons. First, in most of the literature, the – from an economic point of view – less interesting assumption of inelastic, or fixed overall demand for road usage is made. In this paper, elastic demand functions for road usage are applied; inelastic demand is only a limiting case of the models. Second, most of the research in this area assumes that the capacity in road networks is deterministic. In contrast, we will assume that the capacity of the road network might differ from day to day, thereby allowing for the occurrence of incidents – such as accidents, lost cargo, or sudden lane closures[1] – that may decrease the network capacity by a significant amount. It is interesting to note that, recently, a number of researchers have been applying, independently from each other, the assumption of networks with stochastic capacity. See, for example, Al-Deek and Kanafani (1993), Arnott, De Palma and Lindsey (1991), Mirchandani and Soroush (1987).

This paper synthesizes the results of various recent studies in which the impact of road pricing and the provision of traffic information on network efficiency is studied both simultaneously and in isolation. Most of the literature has addressed the effects of these instruments separately. Exceptions can be found in Brett and Estlea (1989), De Palma and Lindsey (1994) and El Sanhouri (1994).

The paper is organized in the following way. First, Section 9.2 discusses the modelling framework with stochastic capacity that is used in the remainder of the paper. Section 9.3 studies the impact of the provision of traffic information on network efficiency, and Section 9.4 addresses the effect of simultaneously implementing information provision and road pricing. This is done by analysing the efficiency of combinations of several information and pricing regimes. Finally, Section 9.5 concludes and provides some policy recommendations.

9.2   THE MODELLING FRAMEWORK

9.2.1   The Demand Side

Demand for using the transport network is, in contrast with most of the prevailing literature, assumed to be elastic. The inverse demand function is given by $D(N)$, where N denotes the number of people undertaking the trip from the origin O to the destination D. For simplicity, it is assumed that the networks to be studied contain one origin and one destination, with either one or two links connecting the two. See Emmerink *et al.* (1997a) for some examples of networks with multiple origin–destination pairs. The function $D(N)$ is supposed to reflect the willingness-to-pay, or private benefits, of the population of travellers.

   Elastic demand implies that the number of travellers using the road network depends on the costs of using the network. If these costs are excessively high for some potential travellers, these will decide to suppress the trip, take another mode, or maybe delay the trip to a later point in time.

9.2.2   The Supply Side

It is assumed that each link in the network has a stochastic capacity. It is assumed that the capacity of a link in the network is Bernoulli distributed, that is, the stochastic link travel cost functions have two possible realizations. The probability of low capacity on link l will be denoted by p_l; consequently, high capacity occurs with probability $1 - p_l$. In the remainder of the paper, high capacity is referred to as state 0; low capacity is labelled state 1. Low capacity occurs due to, for example, traffic accidents, lost cargo, sudden lane closures and so on. The link travel costs of link l in state s are given by the average cost functions $C_l^s(N)$, and these depend on the number of travellers using the particular link. The following relationship between the state 0 and 1 link travel cost functions holds for each link l:

$$C_l^0(N) < C_l^1(N) \text{ and } \frac{\partial C_l^0(N)}{\partial N} < \frac{\partial C_l^1(N)}{\partial N} \text{ for all } N > 0 \qquad (9.1)$$

Hence, given a fixed number of road users, both the travel costs, and the rate at which average travel costs increase with an additional road user are higher under state 1. The latter implies higher marginal user costs in state 1.

9.2.3 The Provision of Traffic Information and the Equilibrium Conditions

To study the impact of information on both informed and uninformed travellers, we will distinguish between two groups of travellers, denoted x and y. The inverse demand function of the group of x-travellers is given by $D_x(N_x)$; inverse demand for y-travellers is denoted by $D_y(N_y)$. Hence, the total inverse demand function follows from the relationship $D_x^{-1}(\mu) + D_y^{-1}(\mu) = D^{-1}(\mu)$ that holds for all levels of travel costs μ.

In order to state the equilibrium conditions based on elastic demand for using the network with stochastic capacity, the important distinction between informed and uninformed travellers has to be made. It is assumed that the so-called uninformed travellers are aware of the shape of all the link travel cost functions and the inverse demand functions for both informed and uninformed travellers. In addition, uninformed travellers know the probabilities of low link capacity. Consequently, uninformed travellers will base their behaviour on *expected* travel costs. Informed travellers are assumed to obtain information on the realizations of the Bernoulli random variables, and therefore know with certainty which state prevails for each link on each day. Thus, informed travellers will base their behaviour on *actual* travel costs.

The equilibrium conditions can now be stated in terms of the travellers' private benefits (the inverse demand functions) and private costs (the link travel cost functions):

(i)   An *uninformed* traveller will use the transport network when his or her private benefits do not fall short of his or her *expected* private costs. If the transport network is used by this traveller, then he or she will use the route that minimizes his or her expected costs.

(ii) An *informed* traveller will use the transport network when his or her private benefits do not fall short of his or her *actual* private costs. If the transport network is used by this traveller, then he or she will use the route that minimizes his or her actual costs.

9.3   THE EFFICIENCY OF THE PROVISION OF TRAFFIC INFORMATION

Using the framework described in the previous section, the efficiency of the provision of traffic information is analysed in the present section. It is assumed that the demand and link travel cost functions are linear over the relevant ranges considered. In this context, it is interesting to note that Arnott, De Palma and Lindsey (1992) have proven that the equilibrium travel cost functions in Vickrey's dynamic congestion model (Vickrey, 1969) of the morning rush hour with two groups and two parallel routes are special cases of our linear cost functions.

The analysis in this section is organized in the following manner. In Section 9.3.1, the most simple case is studied, that is, the one-link network. In Section 9.3.2, the analysis is extended to a two-link network. This will enable us to study effects on *route-split* as well as on *modal-split* (or, overall demand). Finally, Section 9.3.3 considers the case of endogenous information provision. As it is assumed that information is provided to an a priori (and thus exogenously) determined group of travellers in Sections 9.3.1 and 9.3.2, this assumption is relaxed in Section 9.3.3.

9.3.1   The One-Link Network[2]

Assuming that the *x*-travellers are provided with the information on the actual link travel cost function, whereas the *y*-travellers are basing their decisions on expected costs instead, the model, labelled model *P* (perfect information to *x*-travellers), can be described by expressions (9.2) to (9.4) below:

$$
\begin{aligned}
&D_x(N_{P,x}^0) \le C^0(N_{P,x}^0 + N_{P,y}), N_{P,x}^0 \ge 0 \text{ and} \\
&N_{P,x}^0 \cdot \left(D_x(N_{P,x}^0) - C^0(N_{P,x}^0 + N_{P,y}) \right) = 0
\end{aligned}
\tag{9.2}
$$

$$
\begin{aligned}
&D_x(N_{P,x}^1) \le C^1(N_{P,x}^1 + N_{P,y}), N_{P,x}^1 \ge 0 \text{ and} \\
&N_{P,x}^1 \cdot \left(D_x(N_{P,x}^1) - C^1(N_{P,x}^1 + N_{P,y}) \right) = 0
\end{aligned}
\tag{9.3}
$$

$$
\begin{aligned}
&D_y(N_{P,y}) \le (1-p) \cdot C^0(N_{P,x}^0 + N_{P,y}) + p \cdot C^1(N_{P,x}^1 + N_{P,y}), N_{P,y}^0 \ge 0 \text{ and} \\
&N_{P,y} \cdot \left(D_y(N_{P,y}) - \left((1-p) \cdot C^0(N_{P,x}^0 + N_{P,y}) + p \cdot C^1(N_{P,x}^1 + N_{P,y}) \right) \right) = 0
\end{aligned}
\tag{9.4}
$$

The superscripts in the notation denote the state, the first subscript denotes the model under consideration (model *P*), whereas the second subscript denotes the group (*x* or *y*). Expression (9.4) ensures that the equilibrium condition labelled (i) in Section 9.2.3 is satisfied; expressions (9.2) and (9.3) do the same for equilibrium condition (ii).

To analyse the impact of the provision of traffic information, model *P* above is compared with model *N*, in which neither the *x*- nor the *y*-travellers are provided with information. In fact, model *N* reflects the 'no information' situation. The equilibrium conditions for model *N* are given in expressions (9.5) and (9.6).

$$D_x(N_{P,x}) \leq (1-p) \cdot C^0(N_{P,x} + N_{P,y}) + p \cdot C^1(N_{P,x} + N_{P,y}), N_{P,x} \geq 0 \text{ and}$$
$$N_{P,x} \cdot \left(D_x(N_{P,x}) - \left((1-p) \cdot C^0(N_{P,x} + N_{P,y}) + p \cdot C^1(N_{P,x} + N_{P,y})\right)\right) = 0 \tag{9.5}$$

$$D_y(N_{P,y}) \leq (1-p) \cdot C^0(N_{P,x} + N_{P,y}) + p \cdot C^1(N_{P,x} + N_{P,y}), N_{P,y} \geq 0 \text{ and}$$
$$N_{P,y} \cdot \left(D_y(N_{P,y}) - \left((1-p) \cdot C^0(N_{P,x} + N_{P,y}) + p \cdot C^1(N_{P,x} + N_{P,y})\right)\right) = 0 \tag{9.6}$$

It can be seen that in model N both the x- and the y-travellers are basing their behaviour on the *expected* link travel costs. By comparing the equilibrium values and associated levels of social welfare – measured as the sum of the individual private benefits minus the sum of the individual private costs – between model P and model N, the impact of the provision of traffic information to x-travellers in model P can be derived. Proposition 9.1 summarizes the main results; for the proofs, the reader is referred to Emmerink *et al.* (1996a).

Proposition 9.1: Assuming linear inverse demand (D_x, D_y) and average user cost (C^0, C^1) functions, and assuming that expression (9.1) holds, then it can be shown that the provision of traffic information to x-travellers:

(a) does not decrease expected road usage by x-travellers;
(b) does not decrease welfare levels of x-travellers;
(c) does not decrease expected road usage by y-travellers;
(d) does not decrease welfare levels of y-travellers;
(e) does not decrease social welfare of the system.

Proposition 9.1 is illustrated in Figure 9.1, showing the net private benefits in model P minus the net private benefits in model N. First, as stated in Proposition 9.1, none of the travellers is worse off due to the provision of information to the x-travellers. Second, informed x-travellers on the left-hand side of $N_{P,x}^1$ benefit due to a decrease in expected travel costs. As these travellers will use the network independent of the information that is provided, the benefits accruing to these travellers are external in nature, that is, they arise due to a change in behaviour from other travellers. The same holds in fact for the y-travellers. As the y-travellers are not informed, they do not change their behaviour according to the prevailing state. However, as depicted in Figure 9.1, these travellers do incur benefits because the expected travel costs decrease. Consequently, the benefits accruing to y-travellers are also external in nature. Finally, travellers between $N_{P,x}^1$ and $N_{P,x}^0$ incur benefits due to changes in their own behaviour. Without the provision of traffic information, these x-travellers will either never use the network (those close to $N_{P,x}^0$) or always use the network (those x-travellers close to $N_{P,x}^1$). However,

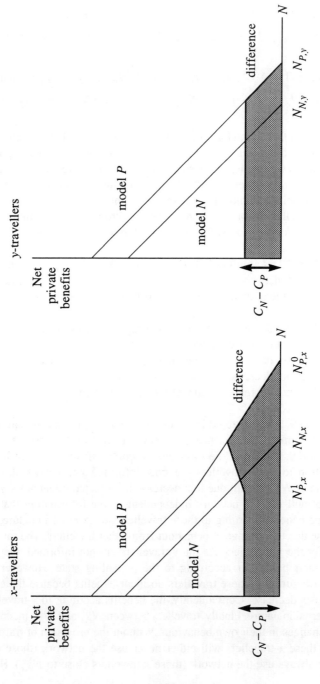

Figure 9.1 *Expected net private benefits for informed and uninformed drivers*

when provided with information in model *P*, these travellers will only use the network in state 0 when the capacity of the network is relatively high. Consequently, (part of) the benefits accruing to these travellers are internal in nature. To summarize the results, in the present model the provision of information leads to a strict Pareto improvement. In order to further investigate the efficiency of the provision of traffic information, the system welfare is compared with system welfare under *the first-best* policy, which can be achieved by fluctuating, state dependent road pricing. The first-best policy is defined as the policy that maximizes system welfare, that is, maximizes the sum of the individual benefits minus the sum of the individual costs. The welfare measure ω is used for this purpose:

$$\omega = \frac{Welfare\ (Model\ P) - Welfare\ (Model\ N)}{Welfare\ (first\text{-}best) - Welfare\ (Model\ N)} \tag{9.7}$$

Hence, ω provides the achievable welfare gains as a proportion of the theoretically possible welfare gains. Clearly, ω cannot exceed the value of one. In addition, it follows from Proposition 9.1 that ω cannot be smaller than zero, as the net benefits do not decrease due to information.

Experiments in Emmerink *et al.* (1996a) with linear demand and cost functions, and various parameter schemes have shown that the ω is most likely to fall in between the interval [0.0, 0.4], that is, with information provision only it is rather unlikely that more than 40 per cent of the achievable welfare gains will be realized.

9.3.2   The Two-Link Network[3]

In the one-link network studied above, welfare gains only arise due to so-called *modal-split* effects, as only one route was available to all travellers. However, the provision of traffic information may also help travellers to find their way in road networks. Or in other words, beside modal-split effects, these information systems can be expected to be able to generate beneficial *route-split* effects as well. In the present section, these are studied using a two-link network. All the travellers still use the same single origin-destination pair; however, they have the choice between two routes, labelled link 1 and link 2.

For the equilibrium conditions of the two-link model, the reader is referred to Emmerink *et al.* (1998). Here, the discussion is limited to presenting the main results that prevailed in most of the experiments. These are depicted in Figure 9.2.

The *x*-axis in the figure shows the percentage of informed travellers, whereas the *y*-axis depicts the expected travel costs. The curve labelled *no information*

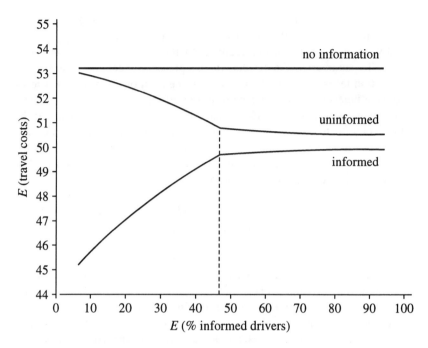

Figure 9.2   Expected travel costs as a function of the expected number of informed drivers

gives the expected travel costs in the situation where no information is available; model N. The curve labelled *uninformed* provides the expected travel costs for the group of uninformed travellers y, when the x-travellers are provided with information. Finally, the curve labelled *informed* provides the expected travel costs for the informed travellers, that is, the x-travellers. First, note that the curves are kinked at a level of approximately 47 per cent of informed travellers, indicated by the point z in Figure 9.2.[4] On the right-hand side of z, the equilibrium travel costs on both routes are identical in each state. The informed travellers ensure that this equality will hold. If the travel costs were not equal on both routes in a particular state, then (some) in-formed drivers would have an incentive to switch to the route with the lower travel costs, thereby increasing the travel costs on this route and lowering those on the other. With a sufficient number of informed drivers, which is the case on the right-hand side of z, this process will continue until travel costs on both routes are the same in each state. Consequently, the benefits to informed travellers on the right-hand side of z are solely due to modal-split effects. These were previously studied in Section 9.3.1. On the left-hand side of z, the equilibrium link travel costs are not the same for both routes in each state. The large benefits incurred by the informed travellers are then mainly caused by so-called route-split effects: all informed travellers who are using the network choose the lower cost route in case of an incident on the other route, see equilibrium condition (ii) in Section 9.2.3. Therefore, these travellers are significantly better off than their uninformed counterparts.

Furthermore, Figure 9.2 reveals again that external effects play an important role. For example, it can be seen that the expected travel costs to uninformed travellers *decrease* as more travellers are informed. This is a clear example of an external effect. In addition, Figure 9.2 shows that the expected travel costs to informed travellers *increase* as more travellers acquire the information. Hence, an additional informed traveller negatively affects the already informed ones, while positively influencing the uninformed ones; see also Emmerink *et al.* (1994).

Concerning the impact of the provision of traffic information on ω, the picture is very much the same as the one in Section 9.3.1. With most parameter combinations, the efficiency gains due to information provision will not exceed 40 per cent of the achievable welfare gains under a first-best policy. However, with totally inelastic demand and identical routes, it can be shown that the ω might be substantially larger than 0.4 (see also Section 9.4).

9.3.3 Endogenous Demand for the Provision of Traffic Information[5]

Thus far it was assumed that the group sizes of informed and uninformed travellers were determined exogenously, that is, these were given as inputs of the model by the respective demand functions. The model clearly gains much in realism if it is assumed that the number of travellers acquiring information depends on the private benefits and costs for the individual travellers buying the information. In this section, this assumption is made. In the model presented hereafter, it is assumed that an individual decides to be informed when the *internal* benefits of buying the information exceed the private costs of being informed. The *external* benefits are (by definition) independent of whether or not that particular individual is informed, and are not accounted for by a utility-maximizing individual in deciding whether to buy information. As we have seen in Section 9.3.1, these external benefits (and costs) were caused by the fact that other road users were informed on the actual traffic situation.

In the model, labelled model E (where the E stands for endogenous), it will be assumed that the price of acquiring the information is equal to π. Due to the static equilibrium nature of the model, the price of information π to be considered is short of any time dimension. In other words, whereas one would intuitively think of π as an individual investment, the internal benefits of which were to be reaped during a subsequent (large) number of travel decisions, such reasoning is not in the spirit of static equilibrium analysis. Hence, for the translation of the present model into more practical terms, one should either interpret π as the daily equivalent of some purchase price capital π (where π reflects daily interest and depreciation), or one should consider π as the real purchase price and take the inverse demand and link travel cost functions to be some discounted measures of the future stream of benefits and costs of road usage.

As shown in Section 9.3.1, the travellers in the interval $[N_P^1, N_P^0]$ are the only ones obtaining internal benefits from the information.[6] Hence, these are the travellers who are potentially interested in buying the information. Leaving the more technical details of the equilibrium conditions of the present model aside – these can be found in Emmerink *et al.* (1996b) – Figure 9.3 depicts the net private benefits due to the endogenous provision of traffic information, that is, the net private benefits in model E minus the net private benefits in model N. On the one hand, drivers in the interval $[N_E^1, N_E^0]$ will buy the information. These will benefit from internal benefits due to the traffic information. On the other hand, drivers on the left-hand side of N_E^1 benefit

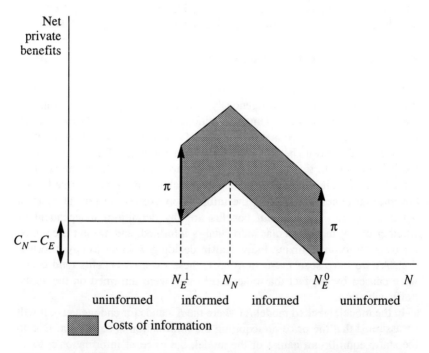

Figure 9.3   Difference in expected net private benefits of the model with endogenous demand for information (model E) and the model in which no information is available (model N)

from an external decrease in expected link travel costs equal to $C_N - C_E$. Finally, drivers on the right-hand side of N_E^0 will not use the road network and will therefore not acquire the information.

It is interesting to note that the traveller positioned at N_E^1 at the x-axis is indifferent between either buying the information and using the network only in state 0 or not buying the information and using the network in both states. The internal benefits due to the information in the former case are exactly offset by the price of the information π in the latter, as can be seen by the arrow in the middle of Figure 9.3. Similarly, the traveller positioned at N_E^0 at the x-axis is indifferent between either buying the information and using the network only in state 0 or not buying the information and never using the network.

The efficiency of the endogenous provision of traffic information, as given by the performance indicator ω, is very much dependent on the price of the information. For most cases, it can be shown that, depending on the parameters used in the model, the efficiency indicator ω lies somewhere in between the interval $[0.0, 0.4]$.

9.4 INFORMATION AND PRICING IN A JOINT FRAMEWORK[7]

9.4.1 General Issues

Thus far, we have only looked at the impacts of information provision on the efficiency of road usage. We now introduce pricing instruments in the analysis. As a matter of fact, pricing and information provision do bear a close similarity. As first-best congestion charges depend on the actual level of congestion, they clearly contain considerable information, and even imply perfect information provided road users are perfectly aware of their private costs. At the same time, first-best fluctuating congestion tolling without proper pre-trip and on-route information provision is likely to have only a limited impact on user behaviour, as many choices (modal choice, departure time, route choice) will then be based on expected rather than actual tolls and congestion levels. In addition, such information provision to a considerable extent determines the social acceptability of fluctuating road pricing (imagine the emotions of a commuter not only ending up in unexpectedly severe congestion, but facing an unexpectedly high toll on top of that ...). As is the case for any market, efficient pricing of road usage only yields its desired optimal effects if individual choices are based on perfect knowledge of the prevailing price and quality of the 'good' to be purchased. Moreover, many proposed practical pricing instruments for the regulation of congestion do not lend themselves for fee differentiation according to the actual level of congestion (peak hour permits, area licences, and so on), and therefore will not reflect perfect information. In these cases, information provision may yield efficiency improvements in addition to those generated with such 'flat' tolling mechanisms.

Therefore, both with perfect and with imperfect tolling, information provision and tolling may be expected to be complementary measures for theoretical reasons. Finally, one may of course envisage technical complementarity of pricing and information systems.

This section investigates the relative performance of, and interactions between, pricing and information provision, on a two-link network with elastic overall demand as considered in Section 9.3.2. Five regulatory 'regimes' will be considered. The first one is no tolling/no information (I), where road users base their behaviour on expected private costs only. The second regime is no tolling/perfect information (II), where road users base their behaviour on actual private costs. The third is non-fluctuating ('flat') tolling/no information (III), where behaviour is based on expected social costs. The fourth regime is a combination of II and III: flat tolling/perfect information (IV). Here, the regulator provides perfect information on prevailing levels of congestion, but charges only one single flat toll in all circumstances, the level of which is determined so as to maximize expected efficiency of road use given the fact that drivers are fully informed. Finally, there is the first-best case of fluctuating ('fine') tolling, reflecting perfect information (V).

The combination of fine tolling and no information will not be analysed explicitly. Still, this combination is actually described by regime III, since it can be shown that the expected value of the optimal fine fees with no information should be equal to the optimal flat fee with no information, rendering the two regimes identical in terms of user behaviour and welfare effects (without information, the actual value of the fee only has an *ex post* redistributive impact, whereas the *ex ante* signal function and the resulting behaviourial impacts then only depend on the expected value of the fine fee).

It is important to stress that, in contrast with the previous sections, only 'public' information will be dealt with: either no driver or each driver has perfect information. In practical terms, this means that, for information without fine tolling, information is given through, for instance, public message signs or radio information (assuming that everybody listens to the radio).

The optimal pricing rules for the three pricing regimes (III–V) can be derived by maximization of expected welfare, given the road users' behaviour under the prevailing availability of information, and dependent on whether fine or flat tolling is used. The resulting optimal pricing rules are discussed in Verhoef *et al.* (1996).

9.4.2 Simulation Results

In order to investigate the properties of the five regulatory regimes, the simulation model presented in Section 9.3.2 was used. Again, it is assumed that all demand and cost functions are linear over the relevant ranges (that is, the ranges containing the levels of usage in each of the possible states and in each of the possible regulatory regimes). As outlined above, these are sufficient to serve the general goal of the simulations, being the assessment of the influence of some key factors related to demand and cost structures on the relative efficiency of non-optimal regulation. The performance of regimes II–IV will be expressed in the 'index of relative welfare improvement' ω (see Section 9.3.1), which is for instance for regime II defined as:

$$\omega^{II} = \frac{\overline{W}^{II} - \overline{W}^{I}}{\overline{W}^{V} - \overline{W}^{I}} \tag{9.8a}$$

where $\overline{W}$ denotes expected welfare. Therefore, ω gives for the regime considered the achievable welfare gains as a proportion of the theoretically possible or optimal efficiency gains; both compared to welfare in regime I. For comparing regimes I and V, the following index of potential relative welfare improvement ω^{V} is used:

$$\omega^{V} = \frac{\overline{W}^{V} - \overline{W}^{I}}{\overline{W}^{V}} \tag{9.8b}$$

Note that the index ω^{V} is not directly comparable to the other indices ω; the reason for including ω^{V} is that it enables a better interpretation of the other ω's.

In Figure 9.4, the impact of the severeness of the cost shocks is considered, represented by the 'volatility' of the congestion cost parameters $\beta_l^1 - \beta_l^0$ (β_l^s gives the slope of the average cost curve on link l in state s). Both links are assumed to be identical. On the left-hand side of the figure, the parameters β are, for both routes, identical in both states, while β_1^1 and β_2^1 simultaneously increase when moving to the right. Therefore, on the extreme left-hand side, there is complete certainty, and we find $\omega^{II} = 0$ and $\omega^{III} = 1$: information provision yields no benefits as there is complete certainty, whereas flat tolling yields first-best efficiency gains because fluctuating tolls would be the same in each possible state, anyway. When volatility increases however, the relative efficiency of information provision (without tolling) increases, due to the increasing value of information (both from a private and from a social point of view). In contrast, flat tolling becomes less efficient due to the increasingly important shortcoming of fee adaptation. At sufficiently high levels of

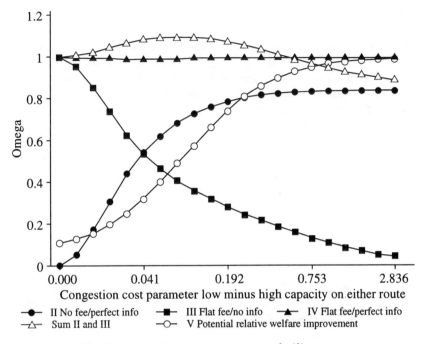

Figure 9.4   Varying congestion cost parameter volatility

volatility then, ω^{II} may exceed ω^{III}. As shown by ω^{V}, this happens in situations where potential efficiency gains are relatively large.

It is important to stress that ω^{II} and ω^{III} show an opposite pattern. This was also found in other simulations, and it indicates that flat tolling and information provision are highly complementary instruments. This is underpinned by the fact that ω^{IV} is very close to unity throughout, indicating that the combination of flat tolling and perfect information provision yields an expected welfare almost as high as does first-best fine tolling .

Finally, the sum of ω^{II} and ω^{III} is shown also, in particular to examine whether the efficiency gains of flat tolling and information provision are sub-additive or super-additive. Over a large range, the efficiency gains of the two instruments are sub-additive; only at extremely high volatility does super-additivity occur.

In the second simulation, in Figure 9.5, demand characteristics are considered. Here, the demand curve is 'tilted' around the original intersection in regime I, varying from high elasticities on the left-hand side to almost perfect inelasticity on the right-hand side. The reason for changing both α and δ simultaneously is to avoid very (small) large levels of road usage when demand approaches complete (in-)elasticity.

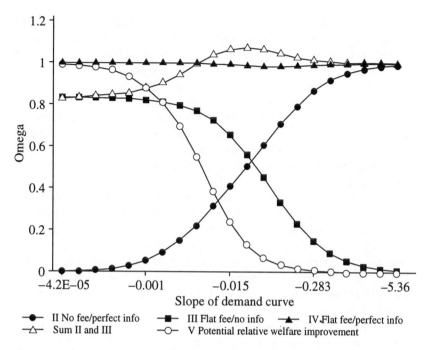

Figure 9.5 Varying demand characteristics

In general, misallocations due to imperfect pricing become more serious with more elastic demand. Hence, in Figure 9.5, ω^V approaches unity in these cases; $\overline{W}^I$ decreases rapidly. For the same reason, ω^{II} is low when demand becomes more elastic; the large majority of the potential efficiency gains can only be obtained by means of tolling. Moreover, when demand is perfectly elastic (implying that marginal benefits are equal to average benefits) and no tolling takes place, expected welfare is zero both in states I and II: without information, marginal and average benefits are equal to expected average costs on both routes; with perfect information, marginal and average benefits are equal to average costs on both routes in all states. In contrast, flat tolling without information provision already yields considerable efficiency gains (see ω^{III}).

When moving to more inelastic demand however, route-split rather than modal-split decisions become increasingly important for overall efficiency, simply because overall demand becomes more sticky. Such route-split decisions are, with otherwise equal routes, especially relevant when a shock occurs on one of the two routes only. As flat tolling without information provision will then have no effect on route-split decisions, ω^{III} falls to zero when approaching completely inelastic demand. Information provision on the other hand does affect route split, and ω^{II} increases accordingly. The reason that ω^{II} even approaches unity in Figure 9.5 is that with inelastic demand and identical routes, equalization of marginal private costs on both routes (user equilibrium) implies equalization of marginal social costs (optimal route split) because of the linear cost functions. Hence, individual optimizing behaviour based on perfect information then results in optimal usage of the network. Indeed, when allowing for free-flow cost differentials between the two routes, this property no longer holds, and ω^{II} reaches a maximum below unity, whereas ω^{III} remains larger than zero, because the route-specific flat tolls can to some extent correct for the expected inefficiency in route split.

Finally, the fact that ω^V is practically zero at inelastic demand suggests that information provision without tolling becomes efficient only when potential efficiency gains become very small. These low values for ω^V however, are to some extent also caused by the fact that total benefits, measured as the area under the demand curve, are extremely large in all regimes due to the extreme steepness of this curve. It is therefore noteworthy that fine tolling, compared to no tolling/no information, still yields a cost advantage of 6.5 per cent on the right-hand side of Figure 9.5.

The almost perfect complementarity of flat tolling and information provision is again clearly demonstrated by the curvature of ω^{IV}. It can finally be noticed that, in Figure 9.5, the efficiency gains exhibit super-additivity at more elastic demand, whereas sub-additivity prevails at more inelastic demand.

Finally, the welfare gains of the various regimes as discussed above are in general a combination of route-split and modal-split (or overall demand) effects. By comparing these welfare gains to those arising on a one-link network, these two effects can be separated. For this purpose, the same simulations were run for a one-link network of comparable capacity as the two-link network considered above. This was accomplished technically by assuming that the probabilities p_1 and p_2 are perfectly dependent.

When re-running the simulations reported in Figure 9.4 for a one-link network, ω^{III} is a bit higher throughout, and for modest cost shocks ω^{II} again is a bit lower. To start with the latter, this reflects that efficiency gains due to voluntary route split adaptation with perfect information, in case of a shock on one of the two links, can obviously not occur on a one-link network. The former reflects that the impossibility of flat tolling to affect route-split in such cases is no longer a relevant shortcoming on a one-link network. For more extreme cost shocks however, ω^{II} for a one-link network slightly exceeds ω^{II} for a two-link network of comparable capacity. This can be explained by noting that with an extreme cost shock on one of the routes of a two-link network, information provision without tolling will lead to serious congestion on the other route as well. This effect cannot occur on a one-link network, where, in case of severe congestion, it will be rational for many informed drivers to abstain from using the network altogether. Finally, ω^{IV} remains practically unaffected; it is only slightly lower for a one-link than for a two-link network of the same capacity.

For the simulations discussed in Figure 9.5, the implications of considering one link instead of a two-link network are more serious. Figure 9.6 illustrates this by comparing ω^{II}, ω^{III} and ω^{IV} for the one-link network with those given in Figure 9.5 for a two-link network. For elastic demand, things remain practically the same; for inelastic demand however, the various ωs diverge quite drastically. In the discussion of Figure 9.5, it was pointed out that for the case of a relatively inelastic demand, it is actually route split that determines overall efficiency. Obviously, on a one-link network, this is no longer an issue. Therefore, when demand becomes more inelastic, it is still only the effect on total demand that determines the relative efficiency of the various regimes. For regime II this depends on the number of users kept out of the system when being informed on the occurrence of low capacity, and

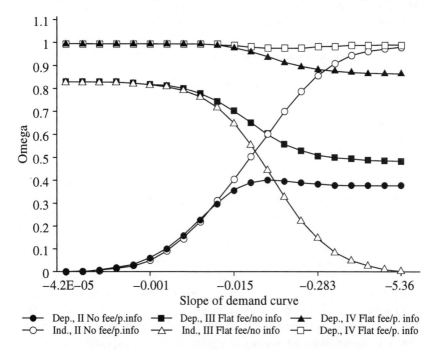

Figure 9.6 Varying demand characteristics: a one-link (dependent probabilities) versus a two-link (independent probabilities) network

for regime III this depends on the number of people kept out of the system due to the flat toll in both states. Apparently, these effects are such that ω^{II} and ω^{III} tend to some maximum and minimum value, respectively.

Furthermore, ω^{IV} is here seen to fall significantly below unity for the first time. However, it is important to stress that when approaching a completely inelastic demand in the case of a one-link network, ω^{V} itself becomes zero, simply because neither tolling nor information provision will affect road usage on the single link anyway. Therefore, ω^{V} approaches zero not only because of the extremely large benefits at inelastic demand; in addition, for the one-link network it was found that the maximum achievable cost advantage at $\alpha = 5.36$ is 0.4 per cent, as opposed to 6.5 per cent for the two-link network. Hence, ω^{II}, ω^{III} and ω^{IV}, being then proportions of practically zero, are not very meaningful measures in this case.

9.5   CONCLUSION

This paper studied the economic impacts of two policy instruments to regulate road transport, information provision to travellers and congestion pricing. In order to do so, a network equilibrium model with stochastic link travel costs was proposed. This model allowed us to study the efficiency impacts of information provision to travellers in isolation and of a combined information provision and congestion pricing system. Various models were discussed, and the regulatory efficiency of each was assessed.

In the model, informed travellers base their trip-making decisions on actual travel costs, while uninformed travellers base their decisions on expected travel costs. Consequently, the equilibrium is based on rational expectations of all actors in the system.

It was found that the effect of information provision on efficiency is unlikely to be higher than 40 per cent of the theoretical possible welfare gains, that is, the welfare gains due to an implementation of the first-best policy of fluctuating congestion pricing. However, it was also shown that both informed and uninformed travellers gain from information provision. In other words, information provision leads to a strict Pareto improvement.

Next, interdependencies between pricing and information provision were studied. When dealing with stochastic congestion, information provision and flat tolling are found to be highly complementary. The combination of these two instruments performs in practically all cases almost as good as the theoretically first-best option of fine tolling. Given the psychological advantages of flat tolling, related to issues of predictability and transparency, it seems plausible that such a combination of instruments might be more attractive than the use of fine tolls. As long as expected congestion remains the same, the regulator might use the same tolls for certain links at certain times of the day, regardless of the actual level of congestion. Moreover, for a smooth usage of fine tolls, one could not do without proper pre-trip and on-route information provision, which means that in both cases the same sort of information technologies would be required anyway.

NOTES

1. Empirical evidence suggests that a considerable share of traffic congestion results from more or less unpredictable events. No less than 44 per cent of traffic jams in The Netherlands, both unweighted and weighted for severeness, directly results from events such as road works, accidents or lost cargo (AVV, 1995).
2. The results in this section are based on Emmerink *et al.* (1996a).
3. This section is based on Emmerink *et al.* (1998).
4. Clearly, the location of point *z* (in Figure 9.2 at 47 per cent) is dependent on the parameters of the respective demand and link travel cost functions used in the experiments.
5. The results in this section are based on Emmerink *et al.* (1996b).
6. Note that the second subscript referring to the group has been dropped here. This subscript was previously required as the information was distributed exogenously.
7. This section is based on Verhoef *et al.* (1996).

REFERENCES

Al-Deek, H. and A. Kanafani (1993), 'Modeling the benefits of advanced traveler information systems in corridors with incidents', *Transportation Research*, **1C** (4), 303–24.

Arnott, R., A. de Palma and R. Lindsey (1990), 'Economics of a bottleneck', *Journal of Urban Economics*, **27**, 11–30.

Arnott, R., A. de Palma and R. Lindsey (1991), 'Does providing information to drivers reduce traffic congestion?', *Transportation Research*, **24B** (3), 209–28.

Arnott, R., A. de Palma and R. Lindsey (1992), 'Route choice with heterogeneous drivers and group-specific congestion costs', *Regional Science and Urban Economics*, **22**, 71–102.

Arnott, R., A. de Palma and R. Lindsey (1993), 'A structural model of peak-period congestion: A traffic bottleneck with elastic demand', *American Economic Review*, **83** (1), 161–79.

Arnott, R., A. de Palma and R. Lindsey (1994), 'The welfare effects of congestion tolls with heterogeneous commuters', *Journal of Transport Economics and Policy*, **28** (2), 139–61.

AVV (Adviesdienst Verkeer en Vervoer), (1995), *Verkeersgegevens; Jaarrapport 1994* (Transport data, yearly report 1994), Ministerie van Verkeer en Waterstaat, DGR, Rotterdam.

Brett, A.C. and J.R. Estlea (1989), 'Electronic route-guidance to electronic road-pricing: The next step?', in *Proceedings of the 17th PTRC Summer Annual Meeting*, 245–52, University of Sussex, UK.

De Palma, A. and R. Lindsey (1994), 'The potential benefits and synergy of advanced driver information systems and road pricing', working paper, University of Genève, No. 1994.6.

EC (Commission of the European Communities), (1995), *Green Paper Towards Fair and Efficient Pricing in Transport: Policy Options for Internalising the External Costs of Transport in the European Union*, Directorate-General for Transport, Brussels.

El Sanhouri, I. (1994), *Evaluating the Joint Implementation of Congestion Pricing and Driver Information Systems*, PhD Dissertation, Massachusetts Institute of Technology.

Emmerink, R.H.M., P. Nijkamp, P. Rietveld and K.W. Axhausen (1994), 'The economics of motorist information systems revisited', *Transport Reviews*, **14** (4), 363–88.

Emmerink, R.H.M., E.T. Verhoef, P. Nijkamp and P. Rietveld (1996a), 'Information provision in road transport with elastic demand: A welfare economic approach', *Journal of Transport Economics and Policy*, **30** (2), 117–35.

Emmerink, R.H.M., E.T. Verhoef, P. Nijkamp and P. Rietveld (1996b), 'Endogenising demand for information in road transport', *Annals of Regional Science*, **30**, 201–22.

Emmerink, R.H.M., E.T. Verhoef, P. Nijkamp and P. Rietveld (1997), 'Information in road networks with multiple origin-destination pairs', *Regional Science and Urban Economics*, **27**, 217–40.

Emmerink, R.H.M., E.T. Verhoef, P. Nijkamp and P. Rietveld (1998), 'Information policy in road transport with elastic demand: Some welfare economic considerations', in *European Economic Review*, **42**, 71–95.

Knight, F.H. (1924), 'Some fallacies in the interpretation of social cost', *Quarterly Journal of Economics*, **38**, 582–606.

Mirchandani, P. and H. Soroush (1987), 'Generalized traffic equilibrium with probabilistic travel times and perceptions', *Transportation Science*, **21** (3), 133–52.

Ortúzar, J. de D. and L.G. Willumsen (1994), *Modelling Transport*, Chichester: John Wiley & Sons.

Pigou, A.C. (1920), *Wealth and Welfare*, London: Macmillan.

Verhoef, E.T., R.H.M. Emmerink, P. Nijkamp and P. Rietveld (1996), 'Information provision, flat- and fine congestion tolling and the efficiency of road usage', *Regional Science and Urban Economics*, **26**, 505–29.

Vickrey, W.S. (1969), 'Congestion theory and transport investment', *American Economic Review*, **59** (Papers and Proceedings), 251–61.

PART III

Political and Social Feasibility

10. Road pricing for congestion management: the transition from theory to policy

Kenneth A. Small and José A. Gomez-Ibañez

10.1 INTRODUCTION

Traffic congestion is a classic externality, especially pervasive in urban areas. The theoretical and empirical relationships governing it have been thoroughly studied. As a result, most urban economists and a growing number of other policy analysts agree that the best policy to deal with it would be some form of congestion pricing. Such a policy involves charging a substantial fee for operating a motor vehicle at times and places where there is insufficient road capacity to easily accommodate demand. The intention is to alter people's travel behavior enough to reduce congestion.

Researchers have long speculated about how to overcome the practical barriers to implementing some form of congestion pricing. The work of William Vickrey (1955, 1963, 1965, 1973) stands out, but is by no means alone: other notable contributions addressing policy design and evaluation include Walters (1961), UK Ministry of Transport (1964), Mohring (1965), May (1975), Gomez-Ibañez and Fauth (1980), Kraus (1989), and Small (1992). A comprehensive two-year study by the US National Research Council (1994) is almost entirely concerned with implementation. Additional recent policy evaluations include Grieco and Jones (1994) and Emmerink *et al.* (1995). Together, these works address technology and institutions for implementation, relationship to road investment, welfare evaluation of ideal and not-so-ideal policies, financial policies for using revenues, and practical steps that could take us from current policies toward congestion pricing.

Public officials have recently become more interested in congestion pricing and other schemes for charging for road use, such as toll roads or parking taxes. This broader group of policies is often called road pricing. The interest in road pricing has been stimulated by the desire to find new revenue sources for transportation investments, and by the failure of alternative policies to significantly stem the growth of traffic congestion.

As a result, practical experience with road pricing has been increasing worldwide. For many years, the only example of congestion pricing was Singapore, a case that has received mixed reviews. Today there is considerably more experience to draw from, as well as several quite detailed plans that made considerable progress towards political approval. These cases cover a wide range of sites, objectives, and details of implementation. Many are described by Hau (1992), Lewis (1993), and Gomez-Ibañez and Small (1994).

This chapter summarizes 13 such cases, including Singapore, and draws lessons about implementation from them. In particular, we examine how well the theoretical advantages of congestion pricing hold up in the transition to practical and politically acceptable policies. The cases are divided into four broad categories: congestion pricing of a center city, center-city toll rings designed primarily to raise revenue, congestion pricing of a single facility, and comprehensive area-wide congestion pricing. Table 10.1 lists our cases according to these categories, and shows whether each case is already implemented, is under study, or, as in one case, is a limited-time experiment.

Table 10.1   Cases of road pricing studied

Type of road pricing	Degree of implementation		
	In place (starting date)	Behavioral experiment (dates)	Under study
City center: congestion pricing	Singapore (1975)		Hong Kong Cambridge, UK
City center: toll ring	Bergen (1986) Oslo (1990) Trondheim (1991)	Stuttgart (1994–95)	Stockholm
Single facility: congestion pricing	Autoroute A1, France (1992) State Route 91, California (1995) Interstate 15, San Diego (1996)		
Area-wide: congestion pricing			Randstad London

10.2 PIONEERS: CONGESTION PRICING OF CITY CENTERS

Three cities have seriously considered congestion pricing of a city center, each pioneering a different method of applying or implementing the concept. Singapore was the first to design and implement a practical, low-tech scheme for congestion pricing. Singapore's initial system was very simple: the priced area is defined by a single cordon line surrounding the city center, the technology consists of paper windshield stickers, and enforcement is through visual inspection by traffic officers. Hong Kong was the pioneer in fully-automated charging; its electronic road pricing (ERP) scheme was a flexible and comprehensive system involving multiple cordons. For Cambridge, England, the new concept was congestion-specific charging, an attempt to more closely approximate the theoretical ideal of congestion pricing by making the charge vary in real time in a manner reflecting the severity of congestion actually encountered while inside the priced area.

Only one of these systems is operational. Singapore's Area License Scheme (ALS) was inaugurated in 1975 and still operates today; the city has recently inaugurated an electronic system to replace its manual charging and enforcement. Hong Kong's ERP scheme was subjected to extensive technological field trials as well as exhaustive desk studies for prediction and evaluation, but was withdrawn due to public opposition. Cambridge has also been the site of a technological field trial but the scheme was abandoned when a new and unsupportive council came to power in 1993.

10.2.1 Singapore's Area License Scheme

Singapore's ALS is part of an extremely stringent set of policies designed to restrict automobile ownership and use in this crowded island city-state of three million people. The national government chose the ALS over conventional road tolls and higher parking charges because space for toll stations was lacking in the city center and it thought higher parking charges would be ineffective in the face of heavy through traffic and numerous chauffeur-driven cars.

The size and structure of the fee has varied over the years. When first implemented in 1975, the fee was imposed only on vehicles entering the restricted area during the morning peak period. Carpools and taxis carrying four or more people were exempted, as were motorcycles and commercial trucks. For cars, the fee has ranged from approximately $1.50 to $2.50 per day in US currency equivalent.[1] In 1989, the charging hours were extended to the afternoon peak (but still in the inbound direction, since that produced the desired effect on through traffic) and the exemptions were eliminated for all vehicles except public transit. In 1994, the hours were extended to include the time between the morning and afternoon peaks. Collection costs have been modest, amounting to about 11 percent of revenue in the early years.

The effects on traffic have been dramatic. Among commuters to jobs in the restricted zone, the share commuting in cars with less than four passengers dropped from 48 percent to 27 percent during the first few months of operation, while the combined modal shares of carpool and bus rose from 41 percent to 62 percent (Watson and Holland, 1978, p. 85). As shown in Table 10.2, the numbers of vehicles of all types entering the zone during restricted

Table 10.2   Effects of the Singapore area license scheme

	1975 initiation: morning only		1989 changes: morning and afternoon	
	Before (Mar. 1975)	After (Sept.–Oct. 1975)	Before (May (1989)	After (May 1990)
Daily traffic entering restricted zone (1000s):				
7:00–7:30	9.8	11.1	9.7	9.7
7:30–10:15[a,b]	74.0	41.2	51.8	44.8
10:15–11:00	NA	NA	22.1	21.8
4:00–4:30	NA	NA	12.9	12.4
4:30–6:30[b]	NA	NA	51.5	23.8
6:30–7:30	NA	NA	22.3	24.1
Average commute time to jobs in restricted zone for those not changing mode (minutes):				
Solo driver	26.8	27.9	NA	NA
Carpool[c]	28.2	31.5	NA	NA
Bus rider	40.4	41.0	NA	NA

Notes:
a   Restraint hours in effect August 1975–May 1989.
b   Restraint hours in effect February 1990–December 1993.
c   Average for carpool drivers, carpool passengers, and other car passengers, weighted by number in sample.
NA = data not available

Sources: Watson and Holland (1978), pp. 41, 133; Menon and Lam (1993), p. 29.

hours declined by 44 percent. During the half-hour preceding the restraint period, in contrast, traffic rose 13 percent, and it probably rose also during the hours after the peak. (In fact, the original restraint hours of 7:30–9:30 had to be extended by 45 minutes after the first month of operation because so many people were postponing trips until just after the restraint period.)

Some of the road space originally released during the restraint hours was taken by trucks, whose peak-period entries increased by 124 percent during the first few months of operation (Watson and Holland, 1978, p. 48). Their use declined markedly after the fee was extended to trucks in 1989. Furthermore, afternoon traffic failed to decline significantly until afternoon restraint hours were established in 1989; before that, many people with destinations on the far side of the zone apparently avoided the zone during the morning but traveled through it during the afternoon. Both truck traffic and afternoon peak traffic illustrate that very specific responses occur to pricing incentives, and any loopholes in the charging scheme are likely to be heavily exploited.

While traffic speeds rose dramatically in the zone itself, a large portion of the resulting time savings appears to have been dissipated by increased congestion outside the zone. As shown in Table 10.2, average commuting time to jobs in the zone increased for each mode of travel from May to October, 1975. We suspect that subsequent road improvements outside the zone have modified this pessimistic finding, but data are lacking.

In 1994 the ALS was extended to a two-tiered structure covering a longer period of the day, with one charge for a weekday permit valid for the midday hours (10:15–16:30) and a higher charge for a permit that also covers the morning and afternoon peak (valid 7:30–18:30). In March 1998, the current paper permit system was replaced by an electronic 'smart card' system; initially it will merely duplicate the current pricing structure but later it may be used to introduce refinements.[2]

The Singapore experience demonstrates that travelers respond dramatically to sufficiently high pricing incentives. However, it does not necessarily prove that a scheme as simple as a single cordon and a single time period is a good idea. Problems of spillover across spatial and time boundaries may make this scheme too crude an approximation of marginal-cost pricing to provide the net economic benefits achievable in theory. On the other hand, the problem could be simply that the fee was set too high, as argued by Watson and Holland (1978), Wilson (1988), Toh (1992), and McCarthy and Tay (1993).

10.2.2 Hong Kong's Electronic Road Pricing Trial

Nearly a decade after the inauguration of the Singapore area license scheme, Hong Kong, a slightly larger city with population 4 million, proceeded with

plans for a more complex system using electronic charging and video enforcement. Hong Kong's field trial proved the ability of electronic charging
mechanisms to operate with very high degrees of accuracy. The system, now
technologically outdated, used radio-frequency communications through loop
antennas buried in the pavement, and required vehicles to be channeled into
lanes when they passed the charging points. Systems for automatic charging,
billing, and enforcement through closed-circuit television all performed extremely well (Catling and Harbord, 1985).

Alternative pricing structures and charging locations were evaluated using
a simulation model designed by the MVA Consultancy in London (Harrison,
1986). Three different schemes were studied (see Table 10.3), each including
at least five charging zones in contrast to Singapore's single zone. (Hong
Kong has two dense commercial districts, one on the tip of the Kowloon
Peninsula and the other on the north shore of Hong Kong Island, making a
single cordon like Singapore's less practical.) Scheme A had five zones and
several cordon 'tails' extending the zonal boundaries to discourage travel
along the outer edge of the zones; 130 distinct charging points would have
had to be equipped, each imposing an identical charge which varied by time

Table 10.3   Predicted effects of Hong Kong electronic road pricing schemes

	ERP scheme		
	A	B	C
Design of restraint scheme:			
Number of zones	5	5	13
Number of charging points	130	115	185
Peak direction more expensive?	no	yes	yes
Average monthly payment (US$ equivalents, 1985)[a]	15.60	18.20	20.80
Predicted effect on travel:			
Change in peak-period car trips	–20%	–21%	–24%
Economic evaluation:			
Gross revenue (US$ millions/year)[a]	51	60	70
Net benefits before collection costs (US$ millions/year)[a]	95	113	119

Note: a   The 1985 exchange rate was HK$1 = US$0.13 (International Monetary Fund, 1992).

Source: Transpotech, Ltd. (1985), pp. 2.69, 2.70, 2.74, 2.79.

of day. Schemes B and C imposed higher charges for crossing in the direction of peak flow than for crossing in the opposite direction. Scheme C also had more zones and more charging points than either A or B. In all three schemes, two levels of charges were to be assessed: a higher one during the morning and afternoon peaks and a lower one before, between, and after the peaks. No charge would be assessed at other times.

Peak travel was predicted to decline by 20 to 24 percent (Table 10.3). Total daily car trips would be reduced by 9–13 percent. In the case of Scheme B, for example, about 41 percent of all daily trip makers would be unaffected by the charging scheme, another 42 percent would pay the charge, and the remaining 17 percent would alter their trips, two-thirds by changing mode and one-third by changing time of day of travel (Transpotech, 1985, pp. 2.69–2.79).

Projected net benefits, ignoring collection costs, are shown in the last row of Table 10.3. Taking the most complex scheme (C) as the benchmark, the simplest scheme (A) achieves 80 percent of the possible net benefits, while Scheme B achieves 95 percent. This suggests that five zones and two charging levels are sufficient to approximate marginal-cost pricing reasonably well; charging more in the peak direction (Scheme B) seems to be more important than further refining the geography (Scheme C).

Ultimately none of the schemes were adopted for a number of reasons. The field trials took place during the early stages of a transfer of power from the British colonial government to popularly elected officials; the government was slow to consult newly elected members of local district boards, giving them an issue on which to assert their independence. A weak economy in the early 1980s had lowered automobile ownership, moreover, and thus relieved some of the urgency for strict policies to reduce congestion. Many people objected to the potential invasion of privacy made possible by the electronic monitoring equipment. Finally, many did not perceive that the revenues from the project would benefit them; only belatedly did the government propose to use these revenues to reduce Hong Kong's high annual vehicle registration fees.

Analysts have debated the extent to which Hong Kong's failure to implement any of the proposed schemes represented tactical errors, bad luck, or an inherent political weakness of congestion pricing.[3] What seems clear is that any successful implementation in a democracy will require anticipating and resolving likely objections early in the planning process, including making clear just how the revenues will be used to benefit the population.

10.2.3 Congestion-Specific Charging for Cambridge, England

Cambridge, a historic city of 100 000 people located 100 kilometers north of London, was the site for a unique proposal that would carry congestion pricing close to its theoretical extreme. Within a ring encompassing the congested city center, charges would vary in real time in accordance with the amount of congestion actually experienced by the individual vehicle (Sharpe, 1993). The rationale was that the amount of congestion experienced by a vehicle is probably closely related to the externalities it imposes on others. (This proposition is debatable given the dynamics of congestion formation.) The proposal, put forth in 1990 by Brian Oldridge, then Director of Transportation for Cambridgeshire, won preliminary approval of the Cambridgeshire County Council.

Real-time pricing was to be implemented by means of an in-vehicle meter, which contains a clock and is connected to the car's odometer. Under one suggested charging regime, for example, the meter would assess a charge of US$0.36 (at the 1990 exchange rate) whenever a distance of 0.5 km was traversed either (a) at a speed less than 25 km per hour or (b) with more than four stops.[4] These criteria were intended to make the charge on a vehicle approximate the externality that vehicle imposes on others. Charges would be deducted from the balance contained in a prepaid 'smart card' or 'electronic purse', thereby preserving the user's anonymity and overcoming one source of resistance encountered in Hong Kong.

When Oldridge retired in 1993 his replacement, J. Michael Sharpe, decided to focus on more conventional forms of road pricing, such as cordon charges or zone fees, as alternatives to congestion metering. Sharpe was concerned about the potential for public outrage when charges are unpredictable. From the user's point of view, real-time charging would have meant that on those very days when travel conditions were unexpectedly poor, a financial penalty would be added to the aggravation already experienced. Many citizens might blame politicians or traffic planners for incidents of severe congestion rather than accepting the principle that they should pay more because they are imposing higher marginal costs on others. In addition, drivers might drive unsafely to avoid triggering the meter (Ison, 1996).

The metering technology was tested in October 1993 as part of the ADEPT project within the European Union's DRIVE-II program (Clark *et al.*, Blythe, 1994). Implementation efforts ended, however, with a change in the shire government earlier that year. Surveys in summer 1994 found that the road pricing concept was viewed as 'acceptable' by only one-third of respondents, a larger proportion than for car bans or parking controls but far less than for public transport improvements (Ison, 1996, p. 120). Modeling studies of road pricing alternatives for Cambridge have continued; preliminary results suggest that the use of congestion-specific charges does significantly increase the benefits beyond those achievable from a cordon-type pricing system (Milne *et al.*, 1994), presumably by increasing the precision with which prices approximate marginal costs.

Cambridge demonstrated the technical feasibility of more sophisticated forms of road pricing. But it also demonstrated the need to develop grass roots support simultaneously with concrete proposals, especially ones as radical as the original Cambridge plan. It seems unlikely that any locality would accept a pricing scheme with unpredictable charges, at least in the absence of lengthy prior experience with less elaborate schemes.

10.3 THE SCANDINAVIAN TOLL RINGS

While Singapore, Hong Kong, and Cambridge have been experimenting with increasingly sophisticated proposals for congestion pricing, Scandinavian cities have developed a more modest type of road pricing which has emerged as an important tool for highway finance. Toll rings now surround three Norwegian cities, and one was planned for Stockholm, Sweden.

The Scandinavian toll rings do not represent congestion pricing. They are designed primarily to generate revenue to finance desired transportation infrastructure improvements; furthermore, congestion management is not among the objectives in Norway, and was only secondary in Sweden. As a result, Norway's tolls are low, ranging from approximately $0.70 to $1.75 per entry,[5] and do not vary much by time of day. Furthermore, the locations of toll stations were chosen not to optimize traffic management, but to achieve a politically acceptable balance between the financial contributions of city and suburban residents while altering trip-making behavior as little as possible. In Stockholm, revenue generation was also the dominant motive for the proposed toll ring, although the reduction in vehicle air pollution was a secondary objective. Congestion management was only a third priority, so tolls were not planned to vary by time of day.

The Scandinavian toll rings may evolve into a system of congestion pricing, despite their modest beginnings. The toll rings are virtually identical to a cordon scheme for congestion pricing except that toll rates are low and do not vary much with congestion. Furthermore, each Scandinavian toll ring is more technologically sophisticated than its predecessor. Two of the three Norwegian toll rings offer electronic toll collection as an option. The Swedes planned to develop electronic collection still further by collecting the tolls from free-flowing traffic on multilane roads without physical lane barriers. This gradual progression of technological sophistication offers the opportunity for local planners to examine a number of practical issues that anyone planning a large scale urban congestion pricing scheme would face.

10.3.1 Norway's Three Urban Toll Rings

Norway has long used tolls to finance individual tunnels and bridges; the toll rings extend the concept of toll finance to entire urban road networks. Each toll ring is part of a financial package of major regional road improvements. In each case it is facilitated by the existence of natural barriers created by mountains and fjords. An operational and financial summary of these rings is contained in Table 10.4.

Bergen, with an urban area population of 300 000, instituted in 1986 a manual system operating 16 hours per day on weekdays. It initially used just six toll stations, with a seventh added following completion of a new highway link. Oslo, the nation's capital with area population 700 000, followed four years later with a system of 19 toll stations charging at all times. The imposition of the tolls was timed to coincide with the opening of the Oslo Tunnel, an express bypass for congested downtown arterials that is one of the road projects to be financed by toll revenues. An electronic charging option, available by subscription at reduced daily or monthly rates, uses a microwave technology pioneered in 1987 at the Ålesund tunnel on the western coast; subscribers are billed monthly and enforcement is by video camera.

Trondheim instituted a more complex system in 1991. It operates 11 hours per day on weekdays. Electronic subscribers, who now account for 95 percent of all tolled crossings, benefit from a discount for trips entering after 10:00 and from ceilings on their charge liabilities in any given hour or month. No seasonal pass is available in Trondheim. These features could enable Trondheim's system to approximate congestion pricing, and public literature from the municipality and the Public Roads Administration even touts this feature.[6] At present, the charges per crossing are only $1.12 for prepaid subscribers and the off-peak discount is only $0.32, so the scheme does not accomplish much congestion management.

One drawback of the Trondheim toll ring as a financing mechanism is that about one-third of the region's drivers live inside the ring and therefore seldom pay charges, yet they benefit from some of the road improvements. In order to better distribute the burden as well as to increase revenues, several changes were approved by the city council in June 1996, to be implemented in 1997 pending approval by the Parliament. The most important is the imposition of new charges for crossing three newly defined screenlines inside the ring. Hence there will be three central zones instead of one. At the same time the existing fee for crossing the ring is to be increased by $0.15 and its period of operation will be extended one hour later in the afternoon (to 18:00). The fee for crossing the internal screenlines has not yet been decided, but will be considerably lower than the fee for crossing the ring, with the goal of achieving overall a 50 percent increase in toll revenues.[7]

Table 10.4   Overview of Norway's toll rings

	Bergen	Oslo	Trondheim[a]
Urban area population, '000s	300	700	136
% inside toll ring	10	28	40
Starting date of toll ring	Jan. 1986	Feb. 1990	Oct. 1991
Number of stations	7	19	11
Entry fee for cars (NOK)[b]			
Single trip (manual or coin)[c]	5	11	10
Per trip (subscription):[d]			
With prepayment[e]	4.50	7.43	7
Off-peak discount (after 10:00)	NA	NA	2
Monthly pass[f]	100	250	NA
Times charges are in effect:			
Days	Mon–Fri	all days	Mon–Fri
Hours	6:00–22:00	all hours	6:00–17:00
Average daily crossings during toll hours ('000s)	68	204.4	40.5
% by subscription	59	63	85
1992 gross revenue, NOK millions	63	628	70.7

Notes:
a   Figures exclude the pre-existing Ranheim toll station, which has higher rates (not shown) applicable in both directions and at all times.
b   For 1992. Exchange rate: NOK 1 = $0.16.
c   Bergen: all stations manned. Oslo: all stations manned, 8 also have coin lanes. Trondheim: 1 station manned, others coin or magnetic card only.
d   In Trondheim, subscribers are charged for no more than one trip per hour, and no more than 75 per month. Trondheim subscription rates rose in 1994 for people making 10 or fewer crossing per month.
e   Charges shown are for the following prepayment quantities. Bergen: booklets of 20. Oslo: 350 trips. Trondheim: NOK 1500 prepayment. A postpayment option is also available in Trondheim.
f   Six- and twelve-month passes are also available, at lower rates.
NA: not applicable.

Sources: Larsen (1988), Waersted (1992), Tretvik (1992), and personal communications with E. Backer-Røed (Bro- og Tunnelselskapet A/S, Bergen), K. Waersted (Directorate of Public Roads), G. Fredriksen (Trøndelag Toll Road Company, Trondheim), and T. Tretvik (SINTEF, Trondheim).

Video license plate enforcement in Norway is effective except in Bergen, which lacks electronic collection and still allows non-stop passage by seasonal pass holders. Privacy for electronic subscribers is protected by the Data Inspectorate, an agency which strictly regulates all government data registers containing personal information. Use of electronic billing information for law enforcement, for example, would require a court order.

As expected, the impact of these pricing systems on traffic has been modest, reducing vehicle crossings by no more than 5–10 percent (Ramjerdi, 1994). The Trondheim system does seem to have induced some afternoon peak spreading, as people delay inbound trips until the end of the charging period at 17:00 (the normal work day ends at 16:00); downtown shop owners have even extended their hours of operation to accommodate this response. There was also a small shift in trip making from weekdays to weekends (Meland, 1994, pp. 16–17, 43–44). The small price reduction at 10:00 in Trondheim appears to have little or no effect on travel.

As shown in Table 10.5, attitudes toward the toll rings in both Oslo and Trondheim were strongly negative, although less so after the systems opened than before. Attitudes toward the entire package of tolls and road improvements in Trondheim, however, are more evenly balanced.

Table 10.5   Public attitudes toward toll rings

	Percentage of respondents		
	Positive	Negative	Unsure
Oslo toll ring:			
Before (1989)	29	65	6
After (1992)	39	56	5
Trondheim toll ring:			
Before (April/May 1991)	7	72	21
After (Dec. 1991)	20	48	32
Trondheim package:			
Before (April/May 1991)	28	28	44
After (Dec. 1991)	32	23	45

Sources: A/S Fjellingjen (Oslo); surveys by NOREAKTA (Trondheim) as reported by Tretvik (1992), p. 7 and fig. 4.

10.3.2   The Dennis Package for Stockholm

Sweden's interest in road pricing has arisen in a quite different political context than Norway's. Its capital city, Stockholm, is more than twice the size of Oslo, with a regional population of 1.64 million. Sweden has little history of toll finance of roads, bridges, tunnels, or even ferries. But it does have a strong environmental movement, and the Swedish program has stressed environmental problems associated with traffic, especially in inner cities.

Since the late 1980s, city politicians have been floating various proposals to restrain automobile traffic in order to reduce congestion, pollution, accidents, and noise, and to increase the speed of transit buses. In 1990 the national government convened negotiations among local leaders of the three chief political parties; the appointed negotiator for the Stockholm negotiations was Bengt Dennis, Governor of the Bank of Sweden. In 1991 the negotiators agreed to invest approximately $6.9 billion over 15 years in urban transportation improvements, to be financed primarily by road pricing (Swedish National Rail Administration *et al.*, 1994). The program, known as the Dennis package, devotes slightly more than half of the funds to road improvements and the balance to public transit, primarily rail.

The road investments include two controversial elements, both designed to divert through traffic from the inner city: completion of an inner ring road within the city limits, and construction of a tolled north–south bypass route west of the city. A third controversial element, designed in part to reduce all forms of inner-city traffic, is the toll ring. It would lie just outside the ring road, charging inbound vehicles, and would require about 28 toll stations. The ring toll was expected to be set initially at $2.55 (1992 prices) and would be adjusted to automatically for inflation. Discounts of an undetermined structure could be offered (Cewers, 1994).

The final package required compromise by each of the three main political parties. The feature most pertinent here is that the Moderate Party (a conservative party) objected to the toll ring, desiring instead to finance the inner ring road as a conventional toll road. The compromise was to place the cordon line just outside the ring road. In this way the toll would help limit traffic coming into the inner city, while still serving partly as a toll on the ring road itself, since most people using the road would come from outside the cordon.

The Dennis agreement stated that toll collection initially would allow for either cash or electronic payment. However, the agreement also directed the Swedish National Road Administration to undertake technical development of a fully automated electronic fee-collection system for eventual use. The system was to allow fees to be varied by time of day and by type of emission control on the vehicle (Social Democratic Party *et al.*, 1991, p. 30). It was eventually to operate in a free-flow multilane environment with video enforcement, and to permit a single smart card to pay for the toll ring, public transport, and parking.

Modeling studies suggest that the toll ring would complement the bypass routes' goal of reducing motor-vehicle travel in inner Stockholm, and would mitigate the effects of additional traffic caused by construction of the new roads (Johansson and Mattsson, 1994). The package therefore offers both improved travel conditions and a limitation on congestion and adverse environmental effects of road traffic.

Construction of the inner ring road and imposition of the ring toll were originally scheduled for 1997, but were subsequently delayed indefinitely.[8] Public opposition to part of the inner-ring construction proved so severe that the entire agreement is in jeopardy.

10.3.3   Lessons from the Scandinavian Toll Rings

Norway and Sweden have adopted a pragmatic approach to road pricing, with limited though gradually expanding objectives. While Bergen's and Oslo's schemes are strictly meant to raise revenue, Trondheim's applies a mild incentive to spread the afternoon rush hour, and Stockholm's was designed to significantly reduce inner-city traffic and pollution.

This pragmatism has produced pricing schemes of impressive scope. Each surrounds an entire large city center, affecting many of the region's motorists. Oslo handles 200 000 crossings per day, while Stockholm anticipated more than 350 000 (Cewers, 1994). This large scale spreads the burden of financing road improvements widely. The use of seasonal passes or ceilings on the number of charges incurred further limits the burden on any one household.

The evolution of these toll rings highlights the benefits of building on others' experience. Each project was carefully planned and used methods and equipment that were sufficiently simple and well tested to promote a smooth, relatively problem-free introduction. At the same time, each has taken advantage of the experience of its predecessors by adding new features that increase the convenience to users and the effectiveness of congestion management. Public confidence has developed through experience, so long as the schemes remained closely tied to well articulated and widely shared objectives.

10.4   CONGESTION PRICING OF A SINGLE FACILITY

Three examples of congestion pricing appeared during the 1990s. In each case, the operator of a crowded expressway has adopted an innovative tolling scheme for a particular limited purpose.

10.4.1 Autoroute A1 in Northern France: Weekend Peak Spreading

Autoroute A1 is an expressway connecting Paris to Lille, about 200 km to the north. It is part of a network of toll expressways operated by the Société des Autoroutes du Nord et de l'Est de la France (SANEF), one of seven govern-ment-owned but quasi-commercial toll road operators. As with many state turnpikes in the United States, vehicles receive a ticket upon entering the expressway and pay at a toll booth upon exiting, the amount depending on the length of the trip.

The A1 is subject to heavy inbound peaking near Paris on Sunday afternoons and evenings. In April 1992, after a period of extensive public consultation and publicity, SANEF confronted this congestion problem by implementing a time-varying toll scheme for Sundays only. A special 'red tariff' is charged during the Sunday peak period (16:30–20:30), with toll rates 25 to 56 percent higher than the normal toll. Before and after the peak there is a 'green tariff' with rates 25 to 56 percent lower than the normal toll. For example, the tariff from Lille to Paris is normally $9.88;[9] but on Sunday it falls to $7.41 at 14:30, then rises to $12.35 between 16:30 to 20:30, then falls again to $7.41 before returning to its normal value at 23:30. These hours and rates were designed so that total revenues are nearly identical to those collected with the normal tariff. This property was believed essential for public acceptance, which in fact has been largely favorable.

The impact of the scheme is mainly on the timing of trips. Comparisons of traffic counts show that southbound traffic at the last mainline toll barrier near Paris declined approximately 4 percent during the red period and rose approximately 7 percent during the green period, relative to a six-year trend for comparable Sundays. The most pronounced shift was from the last hour of the red period to the later green period (Groupe SEEE, 1993, pp. 11, 18). A survey in November 1992 confirmed that many people – about one-fifth of those traveling during the green period – sought to lower their toll by shifting the timing of their trips, sometimes by stopping for meals at service areas along the highway (Centre d'Etudes Techniques de l'Equipement Nord-Picardie, 1993).

Although many people traveling during the early green period (14:30–16:30) said that they had advanced their trips, traffic levels during these two hours grew little if at all. A likely explanation is that as congestion during the red period lessened, some people who previously had traveled early in order to avoid congestion now found it more convenient to travel during the peak and were willing to pay the higher toll to do so. This is an example of the kind of efficient reallocation of peak traffic, to those for whom timing is most important, that is predicted by the theory of congestion pricing (Arnott *et al.*, 1988).

The experiment on Autoroute A1 appears to be successful, and is being imitated by a fully private toll road company, Cofiroute, at other toll booths near Paris.

10.4.2   California's Private Toll Lanes: 91 Express Lanes

The first site of congestion pricing in the United States is a section of highway in southern California which opened to traffic in December 1995. Designed and operated by a private corporation, the project is far more complex than the Paris scheme.

Its history goes back to 1989, when new California legislation authorized four transportation projects to be selected from proposals by private firms. The four selected projects are all for toll expressways, including two on which tolls would vary by time of day.[10]

One of these projects (the only one to be built as of early 1998) is located in the median strip of the existing Riverside Freeway (State Route 91). This is an extremely congested commuter route connecting the employment centers of Orange and Los Angeles Counties with rapidly growing eastern suburbs, primarily in Riverside County. The original four lanes in each direction carried over 200 000 vehicles per day with one-way delays as much as 50 minutes including time in queues at metered entrance ramps. The project added two lanes in each direction in the median along a 16-km stretch in Orange County, for a capital cost of approximately $126 million. While the original freeway lanes remain untolled, users of the new '91 Express Lanes' must pay a fee, except for motorcycles and high-occupancy vehicles (HOVs) with three or more passengers. Profits are constrained by a flexible ceiling on rate of return, negotiated with the State in a franchise agreement; otherwise the toll rates and structure are freely determined by the company. This flex-ibility was crucial to the project's viability and, in particular, to the builders' ability to apply time-varying tolls.

The project was controversial in Riverside County, whose residents will pay most of the tolls, even though it adds new capacity and the original lanes remain free of charge. The reason is that it substitutes for an originally planned single HOV lane in each direction, which was expected to be funded by Orange County. Riverside County had already built HOV lanes on its side of the border, and many of its leaders felt that its residents should not be contributing toward the cost of Orange County's lanes. This objection is partially ameliorated by the stipulation that the new lanes are free to vehicles with three or more occupants, subject to some financial conditions,[11] and the fact that they provide twice the capacity increment of the original HOV plan. In any event, the project has received generally favorable ratings in opinion surveys, with 60–70 percent approving toll finance and 50–60 percent (up from 40–50 percent before it opened) approving time-varying tolls (Sullivan and Mastako, 1997).

The scheme used by this project has come to be known as 'HOV buy-in' or high occupancy toll (HOT) lanes (Fielding and Klein, 1993). In essence, the unused capacity in HOV lanes is auctioned off to lower-occupancy vehicles. Some proponents of HOT lanes argue that one should later incorporate adjacent free lanes, one by one, into the HOT lane facility if there is adequate demand for faster service at a price. Such a scheme was proposed for the Seattle area and accepted by the Washington State Transportation Commission (WSDOT, 1994), although public opposition soon stymied that particular initiative.

The existence of free parallel lanes just a few feet away greatly constrains the tolls that can be charged on HOT lanes. As a result, the company which operates the 91 express lanes is using a complex toll structure. The initial structure, shown for the inbound direction in Table 10.6, had a maximum toll of $2.50. The price is announced on electronic message signs visible prior to the point where motorists must decide whether to opt for the priced or unpriced lanes. The toll schedule was revised in January 1997, primarily by raising the toll $0.25 during the peak and night periods while leaving the shoulder of the peak the same, thereby creating a slightly steeper gradient. At the same time an optional two-part tariff was introduced, by which a flat fee of $15 per month

Table 10.6   Initial toll rates, Route 91 express lanes inbound

Weekdays:	Mon.–Thurs.	Friday
0:00–4:00	$0.25	$0.25
4:00–5:00	1.50	1.50
5:00–9:00	2.50	2.50
9:00–10:00	1.50	1.50
10:00–11:00	1.00	1.00
11:00–15:00	0.50	0.50
15:00–19:00	0.50	1.00
19:00–24:00	0.25	0.25
Weekend:	Saturday	Sunday
0:00–8:00	$0.25	$0.25
8:00–10:00	0.50	0.50
10:00–15:00	1.00	1.00
15:00–18:00	0.50	1.00
18:00–21:00	0.50	0.50
21:00–24:00	0.25	0.25

Source: California Private Transportation Company, Corona, Calif.

entitles the user to a \$0.50 reduction on every toll. Later revisions raised tolls further and introduced some toll variation within the four-hour peak periods.

For the longer term, the operator is considering toll rates that would vary in fine increments in response to real-time measurements of congestion levels. Information about delays on the free lanes would be added to the price information that is already provided on variable-message signs. The fact that users would know the price in advance is an important difference between this scheme and the real-time pricing plan proposed earlier in Cambridge.

The complexity of the pricing structure is made possible by restricting entry to cars equipped for electronic charging. Each car carries a transponder in its windshield with a corresponding account maintained off-site by the operator. The operator claims that only a few percent of users are violators, and they are detected by video monitoring of license plates.

The company reported that over 75 000 users established prepaid accounts and received transponders during the first year of operation. Traffic in the express lanes has grown steadily and was about 26 000 per weekday after a year of operation, with about 20 percent consisting of exempt HOVs.[12] Average one-way peak hour volume appears to have reached around 2400 vehicles,[13] somewhat over half the capacity, after one year.

Delays on the adjacent free lanes have diminished dramatically, often to about 10–20 minutes. One would expect this to release considerable latent demand for the corridor, either through newly generated traffic or diversions from parallel routes. Preliminary findings of a monitoring study showed few such demand effects during the first six months of operation (Sullivan and Mastako, 1997). In part this reflects the mountainous terrain and the consequent absence of close substitutes for the route.

The reduction in traffic delays on the adjacent lanes is good for public relations, but of course tends to undermine the incentive to use the new lanes. Conditions for a successful pricing strategy on a HOT lane are more delicate than in most applications, because the quality differential between the express lanes and the free alternative tends to automatically erode as traffic shifts. A crucial parameter is the extent to which latent demand will permit the expanded peak-hour capacity to be filled while still maintaining some congestion on the free portion of the highway. In a sense the delicacy of the pricing conditions is the price paid for the politically expedient bundling of the pricing concept with the simultaneous provision of new capacity.

10.4.3   Buying Space on Existing Carpool Lanes: I-15 Express Lanes in San Diego

Another HOT lane project, also in southern California, has been proceeding along a completely different path.[14] An existing pair of 13-km-long reversible carpool lanes on a major commuter route into San Diego was underutilized, with peak-hour volumes below 1000 vehicles per lane. Meanwhile a local mayor, subsequently a state legislator, was pressuring the regional transportation planning agency to find a way to finance public transit services to his suburban community located on the same route. The result was a scheme to sell off vacant capacity on the reversible lanes to single occupant vehicles, with the revenue targeted for public transit.

The project has been proceeding in steps. Starting in December 1996, a limited number of monthly permits were sold at $50 each, the permit allowing unlimited use of the reversible lanes during that month. The permits were colored decals for the windshield, with police enforcement by visual inspection (as in Singapore's scheme twenty years earlier). To ensure free-flow conditions, only 500 permits were sold during the first month, and in fact were all sold on the first day they were offered. As of early 1997, officials planned to sell additional permits as they gained experience, and to gradually increase the fee to a projected $110 later that year.[15]

Although a flat monthly fee may not appear to be congestion pricing, there is little incentive for anyone to purchase a permit except for use during peak hours. Thus the price of the monthly permit serves as a somewhat crudely targeted congestion toll.

Officials planned to substitute transponders for decals as the enforcement mechanism in 1997. Later, the monthly pass is to be replaced by an electronically collected fee per trip. The fee schedule will vary in real time with the degree of congestion, subject to stated limits.

The project is managed by the San Diego Association of Governments, in close cooperation with the California Department of Transportation. It has been remarkably free of controversy both because of extensive public participation and consultation and because the HOT lane concept produces few losers. Carpoolers may lose if speeds drop in the former HOV lanes, but these losses can be kept small by strictly limiting the number of paying users. Environmentalists sometimes oppose HOT lanes on the grounds that they might dilute the incentive to carpool.

10.4.4 Lessons and Future Prospects for Congestion Pricing on Single Facilities

France and California have produced the first three instances of true congestion pricing other than Singapore's. Each is a narrowly targeted response to specific problems. Each turned to pricing as a common-sense adaptation of more conventional policies – ordinary toll financing or HOV lanes – to the specific needs of the situation. In France, political considerations called for revenue neutrality and so an intuitive (though non-optimal) three-tiered toll structure was developed. On California's 91 Express Lanes, financial viability in the face of parallel free lanes required a fine-tuned system of time-of-day pricing. On California's Interstate 15, the existence of underutilized HOV lanes permitted even a very rough pricing scheme to raise new revenue and provide travelers with a new option.

A number of other single-facility congestion pricing projects are under consideration in the United States. The New York State Thruway Authority announced plans early in 1997 to collect time-varying tolls on trucks crossing the Tappan Zee Bridge north of New York City. Detailed planning is underway to convert the Katy Expressway's HOV lane, a 21-km reversible single lane in western Houston, into a HOT lane. The Maine Turnpike experimented with time-of-day pricing in the summer of 1995 by offering a discount during certain off-peak hours on Fridays and Sundays (Colgan *et al.*, 1996). Another of the approved private projects in California, thus far held up by environmental and financial considerations, would extend State Route 57 as an all-new elevated expressway along the Santa Ana River channel in Orange County; 18 kilometers in length, it would charge tolls tentatively proposed to vary between $1 at night and $5 during the peak (Gomez-Ibañez and Meyer, 1993, p. 173). Initial planning for congestion pricing on the San Francisco Bay Bridge (Dittmar *et al.*, 1994) was overturned by political opposition, as was the far-reaching HOT lane proposal for the Seattle area mentioned earlier. Preliminary studies of HOT lanes and other congestion pricing schemes are underway in New York, Los Angeles, Minneapolis, Portland (Oregon), Boulder (Colorado), and Lee County (Florida).

10.5   BIG PLANS FOR THE RANDSTAD AND LONDON

Two very large metropolitan areas, in The Netherlands and England, have been the sites of proposals, plans, and studies of comprehensive congestion pricing. The scale and scope of these potential pricing schemes make them qualitatively different from the schemes discussed earlier. Their political history is like the proverbial cat with many lives: each time the concept is defeated, it resurfaces for serious consideration in a new form. Thus, the prospects for implementation are quite uncertain.

10.5.1   The Netherlands' Randstad Region[16]

The Randstad region of The Netherlands, shown in Figure 10.1, is a sprawling urban agglomeration that covers more than 2000 square miles and is home to some 6 million people. It includes the nation's four largest urban areas: Rotterdam and Amsterdam, with one million people each, and The

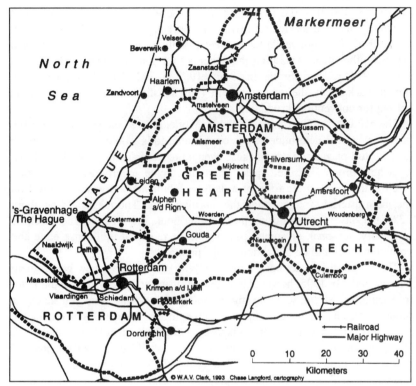

Regions of the Randstad

Source: Clark and Kuijpers-Linde (1994) reprinted by permission

Figure 10.1 Randstad, Holland

Hague and Utrecht, each with over half a million. The Randstad resembles the Los Angeles region in the United States in both its urban form and its degree of road congestion.[17] Both areas are polycentric with multi-directional peak flows, both contain vital international ports and airports, and both have turned to congestion management strategies to cope with growing traffic.

During the late 1980s, the government of the Netherlands developed a proposal called *rekening rijden* ('road pricing') for the region. It involved a multiple cordon system with 140 charging points and time-varying tolls, and was expected to reduce vehicle travel by 17 percent during peak hours. Considerable development work was undertaken on the technology and on models to predict traffic impacts. However, critics questioned its technical feasibility, its security against invasions of privacy, and its ability to prevent traffic from spilling over to local streets. Publicity had focused on technical aspects rather than explaining the benefits to a doubtful public (Grieco and Jones, 1994, p. 1526; Emmerink *et al.*, 1995, p. 598). Unable to obtain support in Parliament, the government in 1990 substituted a more modest plan calling for conventional road tolls.

The Ministry of Transport and Public Works revived the proposal in 1992, however, after it determined that conventional tolls would require too much land for toll plazas and would cause even more traffic congestion. The Ministry's new proposal, called 'peak charging', again incorporated congestion pricing, this time in the form of a daily supplementary license for travel on the main arterial system during the morning peak. The fee would be about $2.85 per day[18] applied during the morning hours 6:00–10:00. The purchase of a daily, seasonal, or annual pass would be recorded by license plate and enforcement would be by random video pictures.

The proposal was set back temporarily in 1994, when a new government was elected. By 1995, however, the new Minister of Transport issued a letter to Parliament strongly proposing *rekening rijden*, this time translated as 'congestion charging', for implementation in the Randstad starting in the year 2001 (Dutch Minister of Transport, 1995). While details remained open, the letter suggested that a substantial charge would be levied on national motorways during the morning rush hour, for the sole purpose of congestion management. The scheme 'has no purpose in terms of financing, as earnings will be returned ... where possible ... [to] the categories of road users who will pay' (p. 2). The letter stated that the Cabinet considered congestion charging essential, and that it 'could lead to a more than fifty per cent reduction of congestion during the morning rush hour on the main road network in urban Holland'. Consultations with local officials would determine whether or not charges would be imposed on parallel local roads in order to limit undesirable diversion of through traffic. An automatic system using anonymous debit cards was envisioned, with technology compatible with emerging European standards.

The Minister's letter gave considerable attention to the need to build public support, acknowledging that 'civilian opposition forms a major and detrimental risk'. Accordingly, the Ministry surveyed peak-period road users about the project in June 1995 (Verhoef, 1996, chapter 10). Half the sample said road pricing was a bad idea, a quarter that it was a good idea. An overwhelming majority – 85 percent – said their opinion would depend on the allocation of revenues. The most favored policies for such allocation were road investments and reductions of vehicle-related taxes, followed closely by public transport investments. About one-third said they would respond to congestion charging in part by rescheduling trips, an option that dominated all other responses (other than no change). As of late 1996, the Ministry of Transport was still committed to implementing congestion charging starting in the year 2001.[19]

10.5.2 Greater London

Greater London, with seven million people and nearly four million jobs, has been the site of a series of comprehensive studies of congestion pricing over the last 30 years. The resulting proposals have garnered considerable political support, but not enough as yet to be adopted.

During the 1970s, the Greater London Council became interested in restraining traffic through a form of 'supplementary licensing' in which a daily license would be required to drive within a defined area during peak hours. The favored options all involved a daily charge of around $2.00 (1973 prices)[20] to drive in Central London between 8:00 and 18:00 on weekdays; in some variations, an additional charge would apply in Inner London (a larger area surrounding Central London) during the morning peak only. Because Central London is only 3.4 miles in diameter and has extensive transit service, these charges were expected to reduce downtown traffic dramatically and to raise peak-hour speeds by as much as 40 percent (May, 1975).

In 1985, the Greater London Council was abolished and its planning functions devolved to the newly created London Planning Advisory Committee, composed of representatives of local boroughs and other authorities. This group in 1988 proposed a transportation strategy with considerably less road building than was planned by the national government. The strategy relied heavily on traffic restraint, including pricing measures. This time the pricing proposal was for three concentric cordon rings, the innermost surrounding Central London and the outermost surrounding Inner London. In addition, screenlines would divide Central London into six cells. A charge of $0.89 (1988 prices) would be assessed for crossing a cordon or screenline; for Central London this would apply all day in both directions, whereas for the outer two cordons it would apply only during the peak period and in the peak direction (London Planning Advisory Committee, 1988).

Analysis suggested that the proposed charges would have reduced inbound traffic by 15 percent into Inner London and 25 percent into Central London (May *et al.*, 1990). More recent analysis shows that the financial burden of the scheme would have been borne primarily by suburban car-owning households. Restricting the charges just to Central London would have lowered total benefits and shifted the adverse impacts more toward poorer households

(Fowkes *et al.*, 1993); it would also have made the benefits more sensitive to the charging level, thus raising the danger of setting the price too high, as apparently happened in Singapore.

The most recent study of congestion pricing in London was a three-year program sponsored by the UK Department of Transport. Concluded in 1994, the study encompassed technology, public attitudes, changes in travel behavior, effects on reliability of travel times, effects on goods vehicles, cost–benefit appraisal, and many other issues. A sophisticated modeling scheme, named APRIL, was developed to distinguish seven time periods and allow for several types of mode, route, and time-of-day shifts. The methods and results were described in a published report and in a series of articles in *Traffic Engineering and Control*.[21] All calculations were based on hypothetical implementation in 1991 and results stated at 1991 price levels.

The simplest pricing scheme investigated was a single cordon charge for Central London, involving 130 charge points. Three charge levels (ranging from approximately $3.50 to $14.00 for an inbound crossing) were considered. This scheme was predicted to achieve substantial traffic reductions for Central London (8 to 22 percent), with correspondingly large improvements in average speed (10 to 32 percent). Annual revenues of $285 to $825 million would be partially offset by annual operating costs of the charging system (including in-vehicle units) of $97 million, as well as by modest changes in parking and public transport revenues.[22] In addition there would be a one-time implementation cost of $150 million for the simplest charging system (read–write tags with central accounting). After taking into account user time savings, lost consumer surplus, accident cost savings, and annualized implementation costs, the net benefits were estimated to be about $60 million (at the low charge) to $105 million (at the high charge). These did not account for any user benefits from increased bus frequency. A charge level about three-fourths of the highest one considered appeared to generate the highest net benefits.[23]

Successively more complex schemes provided significant additional net benefits only when charge levels were high. Adding a more outlying cordon around Inner London and charging outbound trips at half the level of inbound trips would more than double net benefits at the high charge level. A further increase, to $345 million annually, could be attained by adding a third cordon and four radial screenlines, with charges varying in several steps over time. Compared to a single inbound cordon, this scheme has a slightly smaller effect on traffic in Central London but a much larger effect on traffic in the larger Inner London area. The charge levels that maximize net benefits would also be higher. However, this scheme also would be considerably more complex than a single cordon, with nearly three times the implementation and operating costs.

These studies generally verify the behavioral responses expected from theory. However, the technology was sufficiently expensive that charging costs used up an uncomfortable portion of revenues and benefits unless charges were set at levels that the public might consider very high. The technology investigated offered very high reliability, virtually no intrusion on traffic flow, and a high level of convenience and protection of privacy for drivers, however, characteristics considered essential for acceptance of a system affecting so many people.

At the conclusion of the study the Minister of Transport declared that no congestion pricing would be undertaken in London at least for the remainder of the decade. However, results of the study were being considered for application to other British metropolitan areas such as Bristol (Collis and Inwood, 1996).

10.5.3   Assessment

Despite the commitment of some important political figures, neither The Netherlands nor the United Kingdom has put in place any of the ambitious schemes for congestion pricing that have been proposed. The magnitude of the operation has been so large, the technical and operational details so numerous, the effects so far-reaching, and the interest groups so many, that it has proven exceedingly difficult to introduce comprehensive pricing all at once. Nevertheless, much has been learned about how road pricing might be administered and what its effects might be.

10.6   A REAL-LIFE BEHAVIORAL EXPERIMENT: STUTTGART

A unique experiment was undertaken in Stuttgart, Germany, between May 1994 and February 1995.[24] A cordon line was established around the southern entrance to the city center, with three charging points controlling access. Some 400 volunteer motorists agreed not only to test the charging equipment but to subject themselves to actual charges and to participate in a number of interviews and surveys. In return, they received a block allocation of funds that was intended to more than cover expected charges. At the margin, then, these volunteers paid fully for any trip taken, even though they made money from the experiment as a whole. To be sure they realistically perceived the trips as costing them money, they were required to recharge their debit cards each month (for an amount specified by the experimenters) using their own funds, and the block allocation (of the same amount) was paid three weeks later.[25] The charging equipment consisted of an on-board charging unit and a rechargeable debit card. A variable message sign outside the cordon informed participants what the charge was at that particular time.

This scheme cannot test system-wide responses to congestion pricing, but it is ideal for testing individual behavioral responses. Not only did the participants agree to take part in extensive monitoring, but the charging scheme was varied extensively over the course of the experiment, in five distinct phases each lasting two months.

The most dramatic behavioral shifts occurred in response to charging patterns specifically designed to elicit them. When one route was charged a differential of up to $2.50 compared to the other two, for example, about one in eight drivers switched from their usual route to a cheaper one. Similarly, about one in eight switched to cheaper times of day when faced with large price differentials over time. The weekday pricing schedule for this phase of the experiment is shown in Table 10.7.

Table 10.7   Stuttgart weekday fee schedule, September–October 1994

Time	Fee (US$)[a]
0:00–6:00	0.00
6:00–6:45	1.25
6:45–7:15	5.00
7:15–7:45	3.75
7:45–8:15	5.00
8:15–9:00	2.50
9:00–17:00	1.25
17:00–19:00	2.50
19:00–21:00	1.25
21:00–24:00	0.00

Note: Using the 1994 average exchange rate of approximately 1 mark = US$0.625.

Source: Hug *et al.* (1997), fig. 4.

The next most common responses were to shift to public transport or to carpool. Public transport was facilitated by a park-and-ride lot located just outside the cordon and providing frequent subway service to the city center. The shift to public transport varied over the five different phases from 3.4 to 5.9 percent of participants' total weekday trips, the amount depending sensitively on the magnitude of the automobile charges. (Weekend shifts were much larger, up to 15 percent.) Carpooling was a small but steadily increasing response, with participants reporting by the end of the experiment that about 7 percent of their trips were in newly formed carpools.

A less common response was to combine two or more trips into a single tour. Such tours increased in frequency by about 3 percent of all participants' trips on weekdays and 6 percent on Saturdays. Destination shifts were reported to be less than 1 percent of trips. Of course, a permanent system might elicit some additional responses that a limited-duration experiment does not.

The lesson of this experiment was that people will respond to pricing incentives, especially when they are finely targeted. Charging patterns can induce substantial shifts of route and time of day if designed to do so. Significant though somewhat smaller shifts to public transport can also be induced in a situation where good transport service is available.

The city and county of Leicester, England, were planning a similar trial for 1997 on the A47 corridor.[26]

10.7 CONCLUSION

Both studies and actual experience have shown that congestion pricing can substantially affect behavior and reduce traffic congestion. At the risk of over-generalizing, it appears that charges of $2 to $3 per day for entry to a restricted area during peak periods can reduce traffic by 20 percent or more. Charges can be targeted to divert traffic around certain areas or to shift it from one time period to another. In most cases it is feasible to offer customers a choice of collection options. Operating costs can be kept to reasonable levels, around 10–12 percent of revenues.

Careful attention to the details of design and implementation is important. The level of fee, the potential for evasion or diversion, the security of information about people's travel, and the degree of public understanding all greatly influence the project's viability.

Winning political approval for any congestion pricing project is difficult in a democracy, even with careful planning. The most fundamental reason is that many motorists stand to lose, especially if they do not perceive that they are benefitting from the uses of toll revenues. One obvious solution is to use toll receipts to finance widely desired transportation improvements, to lower other taxes paid by motorists, or to reduce other toll charges. When the tolled facility is new and is financed directly by the revenues, people are more likely to understand the relationship between their payments and tangible benefits.

Another reason is that people are suspicious of plans to change arrangements they are comfortable with. In this case, a strategy of incremental change may hold the answer. The Norwegian toll rings began as means of financing transportation infrastructure, but have gradually incorporated traffic management as a subsidiary goal. The accumulated experience has enabled Stockholm to design a conscious traffic management strategy in a city considerably larger than any in Norway, while still giving prominence to the objective of financing infrastructure. It seems likely that similar spillovers from the projects in France and California could easily occur, giving pricing mechanisms the degree of credibility needed for other toll road operators to adapt them to their needs. These considerations increase the importance of demonstration projects.

There is always the danger that an ill-advised project will focus attention on the potential drawbacks of congestion pricing without revealing its potential benefits, and thereby provide ammunition to opponents. One advantage of the comprehensive studies in The Netherlands and Britain is that they enable the essential elements of a successful program to be identified in advance, thereby reducing the likelihood of unexpected problems arising during the course of implementation.

Finally, an experimental approach as in Stuttgart offers the triple advantages of testing the equipment, demonstrating the system to the public, and collecting valuable data on how travelers respond to a variety of pricing schedules.

In sum, the international experience with congestion pricing is both cautionary and encouraging. While suggesting important pitfalls and political limitations, it also demonstrates that pricing can be practical and effective at managing congestion, and that political problems, while difficult, may be soluble.

ACKNOWLEDGMENTS

This paper draws extensively from research supported by the Transportation Research Board and the American Association of State Highway and Transit Officials, through the US National Cooperative Highway Research Program. We are grateful to Timothy Hau for providing valuable details from his research, and to the many individuals who provided additional information on specific cases. An earlier version of this paper was published in Tae Hoon Oum *et al.* (eds), *Transport Economics: Selected Readings*, Korea Research Foundation for the 21st Century, 1995. We are grateful to Richard Arnott, Roy Bahl, Amihai Glazer, and Clifford Winston for comments on a still earlier version that was presented at a Taxation, Resources and Economic Development (TRED) conference sponsored by the Lincoln Institute of Land Policy, Cambridge, Massachusetts. We alone are responsible for the results and opinions expressed.

NOTES

1. The exchange rate between the Singapore dollar and the US dollar was approximately S$1=US$0.48 in 1975, US$0.55 in 1992, and US$0.70 in 1996. For a complete account of changes in fee structure and level over the years, see Gomez-Ibañez and Small (1994), especially Table A-4. For other reviews see Toh (1992) and Menon *et al.* (1993).
2. Expected cost is about US$140 million (at the 1996 exchange rate), including equipment for about 60 charging locations and 700 000 in-vehicle units. Personal communication, Senior Manager for Traffic and Road Management, Land Transport Authority, 25 June 1996.
3. See Ho (1986), Fong (1986), Borins (1988), and Hau (1989).
4. See 'SERC Funds Research' (1990) or Oldridge (1994).
5. We use the average exchange rates for 1992: NOK 1 = US$0.16 for Norway, and SEK 1 = US$0.17 for Sweden.
6. See Norwegian Public Roads Administration and Trondheim Municipality (undated), pp. 14–15.
7. Private communication from Tore Hoven, toll ring project manager, Public Roads Administration, 21 Jan. 1997. Annual revenues as of early 1997 were running about NOK 80 million, or $12 million at the January 1997 exchange rate.
8. Press release by Ulf Lundin, Ministry of Transport and Communications, 2 February 1997.
9. Using the 1992 exchange rate of 1 franc = $0.19.
10. Gomez-Ibañez and Meyer (1993), pp. 172–93.
11. See California Department of Transportation and California Private Transportation Corporation (1992), p. 2; or Fielding (1994), p. 392. In 1998 HOVs began paying half price.
12. The figure for total traffic is from a presentation by Edward Sullivan, Transportation Research Board, Jan. 14, 1997. Of that traffic, 22 percent was exempt HOVs at an unspecified time late in 1996 (Williams, 1996, p. 23); that percentage was steadily declining throughout 1996 as new SOVs were signed up, so it was probably close to 20 percent in early 1997.
13. See Fine (1996).
14. See Duve (1994) and Oropeza and Orso (1996).
15. Presentation by Mario Oropeza to the Transportation Research Board annual meeting, January 1997.
16. The information in this section relies in part on Stoelhorst and Zandbergen (1990), Pol (1991), In't Veld (1991), Hau (1992), and personal communications with H.D.P. Pol, former director of Project Spitzbijdrage, Dutch Ministry of Transport and Public Works, most recently on 5 November 1996.
17. See Clark and Kuijpers-Linde (1994) for an explicit comparison.
18. At 1992 prices, using the 1992 exchange rate of 1 guilder = US$0.57.
19. Dutch Ministry of Transport, Public Works and Water Management (1996), p. 6.
20. Exchange rates per British pound were $2.45 in 1973, $1.78 in both 1988 and 1990, and $1.77 in 1991.
21. UK Department of Transport (1995a, 1995b) consists of a three-volume final report and a 61-page summary. The six articles begin with Richards *et al.* (1996) and continue in the next five issues of *Traffic Engineering and Control* (March through July/August 1996). See especially Bates *et al.* (1996) for many of the results described in the text.
22. UK Department of Transport (1995b), pp. 38–9, 42–3. This figure for operating cost applies to read–write tags, transponders with smart cards, and hybrid systems. We do not report the lower cost estimated for a transponder with electronic cash (also known as an 'electronic purse') because some of its costs are assumed in the study to be borne by financial institutions providing the cards and maintaining the accounts, hence are omitted from the calculations.
23. The foregoing figures are reported in UK Department of Transport (1995b), pp. 21, 37, 39, 42, 45.

24. The description in this section is based on Hug *et al.* (1997).
25. Hug *et al.* (1997) state that the block allocation in a given month depended in part on the expenditures by that driver in the previous month. If the test subjects knew or guessed this, their perception of the money cost of a trip might have been reduced.
26. See 'Testing the Limits' (1996). This was also reported in the newsletter of the UK Transport Research Laboratory.

REFERENCES

Arnott, Richard, André de Palma and Robin Lindsey (1988), 'Schedule delay and departure time decisions with heterogeneous commuters', *Transportation Research Record*, **1197**, 56–67.

Bates, John, Ian Williams, Denvil Coombe and James Leather (1996), 'The London congestion charging research programme: 4. The transport models', *Traffic Engineering and Control*, **37**, 334–9.

Borins, Sanford F. (1988), 'Electronic road pricing: an idea whose time may never come', *Transportation Research*, **22A**, 37–44.

California Department of Transportation and California Private Transportation Corporation (1992), *Amendment 1, Development Franchise Agreement: State Route 91 Median Improvements*, 8 January.

Catling, Ian and Brian J. Harbord (1985), 'Electronic road pricing in Hong Kong: the technology', *Traffic Engineering and Control*, **26**, 608–15.

Centre d'Etudes Techniques de l'Equipement Nord-Picardie (1993), 'Modulation des Péages sur A.1', study prepared for Service d'Etude Technique des Routes et Autoroutes (SETRA), Government of France.

Cewers, M. (1994), 'Stockholm Toll Collection System', in *Proceedings of the International Conference on Advanced Technologies in Transportation and Traffic Management*, Centre for Transportation Studies, Nanyang Technological University, Singapore (May), 143–50.

Clark, D.J., P.T. Blythe, N. Thorpe and A. Rourke (1994), 'Automatic debiting and electronic payment for transport – the ADEPT project: 3. Congestion metering: the Cambridge trial', *Traffic Engineering and Control*, **35**, 256–63.

Clark, William A.V. and Marianne Kuijpers-Linde (1994), 'Commuting in restructuring urban regions', *Urban Studies*, **31**, 465–83.

Colgan, Charles S., Gary Quinlin, Randy Nelson, Thomas Tietenberg, Richard Anderson and Bruce Clary (1996), 'Congestion pricing on the Maine Turnpike: interim report of 1995 field trials and survey', Portland, Maine: Muskie Institute of Public Affairs, University of Southern Maine (January).

Collis, Hugh and Hugh Inwood (1996), 'Attitudes to road pricing in the Bristol area', *Traffic Engineering and Control*, **37**, 580–84.

Dittmar, Hank, Karen Frick and David Tannehill (1994), 'Institutional and political challenges in implementing congestion pricing: Case study of the San Francisco bay area', in US National Research Council, Committee for Study on Urban Transportation Congestion Pricing, *Curbing Gridlock: Peak-Period Fees to Relieve Traffic Congestion*. vol. 2, Transportation Research Board Special Report 242, Washington, DC: National Academy Press, 300–317.

Dutch Minister of Transport (1995), 'Contours of implementation of congestion charging (*Rekening Rijden*)': Abstract of a Letter to Parliament from the Minister of Transport (23 June).

Dutch Ministry of Transport, Public Works and Water Management (1996), *Working Together Towards Greater Accessibility (Short Version)* (September).

Duve, John L. (1994), 'How congestion pricing came to be proposed in the San Diego region: a case history', in US National Research Council, Committee for Study on Urban Transportation Congestion Pricing, *Curbing Gridlock: Peak-Period Fees to Relieve Traffic Congestion*, vol. 2, Transportation Research Board Special Report 242, Washington, DC: National Academy Press, 318–33.

Emmerink, R.H.M., P. Nijkamp and P. Rietveld (1995), 'Is congestion pricing a first-best strategy in transport policy? A critical review of arguments', *Environment and Planning B*, **22**, 581–602.

Fielding, Gordon J. (1994), 'Private toll roads: acceptability of congestion pricing in Southern California', in US National Research Council, Committee for Study on Urban Transportation Congestion Pricing, *Curbing Gridlock: Peak-Period Fees to Relieve Traffic Congestion*, vol. 2, Transportation Research Board Special Report 242, Washington, DC: National Academy Press, 380–404.

Fielding, Gordon J. and Daniel Klein (1993), 'High occupancy/toll lanes: phasing in congestion pricing a lane at a time', Policy Study No. 170. Los Angeles: Reason Foundation.

Fine, Howard (1996), 'Fares may be reduced on 91 express lanes', *Orange County Business Journal*, (9 Dec.), pp. 1, 12.

Fong, Peter K.W. (1986), 'An evaluative analysis of the electronic road pricing system in Hong Kong', *Hong Kong Economic Papers*, **17**, 75–90.

Fowkes, A.S., D.S. Milne, C.A. Nash and A.D. May (1993), 'The distributional impact of various road charging schemes for London', Institute for Transport Studies Working Paper 400, University of Leeds (June).

Gomez-Ibañez, José A. and Gary R. Fauth (1980), 'Downtown auto restraint policies: the costs and benefits for Boston', *Journal of Transport Economics and Policy*, **14**, 133–53.

Gomez-Ibañez, José A. and John R. Meyer (1993), *Going Private: The International Experience with Transport Privatization*, Washington, DC: Brookings Institution.

Gomez-Ibañez, José A. and Kenneth A. Small (1994), *Road Pricing for Congestion Management: A Survey of International Practice*. US National Cooperative Highway Research Program Synthesis of Highway Practice 210, Washington, DC: Transportation Research Board.

Grieco, Margaret and Peter M. Jones (1994), 'A change in the policy climate? Current European perspectives on road pricing', *Urban Studies*, **31** (9), 1517–32.

Groupe SEEE (1993), 'Evaluation quantitative d'une expérience de modulation de péage sur l'autoroute A1: note de synthèse', Note 90601800-4f, prepared for Service d'Etude Technique des Routes et Autoroutes (SETRA), Government of France (April).

Harrison, Bil (1986), 'Electronic road pricing in Hong Kong: estimating and evaluating the effects', *Traffic Engineering and Control*, **27**, 13–18.

Hau, Timothy D. (1989), 'Road pricing in Hong Kong: a viable proposal', *Built Environment*, **15**, 195–214.

Hau, Timothy D. (1992), *Congestion Charging Mechanisms for Roads*, World Bank Working Paper No. WPS-1071, Washington, DC.

Ho, L.-S. (1986), 'On electronic road pricing and traffic management in Hong Kong', *Hong Kong Economic Papers*, **17**, 64–74.

Hug, Klaus, Rüdiger Mock-Hecker, and Julian Würtenberger (1997), 'Transport demand management by electronic fee collection in a zone-based pricing scheme: the

Stuttgart MobilPASS field trial', paper no. 970025 presented to the Transportation Research Board. Ulm, Germany: Research Institute for Applied Knowledge Processing (FAW) (January).

In 't Veld, R.J. (1991), 'Road pricing: a logical failure', in D.J. Kraan and R.J. in 't Veld (eds), *Environmental Protection: Public or Private Choice*, Dordrecht: Kluwer Academic Publishers, 111–21.

International Monetary Fund (1992), *International Financial Statistics Yearbook*, vol. 45.

Ison, Stephen (1996), 'Pricing road space: back to the future? The Cambridge Experience', *Transport Reviews*, **16** (2), 109–26.

Johansson, Börje and Lars-Göran Mattsson (1994), 'From theory and policy analysis to the implementation of road pricing: the Stockholm region in the 1990s', in Börje Johansson and Lars-Göran Mattsson (eds), *Road Pricing: Theory, Empirical Assessment and Policy*, Boston: Kluwer Academic Publishers, 181–204.

Kraus, Marvin (1989), 'The welfare gains from pricing road congestion using automatic vehicle identification and on-vehicle meters', *Journal of Urban Economics*, **25**, 261–81.

Larsen, Odd I. (1988), 'The toll ring in Bergen, Norway – the first year of operation', *Traffic Engineering and Control*, **29**, 216–22.

Lewis, Nigel C. (1993), *Road Pricing Theory and Practice*, London: Thomas Telford).

London Planning Advisory Committee (1988), *Strategic Planning Advice for London*, London.

May, A.D. (1975), 'Supplementary licensing: an evaluation', *Traffic Engineering and Control*, **16**, 162–7.

May, A.D., P.W. Guest and K. Gardner (1990), 'Can rail-based policies relieve urban traffic congestion?', *Traffic Engineering and Control*, **31**, 406–7.

McCarthy, Patrick and Richard Tay (1993), 'Economic efficiency vs traffic restraint: a note on Singapore's area license scheme', *Journal of Urban Economics*, **34**, 96–100.

Meland, Solveig (1994), 'Road pricing in urban areas: the Trondheim toll ring – results from panel travel surveys', Gaudi Project Report no. V2027, Drive Programme, Public Roads Administration, Trondheim, Norway.

Menon, A.P.G. and S.H. Lam (1993), 'Singapore's road pricing systems, 1989–1993', Transportation Research Report NTU/CTS/93-2, Centre for Transportation Studies, Nanyang Technological University, Singapore (November).

Menon, A.P. Gopinath, Soi-Hoi Lam and Henry S.L. Fan (1993), 'Singapore's road pricing system: its past, present and future', *Institute of Traffic Engineers Journal*, **63** (12) (December), 44–8.

Milne, D.S., A.D. May and D. Van Vliet (1994), 'Modelling the network effects of road user charging', in *Proceedings of the International Conference on Advanced Technologies in Transportation and Traffic Management*, Centre for Transportation Studies, Nanyang Technological University, Singapore (May), 113–20.

Mohring, Herbert (1965), 'Urban highway investments', in Robert Dorfman (ed.), *Measuring Benefits of Government Investment*, Washington, DC: The Brookings Institution, pp. 231–75.

Norwegian Public Roads Administration and Trondheim Municipality (undated), 'The automatic toll ring in Trondheim', Oslo: Public Roads Administration.

Oldridge, Brian (1994), 'Congestion metering in Cambridge city, United Kingdom', in Börje Johansson and Lars-Göran Mattsson (eds), *Road Pricing: Theory. Empirical Assessment and Policy*, Boston: Kluwer Academic Publishers, pp. 131–40.

Oropeza, Mario and Pedro Orso (1996), 'I-15 Express Lanes Congestion Pricing Project', San Diego: San Diego Association of Governments and California Department of Transportation (November).

Pol, H.D.P. (1991), 'Road pricing: the investigation of the Dutch Rekening Rijden system', Netherlands Ministry of Transport and Public Works (February).

Ramjerdi, Farideh (1994), 'The Norwegian experience with electronic toll rings', in *Proceedings of the International Conference on Advanced Technologies in Transportation and Traffic Management*, Centre for Transportation Studies, Nanyang Technological University, Singapore (May), 135–42.

Richards, Martin, Clive Gilliam and John Larkinson (1996), 'The London congestion charging research programme: 1. The programme in overview', *Traffic Engineering and Control*, **37**, 66–71.

'SERC Funds Research on Congestion Pricing, with Cambridge a Possible Candidate Site for Demonstration', *Traffic Engineering and Control*, **31** (10), 532–3.

Sharpe, J. Michael (1993), 'Demand management: The Cambridge approach', *Transportation Studies*, Cambridgeshire County Council, Cambridge, UK (May).

Small, Kenneth A. (1992), 'Using the revenues from congestion pricing', *Transportation*, **19**, 359–81.

Social Democratic Party, Moderate Party and Liberal Party (1991), 'The Greater-Stockholm negotiation on traffic and environment: the Dennis agreement', signed by O. Lindkvist *et al.*, transmitted by Bengt Dennis to The Minister of Transportation and Communication, Stockholm, Sweden (23 January).

Stoelhorst, H.J. and A.J. Zandbergen (1990), 'The development of a road pricing system in The Netherlands', *Traffic Engineering and Control*, **31**, 66–71.

Sullivan, Edward C. and Kimberley A. Mastako (1977), 'Impact assessment for the California Route 91 variable-toll express lanes', paper no. 971046 presented to the Transportation Research Board (January).

Swedish National Rail Administration, Stockholm County Council, Greater Stockholm Transport Company, City of Stockholm and Swedish National Road Administration (1994), *Effects of the Dennis Agreement: An Overview*, Sundbyberg, Stockholm and Solna, Sweden.

'Testing the Limits', *The Economist*, (4 May, 1996), p. 59.

Toh, Rex S. (1992), 'Experimental measures to curb road congestion in Singapore: pricing and quotas', *Logistics and Transportation Review*, **28**, 289–317.

Transpotech, Ltd (1985), *Electronic Road Pricing Pilot Scheme: Main Report*, Report prepared for the Hong Kong Government (May).

Tretvik, Terje (1992), 'The Trondheim toll ring: applied technology and public opinion', SINTEP Transport Engineering, Trondheim, Norway. Presented at the joint OECD/ECMT/GVF/NFP Conference on The Use of Economic Instruments in Urban Travel Management, Basel, Switzerland (June).

UK Department of Transport (1995a), *The London Congestion Charging Research Programme: Final Report* (three volumes), London: UK Department of Transport.

UK Department of Transport (1995b), *The London Congestion Charging Research Programme: Principal Findings*, London: UK Department of Transport.

UK Ministry of Transport (1964), *Road Pricing: The Economic and Technical Possibilities*, Her Majesty's Stationery Office, London.

US National Research Council, Committee for Study on Urban Transportation Congestion Pricing (1994), *Curbing Gridlock: Peak-Period Fees to Relieve Traffic Congestion*. Vol. 1: Committee Report and Recommendations; Vol. 2: Commissioned Papers. Transportation Research Board Special Report 242. National Academy Press.

Verhoef, Erik (1996), *Economic Efficiency and Social Feasibility in the Regulation of Road Transport Externalities*, PhD Dissertation, Free University of Amsterdam.

Vickrey, William S. (1955), 'Some implications of marginal cost pricing for public utilities', *American Economic Review, Papers and Proceedings*, **45**, 605–20.

Vickrey, William S. (1963), 'Pricing in urban and suburban transport', *American Economic Review, Papers and Proceedings*, **53**, 452–65.

Vickrey, William S. (1965), 'Pricing as a tool in coordination of local transportation', in John R. Meyer (ed.), *Transportation Economics: A Conference of the Universities – National Bureau Committee for Economic Research*, New York: Columbia University Press, pp. 275–96.

Vickrey, William S. (1973), 'Pricing, metering, and efficiently using urban transportation facilities', *Highway Research Record*, **476**, 36–48.

Waersted, K. (1992), 'Automatic toll ring no stop electronic payment systems in Norway – systems layout and full scale experiences', Directorate of Public Roads, Norway, paper presented to the Sixth Institution of Electrical Engineers International Conference on Road Traffic Monitoring and Control, London (April).

Walters, A.A. (1961), 'The theory and measurement of private and social cost of highway congestion', *Econometrica*, **29**, 676–99.

Washington State Department of Transportation (WSDOT) (1994), 'Public private initiatives in transportation: status report', Public Private Initiatives in Transportation Program, WSDOT (19 August).

Watson, Peter L. and Edward P. Holland (1978), *Relieving Traffic Congestion: The Singapore Area License Scheme*, World Bank Staff Working Paper No. 281, Washington, DC.

Williams, Carl B. (1996), 'HOT lanes, road pricing and HOV doubts: 91 express lanes suggest new directions in highway policy', *Public Works Financing*, **103** (December), 21–5.

Wilson, Paul W. (1988), 'Welfare effects of congestion pricing in Singapore', *Transportation*, **15**, 191–210.

11. The equity impacts of road congestion pricing

Harry W. Richardson and Chang-Hee Christine Bae

11.1 INTRODUCTION

Although the initial discussions of road congestion pricing can be traced back to A.C. Pigou (1920) and Frank Knight (1924), the modern analysis of the topic owes much to Walters (1961, 1968) and Vickrey (1963). Their treatments primarily focused on the efficiency implications of road pricing, but equity considerations were introduced soon after (Vickrey, 1968; Foster, 1974, 1975; Richardson, 1974; Kulash, 1974) and have been debated intermittently (for example, Small, 1983; Else, 1986; Cohen, 1987) up to the present time (for example, Giuliano, 1994; Arnott, de Palma and Lindsey, 1994). This chapter has two goals: to review some of the key issues that have been emphasized in the literature on the equity consequences of road congestion pricing; and to describe an important and very recent application of road pricing in California (the FASTRAK lanes on the 91 Freeway) that is *capable* of addressing most, if not all, of the equity objections to road pricing. Real-world experience on this sophisticated and innovative roadway could make much of the previous research (often based on hypothetical behavior) obsolete.

11.2 PRELIMINARY CONSIDERATIONS

The equity implications of congestion pricing are complex because of all the different options facing travelers under a congestion pricing regime. These options include: no change in travel behavior (that is, paying the charges); increasing travel (because trip times on formerly congested roads are now reduced); unchanged travel behavior combined with attempts to reduce total automobile costs (for example, keeping vehicle longer, or replacing it with a cheaper or more fuel-efficient vehicle); changing travel behavior with the

247

same level of tripmaking (for example, changing trip time, route, or mode, such as carpools, transit); reduce tripmaking (for example, trip chaining, telecommuting, or simply traveling less); and changes in location (for example, residence, workplace, shopping destination). Travelers with different incomes will choose different options in varying proportions, and the distributional impacts will vary widely according to their responses. Also, the types of response will depend upon external conditions, such as whether free carpool lanes are available or on current conditions in the housing market (that affect residential mobility rates).

The general dimensions of the equity impacts of road pricing are well understood. In the absence of redistribution of revenues, assuming identical road users, both road users and those 'tolled off' the road suffer welfare losses, but these are typically smaller for those who stop using the road. When income differences are allowed, some users may benefit compared with the no pricing case. These are likely to be high-income drivers who suffer more from unpriced congestion because of the higher value of their travel time. Of course, once redistribution of revenues is introduced, these can be arranged to achieve pro-equity results or to minimize opposition to road pricing as a policy instrument. However, an important point about congestion tolls is that although revenue redistribution can be arranged in such a way that the lower income groups can gain, some lower-income individuals may nevertheless lose (for instance poor workers living in areas far from transit may pay more in tolls than redistributed receipts).

Moreover, equity mitigation strategies have to be carefully designed from place to place. For example, while using congestion fee revenues to finance transit programs might be effective in some world cities, it is an inappropriate strategy for the Los Angeles metropolitan region. The reason is that the low-income individuals adversely impacted by congestion pricing are unlikely to be the same individuals that might benefit from transit subsidies or employee benefits (such as transit passes or free or heavily subsidized vanpools). Redistribution of resources (including time and money) within the low-income groups as a whole is not an acceptable substitute for compensating the specific drivers that are forced either to pay substantial sums in congestion fees or incur additional time costs resulting from diverted trips. In fact, the standard prescription of designing pro-equity redistributions of toll revenues may be something of a red herring, because most redistributions are not targeted at the affected parties or are unlikely to be implemented because of the public sector's pressure for additional resources.

However, one effective method of directly compensating affected drivers is the cross-subsidization of congestion fees. Using windshield transponders of the kind adopted for the 91 Freeway in Orange County (see below), prices could vary with income upon submission of W-2s (that is, official annual payroll summaries) and income tax returns. The only problem is designing the fee structure for both wealthy and poor drivers to divert enough automobiles from the priced roads to generate enough travel savings benefits and congestion relief to those continuing to use the priced roads.

11.3   LITERATURE REVIEW

Recent overviews of congestion pricing include Levinson (1995), May (1992), Jones and Harvey (1991), Morrison (1986) and Elliott (1986). With respect to equity impacts, Small (1983) presented some of the most detailed results in his analysis of a hypothetical $1.00 peak expressway toll in the San Francisco Bay Area. Without revenue distribution, the average low-income commuter would lose $0.28 per day and the average middle-income would lose $0.13, while the average high-income commuter would gain $0.08. If revenues were redistributed on an equal per capita basis, all groups would gain but the lowest-income group would gain least. However, it is possible to redistribute revenues more progressively in ways that could even make the poorest group of drivers as a whole gain more. However, within the group it is almost certain that some individuals may still lose, for example those with long commutes, few prospects for changing jobs, tight budgets, and no capacity to change either the time or mode of travel.

As pointed out by Giuliano (1994), the equity issues in congestion pricing must consider both the distribution of benefits associated with reduced congestion (including side-benefits such as pollution reduction gains) and the distribution of costs needed to achieve the congestion benefits. However, she also suggests that equity may also be analysed in terms of fairness to population subgroups. For example, working women may be more likely to face more inflexible work schedules that reduce their options in the face of peak congestion pricing.

Giuliano also summarizes the three key findings of previous distributional impact studies. First, net impacts depend on how toll revenues are spent. Second, in most circumstances the rich will benefit more than the poor. Third, it is impossible to compensate everybody, so some groups will be made worse off by tolls (although not necessarily the poor; for example, middle-income commuters in the San Francisco Bay Area would suffer most from peak tolls because of the lack of alternative routes and times of travel).

By considering two hypothetical sets of alternatives for middle-income and for low-income commuters, Giuliano concludes that the distributional impacts of costs and benefits are less related to income than to other conditions (for instance gender, opportunities for flexible work schedules, the availability of transit and high occupancy vehicle [HOV] services). She believes that the obstacles to a widespread introduction of congestion pricing are considerable.

In an earlier paper (Giuliano, 1992, pp. 335–6), she concluded that

> it is unlikely that congestion pricing will be implemented to any significant extent in the U.S. Public skepticism regarding the effects of congestion pricing, resistance to high tolls, and pressures to divert toll revenues to new transportation facilities are barriers to effective congestion pricing programs. More likely are tolls on new capacity, tolls for specific classes of users, and other less direct and less complex auto pricing strategies.

The FASTRAK project described below is a new-capacity toll road, so that it is one of the easier options because of the benefits to non-users. However, success with such projects might spur a much broader adoption.

According to Cameron (1994), congestion costs increase with income for two reasons: high-income individuals spend more time traveling (and consequently are at greater risk from delays) and the value of their time is greater because they earn more. Congestion costs averaged about four percent of income for the highest income group falling to one percent for the lowest (of five) income groups. From this perspective, the better off have more to gain from congestion pricing. Hence, an argument in favor of congestion pricing should pay particular attention to the equity impacts. In particular

> different types of incentive fees, different levels of incentive fees, and different plans for rebating and reinvesting incentive fee revenues would have quite disparate effects on the region's various income groups. ... Market-incentive policies ... are neither inherently equitable nor inherently inequitable. How they are designed and implemented will determine their impacts on income distribution. (Cameron, 1994, p. viii)

He concludes that '(l)ocal and state officials should focus public agency attention on transportation equity. Much less is known about equity than about efficiency' (ibid., p. viii).

Cameron analyses the impact of a 5 cents per mile VMT (vehicle miles traveled) fee. Based on quintile income groups, the lower the income, the greater the cutback in auto travel. Regionwide auto travel would decline by 11 percent, but the lowest-income group would cut trips by 29 percent (the middle-income group would cut trips by 13 percent, while the top quintile would cut back by only three percent). The problem with the huge cutback by low-income households is that essential trips may have to be forgone. Also, the burden is increased by the fact that the initial distribution of the net benefits of the existing transportation system are weighted against the poor. Cameron estimates a net benefit of $650 per year for a person in the lowest quintile compared with a net benefit of $3750 for a person in the highest quintile, although the middle quintiles gain more when net benefits are expressed in percentage of income terms (16–18 percent of income).

Anderson and Mohring (1995) undertook some simulations of the impact of congestion pricing (on freeways and all roads) in the Minneapolis–St. Paul metropolitan region. They examined the impact on four income groups with average annual household incomes of $25 900, $44 900, $65 000 and $87 520 respectively. In all cases the lowest-income group suffers most. For example, in the case of totally inelastic peak-hour travel

> low income travelers would have the worst of all worlds. Seeking uncongested routes to avoid tolls would result in their trips becoming so circuitous that they would be burdened, not only by tolls, but also by spending more time on the road than they would in the absence of tolls; their time *plus* money costs of travel would almost double. (Anderson and Mohring, 1995, p. 16, original emphasis)

On the other hand, applying tolls to the whole road network would generate $1.54 of revenue for each dollar of surplus travelers would lose. Finally, Anderson and Mohring point out an important feature of almost all the estimates of the value of travel time: they are typically based on modal choice decisions (transit vs. auto) of commuters, a strange focus given that about three-quarters of trips are non-work trips and that many of these trips take place in peak travel hours. Giuliano (1994) challenged this position by quoting surveys on three Los Angeles freeways that suggested that the vast majority of trips were work-related. But the data referred to the morning peak; non-work trips are much more common in the afternoon peak, although some of these may be diverted off the most congested routes.

In an analysis of roads with congestion tolls compared to HOV services (for example, carpool lanes) and regular untolled roads, Gomez-Ibañez (1992) identified three groups of winners, three groups of losers and an indeterminate seventh group. The winners include: solo drivers who gain because the toll is more than offset by time savings; continuing users of HOV lanes; and recipients of toll revenues. The losers are: solo drivers with time savings valued less than the toll; those who shift to a less convenient road or route; and those already using these alternative, now more congested, roads. The impact on the solo driving group that shifts to HOV modes is unclear because the answer depends on a comparison of the toll saving with the degree of inconvenience associated with using the HOV mode.

Verhoef (1996) explored some of the equity implications of road pricing via a survey of peak road users in the Randstad area of the Netherlands, covering 1327 respondents (a 40 percent response rate). Although about one-half of the respondents were opposed to road pricing, most (83 percent) stated that their opinion depended upon how revenues would be allocated. The study revealed that the most important alternative to even 'prohibitive' road pricing was 'no alternative' with rescheduling the trip a distant second. If many road users decide to bear the congestion charges, the use of revenues becomes even more critical. The survey indicated a preference for the following uses (in descending order): investment in new roads, reduction in vehicle ownership taxes, fuel tax cuts, public transit subsidies, investment in carpool facilities, general tax reductions, general public investment, and government budget relief. As a generalization, respondents preferred allocations of the revenues in ways that directly benefit them as road users. Possibly, the most progressive use of the revenues would be to replace some of the vehicle ownership taxes used to finance roads, especially by reducing these taxes more on the smaller and cheaper vehicles predominantly owned by the lower income drivers.

Revenue redistribution is not an insignificant item; Small (1992) estimates that regionwide congestion pricing in Los Angeles could generate toll revenues of $3 billion per year. One pro-equity approach is to use toll revenues to offset regressive taxes, especially those used to finance transportation projects, such as gasoline and sales taxes. Another idea is that if the commuters adversely affected are concentrated in limited geographical areas, revenues could be targeted to those locations in the form of commuter subsidies, tax rebates or improvements in local transportation. Small (1992) suggested a three-way distribution of toll revenues in a hypothetical Los Angeles road pricing program: one-third in the form of rebates to drivers, one-third to taxpayers in the form of tax reductions, and one-third as transportation (especially transit) improvements.

A neglected aspect of the equity impact of congestion pricing is how it affects transit use. If extensive modal shifts towards transit occurred, it is possible that transit services might become more congested. But more probable impacts are improvements in transit services if toll revenues are redistributed to transit agencies and faster traffic flows for transit resulting from congestion relief (Kain, 1994).

11.4   CONGESTION PRICING, AIR QUALITY AND EQUITY

Most transportation measures, including congestion pricing, have been justified in terms not only of congestion relief but also of air quality improvement. However, the link between congestion pricing and reductions in air pollution is very complex. In fact, it is not proven that congestion pricing would result in significant improvements in air quality (Bae and Richardson, 1994; Richardson and Bae, 1994).

Preliminary considerations include: measures to reduce VHT (vehicle hours of travel) are more effective in cutting emissions than VMT-reduction measures; congestion pricing may not reduce emissions because it may stimulate more and/or longer trips; and congestion pricing may have an unclear impact on the 'jobs–housing balance' effect by inducing more people to change homes or workplaces either to shorten trips or to switch them to unpriced roads. On the other hand, some studies (for example Cameron, 1991) have suggested emission reductions in the 8–15 percent range.

Guensler and Sperling (1993) identified several different impacts of congestion pricing that might affect vehicle emissions: its effects on: (i) the number of trips; (ii) the length of trips; (iii) vehicle miles of travel; (iv) the reduction in congestion and the associated smoother traffic flow; (v) traffic speeds; (vi) the distribution and relative speed of traffic between freeways and local roads; (vii) the distribution between peak and off-peak travel; (viii) the amount of trip-chaining; and (ix) the impact on carpooling and transit use.

What are the key research results? First, the impact of congestion pricing on the number of trips is critical. The reason is that trip-end emissions (cold starts and hot soaks) account for 65 percent of total hydrocarbon emissions on a ten-mile average speed trip. Second, a congestion price of $0.15 per mile might reduce automobile emissions by only 4 percent (Harvey, 1991). Third, if congestion pricing affects the tripmaking behavior of the lower-income groups, the impacts (whatever they are) may be magnified because the poor are more likely to drive older, more polluting vehicles. Fourth, time-specific pricing might worsen air quality if it results in changes from moderate (for example, 30–40 mph) to high free-flow travel speeds. Fifth, high acceleration and deceleration rates increase emissions significantly so much depends on the extent to which congestion pricing reduces stop-and-go traffic. Sixth, air pollution gains from freeway pricing may be outweighed by the effects of more congestion and reduced speeds on unpriced arterial roads. Seventh, it is impossible to draw clear conclusions from current emissions modeling efforts about the impact on emissions of policies that change travel speeds, because of the wide range of uncertainties about the size of these impacts.

This brief review suggests that in the current state of knowledge it is difficult to measure the favourable impact, if any, that congestion pricing might have on air quality. This is so, despite the almost universal citing of air quality benefits as a side-effect of road congestion charges. However, if these benefits are shown to exist, would they have a pro-equity impact or not? Bae (1996) has shown that measures to improve air quality in the Los Angeles metropolitan region have progressive income distribution impacts. One explanation is that air quality varies widely from one community to another within the region, and the poor tend to congregate within currently polluted neighborhoods that will become cleaner by the attainment of Federal clean air standards. The improvement would be greater for ozone than for other pollutants (smog levels in Los Angeles are about three times the Federal standard), and mobile sources are the major contributor to smog precursors. Another explanation is that even within the same community poor people would usually benefit more than the rich because at moderate income levels health benefits swamp the modest unemployment risks, and price and tax impacts (see Bae, 1996, for the technical analysis underpinning these conclusions).

11.5   INTERNATIONAL APPLICATIONS

There are at least six types of congestion pricing: point pricing (a road user passing a point is charged a fixed fee regardless of distance traveled); cordon pricing (a fee charged to enter a congested area at each entry point); zone pricing (differential charges within a cordoned area); variation of parking charges with the degree of congestion; charges for distance traveled; and congestion charges related to both time spent and distance traveled. Among the cases mentioned here, Singapore uses cordon pricing as does Trondheim (Norway), while the A-1 toll road outside Paris charges for distance traveled. The 91 Fwy scheme in the Los Angeles metropolitan region (discussed in detail below) uses a point pricing approach.

The oldest and most well-known application of road pricing is the Singapore scheme first introduced in 1975 (Hau, 1992). The low-technology approach, a windshield sticker with a fixed cost per day for entering the CBD at 33 access points, has been quite effective in reducing congestion (by about 25 percent) and the compliance rate is very high.

France's A-1 toll road scheme varies the standard toll by giving a discount in low-traffic periods and applying a premium at congested times at levels that are revenue-neutral. Its impact was to induce some changes in the time of travel not to divert traffic to alternative routes.

In Norway, Oslo and Trondheim have implemented an electronic road pricing scheme that is similar to that adopted in the 91 Fwy scheme (FASTRAK). The differences are that: the programmes are aimed at raising revenue rather than reducing congestion (although in Trondheim a small premium is charged in peak traffic periods) and that users can pay tolls manually (in the FASTRAK scheme even three-person carpoolers who ride free have to have a windshield responder). Hong Kong also experimented with the technology of electronic pricing between 1983 and 1985, but a real-world congestion pricing scheme was never introduced after the proposal was rejected by the vote of neighbourhood councils. Congestion pricing schemes have also been seriously considered in Stockholm, the Randstad region in Holland and in London.

11.6 FASTRAK: REAL WORLD CONGESTION PRICING AT LAST

With the introduction of FASTRAK, a privately financed 10-mile toll road in Orange County, California in December 1995, we now have a real-world experiment in congestion pricing. FASTRAK was facilitated by several favorable conditions: high traffic volumes, strong local support, prospects for early implementation, and access to financing. Features of the system include: a transferable windshield transponder of about 3.5 inches square that automatically collects tolls without human intervention (that is an AVI/ETC [automatic vehicle identifier/electronic toll collection] system); an infinitely flexible dynamic congestion pricing mechanism that could change toll levels at the push of a button as frequently as required to maintain the goal of 65 mph free flow of traffic on the priced road (although in its initial phase, the road used only 5 preset toll levels between $0.25 and $2.50, with the peak toll increased in early 1997 to $2.75); the potential for cross-subsidization by charging different rates to different transponder serial numbers (this is not planned, but it is critically important from the equity perspective because users with different incomes could be charged according to their willingness to pay); a free carpool lane for vehicles with three or more occupants (although such vehicles still require a transponder).

As of December 1996, 70 000 transponders had been leased. However, daily weekday ridership is less than the number of lessees: 25 000 vehicles, with 41 000 riders. The peak-hour flow is currently about 2400 vehicles per hour. The technology permits processing of 2500 vehicle transactions per hour and stores more than 65 000 transactions. Hitherto, the road is a win–win situation for both users and non-users, because it increased freeway capacity by 50 percent so that traffic speeds have improved on both the toll road and the free road (improving from congestion level F3 to D; F3 is the worst level of congestion implying 3 or more hours of traffic at 30 mph or less, while level D implies the heaviest degree of uncongested traffic). Prior to the opening of FASTRAK, hourly traffic flow was in the congested range (7250–8500 vehicles per hour) between 4:00 a.m. and 9:00 a.m. and between 2:00 p.m. and 7:00 p.m. However, as the pace of development picks up in Riverside County, the improvement on the untolled sections of the road may not last. The time savings per vehicle in the peak are estimated at 20 minutes one-way. Prices are not regulated but the corporation is limited to a maximum internal rate of return of 17 percent, with any excess revenues going to State and local highway projects. There is a small revenue shortfall below expectations. The prime reason is that too many free 3-rider or other HOV users are on the road in peak hours, undermining the 20-minute trip saving guarantee. This explains the 25 cents increase in the peak rate as an attempt to shift some users to near-peak times.

It could be argued that the toll road is more equitable than 'free' publicly financed highways, financed by revenues (for example, Federal and State gasoline taxes, State user fees, State and local sales taxes, property taxes) that are mainly regressive; the exception is Federal and State income taxes which are, nominally at least, progressive. The cost of the road was $126 million, including the technology component. The operations and maintenance costs over the lifetime of the project (after 35 years the ownership of the road reverts to the State of California) are estimated to amount to $120 million, including payments to Caltrans (the State of California Department of Transportation) to maintain the road and to the California Highway Patrol to police it. Although violators may be caught manually, the licence number of any vehicle without a transponder is automatically videotaped, and penalties (ranging from $100 for a first offence to $500 for a third offence) are imposed by mail using Department of Motor Vehicle ownership records. The road has specific appeal to certain groups such as workers with inflexible work schedules and independent contractors with variable work hours (for whom time directly means money).

The FASTRAK system is consistent with equity goals because it offers drivers an option demand on every trip (provided that they have had the foresight to obtain a transponder in advance). There is at each of the three entry points one-and-a-half miles of road during which the decision to use the priced road can be made. In making this decision, drivers will take into account the flow of traffic on the 'free' road, the prevailing toll, and – most important – their own needs for time savings on that particular day. Most of the motorists that have obtained transponders use the toll road relatively infrequently, and only a very small proportion pay the maximum toll of $27.50 for five peak round trips per week. A slightly regressive characteristic of FASTRAK is that users without credit cards have to pay a $40 refundable cash deposit to lease a transponder whereas credit card users can post the deposit without it being charged. However, under an agreement between the operating company (California Private Transportation, Inc.) and Riverside County, county employees are exempt from the deposit.

Unfortunately, there has not yet been any research on who uses FASTRAK and why. The operators are reluctant to release information because they are probably competing for contracts on new toll roads (for example in Minnesota, Texas and Washington State), and they have not collected income or related data from their customers (at best, they have only the poor proxy of car model and year). Such information would be valuable because the system offers favorable conditions for a relatively clean test. There are almost no alternative routes or modes. The adjacent road (literally feet away) offers the same level of service with the critical exceptions of slower speed but no toll. In addition, there is enough variation in tolls by time of day to illustrate willingness to pay under different conditions and times. The information made available would be based on market decisions rather than on hypothetical stated preferences or assumed alternative responses by equity-impact analysts. Furthermore, the technology permits research results to be obtained without manual traffic counts or other costly research methods: the only requirement would be the ability to assign income classes and commuter status to transponder numbers; also, the operator's records will automatically show use of the road, while for commuters non-use could be assumed to reflect choosing the 'free' road (after allowing for absenteeism, illness and other irregularities in commuting behavior). Finally, the results would be independent of alternative uses of the toll revenues because in this case the use is fixed (to repay for the costs of building, operating and maintaining the toll road). Of course, a comprehensive distributional impact analysis would require analysis of many other variables, such as the extent to which faster speeds generate new traffic, the impact of the toll road on land values, and induced changes in location.

The appeal of the FASTRAK and similar systems is that the standard hierarchical choice of adjustments (first choice: change the travel time [easier for higher-income commuters, males and certain occupations – especially sales workers who in the United States because of longer shopping hours have very flexible schedules, Giuliano, 1994]; second choice: change the route; third choice: change the mode) is unnecessary. The only adjustment needed is to choose to take the toll road or its contiguous untolled road, a decision that has to be taken in a couple of minutes by estimating expected traffic on the FASTRAK stretch on the basis of traffic flow near the entry point.

Changing the transportation mode is either impossible or unappealing in a metropolitan area such as Los Angeles where alternative modes, especially in public transit, are often not available. The advantage of the privately financed toll roads is that they juxtapose two viable alternatives side-by-side; of course, the absence of rights-of-way may limit their applicability to certain locations. The FASTRAK solution was viable only because the freeway had wide medians and because Caltrans (the California Department of Transportation) ceded the rights-of-way to the operator.

Another feature of FASTRAK is that it is not available to heavy trucks. This step was necessary to sustain the claim of 65 mph free-flow traffic, and also enabled the contractors to hold road construction costs down by substituting asphalt for concrete. However, evidence suggests that the trucking industry attempts to avoid peak-hour congestion.

The preparations for FASTRAK included analysis of focus groups stratified by income level. Interestingly, the $50 000-plus focus group worried about what other motorists might think of them driving on the toll road.

However, the $30 000 focus group recognized the value of time savings because of the precious use of the saved time (for instance time spent with family); the traditional view that the value of travel time increases with income may be incorrect for moderate and low income families with long commutes, double income jobs and other constraints eating into leisure and 'quality' time.

Giuliano (1992) identified three major pitfalls in the implementation of congestion pricing, each of which is specifically addressed by FASTRAK. The first problem is setting the correct toll (poorly set tolls could result in too much diversion or insufficient reduction in congestion); but FASTRAK has the technology to change the toll at will (infinitely adjustable). The second problem is that tolls could redistribute congestion to other roads, but FASTRAK adds 50 percent capacity to an existing road. The third problem is serious doubts about how the toll revenues would be used, but FASTRAK uses them to pay for the costs of constructing, maintaining and operating the toll road that currently benefits both the users of the toll road and the users of the adjacent 'free' road.

In the words of one observer: 'For all the loose talk about "Lexus lanes" and "pricing the poor off the road", the direct impacts of congestion charges on the poor would be small and mostly favorable. The indirect impacts in job creation would be larger and even more favorable' (Elliott, 1995, p. B9).[1]

Congestion pricing by day and by time of day avoids all the disadvantages of a VMT (vehicle miles traveled) charge based on annual odometer readings. The latter has little influence on decisions to take or not to take a particular trip. They are also very weak as pollution charges because they do not allow for differences in emission levels by time and place (for instance in Los Angeles summer morning driving into the wind does thirty times more damage that winter evening driving with the wind behind). They charge for non-local driving by drivers but do not charge for non-local drivers driving locally. They do not capture the high emission levels associated with trip-ends, that is the cold starts and the hot soaks. They invite tampering with the odometer.

Calfee and Winston (1995) have recently cast doubt on the viability of congestion tolls by arguing that 'estimated commuters' value of travel time is low – much lower than previous estimates derived from transportation mode choice models – and is surprisingly insensitive to travel conditions and how toll revenues are used. It appears that commuters, having adjusted to congestion through their modal, residential, workplace, and departure time choices, simply do not value travel time savings enough for them to benefit substantially from tolls' (Calfee and Winston, 1995, p. 4). Their findings were based on a questionnaire involving 13 different scenarios offering combinations of: private vs. public vs. unallocated toll roads, specified vs. unspecified use of revenues, traffic conditions, and 'smart' cars. Scenario 11 (a private toll road, revenues used for construction and maintenance, no trucks) best approximates the conditions on FASTRAK. The mean value of congested travel time (there is some variation, depending on the length of the commute) was $3.34 per hour. Given the estimated travel time savings on FASTRAK of 20 minutes on a one-way trip, this implies a willingness-to-pay of only $1.11. If this result was accurate, the average commuter would not choose the toll road in peak hours, and probably never at all because the time savings at the $1.00 toll zone period would be much lower than the peak saving. Even the highest income commuter ($125 000–$175 000 per year, and there are very few of these on this particular road) would value the peak-hour time savings at a little less ($2.37) than the peak toll ($2.75, in operation between 5:00 a.m. and 9:00 a.m. westbound, and between 4:00 p.m. and 7:00 p.m. eastbound, Monday to Friday). Because the toll road is being used by an increasing number of commuters, so much for even the most precise and careful of contingent valuation estimates! However, it is still possible to agree with Calfee and Winston that those commuters who have a very high WTP to reduce travel time will have already made the workplace/residence locational adjustments that reduce the worktrip and/or congestion to the extent that they were excluded from their sample.

Finally, the coexistence of a toll road and an adjacent untolled road (the FASTRAK situation) raises another issue: tolling only one of the roads may be a second-best policy if the roads are subject to congestion (Verhoef, 1996, Chapter 4; Arnott, De Palma and Lindsey, 1992; Bernstein and El Sanhouri, 1994; Liu and McDonald, 1996). In the FASTRAK case, this would be a practical issue only if congestion pricing were introduced on the Los Angeles freeway system as a whole and perhaps if additional privately-run tolled sections were built (a section of another toll road [the San Joachim Transportation Corridor] was opened in July 1996, but it cuts across open countryside and has no parallel road). However, tolling two parallel roads would normally increase efficiency. In this particular case, they could almost be treated as a single 12-lane highway; however, the fact that FASTRAK is not available for truck traffic suggests that efficiency would dictate differential tolls because the two roads offer differential speeds (even under free-flow conditions). Also, the fact that FASTRAK is private suggests that the tolls might vary because of differences between the price-setting goals of a private company (for example, revenue maximization) and the goal (for example, maximization of social welfare) of the public agency (CALTRANS) controlling the adjacent freeway. This might generate adverse route split effects, but the risk in California would be slight because the private tolls are indirectly regulated via rate-of-return ceilings (hence, revenue maximization is not an option).

The equity argument for tolling only one road even if efficiency criteria would justify tolls on both roads is simply to offer low-income drivers a zero money-cost option. However, given the assumption that low-income drivers will overwhelmingly prefer the lower-cost alternative, it may be feasible to trade off efficiency and equity in an acceptable, if not necessarily an optimal, manner by tolling both roads but with a wide enough differential between the two roads both to satisfy equity goals and to approximate marginal social cost pricing criteria on both roads (after taking into account the differences in the value of travel time among income groups). Also, as pointed out above (p. 248–9), FASTRAK technology would permit cross-subsidization via differential tolls, even on the same road.

11.7 CONCLUSION

Although the case for road congestion pricing has rightly stressed its efficiency benefits, the equity consequences have continued to receive attention and have often been used as an argument to justify the political unacceptability of road pricing. However, the FASTRAK system has changed the focus of the discussion. It shows that the objections disappear in cases where the priced road adds to capacity; of course, this is not always possible. A privately financed road also deals directly with the revenue distribution problem according to the benefit principle. It also demonstrates that the technology is now available to permit instantaneous adjustment of the prices in response to changes in traffic conditions and to charge different rates to different road users, a feature that if adopted could deal with the equity issue once and for all. However, the FASTRAK scheme will still need to be evaluated after more experience with the system (for example its first two years of operation). From that perspective, it is a pity that the operators did not collect more information (for instance on socioeconomic characteristics) from the transponder applicants. The survey research required will be expensive to undertake from scratch, but the shift from contingent valuation studies to real-world behavior would make it very worthwhile.

NOTE

1. The term 'Lexus lane' derives from the name of Toyota's luxury car division.

REFERENCES

Anderson, D. and H. Mohring (1995), 'Congestion costs and congestion pricing', paper presented at the Conference on Congestion Pricing at the Beckman Center, Irvine, California, 6–8 July.

Arnott, R., A. de Palma and R. Lindsey (1992), 'Route choice with heterogeneous drivers and group-specific congestion costs', *Regional Science and Urban Economics*, **22**, 71–102.

Arnott, R., A. de Palma and R. Lindsey (1994), 'The welfare effects of congestion tolls with hetrogeneous commuters', *Journal of Transport Economics and Policy*, **28**, 139–61.

Bae, C.-H.C. (1996), 'The equity impacts of Los Angeles' air quality policies', *Environment and Planning A*, **29**, 1563–84.

Bae, C.-H.C. and H.W. Richardson (1994), 'Automobiles, the environment and metropolitan spatial structure', Cambridge, MA: Lincoln Institute of Land Policy Working Paper.

Bernstein, D. and I. El Sanhouri (1994), 'Congestion pricing with an untolled alternative', Cambridge, MA: Massachusetts Institute of Technology.

Calfee, J.E. and C.M. Winston (1995), 'The value of automobile travel time: implications for congestion policy', Brookings Institution Working Paper, September.

Cameron, M.W. (1991), *Transportation Efficiency: Tackling Southern California's Air Pollution and Congestion*, Oakland, CA: Environmental Defense Fund.

Cameron, M.W. (1994), *Efficiency and Fairness on the Road: Strategies for Unsnarling Traffic in Southern California*, Oakland, CA: Environmental Defense Fund.

Cohen, Y. (1987), 'Commuter welfare under peak period congestion tolls: Who gains and who loses?', *International Journal of Transport Economics*, **14** (3), 239–66.

Elliot, W. (1986), 'Fumbling toward the edge of history: California's quest for a road pricing experiment', *Transportation Research A*, **20A** (2), 151–6.

Elliott, W. (1995), 'Toll lanes aren't elitist; they're smooth riding for all', *Los Angeles Times*, 8 December, p. B9.

Else, P. (1986), 'No entry for congestion taxes?', *Transportation Research A*, **20A** (2), 99–107.

Foster, C. (1974), 'The regressiveness of road pricing,' *International Journal of Transport Economics*, **1**, 133–41.

Foster, C. (1975), 'A note on the distributional effects of road pricing: a comment,' *Journal of Transport Economics and Policy*, **9**, 186–7.

Giuliano, G. (1992), 'An assessment of the political acceptability of congestion pricing', *Transportation*, **19**, 335–58.

Giuliano, G. (1994), 'Equity and fairness considerations of congestion pricing', in *Curbing Gridlock: Peak-Period Fees to Relieve Traffic Congestion*, Transportation Research Board Special Report 242, Vol. 2. Washington, DC: National Academy Press, pp. 250–79.

Gomez-Ibañez, J.A. (1992), 'The political economy of highway tolls and congestion pricing', in Federal Highway Administration, *Exploring the Role of Pricing as a Congestion Management Tool*, Washington, DC: FHA.

Guensler, R. and D. Sperling (1993), 'Congestion pricing and motor vehicle emissions: an initial review', Paper prepared for the TRB/CBASSE Congestion Pricing Symposium, Washington, DC.

Harvey, G. (1991), 'Pricing as a transportation control strategy', Berkeley, CA: Deaki, Harvey, Skarbardonis.

Hau, T. (1992), *Congestion Charging Mechanisms: An Evaluation of Current Practice*, Washington, DC: World Bank.

Jones, P. and S. Harvey (1991), 'Urban road pricing: dealing with the issue of public acceptability – a UK perspective', University of Oxford, Transport Studies Unit, WP TSU669.

Kain, J. (1994), 'Impacts of congestion pricing on transit and carpool demand and supply', in National Research Council, op. cit., 502–53.

Knight, F.H. (1924), 'Some fallacies in the interpretation of social cost', *Quarterly Journal of Economics*, **38**, 582–606.

Kulash, D.J. (1974), *Income Distributional Consequences of Roadway Pricing*, Washington, DC: The Urban Institute.

Levinson, H.S. (1995), 'Freeway congestion pricing: another look', *Transportation Research Record*, No. 1450, 8–12.

Liu and McDonald (1996), 'Efficient congestion tolls in the presence of unpriced congestion: some simulation results', mimeo, University of Illinois at Chicago.

May, A.D. (1992), 'Road pricing: an international perspective', *Transportation*, **19** (4), 313–33.

Morrison, S. (1986), 'A survey of road pricing', *Transportation Research A*, **20A** (2), 87–96.

Pigou, A.C. (1920), *Wealth and Welfare*, London: Macmillan.

Richardson, H.W. (1974), 'A note on the distributional effects of road pricing', *Journal of Transport Economics and Policy*, **8** (1). 82–5.

Richardson, H.W. and C.-H.C. Bae (1994), 'Brown sky blues: are transportation Rxs a cure', La Jolla: 1994 ITE International Conference Paper.

Small, K.A. (1983), 'The incidence of congestion tolls on urban highways', *Journal of Urban Economics*, **13**, 90–111.

Small, K.A. (1992), 'Using the revenues from congestion pricing', *Transportation*, **19**, 359–81.

Verhoef, E.T. (1996), *The Economics of Regulating Road Transport*, Aldershot: Edward Elgar.

Vickrey, W.S. (1963), 'Pricing in urban and suburban transport', *American Economic Review, Papers and Proceedings*, **53**, 452–65.

Vickrey, W.S. (1968), 'Congestion charges and welfare', *Journal of Transport Economics and Policy*, **2**, 107–18.

Walters, A.A. (1961), 'The theory and measurement of private and social cost of highway congestion', *Econometrica*, **29** (4), 676–97.

Walters, A.A. (1968), *The Economics of Road User Charges*, Baltimore: Johns Hopkins University Press.

12. Urban road pricing: public acceptability and barriers to implementation

Peter Jones

12.1 INTRODUCTION

As other chapters in this volume and elsewhere have demonstrated (for example Goodwin and Jones, 1989), the theoretical benefits of road pricing have been well known to economists for decades, and over recent years have become gradually accepted by transport professionals from other disciplines – either on economic efficiency grounds or with an eye on the revenue stream generated by the charges.

There have been many attempts to introduce urban road pricing around the world over the last 40 years – and most have failed. Examples of schemes that were never implemented include London (May, 1975) and Kuala Lumpur (both supplementary licensing), electronic road pricing schemes for Hong Kong (Harrison, 1986) and the Netherlands (Stoelhorst and Zandbergen, 1990; Emmerink *et al.*, 1995) and various proposals in the United States. In most cases extensive professional studies had demonstrated the technical feasibility and economic benefits of introducing the scheme, but the stumbling block was public and political acceptability. Too often this aspect was given inadequate attention, in the mistaken belief that a scheme which showed strong social and economic benefits would sell itself.

While there are still some important technical and operational issues to be resolved, it is now generally accepted that probably the greatest barrier to implementation is public (and, linked to this, political) acceptability. The argument behind this paper is that issues of public and political acceptability should be at the forefront when debating and designing road pricing schemes – and not left as an afterthought, once a scheme has been selected on other grounds.

This pushes to the forefront perhaps the most fundamental question of all: is it possible to design an urban road pricing scheme that is both publicly/ politically acceptable *and* effective at meeting policy objectives? At face value these two objectives seem to be in opposition. Public acceptability is likely to be increased by lowering charges or broadening the range of exemptions, but with the consequence of 'watering down' the effectiveness of the scheme, perhaps to the point where there may be little to gain from its introduction.

In the past, the limitations of manual schemes meant that there were only a few practical options for introducing urban road pricing and hence a 'take it or leave it' attitude was perhaps inevitable. Now, however, with rapid developments in technology (for example electronic vehicle identification, on- and off-vehicle toll collection and enforcement), this is no longer a constraint and there are almost limitless possibilities for scheme design. This greatly increases the possibilities of finding solutions that are both effective and acceptable.

This chapter looks at the issue of road pricing through the eyes of the public, drawing on a number of published and unpublished public attitude studies from the UK and elsewhere (see also Jones, 1995). It first summarizes the range of concerns that have been expressed about urban road pricing in public attitude surveys (Section 12.2). Drawing on this data, Section 12.3 then identifies four key issues that it is argued will have to be satisfactorily addressed if road pricing is to be introduced with public support. Section 12.4 reviews the key parameters of scheme design that can be adjusted to produce solutions that can gain public support, and Section 12.5 gives some examples of specific schemes that would address particular concerns and give priorities or discounts to particular groups. Finally, Section 12.6 considers the wider policy context and suggests some areas for further research.

The examples of possible schemes in Section 12.5 are purely illustrative. It is only through carrying out detailed research with members of the public locally that an acceptable and effective urban road pricing scheme for a given area is likely to result.

12.2   PUBLIC CONCERNS ABOUT ROAD PRICING

Many countries impose tolls on parts of their road system, either to pay for the creation of a high capacity/performance network (for example motorway tolling in France and Spain), or to recoup investment in particularly expensive links (for example estuarial river crossings or tunnels through mountains). While most drivers have come to accept this principle, and the experience of paying such tolls can assist drivers in relating to the concept of urban road pricing, at the same time it can lead to serious confusion, in two respects. First, the objectives of motorway tolling (that is to pay for improved road infrastructure) and urban road pricing (that is to suppress demand and fund improvements to alternative modes) are different. Second, conventional toll plazas are often very space consuming and this can cause anxiety in the public mind as to how charging could be implemented in urban areas.

There have been public attitude surveys in many countries that collectively have identified a wide range of concerns about proposals to charge drivers directly for road use in urban areas (for example Borins, 1988;·Verhoef *et al.*, 1997). These can be grouped under eight headings.

12.2.1 Drivers find it Difficult to Accept the Notion that they Should be 'Charged for Congestion'

When first introduced to the concept of 'congestion charging' many drivers react strongly against the idea that they should be charged on the basis of the amount of congestion they encounter (or based on related measures, such as travel time on the network): this seems to them to be irrational and inappropriate.

Further probing identifies three factors underlying this reaction:

(i)   People expect to be charged for things they wish to acquire, not the things they wish to avoid; the notion of congestion charging is simply interpreted as being asked to pay for congestion, which is the last thing that drivers want!

(ii) This is compounded by the fact that most drivers see themselves as victims of congestion, not contributors to it. There is usually a recognition that collectively the volume of traffic results in the observed level of congestion on the network, but most see this as an internality of the system, not an externality: it is something that is collectively tolerated, because the alternatives are less attractive. Drivers feel they are already 'paying for congestion' in terms of the delays encountered en route and the additional stress of driving in congested conditions – why should they pay twice?

(iii) There is a concern that any attempt to charge drivers directly in proportion to the congestion they are experiencing (either using a congestion meter, as proposed in the Cambridge trial or on the basis of travel time) would encourage bad driving and would increase stress and traffic accidents. This effect has recently been confirmed in a series of trials using a driving simulator.

12.2.2 Urban Road Pricing is not Needed

The instinctive reaction is often to argue that introducing urban road pricing is a very extreme measure – charging for the use of the public road network that people have come to regard as free at the point of use – and should only be contemplated in extreme circumstances. In most cases it is not needed.

This lack of need for road pricing is argued on two grounds:

(i) Road traffic conditions are not bad enough to warrant the use of such an extreme measure, people would rather put up with the delays; or
(ii) Traffic containment or reduction is needed, but it could be better or more appropriately achieved in other ways. Either by simply improving modal alternatives (for example 'better public transport') or through the use of other restraint measures such as bans on road traffic in major shopping streets, or restrictions on access to certain parts of the road network. Something less 'draconian' will suffice.

12.2.3 Pricing will not Get People Out of Their Cars

Drivers often express the opinion that pricing will be a very ineffective means of discouraging car use, or in economic terms that drivers will be inelastic to road charges. This is based on the belief that, having paid for their car and its running costs, the costs of use represent a small proportion of the total and that drivers will want to maximize the benefit from their investment. This view is strengthened by the feeling that, however high the charges, most drivers will be 'forced' to carry on driving as the alternative transport modes are inadequate (that is they do not provide an adequate level or quality of service) or are inappropriate (for example not suited to carrying large loads or transporting young children).

Interestingly, driver attitudes to charging are inconsistent, as one of the most popular suggestions for getting car drivers to switch to public transport is to reduce the price of the fares – suggesting that, in this direction at least, car drivers are highly price elastic. Although it is possible to conceive of an asymmetrical demand curve, the evidence suggests that this is largely a perceptual distortion rather than an observed behavioural response.

12.2.4 The Technology Involved in Electronic Road Pricing will not Work

Although the Singapore urban road pricing scheme has successfully operated using a paper disk for over 20 years, and the Bergen toll ring uses no more advanced technology than a video camera, it is generally accepted that in most urban areas some form of electronic recognition, payment and enforcement system would be needed for a comprehensive road pricing scheme. Recently implemented schemes in Norway and the USA have all used electronic payment systems.

In some societies, this can raise a set of concerns about the reliability of the technology and about the privacy issues that may arise (see also Section 12.2.5). In the UK in particular, there is still relatively little experience of electronic tracking and debiting technology, and an electronic form of urban road pricing raises two kinds of concern:

(i)   That the technology may misfunction, either by not correctly recording the passage of a particular vehicle or by making an incorrect charge for the use of the road network. In a large city such as London the sheer scale of the exercise also results in some scepticism about the practicality of the exercise. Well publicized failures, ranging from new computer systems for the London Stock Exchange and the London Ambulance Service, heighten public concerns.

(ii)   Even were the technology to be very reliable some people argue that 'it would not work' because large numbers of drivers would refuse to pay. Doubts are expressed either about the ability of the system to detect non-compliance (including the possibility of forged payment cards), or that it would become administratively overloaded by the volume of offenses committed.

These problems are compounded by confusion in the public mind by the wide range of technologies on offer (including different on- and off-vehicle charging systems, various communications and tracking procedures, and so on), and the lack of first-hand experience of their successful operation.

12.2.5   Electronic Road Pricing can Result in Unacceptable Privacy Issues

Concerns about the tracking of individual car trips by authorities and the potential invasion of privacy feature strongly in public discussions about road pricing, but in a way that leads to a 'Catch 22' situation.

On the one hand drivers worry about the ability of the system to identify individual movements and potentially disclose or otherwise misuse information of a personal nature. On the other hand, if no record is kept of individual movements, there is a worry that drivers may be incorrectly charged with no basis on which that charge can subsequently be checked and challenged.

Technological solutions to this conundrum are becoming available, whereby the movement information is stored on a smart card normally kept by the driver, but it is an issue that is still important in the public mind.

12.2.6   Road Pricing will Cause Severe Boundary Problems

The simplest forms of road pricing that can be explained to the public, and the ones that have been introduced to date in Norway and Singapore, involve a cordon or boundary charge for entering an area. One concern that this raises is that in response to such a scheme many drivers will park just outside the area and complete their journey on foot or by public transport, and that large volumes of through traffic will divert around the area – bringing congestion to previously uncongested areas.

There is some evidence of this having occurred in Singapore (and also in cities with central access restrictions), but less so in Norway which has a lower charge and where the cordon is further out from the city centre and the cordon is located so as to minimize the possibilities for diversion. This is an important issue, but not one that is unique to restraint schemes based on road pricing.

12.2.7   Road Pricing is Just Another Form of Taxation

One feature of many Western democracies is a growing suspicion of government and its (mis)use of tax raising powers. In the UK, for example, the annual Vehicle Exercise Duty (VED), which is payable for the use of a vehicle on the public highway, was originally designated as the Road Fund License, with revenues hypothecated for new road building. While this link was severed many decades ago, it is still remembered by most drivers.

Not only is the UK Treasury very resistant to the idea of hypothecating road pricing revenues for particular purposes, but the public are also very wary about the government keeping their word in the longer term. There is a fear that a hypothecated road pricing charge might just become an 'easy option' for absorption when additional tax revenues need to be raised.

12.2.8   Road Pricing is 'Unfair'

When the other concerns about road pricing have been addressed, there is usually one remaining issue that people find difficult to articulate, but has broadly to do with equity and can be summed up in the phrase: 'It isn't fair'. What is meant by this depends on the objectives behind the road pricing scheme.

In situations where a scheme is proposed in order primarily to reduce traffic levels (that is some form of charging to meet congestion or traffic reduction objectives) this concern about fairness is primarily *social* in nature and derives from two sources:

(i) The urban road network (unlike motorways) is implicitly viewed as a general purpose public space, which all are free to share. With the encroachment of the market on other areas that were previously in the public domain (for example the growth of shopping malls and other places where public access is controlled), it represents one of a diminishing number of situations where people are treated equally. As car drivers, all have equal access to the road network, regardless of income, status, and so on.

(ii) The aim of congestion pricing is explicitly to take some traffic off the road network. The question is whether those least able to pay the charges represent the types of traffic that in social terms are regarded as the least essential. In the minds of many, ability to pay and the importance of the trip are not synonymous; drivers often cite the need for poorer people with a car to get to work, visit sick relatives, and so on. In this context, congestion may be viewed as a socially preferable form of rationing (using time) rather than introducing rationing by money.

As a consequence, there is pressure to exclude certain groups from incurring charges (or to offer them discounted charges) in order to address social equity issues.

Conversely, where road pricing is being introduced primarily as a revenue raising mechanism, as has been the case with the Norwegian toll rings, and there is no direct intention of using charging as a means of removing drivers from the road network, then the issue of equity is primarily *geographical* in nature.

Here the concern is that not everyone who will benefit from the investments paid for by the toll rings are contributing their fair share in charges. In Trondheim it is estimated that one-third of drivers contribute two-thirds of the income and a third virtually nothing, though all stand to gain. The problem is that not enough drivers are contributing their 'fair' share and hence the pressure is to include additional groups. In this situation the solution may be to introduce additional rings, to capture a higher proportion of existing car trips.

12.3 OVERCOMING BARRIERS TO PUBLIC ACCEPTABILITY

Based on the concerns expressed by the public, it is evident that four general arguments have to be won before road pricing can be introduced into urban areas with majority public support. Namely that:

1. there is a need to take some action to restrain traffic levels;
2. the alternatives to road pricing are ineffective or insufficient;
3. road pricing is a practical and effective measure; and
4. equity concerns can be addressed.

12.3.1   An Agreed Need for Action

There is considerable public concern about the growth of road traffic and its consequences, and this level of concern is increasing in many countries (Jones, 1995).

Various opinion surveys carried out in the UK in the last few years have confirmed that traffic congestion, and the road safety and environmental implications of traffic, are at the forefront of most people's minds. Nationally, around 80 per cent of adults regard current traffic levels in general as posing a 'Very' or 'Fairly Serious' problem. Concern about traffic-related problems rises to an overwhelming 95 per cent when people are asked about congestion and pollution in larger towns and cities. In a survey in London in 1991, traffic congestion was more often cited as a serious problem than house prices or crime. There is also a general perception that conditions are deteriorating, both in terms of worsening traffic congestion and the other traffic-related externalities.

While traffic congestion and the unpredictability of journey times ranks as the major traffic-related concern of businesses in the UK, this is not the case among the general public. Quimby and Downing (1991) asked how concerned people felt about a wide range of social issues, including some traffic-related problems. Overall, 56 per cent reported being 'Very Concerned' about pollution of the environment (the highest score), 41 per cent about road safety, and 35 per cent said they were 'Very Concerned' about traffic congestion. The 1996 Lex Survey of UK drivers and non-drivers (Lex, 1996) found that around 70 per cent of both groups saw traffic congestion in cities and air pollution as major problems; however, when asked which issue they were most concerned about, more than twice as many opted for air pollution than for traffic congestion.

This rank ordering seems to reflect the relative concern found for these issues in several other national surveys; although traffic congestion may have a higher profile in everyday discussion, deeper concerns are generally felt about environmental deterioration and injury or loss of life. This is supported by findings from UK qualitative surveys too, where drivers seem more willing to contemplate measures that may in some way restrict or penalize them, if they result in clear safety or environmental benefits (Jones *et al.*, 1996). This also seems to be borne out politically, in that cities that have taken action against the car (for example Athens or Milan) have done so primarily because of concerns about deteriorating air quality rather than about traffic levels *per se*.

At the European level, the International Union of Public Transport (UITP) and the European Commission sponsored a study of European attitudes towards 'Access to City Centres', in all member states of the European Union. The study comprised a public attitude survey (1000 adults per country), and a smaller study of decision makers' attitudes. Respondents were asked about the effects of car traffic in the urban area in which they lived/worked/shopped on their ability to carry out such activities. Across Europe as a whole, 59 per cent described these consequences as 'Hardly bearable' or 'Unbearable', with this proportion ranging from a low of 27 per cent in Denmark to a high of 84 per cent in Italy. For political decision makers across Europe, 73 per cent rated the consequences of urban car traffic as being 'Hardly bearable' or 'Unbearable', and all mentioned some traffic-related problem in their city.

When asked more specifically about what contribution they thought that car traffic in the city centre made to a deterioration in the quality of the air, 78 per cent of adults across Europe as a whole saw this as the main cause or an important cause of the deterioration, with percentages ranging from a low of 57 per cent in Ireland up to 95 per cent in Italy. Among decision makers the mean percentage across Europe was higher, at 92 per cent.

Urban transport policies are increasingly designed to contribute to achieving a number of objectives, which typically include:

(a)　Reducing traffic congestion.
(b)　Maintaining and enhancing the economic attractiveness of urban areas.
(c)　Reducing the local environmental impact of traffic (in terms of noise levels, air pollution, and so on).
(d)　Reducing road traffic accidents.
(e)　Reducing CO_2 emissions.
(f)　Improving public transport and non-motorized modes.

There seems to be public and professional agreement that further action is needed in many urban areas to achieve most of these objectives, so the case for some additional measures has already been established. The introduction of urban road pricing charges has two general effects[1] that can contribute directly or indirectly to achieving several of these objectives:

(i)　it reduces the volume of road traffic in the charged area;
(ii)　it raises substantial net revenues.

The Area Licence Scheme (ALS) in Singapore was introduced primarily to reduce city centre traffic levels (effect (i)), with little discussion of how the revenues would be spent, while the various urban toll ring schemes in Norway were designed to raise revenue for local transport investment (effect (ii)).

Road pricing can directly assist with meeting several of the urban policy objectives outlined above within the charged area – though, depending on the type of scheme, at the expense of exacerbating these problems outside the area – and through the revenue raised can provide resources to introduce measures to advance some of the other transport objectives.

Leaving aside the question of impacts outside the charged area, urban road pricing schemes will typically reduce traffic congestion (a) and the environmental effects ((c) and (e)); but there are concerns that the economic viability of the city centre may be damaged (b), and that the higher traffic speeds resulting from the reduced congestion might increase road accidents (d).

The revenues raised can be used in various ways to further assist in meeting these objectives, both through strengthening the positive impacts of road pricing and reducing the negative ones. For example, problems of increased road accidents could be countered by the introduction of physical traffic calming measures, enhanced provision of safe pedestrian and cycle routes, and the installation of speed cameras. Congestion reduction can be aided by selective increases in road capacity, alongside the reductions in demand brought about through pricing; and net revenues can be used to improve the public transport and non-motorized mode networks (f).

12.3.2   The Inadequacy of the Alternative Solutions

Urban road pricing is not one of the more popular solutions for dealing with urban traffic problems, though its popularity is rising in the UK over time. Overall, UK surveys show strongest support for policies that provide alternatives or supplements to car use, without directly constraining the person's ability to continue travelling by car: these policies include Park and Ride schemes, general public transport improvements, and encouraging walking and cycling. Next come traffic regulations, comprising both better enforcement of existing regulations (for example better parking enforcement), and the introduction of new regulations (for example new restrictions on cars entering central areas), which generally have majority support.

This ranking of public support is mirrored to a large extent by the measures that local authorities in several European countries are currently pursuing in urban areas: public transport improvements (including new Park and Ride schemes), better cycling and walking facilities, access restrictions through enhanced pedestrianization and bus only streets, and increased parking enforcement.

For several years, UK surveys have shown that about a quarter to a third of the population support urban road pricing, with around a half or more opposed. Recently this gap has narrowed significantly and in the 1996 Lex Survey there was net opposition (that is percentage support minus percentage opposed) of only 10 per cent among car drivers and 5 per cent among non-drivers. Urban road pricing has now become much less unpopular than major new road building or than motorway tolling – a very significant shift politically.

A recent in-depth study for the UK Department of Transport of public attitudes to transport policy and the environment (Jones *et al.*, 1996) found that drivers were more likely to support road pricing and higher parking charges after they had considered the effectiveness of the measures, both in terms of influencing their own behaviour and generally reducing traffic problems in urban areas. This suggests that informed public debate is likely to further increase support for an urban road pricing policy.

Thus, while public opinion is moving towards accepting road pricing as a potential solution to urban traffic-related problems, more efforts are likely to be needed to achieve a clear majority support for implementation. This is not simply a question of 'selling' road pricing, but of identifying situations in which road pricing is a more appropriate tool than other traffic restraint measures. It is not a panacea for all problems and should not be regarded as such.

Whether road pricing is needed will depend on local circumstances, including network conditions and policy objectives. But there are good arguments in favour of road pricing. Parking controls do not deal with the congestion and air quality problems caused by through traffic or commuters with their own PNR space; and access restrictions do not raise funds to invest in public transport or traffic calming measures – indeed, the associated enforcement may be a further drain on local resources.

12.3.3   The Practical Feasibility of Road Pricing

Public concerns about the practical and technical feasibility will need to be addressed on at least three levels:

(i)   that direct road user charges will result in reduced traffic volumes – at levels of charging that are not viewed as punitive;
(ii)   that schemes can be devised that will not simply create or add to problems elsewhere, through boundary or displacement effects (as has occurred in Singapore);
(iii) that the technology will be reliable and the system will be enforceable.

Although there remains some scepticism among traffic engineers as to whether road traffic levels are sensitive to the price of travel (or to other factors such as the level of service), there is growing evidence that road pricing 'works' as a mechanism for reducing traffic volumes. The Singapore scheme reduced car traffic by well over 50 per cent after its introduction (Holland and Watson, 1978) and significant reductions in car use inside the charged area have been maintained for over two decades. Stated preference and modelling exercises in Hong Kong (Harrison, 1986) and London (MVA Consultancy, 1995) also showed that charging could significantly impact on traffic levels.

However, what is less certain is whether the desired level of reduction can be achieved with a level of charge that is below a politically acceptable threshold – even assuming it is perceived to be the most appropriate restraint measure. One difficulty here is that traffic in peak periods tends to be more inelastic than in the off-peak, so that higher charges are needed to reduce traffic levels at the most congested times of day.

Boundary effects have long been a problem with road pricing proposals, and here the moves towards electronic-based charging are likely to reduce the magnitude of the problem: time, distance or congestion-based charging have far fewer boundary problems than a cordon or area-based scheme. In addition, measures such as Controlled Parking Zones outside the charged area could be used to mitigate boundary effects.

Concerns about technological reliability will doubtless be overcome in time, but as noted in Section 12.2.4 there is considerable public scepticism about whether a large scale road pricing scheme would work. In addition, surveys by the Royal Automobile Club and others have suggested a strong conservatism regarding methods of payment, with little support for electronic payment systems. As the latter become more familiar to travellers through cashless parking and public transport Smartcard systems, it is likely that attitudes will shift quite quickly towards a greater acceptability.

12.3.4 Dealing with Equity Concerns

Equity has both an input and an output dimension: who pays? and, how should the money raised be spent? Equity concerns apply particularly in countries like the UK where the majority of the population lives in households with a car and where travel by car is regarded as a necessity for meeting the demands of daily life. It has not proved to be such a major issue in countries with much lower levels of car ownership and high levels of public transport provision such as Hong Kong or Singapore.

Who pays
As noted in Section 12.2.8, the nature of the equity concern depends on the primary objectives of the scheme and the level of charge. In the Norwegian situation, where charges are relatively low and the primary objective is to

raise revenue not decrease traffic levels, the issue is one of ensuring that the burden is shared as equally as possible. In cases where the primary aim is to reduce traffic levels (for congestion relief, environmental improvement, or both), then the issue is one of social equity: to put it in extreme form, is it fair that 'essential' car trips made by poor people should be priced off the road at the expense of non-essential trips made by rich drivers?

What this second situation leads to, when the policy objective is to reduce traffic levels, is whether pricing is the best or fairest means of achieving this reduction: does pricing take off the traffic that is generally felt to be of lowest priority? This is the core issue, determining both the most suitable form of road pricing scheme – and, indeed, whether urban road pricing is the most appropriate tool to achieve the desired reduction in traffic levels.

It is often argued that rationing on the basis of ability to pay is not only economically efficient, but also will become publicly acceptable since drivers have got used to paying for parking, and that the same would happen in time with road pricing. However, closer inspection shows that only a minority of those vehicles/drivers stopping in an area are paying for doing so at the point of use:

- Residents and employees often have free, private off-street parking spaces.
- Free private parking spaces are also sometimes provided for customers.
- Free (or reduced price) on-street parking is often provided for disabled drivers and residents when spaces are in short supply.
- On- and off-street loading activities usually take place without charge.

Were similar categories of residents, employees, disabled drivers, some customers and goods vehicles exempt from road pricing charges, then it is probable that the base would be too narrow to achieve worthwhile reductions in traffic – and it would be largely the same groups that would be affected by both road pricing and parking charging policies.

To be effective, road pricing would need to include and affect the behaviour of some groups who currently avoid paying for parking. This is likely to increase support for road pricing among some groups and decrease it among others – but it would be unwise to regard parking charges as a precedent.

The use of the revenues
In relation to the use of revenues, the evidence from public attitude surveys in the UK is clear (Jones, 1991): road pricing will not be publicly acceptable unless the money raised is hypothecated for local transport and environmental projects:

- At the national level, one survey found that 30 per cent of adults supported road pricing as a stand alone measure (with a net rejection of –27%). This support increased to 57 per cent for a road pricing based package (net support of +27 per cent), where the money raised was used to fund public transport improvements, traffic safety measures and better facilities for pedestrians and cyclists.
- In London, a survey using a similar question found 43 per cent supporting road pricing as a single measure, rising to 63 per cent when the money raised was used for purposes of which the respondents had approved.

Most professional and governmental bodies in the UK now accept that hypothecation of revenues will be part of the price that will have to be paid to gain sufficient public support for urban road pricing to ensure its introduction in this country.

Where road pricing is introduced primarily to raise revenue for specified purposes (for example for new transport investment), then its use is largely predetermined by the policy. However, where it represents a by-product of another policy objective, such as reducing traffic congestion, then revenues could be used in several ways. For example, by:

- Building additional road capacity, at junctions or by widening links.
- Installing advanced traffic control systems to enhance network capacity.
- Improving other modes, to encourage further reductions in car use: better public transport systems, improved facilities for walking and cycling, and so on.

Or in terms of meeting more general social equity concerns, by:

- Reducing general motoring taxation, at the limit by giving a near neutral effect on average motoring taxation (allowing for collection costs).
- Reducing domestic and business rates within the charged area, to counter increased costs/loss of profit.
- Improving the modal alternatives, to provide acceptable travel conditions for those displaced from cars by the road pricing charges.

There is this thus considerable scope for using revenues in a variety of ways to further policy objectives and to ameliorate the negative effects of road pricing on particular groups of travellers. The issue still remains, however, of how schemes can be designed that protect certain vulnerable road user groups and concentrate the effects on others. Section 12.4 looks at the various elements of scheme design that can be varied, and Section 12.5 illustrates how this flexibility could be used to address various concerns.

12.4   ELEMENTS OF SCHEME DESIGN

There are five key questions that need to be addressed when designing an urban road pricing scheme, and where the decisions taken give considerable scope for designing locally acceptable schemes:

1.   Who should be charged?
2.   How much should they pay?
3.   Where should they be charged?
4.   When should they be charged?
5.   How should they be charged?

12.4.1 Categories of Traveller to be Charged

At one extreme, it could be argued that all road users who benefit from the use of a section of road should make a payment, including pedestrians. This is the case for certain bridges where tolls are charged to cover construction and maintenance, and it might be argued that the same principle should apply if an objective of introducing charging is to reduce congestion, since all road users contribute (including pedestrians, who delay road traffic when crossing the road!).

On the other hand, a case can be made for exemptions, on various grounds, depending on local priorities:

- Where air quality improvements are a primary objective, then pedestrians, cyclists and drivers of electric vehicles might be excluded.
- Where road pricing forms part of a policy package to discourage car use, then pedestrians, cyclists and public transport vehicles might be excluded.
- According to 'need' to use vehicles: on this criterion, goods vehicles and disabled drivers might be exempted.

12.4.2   Levels of Charge

General levels of charge are determined by the policy objectives and local circumstances; within this, variations can be introduced for different categories of user. Where the primary aim is to raise revenue without affecting traffic patterns, then charges will be considerably lower than where the objective is to reduce traffic levels. In the latter case, charges will need to be higher where there are fewer alternatives (modes, destinations, and so on), and where the aim is to deal with wider environmental problems rather than just traffic congestion (as the former generally requires lower traffic volumes than the latter).

Exemptions can be viewed as one extreme of a continuum of price reductions. Reductions might be offered to certain groups on several grounds:

- to reflect the varying costs they impose (in relation to road construction requirements, environmental externalities, and so on);
- to take account of behavioural resistance to a charge (typically, price elasticities are lower in peak than in off-peak periods); or
- to reflect political/public sensitivities (for example reduced charging rates for local residents).

12.4.3 Area to be Charged

The spatial extent of the charged area is closely dependent on the objectives of the scheme, plus local geographical factors. In the past it was also limited to a small number of roads or a limited geographical area by the practicalities of manual charging (for example in the case of the Singapore Area Licensing Scheme).

Where the aim is primarily to control traffic congestion, then the charged area may well be smaller than if wider environmental objectives lie behind the scheme. When revenue raising for transport investment is the key objective, the charged area will need to relate to the area that will gain directly from the new investment. In the latter case the boundary of the area will be selected to maximize the number of journeys intercepted and to minimize opportunities for diversion to avoid the charge; where congestion reduction is the primary objective, boundaries might be chosen to encourage diversion.

The introduction of electronic road pricing provides the opportunity to extend the area of coverage of proposed schemes, for a number of related reasons:

- The relaxation of the constraint of a limited number of entry points.
- In some circumstances, boundary effects can best be handled by extending the area that was initially intended to be covered.
- Once the decision has been taken to equip regional vehicle fleets with appropriate technology, extending the area of coverage is relatively cheap.

12.4.4 Times of Day of Operation

This is closely related to the objectives of the scheme. Congestion reduction will in general involve charging for shorter periods of time than when environmental improvements are the key issue. Similarly, where the objective is revenue raising, then a 24 hour charge may be an appropriate option.

Electronic road pricing provides opportunities to vary charges by time of day, to a much greater extent than is practical for manual charging. Variable charging by time of day may be important for three reasons:

(i)   To achieve desired reductions in traffic levels: off-peak traffic may need to be reduced by a smaller proportion than peak traffic (to encourage switching of travel to off-peak periods), and/or may be more price sensitive thereby requiring a lower charge to achieve the same effect.

(ii)   To reduce the negative effects of road pricing in relation to other policy objectives (for example impacts on the local economy): both the Bergen and Trondheim schemes have periods of the week during which city centre shops are open when no charges are levied, so reducing the impact of the charges on city centre trade.

(iii) To address social equity concerns: all proposed or implemented schemes (except the Oslo toll ring) have periods of the week when there are no charges, so that drivers have some 'free' use of the road network.

12.4.5 The Basis of Charging

It is here that electronic road pricing offers the greatest flexibility, by opening up some options for charging that would not be feasible by any other means over a substantial urban road network.

We can identify five main principles for road user charging:

(i)   *Point*-based charging, at key links or nodes in the road network; this commonly occurs already at bridges and tunnels, and the principle could be extended to major road junctions.

(ii)   *Cordon/boundary*-based charging, for crossing into or out of sectors or enclosed areas. Under the Singapore ALS, there is a one-off charge for unlimited inbound crossings during the period of validity of the permit. For the Hong Kong proposals, the charge would have been levied on a per crossing basis, in both directions but with surcharges in the peak direction of travel.

(iii) *Area*-based charging, giving right of travel *within* a defined area. This is more restrictive on behaviour than the Singapore ALS (because it controls travel inside as well as to/from the area), and at one time was proposed as a manual scheme in Stockholm, but dropped because of enforcement problems.

(iv) *Length*-based charging, defined either in terms of the *time* taken to make the journey or the *distance* travelled. There has been strong public reaction against time-based charging, on the grounds of the unpredictability of the charge, the incentive it gives to speed and drive inconsiderately (for example, not stopping for pedestrians or to let cars out of side streets), and the effect of events outside the control of the driver (for example, delays due to road works or accidents).

(v) *Externality*-based charging, whereby the charge is linked directly to the negative impact being caused by the vehicle. The only practical example to date has been the trial of congestion pricing in Cambridge (Ison, 1996), but in principle the same idea could be related to exhaust emissions from vehicles, for example.

In each case, the technology allows modifications to be made to the level of charge by time of day, vehicle/person type, and so on. It is also possible to cap the maximum charge payable by a vehicle or driver in an hour, a day or a longer period of time.

12.5   DEVISING ACCEPTABLE AND EFFECTIVE ROAD PRICING SCHEMES

There are clearly a very large number of permutations of road pricing scheme that could be devised from the elements discussed in Section 12.4, to meet different local circumstances, policy objectives and social concerns. Where traffic reduction is a key objective behind the introduction of urban road pricing, for whatever reason, then the basic issue remains: *which* traffic is removed from the network?

The concerns about fairness and equity, and the effects on local trade have already been noted, and with advances in technology it is possible to address them to a considerable extent through the way in which road pricing is implemented. Four simple examples are given here, based on different priorities for access to the network inside the charged area:

Priority: 'All vehicle owners should be given some free access to the network'

This requirement could be met in two ways. First, by limiting the charging period to certain hours of the day and days of the week, so that all road users can travel at some times of the week for no charge.

Second, car owning residents living within the charged area and other selected population groups might be given a number of free Travel Units per month (either using a smartcard debiting system, or through an account held by each person). Additional units could be purchased at the standard rate or at a discounted rate (though in principle there could be differences here according to category of user). By taking the idea further and making these free Travel Units available to all residents (with and without a car) and openly tradeable, then there would be a further redistribution mechanism from the rich to the poor.

Priority: 'Impacts on shopkeepers and businesses should be minimized'
This can be achieved by both direct and indirect means. The former might firstly include some free access to the charged area during shop/business opening hours (as is the case in Bergen, Singapore and Trondheim), possibly linked with an extension of shop opening hours into the evening uncharged period (as has happened in Trondheim). The growing trend in several countries to permit the opening of shops on Sundays increases the scope for offering uncharged access periods.

Second, by introducing road pricing in the particular form of an 'Area Parking Charge'. Here all drivers pay a fixed amount to enter the charged area, but in return are provided with a short period of free on- or off-street public parking, thereby minimizing the effect on short-term shoppers and those making service calls, most of whom would probably have had to pay to park anyway. Those with free off-street parking at work would now have to make some payment and long-stay public parking charges might be increased – so that all groups other than short-stay public parkers would be affected by the introduction of the road pricing charge.

Indirect means of mitigating the effects of road pricing charges might include enhanced non-car accessibility through better public transport provision, possibly including new Park and Ride services from outside the charged area, and reductions in business rates.

Priority: 'Service and goods vehicles should get priority, and car commuters and shoppers discouraged'
Most proposed electronic road pricing charging systems (including those proposed for Hong Kong and London) relate the charge incurred directly to the amount of use of the road network (number of cordon crossings, length of journey, and so on).

This clearly makes sense if all traffic is regarded as having equal priority, but in central city areas it is often the lower mileage traffic (car commuters, shoppers) which is viewed as having less priority than the high mileage delivery vans, sales representatives, service engineers and public transport vehicles. While it can be argued that if the journeys are important enough, businesses will pay, this nevertheless puts up costs and may not be a very efficient way of achieving priority for the latter classes of road user. It may also encourage out-migration of businesses from the area.

One option would be to give free or reduced price access to some types of motor vehicle (for example buses, vans), but this cannot distinguish the car used for shopping or commuting from the one used for service calls. Here something similar to the existing Singapore ALS charge provides an option: a high daily permit charge that allows unlimited entries would be much more of a deterrent to someone making one journey into the area per day than to drivers making 'essential' journeys to/from the area throughout the day.

Priority: 'Drivers should know what they are paying for'

This proposition deals with the principle that drivers should be given reliable information about the travel conditions that they will incur if they pay the charge – so they know what they are getting for their money. It is about knowing what they are buying, rather than about addressing an equity concern.

With the increasing deployment of comprehensive ITS systems in urban areas, it is becoming possible to give accurate estimates of current travel times by car, and by alternative modes of transport, so that informed travel choices can be made. Coupled with advanced route guidance, a parking booking system, and a network forecasting capability, it should also become possible to offer a prospective driver a given journey scenario for a certain price (with refunds if performance targets are not met?) – perhaps going further and offering alternative journey routings and timings at different prices. Reductions might also be offered for 'APEX' purchases.

There is no suggestion that *any* of these priorities is correct. Rather, they are intended as examples to give some idea of how much scope now exists for designing schemes that are sensitive to different policy concerns.

One general point to bear in mind is the trade-off between acceptability and effectiveness noted in Section 12.1: the more concessions that are made to user groups to 'buy' acceptance, the less effective the scheme will be in reducing traffic levels, or the more it will need to cut back on journeys made by a few road user groups in order to achieve significant overall reductions. Thus, if taxis, buses and goods vehicles are exempted from charging in city centres, then a high proportion of car trips would need to be suppressed. The equivalent problem arises with parking policy, where spaces under public control are often in a minority.

12.6   ASSESSMENT AND CONCLUSIONS

The paper has demonstrated that there is growing public support for additional measures to deal with the negative effects of road traffic in urban areas, and the gradual increasing recognition of the possible role for urban road pricing. Aside from concerns about practicality, the main stumbling block to public acceptability seems to be how the issue of equity is handled.

While much has been learnt in recent years about the likely effectiveness of road pricing, through major studies in Hong Kong and London and elsewhere, there is still a dearth of research into public attitudes to road pricing and little knowledge about how to devise schemes that best meet local needs.

More work is needed in particular on equity issues, both in terms of establishing the nature of the problem and in devising acceptable solutions, along the lines suggested in Section 12.5. There are also important research issues concerning the future role of ITS and how advances in traveller information and payment/booking systems might impact on road pricing options.

In policy terms there are two main issues which need to be addressed more fully before deciding in favour of a road pricing scheme for an urban area. In particular:

- whether road pricing offers the most appropriate solution in given circumstances;
- what measures are needed to complement the introduction of urban road pricing.

Road pricing is likely to be an attractive option in a range of urban areas, due both to its restraint and revenue raising capabilities, but it should not be oversold, and needs to be implemented with an appropriate package of complementary transport and land use measures, to address the issues identified in Section 12.3.

NOTES

1. In addition, there are potential secondary effects, depending on what happens to the 'displaced' traffic. These might include re-timing of car-based trips, or changes in the mode of travel used to reach the charged area; and the re-routing of trips or changes in trip destination to avoid the charged area altogether, with various additional boundary effects outside the charged area (for example increased local parking pressure).

REFERENCES

Borins, S.F. (1988), 'Electronic road pricing: an idea whose time may never come', *Transportation Research*, **22A**, 37–44.

Emmerink, R.H.M., P. Nijkamp and P. Rietveld (1995), 'Is congestion pricing a first-best strategy in transport policy? A critical review of arguments', *Environment and Planning B: Planning and Design*, **22**, 581–602.

Goodwin, P.B. and P.M. Jones (1989), 'Road pricing: the political and strategic possibilities', in *Systems of Road Infrastructure Cost Coverage*, Round Table 80, European Conference of Ministers of Transport, Paris.

Harrison, B. (1986), 'Electronic road pricing in Hong Kong: estimating and evaluating the benefits, *Traffic Engineering and Control*, **27**, 13–18.

Holland, E.P. and P.L. Watson (1978), 'Traffic restraint in Singapore: measuring the impacts of the area license scheme', *Traffic Engineering and Control*, **19**, 14–17.

Ison, S. (1996), 'Pricing road space: back to the future? The Cambridge experience', *Transport Reviews*, **16** (2), 109–26.

Jones, P.M. (1991), 'Gaining public support for road pricing through a package approach', *Traffic Engineering and Control*, **32**, 194–6.

Jones, P.M. (1995), 'Road pricing: the public viewpoint', Chapter 9 in B. Johannson and L.G. Mattsson (eds), *Road Pricing: Theory, Empirical Assessment and Policy*, Boston: Kluwer Academic Publishers.

Jones, P., T. Grosvenor and D. Wofinden (1996), 'Public attitudes to transport policy and the environment', Summary Report to the Department of Transport, April 1996.

Lex (1996), Lex Report on Motoring 'Listening to *all* road users', published by Lex Service PLC, with research by MORI.

May, A.D. (1975), 'Supplementary licensing: an evaluation', *Traffic Engineering and Control*, **16**, 162–7.

MVA Consultancy (1995), 'The London congestion charging research programme: principal findings', Government Office for London, HMSO.

Quimby, A. and C. Downing (1991), 'Road users' attitudes to some road safety and transportation issues', Transport and Road Research laboratory, Contractor Report 227.

Stoelhorst, H.J and A.J. Zandbergen (1990), 'The development of a road pricing system in the Netherlands', *Traffic Engineering and Control*, **31**, 66–71.

Verhoef, E.T., P. Nijkamp and P. Rietveld (1997), 'The social feasibility of road pricing', *Journal of Transport Economics and Policy*, **31** (3), 255–76.

13. Social feasibility of policies to reduce externalities in transport

Piet Rietveld and Erik T. Verhoef

13.1 INTRODUCTION

Although the principles of Pigouvian regulation of externalities and its attractive efficient properties have been known for some 75 years now, practical applications in regulatory policies in road transport, as well as in other sectors, remain scarce. One of the basic lessons in environmental and transport economics courses is the first-best character of regulatory taxation according to marginal external cost rules. Nevertheless, in the context of congestion pricing, Lave (1995) rightly observes that '[it] has been a commonplace event for transportation economists to put the conventional diagram on the board, note the self-evident optimality of pricing solutions, and then sit down waiting for the world to adopt this obviously correct solution. Well, we have been waiting for seventy years now, and it's worth asking what are the facets of the problem that we have been missing. Why is the world reluctant to do the obvious?' (p. 465).

This important question has recently been addressed in a number of papers on the social and political feasibility of the regulation of road transport externalities, in particular related to congestion and road pricing. Apart from congestion, the same sort of question of course could be asked in the context of the regulation of environmental externalities of road transport – and, indeed, for any economic sector. This paper studies such questions both from theoretical and empirical perspectives. Section 13.2 starts off with a discussion of the welfare economics of regulation, in which the trade-off between efficiency and social feasibility of regulation will be the central theme. Section 13.3 takes a political economy perspective. In this section, we discuss the relevance of contributions in the field of public choice theory. Section 13.4 discusses some empirical research that has recently been carried out on these topics in The Netherlands. We will pay attention to empirical evidence on the social feasibility of policies addressing congestion (especially road pricing), environmental pollution and traffic safety. Section 13.5 contains the conclusions.

13.2   A WELFARE ECONOMIC PERSPECTIVE

It is broadly accepted that economic science should aim at providing preferably 'value free' descriptions and analyses of human choice, and the associated social processes, under conditions of scarcity. As it is not possible to
construct a value free social welfare function according to some ethically
objective criterion, welfare economists have an inherent tendency to rely on
quite humble welfare criteria for the evaluation of different possible outcomes of the economic process; for instance, under different forms of government intervention.

Among these, the strict and potential Pareto criteria are without doubt the
ones most often employed. The *strict Pareto criterion* classifies some policy
(change) to be socially desirable if, as a result, everyone is made better off (in
its weak version), or at least if one person is better off, while no one else is
made worse off (in its strong version). For most policy choices however, both
losers and gainers will be involved, and the strict Pareto criterion becomes of
limited use in the sense that it does not provide any basis for choice between
these alternatives. In such cases, stronger criteria are needed if one yet wants
to make a choice among sensible alternatives. Therefore, one usually relies
on the well-known *potential Pareto criteria*, or compensation criteria, as
suggested by Kaldor (1939) and Hicks (1939). According to these criteria, a
change is classified desirable if the winners are able to compensate the losers
such that everyone is better off after the change has occurred (Kaldor), or if
the losers are in the initial situation unable to compensate the winners such
that both groups would prefer to stay in the initial situation (Hicks). Actual
compensation however, needs not occur according to these principles.

The related concept of *Pareto efficiency* is defined as a feasible situation,
usually in terms of a certain allocation of goods and production factors, for
which there exists no other feasible situation that is weakly preferred to it by
all agents. Therefore, if an economy attains a Pareto-efficient allocation,
there remain no mutually beneficial exchanges to be exploited. The criteria of
Pareto efficiency and potential Pareto improvements have become – among
economists – the standard criteria for the welfare economic evaluation of
(regulatory) policies.

Applying the strict Pareto criterion, no single form of external cost regulation can be justified, as it leaves its generator worse off, unless he or she is
directly compensated. The major advantage of the potential Pareto criterion
over the strict criterion, in contrast, is that it 'allows' regulators to intervene
as soon as the free market fails to achieve optimal social welfare in terms of
efficient use of scarce resources. Externalities – the central theme in this book
– are an important form of such market failures. This major advantage of the
potential Pareto criterion, however, at the same time is a major weakness

when it comes to the social feasibility of policies. Just because the criterion is concerned only with overall social welfare, summed over individuals, and not with the distribution of welfare, it ignores the simple fact that regulators often are democratically elected, and would therefore not be keen to increase efficiency in such a way that only a happy few strongly benefit, but most people are made worse off. Whereas the strict Pareto criterion is probably over-sensitive for such distributional considerations by not allowing any (policy) change that leaves any single person worse off, unconditional adherence to the potential Pareto criterion suffers from a complete neglect of these considerations. Although the 'odd footnote', stating that a potential Pareto improvement can be turned into a strict one by means of appropriate lump-sum redistributions may be valid in theory, it is not of great practical relevance, in particular because the concept of 'lump-sum' distributions is only a highly theoretical bench-mark, with little practical relevance.

Figure 13.1 summarizes these problems for road transport in an ordinary demand–supply diagram. The market equilibrium N^0 is at the intersection of the demand curve, which is equal to the marginal private and social benefits

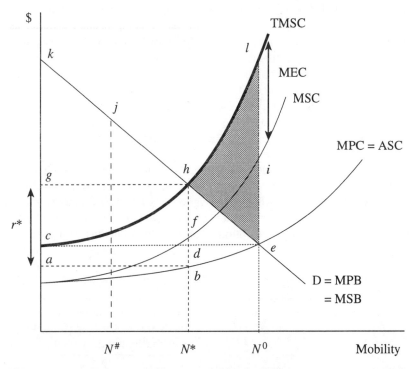

Figure 13.1   Welfare implications of regulating road transport externalities

(D=MPB=MSB),[1] and the marginal private cost curve (MPC). With identical road users, MPC may be equated to average social cost (ASC); it is positively sloped because of intra-sectoral externalities such as congestion. Taking account of intra-sectoral externalities, MSC represents marginal social costs; when accounting for the marginal environmental external costs MEC, TMSC gives the 'total marginal social costs'. Optimal road usage is therefore at N^*, where net social benefits, given by the area between the curves MPB and TMSC, are maximized, and the shaded welfare loss *hel* is avoided. Although diagrams such as Figure 13.1 are usually taken to represent the situation on a certain road on a certain time of day, the figure can also be seen as an abstraction for the more general road transport issue.

The identification of N^* as 'optimal' is of course contingent on the application of the potential Pareto criterion. According to the strict Pareto criterion, the reduction from N^0 to N^* cannot be evaluated as a welfare improvement (nor as a deterioration), because some people are worse off (road users), and some are better off (victims of the environmental externality).

The social feasibility of regulation is not so much dependent on the question of whether society at large benefits from regulation, but rather on the distribution of such a net welfare improvement – expressed, for instance, in the numbers of winners and losers, combined with the intensities of individual welfare changes. For example, in a very simple democracy where all decisions are taken by referendum, a rule of thumb might be that at least half of the voting population should benefit from a certain policy (change); otherwise it would not be accepted. Of course, most democracies do not operate in such a simple manner. Nevertheless, comparable decision and policy mechanisms will apply. In general, there will be some limit to the freedom of a democratically elected government, aiming at being re-elected, in the choice of their regulatory policies.

To illustrate this, consider the optimal instrument for achieving N^* in Figure 13.1, which is the optimal effluent fee r^* (see Verhoef, 1996, for a discussion of the relative efficiency of various regulatory instruments in road transport). The distributional impacts of this policy are given in Table 13.1. The road users generating the optimal mobility N^* will in the first place enjoy a welfare gain due to decreased congestion costs, represented by the rectan-

Table 13.1   The welfare effects of optimal fees

Road users: $0 - N^*$	Road users: $N^* - N^0$	Victims of the environmental externality	Regulator	Social (total)
$abdc - abhg = -cdhg$	$-beh + beif - abdc$	$+filh$	$+abhg$	$+hel$

gular *abdc*. However, the total tax revenues *abhg* necessarily exceed this reduction in congestion costs, so that an overall loss of *cdhg* results. These tax revenues of course accrue to the regulator, or more generally, to the government. Next, the mobility foregone – between N^* and N^0 – incurs a loss of benefits equal to area N^*N^0eh and a reduction of internal private costs of N^*N^0eb, yielding a negative subtotal of *beh*. In addition, external congestion costs within this group will disappear, equal to the total reduction in external congestion costs *beif* minus the fraction *abdc* enjoyed by the remaining road users. Thus the total welfare effect given in the second column in Table 13.1 results. Finally, the reduction in the environmental externality implies a welfare gain to its victims equal *to filh*. Summing over the four groups, a social welfare gain equal to *hel* can then be derived.

Both sub-groups of road users lose because of this policy, and the victims of the environmental externality and the regulator gain. Considering congestion only, it is easy to see that all actors involved, apart from the regulator, would incur net welfare losses due to road pricing. It is, however, important to stress that the tax revenues are implicitly assumed to remain with the regulator, and that the various groups in society do not consider the possibility of benefitting from possible allocations of these financial means. Given the usual response to regulatory taxation ('the car as a cash-cow' or 'yet another tax', instead of: 'more money for beneficial public projects'...), governments should formulate convincing policy packages if such scepticism of tax payers is to be overcome (see also Section 13.4).

It has been observed that such redistributional effects of Pigouvian taxation may dominate the efficiency gains (Segal and Steinmeier, 1980; Evans, 1992). Evans (1992) questions the desirability of road pricing for this reason, among other reasons such as the possibility of monopolistic pricing. The latter seems less of a serious concern in reality, given the revealed reluctance of most governments to use price instruments to any significant extent anyway. Borins (1988) goes a step further, and draws the pessimistic conclusion that road pricing will therefore 'inevitably fail because it is an intrinsically unpopular policy in any democratic urban policy' (p. 43).

A well-established result from the literature, however, is that some road users may benefit from road pricing when heterogeneity of road users is allowed for. The typical case considered concerns income differences. Starting with Richardson (1974), most authors conclude that road pricing is likely to be regressive due to the generally higher value of time for higher income groups (Layard, 1977; Glazer, 1981; Niskanen, 1987; Arnott, De Palma and Lindsey, 1994).[2] Clearly, stated this way, the non-intervention outcome is taken as a reference. Another way of looking at it is that higher income drivers suffer disproportionally from unregulated (excessive) congestion. From that perspective, it is of course questionable whether the progressive incidence of welfare losses due to unregulated congestion provides a sound basis for leaving this inefficiency in existence.

Giuliano (1992) notes that such equity considerations may merely 'present an apparently legitimate basis for opposition that is actually motivated by other reasons' (p. 349), and Small (1983, 1992) stresses at several places that road pricing may actually be progressive given certain redistributions of revenues. Nevertheless, the income transfers as such due to road pricing have played an important role in the discussion of its feasibility (Evans, 1992). Various authors have proposed schemes of spending the funds raised by road pricing in such a way that as many actors as possible eventually benefit, so that the opposition be minimized (Goodwin, 1989; Jones, 1991; Small, 1992). Still, May (1992) asserts that 'it has to be expected that any form of road pricing will introduce some inequities. The key is to keep these to a minimum' (p. 328). Daganzo (1995) approaches the issue from the other side, by proposing a combination of rationing and pricing that reduces the size of money transfers. Else (1986) mentions the possibility of leaving road users a choice between paying a toll or queuing (see also Verhoef, Nijkamp and Rietveld, 1996). Others (Starkie, 1986; Poole, 1992; May, 1992) concentrate on various other aspects of road pricing, especially related to its introduction, that may help improving the public acceptability.

From a welfare economic perspective, then, we can conclude by summarizing the two major problems of Pigouvian taxation for the social feasibility of regulation. Both problems are narrowly related to the fact that the potential Pareto criterion, in the spirit of which the concept of optimal Pigouvian taxation is derived, is concerned with overall welfare only, and is insensitive to the distribution of welfare. It therefore overlooks social resistance against (1) the inequitable impact of taxes, *ceteris paribus* harming lower incomes, with a higher marginal value of money, more strongly than others; and (2) the relatively large transfers from the public at large to the regulator due to taxation.

13.3   A POLITICAL ECONOMY PERSPECTIVE

In the preceding section we discussed the welfare effects of the introduction of pricing to correct for various externalities. The welfare implications for the actors distinguished are quite different. In the present section we address the link between the welfare analysis and the issue of political feasibility of such taxation measures.

13.3.1   Actors' Play in Politics

When we compare the actors in an economic system with the actors in a political system, we observe that there is not a one-to-one correspondence between them. Actors in the economic system are for instance consumers, producers, employers, employees, and victims of externalities. Actors in the political system are: voters, pressure groups, politicians, governments at various levels, civil servants, and so on. As explained, among others, by Frey (1983), the actual policies taken are the result of a complex interplay of these actors given the formal and informal rules of decision making in the public sector. In the present section we will not discuss the various elements and relationships within such a system, but only deal with one particular aspect: the role of voters.

Even in the simple case of a taxation of road transport discussed in Section 13.2, the voting population consists of various relevant combinations: road users versus non-road users, and people who are victims of externalities versus non-victims (see Table 13.2). For voters of type II, taxation of road transport would be against the immediate self-interest as indicated in Table 13.1 in the previous section. Furthermore, taxation would be favourable for voters of type III, neutral for type IV and ambiguous for type I. A relevant additional dimension would be the (perceived) welfare effect of the public sector receipts by the various groups. The extent to which voters would positively value these receipts (because of the useful government expenditures or reductions of other types of taxes) may be expected to play a considerable role in their evaluation of transport related taxes. Thus we arrive at (at least) three viewpoints voters have to integrate when they judge transport tax proposals: as a consumer of transport services, as a victim of externalities, and as a general tax payer.

In the remainder of this section, we will discuss some aspects of voting behaviour that are relevant in this respect: the question as to what dimensions voters seem to weigh in their valuation, the weight attached to the 'general

Table 13.2   Various types of voters and their position as actors in the economic analysis

	victim of environmental externality	
	yes	no
road user	I	II
non-road user	III	IV

interest' compared with the 'private interest', and the perception of the transport problems as well as of the policies proposed.

13.3.2 Voting Behaviour in a Multidimensional Preference Space

An important contribution to the analysis of the impact of voter's preferences on the behaviour of political parties has been given by Downs (1957). Downs studies the situation of two political parties, trying to formulate political programmes so as to maximize their share of the votes. Under the assumption that the preferences of voters can be measured according to some one-dimensional ideological scale, one can draw the conclusion that finally the two parties will look for ideological positions that are very similar, and represent that of the median voter. This theory, which is very similar to the Hotelling model on spatial location in a one-dimensional market (compare Beckman and Thisse, 1986), is appealing as long as there is only one major ideological dimension, and when there are only two political parties that are entirely flexible in the formulation of their political programmes.

However, in many democracies, there are more than two important political parties, and there is evidence that a one-dimensional approach to describing voter's ideologies is an unrealistic simplification (compare Enelow and Hinich, 1984). Thus we need a multi-dimensional representation of ideologies. Which dimensions have to be distinguished is essentially an empirical matter. The one-dimensional model is usually interpreted in terms of an economic dimension ('left' versus 'right', being essentially the difference between priority on equity versus priority on economic growth). In the present context of transport externalities, another relevant dimension is the attitude *vis à vis* the seriousness of environmental problems and the need that the government should correct these. Thus we end up with multiple relevant political dimensions as depicted in Figure 13.2.

In this scheme, voter A gives a high priority to environmental issues, C is keen on equity issues, and D gives a high rank to economic growth. Voter B combines a high preference for economic growth with that for solving environmental problems. Many other intermediate positions are possible.

This scheme implies that green political parties that want to receive support from a broad range of voters will have to formulate policy programmes that to a reasonable extent also come to meet the priorities of voters that also attach a certain priority to economic growth and/or social equity. This is another illustration of the fact that equity issues are important in transport policies.

According to Figure 13.2, voters' preferences cannot be represented simply by means of a score on a one-dimensional line indicating their narrow economic interests. In addition to their own interests, voters seem to take into account broader ideological principles, among other issues related to growth,

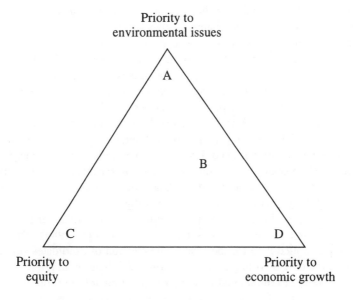

Figure 13.2   A multi-dimensional representation of voters' priorities

equity, and the quality of life. The question arises how the narrow economic interest and the broader ideological principles are combined in voting behaviour. This is the subject of the next section.

13.3.3   Balance between Selfishness and Altruism in Voting Behaviour

Margolis (1982) gives an interesting analysis of the issues of selfishness, altruism and rationality of economic actors when they are voting. He develops a theory to address the 'voting paradox': although in an election with millions of other voters, the probability that one's vote makes a difference to the outcome is extremely small; nevertheless usually most people having the right to vote indeed do so. A simple rational model, in contrast, would predict that a citizen would not vote, since the inconvenience of voting is not outweighted by the probability of a better outcome.

For an explanation it is helpful to consider the economic impact of the act of voting on the personal welfare. This can be defined as the product of the chance that by voting the outcome of an election will be different, and the value of the difference between alternative candidates (see Mueller, 1989). The first factor is extremely small, as indicated above, and the second factor will be limited. As a consequence, the effect on personal welfare will be very small so that citizens maximizing net private benefit would choose to be free

riders by not voting and nevertheless enjoying the benefits of the choice of a
good candidate. If one yet wants to give an economic explanation of why
people take the effort to vote, one seems to need the notion of altruism. In
certain situations, people are not entirely selfish. They attach some weight to
the interest of other people. People vote because they do not only take into
account their personal interest, but also attach utility to group interest.

This theory also has implications for the specific choices people make
when they are voting. Margolis' theory leads to the conclusion that in the
case of a conflict between personal interest and group interest, people do not
necessarily vote for the candidate who is best representing their personal
interests. The reason is that a rational voter observes that he gains very little
by voting for his most preferred candidate since the chance that his vote is
decisive is very small. If voters are driven by a certain degree of altruism,
they may prefer the candidate representing the perceived general interest.
Some evidence of this result is reported by Mueller (1989). The line of
reasoning applied here for the case of the election of candidates can also be
used for the case of voting between alternative policies with referenda.

This theory of rational voting implies that voting does not solely take place
on the basis of self-interest. The perceived general interest will also play a
role. This supports a multi-dimensional approach to voting behaviour. Political parties are not only judged according to the extent they come to meet the
personal interest of a voter. They are also judged according to other relevant
social dimensions, one of them possibly being the environmental quality
issue. A problem is, however, that the general interest is not something
objectively given, but depends on convictions and perceptions. This will be
taken up in the next section.

13.3.4   Perceptions of Private and Social Costs in Transport

It is a well-known result of transport studies that many persons are badly
informed about the costs and benefits of transport alternatives (compare
Blaas *et al.*, 1992). For example, car users are not aware of the full monetary
costs of a trip. The fixed costs are often ignored, but also even petrol costs are
sometimes overlooked, the only remaining cost component considered being
the out of pocket costs for parking. Another example of information and
perception problems concerns the long-run development of the real price of
car use. Contrary to the perception that this price has increased during the
past decades, a careful examination reveals that it has remained remarkably
stable in the long run in the Netherlands (Hopstaken *et al.*, 1991). Comparisons of objectively measured versus perceived quality aspects of transport
systems have been carried out by the Ministry of Transport (1996) and
Bruinsma and Rietveld (1996).

These examples relate to the perception problems of people concerning the *private* costs and benefits of transport alternatives. In the field of *social* costs these perception problems will be even more severe. Observability is an important factor here. Noise and stench can be observed immediately, but emissions of many pollutants and greenhouse gases are difficult to observe by non-experts. Also the damage these emissions may cause is far beyond the knowledge of ordinary people (and it is fair to acknowledge that even experts often do not agree). These perception problems can in principle be improved by increasing the educational level of people, and by providing information.

Perceptions may be rather unstable, however. For example, in The Netherlands, the share of voters that considered 'the environment' as a major political problem was 7 per cent in 1986 (CBS, 1990, 1994). There were no less than 9 themes that received higher scores. But by 1989, the situation had changed drastically: 'the environment' reached rank 1 and was mentioned by no less than 58 per cent as a major problem. In 1994, however, the score for environment as a major problem was down again to 22 per cent. For other issues relevant in this context, the fluctuations were less extreme. For example, the share of voters considering 'transport' as a major problem increased from 2.3 per cent to 4.8 per cent during this period; similarly, the share of voters perceiving 'taxes' as a problem increased from 0.7 per cent to 2.2 per cent.

Such cycles in the perception of environmental and related problems are not entirely random; they can be explained in a way similar to the infrastructure investment policy cycles as mentioned by Frey (1983). Part of the cycle can be explained by business cycles: in periods of economic recession, congestion problems are less severe so that voters tend to give priority to the immediate solution of economic problems. Then, when economic recovery starts, congestion problems tend to become gradually more severe. At a certain point in time, the pressure becomes strong enough to make congestion a political issue. The perception of political parties will tend to follow this trend. This will lead to a stronger democratic support for policies to overcome congestion problems. These policies may have a rather long-lasting impact on infrastructure quality because of the nature of the measures taken, which may last longer than the period of high congestion awareness of the public. Then, gradually the policy momentum for congestion issues will erode due to the emergence of new political issues. A new cycle will occur when finally congestion problems become so urgent that the general public again starts to attach high priority to it. A similar reasoning can be applied to the case of policy cycles with respect to environmental issues.

13.3.5   Conclusion

A simple theory of public decision making would suggest that when majority voting is the decision rule, policies are only politically feasible when more than 50 per cent of the voters would be in favour of them. However, the theories briefly discussed above indicate that there is more at stake here. When voting, voters do not only pay attention to their immediate self interest, but also to the perceived social interest. Here several ideological dimensions play a role, including the priority attached to a high quality of the environment. Thus, there is some scope for environmentally friendly policies, even when these would be against the immediate self interest of a majority of the voters.

13.4   SUPPORT FOR TRANSPORT POLICY MEASURES

For an analysis of the support for transport policy measures we will make use of a model as described in Figure 13.3. Our main point of interest is the acceptance of (or support for) particular policy measures in the field of transport. This acceptance will depend on the perception of the seriousness of transport problems, where both an individual and a social component can be distinguished (see also Section 13.3). Another factor influencing the accept-

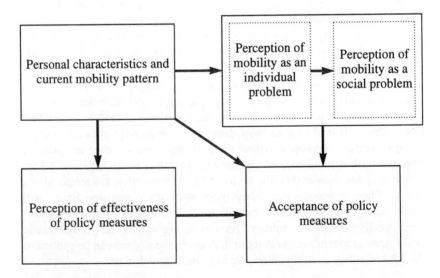

Figure 13.3   A conceptual model of factors influencing the acceptance of policy measures

ance of the measures is the perceived effectiveness of the measures. Finally, in the model we distinguish various individual features and the current mobility pattern of the individual as determinants of the other variables. Given the theoretical framework presented in Section 13.2, we would expect that especially the present income level will play a role as a determinant of the valuation of transport problems and policy measures because of, for instance, its impact on the value of travel time, and – more generally – on the marginal utility of money.

In the present section, we will report the results of two surveys on the social acceptance of transport policy measures carried out in The Netherlands in the years 1992 to 1995. Table 13.3 contains a short description of both surveys. The most complete coverage of the model described in Figure 13.4 is given by the first one. Therefore, we will focus our presentation on this survey and, where appropriate, add results from the second one.

Table 13.3   Two surveys on the acceptance of transport policies in The Netherlands

Survey	Theme	Year	Respondents	References
1	congestion safety environment	1992, 1994, 1995	700–1100 inhabitants each year	Veling (1995), Rienstra *et al*. (1996)
2	congestion	1995	1327 car drivers	Verhoef *et al*. (1997)

13.4.1   Perception of Transport Issues as an Individual or Social Problem

Tables 13.4a and 13.4b give some results on the perception of congestion and safety problems from a social and a private perspective based on survey 1. It appears that as far as safety is concerned, the majority of the respondents actually experience traffic safety problems (some 60 per cent). However, only some 40 per cent considers traffic safety as a social problem. For congestion and pollution, this pattern is reversed. For example, 48 per cent of the respondents experience congestion problems on express ways, but 69 per cent of the respondents consider congestion on express ways as a social problem.

In the upper-right corner of Figure 13.3, the question is raised of how strongly individual and social perceptions of transport problems are related. Tables 13.4a and 13.4b show that there is a strong correlation. For example, of those respondents who say that they experience safety problems, 50 per cent considers traffic safety as a social problem. For those who do not personally experience safety problems, this percentage is only 30. Similar results are

Table 13.4a   *Perception of traffic safety in residential areas as a private versus a social problem, 1992–1995 (in %; for the inner cells, rows sum up to 100%)*

	Safety is not considered as a social problem	Safety is considered as a social problem	Total
Safety is not considered as a private problem	70.1	29.9	41.0
Safety is considered as a private problem	50.4	49.6	59.0
Total	58.5	41.5	100.0

Table 13.4b   *Perception of express way congestion as a private versus a social transport problem, 1992–1995 (in %; for the inner cells, rows sum up to 100%)*

	Congestion is not considered as a social problem	Congestion is considered as a social problem	Total
Congestion is not considered as a private problem	39.1	60.9	51.9
Congestion is considered as a private problem	23.2	76.8	48.1
Total	31.5	68.5	100.0

found for congestion problems. For those who do not personally experience congestion problems on highways, 61 per cent of the respondents report that they consider congestion as a social problem. For those who do experience congestion problems themselves this percentage is as high as 77.

From these tables we infer that the perception of certain transport problems (congestion, safety) as a social problem is shared by substantial parts of the population. Also among those parts of the population who do not experience these problems themselves, quite a number of people consider these problems as a social problem. However, it is clear that the individual experience certainly shapes the social perception. This is a confirmation of the conjecture formulated in Section 13.3.4.

When we take into account other factors to explain the perception of problems (for a detailed account we refer to Rienstra *et al.*, 1996), we find that the transport issues are particularly considered as problematic among younger people, women, people with higher education, residents of large cities, and people with higher incomes. This latter result is in agreement with the discussion in Section 13.2, where the value of time (which depends on income) is an important determinant of welfare losses due to congestion. Another result is that (not surprisingly) commuters and car owners more frequently experience individual transport problems than other respondents. However, they are less inclined to consider these problems as *social* problems. Therefore, although the private experience of problems certainly influences the public perception, commuters and car owners seem to relativize their problems to some extent when they consider their problems from a social perspective. Alternatively, it could to some extent be the case that people who find these problems important already have changed their behaviour so as to avoid having to face these problems personally.

In a study based on survey 2, Verhoef *et al.* (1997) found similar impacts of age, education and income on the perception of transport problems, in this case congestion problems. Thus younger people, people with higher education and people with higher incomes tend to take congestion more seriously than other people. The result for income confirms the notions put forward in Section 13.2. Additional factors influencing the perception of congestion problems found in this study are the travel motive and the length of trips (people on business trips, and people making long trips have higher perceptions of the seriousness of congestion problems). This closely ties in with research results on travel behaviour, according to which values of time in business trips tend to be higher than with other trip purposes.

13.4.2 Perception of the Effectiveness of Policy Measures in Transport

Some results on the perceptions of Dutch residents concerning the contribution of policy measures to the solution of transport problems, based on survey 1, can be found in Table 13.5. The perception of safety related measures such as better education to drivers, more surveyance, and so on, is rather positive. For example, some 92 per cent of the respondents believe that better education to drivers does contribute to the solution of traffic safety problems. For the other problem fields (congestion and the environment), the respondents are usually less optimistic. An extremely negative view is found for the contribution of an increase of EU fuel prices to the solution of congestion problems and the environment. Thus respondents appear to expect little from financial instruments to solve transport problems. There are several explanations for this result: respondents believe that transport demand is inelastic so that taxation only leads to higher revenues for the government. Another explanation is that respondents have a tendency to give strategic answers: they indicate low expected effectiveness for

*Table 13.5   Perception among Dutch residents of the contribution of policy
measures to the solution of transport problems, 1992–1995*

Policy measure	Share of respondents who believe that policy contributes to the solution of transport problem (%)
congestion	
– 30% increase in EU petrol taxes	37.2
– road pricing	53.4
– improve public transport	79.8
– car pooling	92.5
– telematics introduction	81.5
safety	
– better driving education	92.4
– more intensive surveyance	90.3
– low speed design of residential areas	88.6
environment	
– improved car technology	95.0
– 30% increase in EU petrol taxes	43.3
– doubled parking tariffs	32.5
– more bicycle lanes	80.1

those policies that they do not like. This tendency may be the result of a conscious misrepresentation of their perception of effectiveness, but not necessarily so. Still, another explanation would be that respondents anticipate that unpopular policy measures will not materialize and hence will not contribute to the solution of transport problems. Very positive results are found for the possible contribution of technology to the solution of transport problems. Also policies stimulating environmentally friendly transport modes contribute considerably according to the respondents.

Thus we arrive at the conclusion that, in the view of the respondents, demand for car traffic is very inelastic in terms of its own price, whereas it is very elastic in terms of the quality of other transport modes. This leads to very optimistic views on the effectiveness of 'pull measures' (improvement in the supply of alternative transport modes), and to negative views on the effectiveness of 'push measures' (higher costs of car use).

This is a rather uncomfortable conclusion, since modelling exercises with transport policies give rather different results. For example, Bovy (1991) reports that, according to model based studies in The Netherlands, pull measures are rather ineffective as a means to reduce car traffic, whereas push measures are more effective (compare Rietveld, 1993). Thus, there seems to be scope for some effort to improve the understanding of the general public in this respect.

13.4.3   Acceptance of Policy Measures

Some results of survey 1 concerning the support for transport policies are presented in Table 13.6. A high support is found for safety related measures compared with congestion and environmental policy measures. When we compare various types of measures (fiscal, technical, and so on), fiscal measures receive a low level of support; it is interesting to note that road pricing is valued more positively than an increase in fuel taxes. The explanation is probably that it is a more focused type of instrument, so that it will not affect all drivers and all trips. Relatively high support is found for

Table 13.6   Support among Dutch residents for transport policy measures, 1992–1995

Policy measure	Share of respondents who (strongly) support policy measure (%)
congestion	
– 30% increase in EU petrol taxes	20.1
– road pricing	36.9
– improve public transport	76.4
– car pooling	93.5
– telematics introduction (the car driver has to pay the costs)	77.0
safety	
– better driving education	89.7
– more intensive surveyance	85.2
– low speed design of residential areas	82.7
environment	
– improved car technology	90.9
– 30% increase in EU petrol taxes	24.5
– doubled parking tariffs	18.3
– more bicycle lanes	95.0

technological solutions and for pull measures (stimulation of alternative transport modes).

When we take into account the personal features of respondents, we find that the following types of persons tend to give strong support to the policy measures: older persons, highly educated persons, residents of large cities, people who do not have a driving license, people who do not own a car, high income earners, people who perceive transport issues as an individual problem, and people who perceive transport issues as a social problem. Concerning the latter two variables, it is interesting to note that the impact of the *social* perception appears to be significantly larger than that of the *individual* perception (see Rienstra *et al.*, 1996). This confirms the theoretical notions discussed in Section 13.3.3, that respondents do attach a weight to the perceived general interest in their decisions. The larger support for policies among high income earners confirms the discussion given in Section 13.2.

In a study on road pricing among car drivers based on survey 2, Verhoef *et al.* (1997) found that support for road pricing is highest among respondents with the following features: people in single person households (a possible explanation is that their time budget is tight), people who travel long distances by car, drivers who experience a big time loss due to congestion, people with a high value of time (this is the by far most significant factor), drivers who consider carpooling or public transport as feasible alternative transport modes, people who perceive congestion as a social problem, and people who get compensation for the road price from their employer. In this list, again a mixture of private and public interests is found.

As shown in Table 13.1, road pricing has a negative impact on the welfare of drivers (independent of whether they are tolled off the road). However, their welfare position may improve when the government redistributes the toll revenues. An important question in this respect then of course concerns the way in which the revenues are redistributed to society (see Figure 13.4). Drivers strongly favour expenditures which are directly beneficial to road transport (additional road investments, reductions of vehicle taxes or fuel taxes). Moderate support is given to improvement of transport alternatives (investments in public transport, subsidies to public transport, carpool facilities). According to the opinions of car drivers, the least favourable allocation of the receipts would be a general reduction of taxes, an increase in government expenditures, or an unspecified increase of the government budget. As explained in Verhoef *et al.* (1997), certain patterns can be found in the opinions of car drivers on the best way to allocate the money. For example, low income earners are more positive about general and fuel tax reductions; drivers who expect to get compensation from the employer are more positive about road investments. Thus, a clever mixture of alternative uses of the revenues would be needed to maximize the support for an introduction of road pricing.

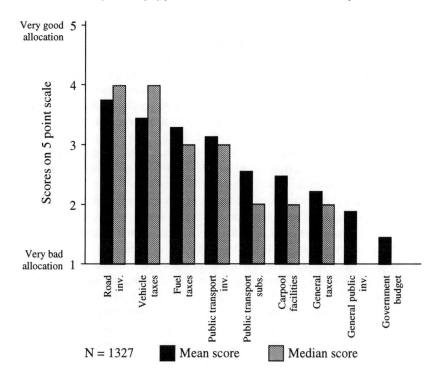

Figure 13.4   Road users' opinions on various allocations of revenues raised with road pricing

13.5   CONCLUSION

In this chapter, we attempted to shed some light on the issues of the social and political feasibility of regulation of road transport externalities. For some 75 years, economists have recognized the first-best features of the Pigouvian solution to the problem of externality regulation; nevertheless, practical applications in transport remained scarce. As a consequence, economists have broadened their view beyond the domain of the concepts of 'potential Pareto improvements' and 'allocative efficiency', to see what are the factors that prevent policy makers as well as the public at large from embracing this 'obviously correct solution', and to investigate how social resistance against regulatory pricing can be overcome. Given the size of the problems caused by road transport externalities, and the expected continuing growth of these problems, the importance of such research, we think, can hardly be overestimated. Clearly, these sort of questions can be studied from a variety of perspectives. Two of them were presented in this paper, namely a welfare economic perspective, and a political economy perspective.

From a welfare economic perspective, two main objections against Pigouvian taxation can be raised. Both problems are narrowly related to the fact that the potential Pareto criterion, in the spirit of which the concept of optimal Pigouvian taxation is derived, is concerned with overall welfare only, and is insensitive to the distribution of welfare. It therefore overlooks social resistance against (1) the inequitable impact of taxes, *ceteris paribus* harming lower incomes, with a higher marginal value of money, more strongly than others; and (2) the relatively large transfers from the public at large to the regulator due to taxation.

Transferring this finding to the political economy framework, it is not surprising that vote-maximizing politicians are in principle not keen on such instruments. It is evident that, in a simple two-dimensional voting space, such policies are very vulnerable to competition from a competing politician, and are therefore hard to maintain in a democracy. However, there is more at stake in the political arena. In the first place, competition among political parties often takes place in a multi-dimensional context. This on the one hand complicates matters considerably, but on the other hand provides politicians with the opportunity to imbed pricing policies in a relatively attractive overall policy package (for instance, including simultaneous reductions of wage taxes, possibly stimulating employment), that may seduce the voters to nevertheless vote for the particular package provided – although these voters may not like every single aspect of that package. Secondly, building on insights from rational voting models, it seems that voters often are not entirely selfish, like simple welfare economic models of individual utility maximizing usually assume. Thus, there may be scope for, for instance, environmental policies, even though these need not be in the primary interest of the majority of voters themselves.

In the final section, some empirical evidence of the above ideas was given. It is interesting to see that many of the theoretical notions indeed seem to be supported by the outcomes of two studies on the social feasibility of various policy instruments. The income effect on the acceptance of (pricing) measures was reproduced by the data, and also the individuals' concern with the allocation of Pigouvian tax revenues was clearly present. Other important elements were the perceived effectiveness of policy instruments, and the perceived seriousness of the problems at hand. In this latter respect, evidence was found that individuals care about transport problems for both private and social reasons; often, the social element was found to be even more significant in the explanation of the acceptability of policy measures than the individual disutility.

These results may give some clues as to how the idea of Pigouvian regulation should be communicated and, so to speak, 'sold' to the public at large. A key element is that a convincing policy package should be offered, in which it is clear what will happen with the tax revenues raised. This might take away much of the voters' scepticism on regulatory taxation. Second, the regulator should take sufficient effort in communicating both the scale of the problems concerned, and the effectiveness of the measures proposed. This latter element may include the provision of relatively attractive alternatives to current behaviour, making the demand for (road) transport more elastic and hence the policies more effective. Third, great care should be taken to account for the regressiveness of policies. Although one could be sceptical about the real motivation behind such arguments against pricing policies, a clear regressive element is certainly present and could be dampened, in particular, by certain allocations of tax revenues.

NOTES

1. Significant external benefits of road transport are not likely to exist; the benefits are usually either purely internal or pecuniary in nature (see Verhoef, 1994). Hence, MPB and MSB are assumed to be identical in Figure 13.1.
2. The higher value of time for higher income groups may actually arise from two separate reasons: a lower marginal utility of income, and a higher marginal utility of time (see Verhoef, Nijkamp and Rietveld, 1996).

REFERENCES

Arnott, R., A. de Palma and R. Lindsey (1994), 'The welfare effects of congestion tolls with heterogeneous commuters', *Journal of Transport Economics and Policy*, **28**, 139–61.

Beckman, M.J. and J.F. Thisse (1986), 'The location of production activities', in P. Nijkamp (ed.), *Handbook of Regional and Urban Economics* (1), Amsterdam: Elsevier Science Publishers, 21–96.

Blaas, E.W., J.M. Vleugel, E. Louw and T. Rooyers (1992), *Autobezit, Autogebruik en Rijgedrag* (Car ownership, car use and driving behaviour), Delft: Delftse Universitaire Pers.

Borins, S.F. (1988), 'Electronic road pricing: an idea whose time may never come', *Transportation Research*, **22A** (1), 37–44.

Bovy, P. (1991), *Verkeerskundige Onderbouwing van Infrastructuur* (Traffic-engineering fundamentals of infrastructure), Rotterdam: Ministry of Transport.

Bruinsma, F. and P. Rietveld (1996), 'The accessibility of European cities, theoretical framework and comparison of approaches', mimeo, Vrije Universiteit, Amsterdam.

CBS (Central Bureau of Statistics) (1990, 1994), *Nationaal Kiezersonderzoek*, The Hague: CBS.

Daganzo, C.F. (1995), 'A Pareto optimum congestion reduction scheme', *Transportation Research*, **29B** (2), 139–54.

Downs, A. (1957), *An Economic Theory of Democracy*, New York: Harper and Row.

Else, P.K. (1986), 'No entry for congestion taxes?', *Transportation Research*, **20A** (2), 99–107.

Enelow, J.M. and M.J. Hinich (1984), *The Spatial Theory of Voting*, Cambridge: Cambridge University Press.

Evans, A.W. (1992), 'Road congestion pricing: when is it a good policy?', *Journal of Transport Economics and Policy*, **26**, 213–43.

Frey, B.S. (1983), *Democratic Economic Policy*, Oxford: Martin Robertson.

Giuliano, G. (1992), 'An assessment of the political acceptability of congestion pricing', *Transportation*, **19** (4), 335–58.

Glazer, A. (1981), 'Congestion tolls and consumer welfare', *Public Finance*, **36** (1), 77–83.

Goodwin, P.B. (1989), 'The rule of three: a possible solution to the political problem of competing objectives for road pricing', *Traffic Engineering and Control*, **30** (10), 495–7.

Hicks, J.R. (1939), 'The foundation of welfare economics', *Economic Journal*, **49**, 696–712.

Hopstaken, P., M.J. Bennis and H.P.C. van Ooststroom (1991), 'De kosten van de auto en het openbaar vervoer vergeleken', in *Proceedings of the Colloquium Verkeersplanologisch Speurwerk*, CVS, Delft, 135–47.

Jones, P. (1991), 'Gaining public support for road pricing through a package approach', *Traffic Engineering and Control*, **32** (4), 194–6.

Kaldor, N. (1939), 'Welfare propositions of economics and interpersonal comparisons of utility', *Economic Journal*, **49**, 549–52.

Lave, C. (1995), 'The demand curve under road pricing and the problem of political feasibility: author's reply', *Transportation Research*, **29A** (6), 464–5.

Layard, R. (1977), 'The distributional effects of congestion taxes', *Economica*, **44**, 297–304.

May, A.D. (1992), 'Road pricing: an international perspective', *Transportation*, **19** (4), 313–33.

Margolis, H. (1982), *Selfishness, Altruism and Rationality: A Theory of Social Choice*, Cambridge: Cambridge University Press.

Ministry of Transport (1996), *International Comparison of Infrastructure*, The Hague: Sdu Publishers.

Mueller, D.C. (1989), *Public Choice II*, Cambridge: Cambridge University Press.

Niskanen, E. (1987), 'Congestion tolls and consumer welfare', *Transportation Research*, **21B** (2), 171–4.

Poole, R.W. jr (1992), 'Introducing congestion pricing on a new toll road', *Transportation*, **19** (4), 383–96.

Richardson, H.W. (1974), 'A note on the distributional effects of road pricing', *Journal of Transport Economics and Policy*, **8**, 82–5.

Rienstra, S., P. Rietveld, and E.T. Verhoef (1996), 'The social acceptance of policy measures in transport', mimeo, Vrije Universiteit, Amsterdam.

Rietveld, P. (1993), 'Transport policy and the environment, the case of the Netherlands', in D. Banister and K.J. Button (eds), *Transport, the Environment and Sustainable Development*, London: Chapman and Hall, 102–13.

Segal, D. and T.L. Steinmeier (1980), 'The incidence of congestion and congestion tolls', *Journal of Urban Economics*, **7**, 42–62.

Small, K.A. (1983), 'The incidence of congestion tolls on urban highways', *Journal of Urban Economics*, **13**, 90–111.

Small, K.A. (1992), 'Using the revenues from congestion pricing', *Transportation*, **19** (4), 359–81.

Starkie, D. (1986), 'Efficient and politic congestion tolls', *Transportation Research*, **20A** (2), 169–73.

Veling, I.H. (1995), 'Draagvlak bij het Nederlandse publiek voor het SVV-beleid in 1992–1995', Report TT95-20, Traffic Test, Veenendaal.

Verhoef, E.T. (1994), 'External effects and social costs of road transport', *Transportation Research*, **28A** (4), 273–87.

Verhoef, E.T. (1996), *The Economics of Regulating Road Transport*, Cheltenham: Edward Elgar.

Verhoef, E.T., P. Nijkamp and P. Rietveld (1996), 'Second-best congestion pricing: the case of an untolled alternative', *Journal of Urban Economics*, **40** (3), 279–302.

Verhoef, E.T., P. Nijkamp and P. Rietveld (1997), 'The social feasibility of road pricing: a case study for the Randstad area', *Journal of Transport Economics and Policy*, **31** (3), 255–76.

Index

316   *Index*